University College of the Fraser Valley

	DATE DUE		

c.1 Ch

Culture and Family Violence

Fostering Change Through Human Rights Law

Roger J. R. Levesque

AMERICAN PSYCHOLOGICAL ASSOCIATION

WASHINGTON, D.C.

Published by
American Psychological Association
750 First Street, NE
Washington, DC 20002

Copies may be ordered from
APA Order Department
P.O. Box 92984
Washington, DC 20090-2984

In the U.K., Europe, Africa, and the Middle East, copies may be ordered from
American Psychological Association
3 Henrietta Street
Covent Garden, London
WC2E 8LU England

Typeset in Times Roman by EPS Group Inc., Easton, MD

Printer: Sheridan Books, Ann Arbor, MI
Dust jacket designer: Berg Design, Albany, NY
Technical/Production Editor: Amy J. Clarke

The opinions and statements published are the responsibility of the authors, and such opinions and statements do not necessarily represent the policies of the American Psychological Association.

SEP 2 4 2002 Q1636335

Library of Congress Cataloging-in-Publication Data
Levesque, Roger J. R.
    Culture and family violence : fostering change through human rights law / by Roger J. R. Levesque.
        p.   cm.— (Law and public policy)
    Includes bibliographical references and index.
    ISBN 1-55798-682-7 (cb : acid-free paper).
    1. Family violence—Law and legislation—United States.
    2. Family violence—Law and legislation.   3. Culture and law.
    4. Human rights.   I. Title.   II. Series.

    KF9322 .L48 2000
    345.73'02555—dc21   00-033195

British Library Cataloguing-in-Publication Data
A CIP record is available from the British Library.

Printed in the United States of America
First Edition

For my wife Helen and our children Marc and Henry

CONTENTS

ACKNOWLEDGEMENTS

This book would not have been imagined without Mark Fondacaro's suggestion that I contribute to a *Law & Policy* special issue on family violence. I got so caught up in the idea that I actually ended up drafting the first part of this book. Mark and Murray Levine, editor of *Law & Policy*, provided detailed critiques of what would become the article for their journal. Their comments helped me refocus my arguments and seek the type of supporting evidence that found its way into this book. For the second part of this book, I owe much to Gary Melton. Several years ago, he invited me to present a paper exploring how U.S. family policy compares with international human rights law. That paper ended up being quite short because the United States essentially has no comprehensive family policy. That short paper, however, served as the spark for much of my work since then and clearly shows through the expression in my views of how human rights law may affect domestic approaches to family life, including family violence.

For my understanding of how the United States should respect cultural differences in family life, I owe much to Mark Chaffin. His insightful comments on an article I wrote for his journal, *Child Maltreatment*, helped me understand the need to examine how practitioners use cultural evidence and the need to offer guidelines for those who inevitably do make value judgments. For my firm belief that law can help reshape family life, especially in nonintrusive ways, I owe much to Alan Tomkins. It was my work with him that helped me focus on the need to harness laws that may seem precatory but in reality are quite dispositive in influencing policy making and peoples' everyday lives. Bruce Sales also deserves considerable credit. He was the first to notice this project's potential. In his effort to secure a contract for the book, he helped structure the book's format as he guided me through rewriting the proposal. The format that emerged from our discussion served as a solid plan of action. As I wrote, I could not help but feel he should have been the book's coauthor simply because of that singular contribution. With Bruce's guidance and the initial input by those mentioned above, this book turned out to be a wonderful intellectual endeavor I never thought I would experience.

The APA Books staff and outside reviewers and editors also deserve considerable credit. Three anonymous reviewers helped ensure that the book remained faithful to its central goal: addressing the cultural roots of family violence. Their comments helped me think through more clearly what I meant by culture and realize how my views of cultural life diverge dramatically from conceptions held by psychologists interested in cultural issues. Distinguishing my views from those of others has helped me to construct more effective arguments, analyses, and proposals. I am grateful for Adrian Harris Forman's close reading of the original manuscript and her perceptive comments, even though she ended up requiring (twice!) that I restructure the manuscript's presentation. The final product is much better because of her efforts. Amy Clarke also deserves considerable thanks for her helpful comments and for being so patient with my many requests as she guided the manuscript through the production process. An anonymous copyeditor's skill in sharpening sentences and asking insightful queries helped make the book a much more precise and careful analysis than I would have written. I greatly appreciate all of the reviewers' and editors' guidance, which was provided in ways that made meeting their high standards feel necessary and natural yet effortless.

Given the large number of talented people who contributed to this book, it should not be surprising that the text sometimes speaks as though society could conquer almost anything. Although the book expresses considerable optimism, it is hard to get away from the fact that violence remains a truly depressing topic. I continue to be amazed when I think of the time spent thinking, writing, and teaching about violence without getting too depressed about it. My understanding of family violence and family life constantly leaves me with considerable optimism. That optimism opens my views to the charge that my observations and analyses of reform efforts are simply too idealistic. Yet I cannot help but feel that much more can be done to prevent and deal with the consequences of violence. That feeling derives as much from research as it does from everyday experiences with my own family. Marc and Isabelle (my parents); Yves, Gilles, and Linda (my brothers and sister); and now my siblings' own families all deserve credit for making me feel the importance of family and understand why familial care remains so crucial to healthy development. My wife Helen and our children Marc, Henry, and their sibling soon to be born are probably the most to blame for my sustained optimism about the world. They are so full of support, energy, love, and passion for life that it is difficult to imagine that life simply cannot be wonderful.

Culture and Family Violence

INTRODUCTION:
Family Violence and Human Rights

Families occupy a paradoxical position in the contemporary world. Despite important cross-cultural differences in the nature and structure of families, cultures attach great significance to family life and the need to protect it. Ideals portray families as the primary source of social, emotional, and economic support for individuals throughout their entire lives. Given the significance of that role, much rhetoric about family life expresses concern for the family, enshrines it with rights, and heralds it as the center of society and as society's most fundamental resource.

Consistent challenges to idealized conceptions of family life do little to dislodge idealized images. Individuals suffer from family violence throughout their lives. Children endure the most frequently documented abuses, which range widely from infanticide, physical maltreatment, sexual exploitation, and slave labor to medical and emotional neglect.[1] Although the plight of children receives the most documentation, other vulnerable groups may suffer as much at the hands of family members. Globally, elderly people also endure similar abuses that arise from lack of adequate care and lead to early deaths.[2] Women disproportionately experience spousal violence, stalking, and poverty, which many commentators view as a cross-cultural universal linked to women's family care-taking roles.[3] Adolescents also suffer at the hands of family members: Families play critical roles in adolescents' sexual violence, drug use, and suicide rates, and they exacerbate negative consequences (e.g., through educational neglect).[4] Globally, abuses are manifested differently. Abuses may take the form of virginity exams, genital mutilation, bride burning, foot binding, slavery, mandatory face hiding, honor killing, forced pregnancy, forced abortion, body trafficking, and forced marriage.[5] Regardless of which group suffers the most and regardless of the form of abuse, the study of violence reveals the general rule that families constitute a pervasive source of violence and contribute to victimization not usually associated with families.

The extent to which ideals of family life persist, despite evidence that families are not necessarily safe havens, reflects the apparent reasonableness of the beliefs that ideals sustain. The reasonableness of those beliefs ensures the failure to recognize the extent of family violence and the inability to respond to even the most recognized forms of family violence. Indeed, the beliefs often result in unintended outcomes: Although beliefs may lead to protection, they also may lead to abuses. The beliefs and the diverse outcomes they catalyze are as paradoxical as the family ideal itself. Five components of currently prevailing family ideals illustrate well how ideals of family life guide family policy making even as they also may unwittingly contribute to maltreatment.

The belief in the power of parental rights infuses numerous policy mandates and reflects ideal societal perceptions that parents should, can, and do control their children. The reality, for example, that parents have a physical and psychological advantage over their young children allows for the belief that parents can mold and direct their children's upbringing. Yet adherence to parental rights allows parents to engage in dubious practices. For example, the United States' legal system pervasively condones corporal punishment. In addition, other countries now legally prohibit the practice and recognize what emerging research now suggests: This form of punishment is linked to numerous other forms of violence and the perpetuation of violence.[6]

The belief that families act in the interest of those who are incompetent and in their charge also continues to guide family policy making. The belief properly recognizes that those who may care more for individuals would be expected to act in those individuals' best interests. Yet the invocation of incompetence allocates considerable power to family members and the possibility that they may misuse it. For example, individuals' rights to physical integrity and control of their own lives diminish as they age, and loss of those abilities and rights increases the risk of individuals' victimizations. Globally, as elders become "decrepit," they lose rights and may even be viewed as already dead and gone.[7] The social processes through which humans become recognized people also affects the level of maltreatment. All cultures recognize personhood incrementally as they usher individuals through a series of culturally meaningful transitions before birth, at birth, through childhood, and often through adulthood, and those transitions affect the extent to which individuals receive protection.[8]

The belief that cultural traditions allow families to thrive also surely constitutes an important part of the family ideal and policy responses to family life. Families rooted in cultural traditions are perceived as cohesive, strong, and worthy of utmost protection from governmental intrusion. Paradoxically, however, the belief also justifies abusive practices. For example, cultural beliefs legitimize problematic practices that reinforce gender roles that perpetuate violence from birth to old age, as reflected by numerous variations of dowry practices that contribute to family violence as they secure women's dependency on their husbands and their families.[9] The opposite is also true. The belief that traditions alone protect vulnerable individuals actually leaves vulnerable some who fall outside of traditional family patterns. The extent to which mentally disabled parents and those who are traditionally viewed as potentially abusive (e.g., gay and lesbian parents) continue to be presumed inadequate parents allows for removing children from functioning, capable families and placing them in harmful situations.[10] Likewise, gay men and lesbians are often viewed as having illegitimate relationships, which renders them essentially unable to seek assistance from social services and legal remedies for violence from their partners.[11] Maintaining tradition, then, far from completely protects individuals from family violence.

Another ingrained belief is that societies should respect individual dignity in the form of the broad right to be let alone or right to privacy. Without doubt, these two rights protect individuals from unwise societal intervention. Yet these venerable beliefs that often serve as foundations for family policy making also allow for the exclusion of needed societal assistance. For example, older citizens may lack social and medical services and may impose a burden on their families. The extent to which they view themselves as burdens relates to their willingness to consider themselves candidates for euthanasia, much as the extent to which they are viewed by others as burdens relates to societal willingness to consider "euthanasia." Thus, although the issue of euthanasia may be viewed narrowly as a way to die with dignity and supported by the right to be let alone, it also involves the allocation of scarce societal resources.[12] Societies find several other justifications to deny elders resources and even permit "homicide" by a family member.[13] Similar social dynamics are at work when societies deal with the other end of the life cycle. Children may be disposed of in numerous ways that may be framed around the right to be let alone and the right to privacy. These rights support the traditional right of parents to raise their children as they see fit, including the right of parents to abort fetuses.[14] The extent to which euthanasia and abortion remain controversial serves to highlight the point that what constitutes violence and harm varies and that different societies (and groups within societies) use different mechanisms to weigh the significance of individual rights and costs they may impose on others.

A last frequently proposed tenet related to family life involves the belief that individuals must contribute to society and properly support their own families. The belief allows for producing families that support themselves when governments cannot. Yet the belief also allows for discrimination against those whose contributions to family life are not overt or whose contributions do not derive directly from social structures outside of family life. The problematic focus on contribution has been well understood and reported by several writers who note the pervasive failure to view mothers' work inside the home as worthy (or more worthy) as the work outside the home.[15] These differences in productivity and societal participation differentially affect the nature of family violence across the life span as they affect the dependency of certain family members on others. Cross-culturally, for example, women arguably are the ones most likely to abuse elders left in familial care. Yet women's apparently singular roles in elder abuse mask the extent to which social forces contribute to the abuse: Female caretakers seemingly abuse primarily because they are the ones entrusted with family care and often do so without external sources of support.[16] Mothers also have been identified as those most likely to abuse children[17] and those most likely to kill their infants,[18] a distinction related to their position in families.

All rationales that uphold the family ideal paradoxically serve to justify what otherwise could be construed as violent, abusive, and worthy of intervention. Much violence remains hidden and justified in families viewed as precious. Indeed, even the view that families are precious remains paradoxical in light of the actual support offered to them. As I demonstrate throughout the text, recognition of the importance of families does not result in services, assistance, and protection for needy family members. Equally true is the failure of families to protect vulnerable members: Vulnerable individuals seemingly occupy a place far in the queue behind other familial and social needs.

Exceptions to myths of family life's inherent protective features do not mean that idealized attachments to family life are irrational and devoid of merit. The beliefs and policies that support ideals of family life do buffer several from maltreatment. Indeed, the extent to which mythic ideals often work makes difficult any attempt to rethink their assumptions and implications. The extent to which the beliefs function and appear right, normal, moral, and appropriate challenges intervention and reform. Families pervasively do shield their members from violence and often may offer emotional refuge. The vast majority of potentially abusive yet rational beliefs continue to be condoned and viewed as essential to the proper functioning of families, societies, and even governmental life. Thus, even when some forms of violence become viewed as unacceptable, they run the danger of also being viewed as a cost to the need to protect families. For example, the need to protect family privacy and the private sphere of social life finds wide cross-cultural (and apparently universal) acceptance, although privacy takes on various institutional forms and differently emerges across cultures and societies.[19] Respect for the various forms of privacy continues, even though it means that individuals are allowed to suffer inside families and the private sphere.

The extent to which the above ingrained beliefs and policies are seen as normal and appropriate is exemplified by the absence of viable alternatives to care for others and by the challenges faced by those who champion alternatives. Although viable options and alternatives to family life may not exist, attempts to rethink the legal nature of family life are far from absent. Some leading commentators in the United States, for example, champion radically different images of the law's role in family life. Some would go so far as to abolish the legal notion of marriage because the legal protections bestowed on families pervasively fail to protect vulnerable individuals. For example, the focus on marriage may mean that its failure leads to inequitable distributions of property and care taking and that abuses inside families are not taken seriously enough.[20] Others would aim to narrow conceptions of what constitutes families so as to exclude groups of individuals from legal protection granted to "traditional" families. These commentators frequently champion the belief that traditional, heterosexual families offer the greatest protection to individuals and reflect the wisest and most moral policy.[21] For the purposes of this book, the most important development involves attempts to harness the power of human rights law to reformulate the place of families in contemporary societies so that legal systems approach the pervasive failures of families and the global and cross-cultural dimensions of those failures. Although attempts to approach families and family violence from the perspective of human rights remain sporadic and limited to groups of individuals who happen to be in families (e.g., women and children), human rights law gains currency. Indeed, the human rights movement theoretically offers unusual opportunities to reconceptualize family violence and respond to the needs of families' vulnerable members. Yet the human rights approach remains plagued by difficulties as it moves from theory to practice.

Human Rights Theory and Practice

The paradoxical ideal and reality of family life finds parallels with current visions of human rights principles. Human rights are envisioned as noble, idealized images of how governments treat citizens. Most people reserve their image of human rights violations for formal governmental actions, such as those of repressive regimes that torture political prisoners and suppress fundamental freedoms of expression and assembly. The thought of a maltreated child, a battered spouse, a physically neglected grandparent, or a family trapped in violence does not conjure images of international human rights violations. Yet modern human rights law actually seeks to protect individuals from such violence.

Expansive Developments

Notions of human rights increasingly expand and place previously ignored forms of violence and relationships within the reach of human rights law. Indeed, human rights developments have been dramatic, even exuberant. Chapters 1, 4, and 5 report these developments in a systematic and comprehensive fashion; here I emphasize the contours of the developments. Reduced to its core mandates, the human rights movement consists of two critical developments: (a) the growing obligations placed by the international community on itself, individual societies, local communities, families, and individuals to respond to human rights abuses and (b) the protections from family violence provided by modern human rights law. The examples given below illustrate the development of different forms of human rights, which are differentially enforceable and which differentially place obligations on actors.

Several international treaties now document the rights of individual family members, including their right to protection from family violence. The most widely ratified and enforceable human rights convention in the history of the world—the United Nations Convention on the Rights of the Child of 1989[22]—delves into family life and directly addresses family violence. The Convention finds that children possess a right to protection from "all forms of physical or mental violence, injury or abuse, neglect or negligent treatment, maltreatment or exploitation including sexual abuse, while in the care of parent(s), legal guardian(s) or any other person who has the care of the child."[23] The convention also offers explicit protections from sexual maltreatment[24] and broad protections against all forms of exploitation prejudicial to any aspects of the child's welfare.[25] To ensure those rights, *State Parties*—countries that sign and pledge to follow the treaty—must "undertake all appropriate legislative, administrative, and other measures."[26] In addition, to ensure those rights, State Parties are to recognize the responsibilities of parents and others who care for children and assist them in efforts to recognize, respect, and ensure the rights of children.[27]

In addition to directly enforceable human rights conventions, the United Nations recognizes human rights developments dealing with family violence through the adoption of declarations that directly confront violence. Most notably, for example, the United Nations' governing body—the General Assembly—adopted the Declaration on the Elimination of Violence Against Women of 1994.[28] The Preamble of the Declaration defines *violence against women* as "any act of gender-based violence that results in, or is likely to result in, physical, sexual, or psychological harm or suffering to women, including threats of such acts, coercion or arbitrary deprivation of liberty, whether occurring in public or private life."[29] The Declaration also rejects cultural relativism by prohibiting *Nation States*—countries that belong to the United Nations—from invoking "any custom, tradition or religious consideration to avoid their obligations."[30] Under Article 4, an effective policy of eliminating violence requires that the State use due diligence to prevent, investigate, and punish acts of violence against women. Nation States, then, must pursue a policy that eliminates violence by all appropriate means and without delay.

In addition to directly enforceable treaties, the world community marks progress in its efforts to protect individuals from family violence through several conferences that have established strategies and plans of action. Most notably, for example, a series of conferences on women's rights now detail the rights of women to protection from violence, including family violence. The Vienna Declaration and Programme of Action of 1993,[31] adopted by the Fifth World Conference on Human Rights, expressly proclaims the indivisibility of all human rights and makes a number of recommendations relevant to protections from violence. These rights include the right to protection from gendered violence, both in private and in public; protection from domestic violence; and protections from harmful cultural and religious practices. The rights were further recognized at the Fourth World Conference on Women, which culminated in the adoption of the Beijing Declaration and Platform for Action of 1995.[32] The Beijing Declaration calls for international, national, and regional efforts to address violence against women and girls, in the form of physical, sexual, and psychological abuse. No nation objected to the need to recognize women's right to be free from violence, including different types of violence specific to women. The need to understand, stop, and prevent family violence has become the women's rights movements' highest priority.

Regardless of their levels of enforceability and the extent to which they recognize the need to protect individuals from family violence, all new and evolving human rights mandates are of significance. The formal treaties directly bind States Parties and the international community. As such, they express a global standard of the manner in which individuals must be treated. Although declarations and platforms from conferences may not directly bind nations, they nevertheless mark the universal transition to a human rights agenda that includes family violence. These consensus agreements add new weight to efforts to recognize the rights to protection from family violence. Although these developments are somewhat recent, they continue the tradition of modern human rights and enumerate how family violence conflicts with numerous fundamental human rights principles, not the least of which include principles of equality and the right to human dignity. As I demonstrate in chapters 1, 4, and 5, these and other traditional human rights protections figure prominently in international human rights law's attempt to regulate family relationships and address the conditions of vulnerable individuals and groups.

All mandates, both new and old, contribute to evolving human rights standards and to the development of customary international law and eventually will serve to bind nations and provide a viable means to hold Nation States (and through them, individuals within Nation States) accountable for violence within families. Consensus evidenced by agreement at an international forum, combined with other forms of evidence, ultimately provides evidence of a binding, enforceable legal obligation. The consensus is significant because nations create international law through their actions. When a sufficient number of nations follow a practice for it to be considered an obligatory norm, it becomes binding international law.[33] The various mandates and approaches to family violence all add impetus to the development of a group of international rights that protects individuals from family violence.

Restrained Responses

Despite these and numerous other mandates that broaden conceptions of human rights abuses and that expand the reach of international law, human rights obligations remain generally invisible. The failure of human rights protections against family violence to infiltrate popular consciousness reflects the failure of human rights experts, policy makers, and those who implement laws to grasp the manner in which human rights law addresses family violence. The failure runs rampant, particularly in the United States.

Commentators and analysts of international law pervasively ignore the manner in which international human rights now deals with maltreatment within families. Leading texts and reviews of human rights law,[34] international relations,[35] international law,[36] the nature of the United Nations[37] and international criminal law[38] do not even mention family violence. The marginalization of international law from jurisprudential analyses exacerbates the failure of leading commentators to consider family violence. Leading scholars interested in human rights as protected in the United States, for example, rarely enter the realm of international human rights law, let alone detail how it could protect individuals from family violence.[39]

Where experts in international law have failed, activists in the United States have not taken the lead to push a human rights agenda in their efforts to combat family violence or enhance the rights of the most vulnerable. The failure occurs at two critical points in responses to international human rights treaties. International human rights first fail during the ratification process. Activists persistently fail to ensure that U.S. ratification of documents makes a difference. Paradoxically, the most prominent commentators who do champion human rights go to great lengths to argue that international rights actually have little impact on U.S. law and policy. For example, commentators played down the potential domestic impact of the Convention on the Elimination of Discrimination Against Women of 1979[40] to such an extent that domestic women's rights groups had no incentive to promote the treaty's ratification.

The result was that even though the United States has one of the most active women's rights movements, efforts to ratify the treaty were unable to mobilize enough popular support to secure ratification of the chief international treaty that protects women's rights.[41] Analyses of attempts to ratify other leading human rights treaties, including the Covenant on Economic, Social, and Cultural Rights of 1966[42] and the Convention on the Rights of the Child of 1989,[43] reveal a similar failure: The pervasive understanding that ratification would have absolutely no consequences whatsoever for the United States (see chapter 6). International human rights treaties also fail once ratified. Even when treaties do gain ratification, their impact remains negligible because they simply remain largely ignored. For example, the United States has ratified four critical human rights treaties (see chapter 6), yet few advocates have used human rights standards to champion the development of legal rights in this country,[44] and even fewer U.S. courts have ventured as far as to rely on them to expand human rights protections.[45] To be sure, several reasons account for the pervasive failure to use existing documents. Those reasons also account for resistance to customary law—law recognized by the international community as *jus cogens*, as peremptory norms that can never be violated. Despite those reasons, it is puzzling that commentaries do not consider the potential benefits of taking human rights law seriously and dismiss the need to detail specific contributions and policy developments that may arise from simply pursuing a human rights agenda.

Where international experts and local activists have failed, the courts have not interceded to champion human rights. Although courts remain free to act *sua sponte* (on their own volition) and may turn to human rights law, they too rarely do so. Courts pervasively ignore international law and its human rights documents. In the United States, the failure to embrace international norms relates to the Supreme Court's indifference to international human rights instruments. Neither international treaties nor customary law figures prominently in American jurisprudence. According to Supreme Court justices themselves, the court continues to show "something less than 'a decent respect to the opinions of mankind.' "[46] Even though the court may have turned to human rights principles in the past, its current approach aims to ensure that "it is American conceptions of decency that are dispositive." [47] U.S. judicial and administrative branches adopt a "dualist" view of the relationship between domestic and international law—an approach that views international and domestic law as distinct, with each nation determining the status of international law within its own borders by its own domestic law. [48] Thus, although many government actors do not deny the importance of international law, they evaluate the domestic effects of international law through the lens of domestic law. [49]

Compared with scholars, activists, and the courts, those who do legislate actually do adopt an active stance. Their posture, however, does not embrace human rights. Rather than ignoring human rights protections, legislators generally aggressively seek to resist international mandates. The resistance and politics of exclusion reflect the United States' long-standing determination to insulate itself from the influence of international law. Yet and again paradoxically, the United States still exerts considerable force in the development of human rights treaties, as much as it did to the actual founding and persistent use of the United Nations itself.

Commentators, activists, legislators, courts, and the general public pervasively ignore and resist developments in universal human rights for several reasons, as explored in the chapters that follow. In terms of family violence, however, two principal factors explain why human rights law does not provide legal authority or foster an appropriate social response. First, international law construes family violence as a domestic issue. Despite developments highlighted above, family violence continues to be construed as a nation's domestic concern, as a matter outside the purview of international law that traditionally concerned itself with interstate actions and the regulation of State behaviors toward one another. [50] Second, and despite measurable progress, family violence still pervasively remains viewed as a domestic, private matter outside of the governmental control of individual Nation States. Thus, the reasons international obligations regarding family violence remain ignored parallel those reasons given in recent commentaries on individual countries: Family violence is (wrongly) construed as a private matter better left to private resolution. [51] Although progress has been made in various countries to respond to "private" violence, [52] the violence generally continues to be deemed as outside of formal human rights law. The move to include protections from family violence into human rights law, despite existing mandates that recognize the protections, undoubtedly remains fraught with numerous controversies, obstacles, and concerns. These challenges serve as the foundation for this text.

Unaddressed Issues and Concerns

Although current international human rights law does protect individuals from family violence, understanding how human rights actually may assist in responses to family violence requires further analysis. Family violence appears to be an indisputable, universal concern, but it creates a minefield of controversies. These controversies cut to the heart of major issues in international relations today, including State sovereignty, economic development, international labor rights, cultural sovereignty, poverty, racism, inequality, and (often ignored) family life. Left to be determined are the standards used to resolve which forms of violence actually fall under human rights law's ambit and the nature of the intervention if the actions do constitute human rights violations. In other words, the central concern of human rights analyses and policy making now involves resolutions of when violence counts as a human rights violation and determinations of the nature of responses mandated by human rights law.

Determinations of what counts as a violation, and what to do about matters that do count, are far from straightforward and are not immune from controversy. Legal reform requires strategic choices that actually implicate conflicting short-term and long-term interests. For example, arguments based on rights associated with the protection of the family or with the protection of privacy may promote the construction of gender roles that are antithetical to the rights of members within those families. Likewise, arguments that champion civil and political rights without including applicable economic and social rights may meet short-term demands but, in the long term, contribute to the neglect of social and economic rights.

Strategic determinations of what counts as a violation and its appropriate response must be made in light of the reality of victims and offenders' lives as well as their cultural location. Addressing family violence from the perspective of human rights necessarily means understanding the nature of families, violence, human rights, and societies. That understanding must be grounded in specific factual contexts and emerging theoretical frameworks. These efforts require a flexible relationship between legal definitions of the scope of human rights obligations regarding family violence and fact-findings that monitor and encourage the actual development of rights. That analysis necessitates reflection on four central issues and concerns.

The first concern relates to conceptions and analyses of violence and family life. What constitutes families and family violence has been subjected to cross-cultural inquiry, but those investigations tend to remain limited to specific forms of family violence, such as violence against elderly people[53] or women.[54] Equally limited are investigations of what to do with individuals outside of formal families, such as those abandoned or rejected by their families, including youth sold for sex and those offered as slaves or wives to temple priests.[55] Regardless of whether individuals are in or out of families, their status requires societies to consider how families contribute to individuals' place in society and the protections from violence individuals receive. The limited information on different forms of family violence undoubtedly remains useful, but its links to human rights law remain to be articulated and resolved.

The second issue involves the cultural dimensions of family violence and the challenges faced by efforts to harness our understanding of cultural forces onto legal responses to family violence. The most pervasive model that guides current intervention efforts and family policy making locates the causes of violence within the family.[56] The approach differs fundamentally from models that take seriously the cultural forces affecting family life. Such approaches would seek to understand and respond to the web of family violence that derives as much from economic, religious, and other institutional pressures. These pressures emanate from outside of family life but affect family dynamics, resources, structures, and the level of risk to individual family members.[57] It is this multilayered understanding of family violence that makes the current and emerging human rights regime applicable and significant. Unlike domestic policy making, the human rights model comports well with this culturally embedded view of violence within the family. The human rights movement can affect several cultural institutions, including religious, economic, legal, and even familial institutions, that impact the extent and nature of family violence.

The third concern relates to legal mandates. This concern operates at several levels. Most notably, it deals with the proper reach of international law and the extent to which nations themselves must address issues of family violence. It also deals, for example, with the manner and extent to which nongovernmental actors may be held accountable, such as international financial institutions and multinational corporations that directly effect policies and programs related to family life. The concerns also touch on the need to decide more precisely what is worthy of intervention and the problem of defining the proper role of law toward other cultural institutions.

The last critical issue deals with the enforcement of human rights that have been deemed worthy of support. These concerns relate to the fundamental purpose of law and how it must balance proactive and reactive attempts to deal with violence and with determinations of the type of system to be used—criminal, civil, or combinations of both. In addition, these concerns necessarily involve the allocation of resources and the extent to which law can operate in the absence of social and economic resources. Likewise, issues of enforcement concern the dangers of intervention and the need to balance important societal concerns (such as the protection of family and individual privacy as well as the protection of defendants' rights and cultural traditions) in efforts to address individuals' victimization and to pinpoint an appropriate site of intervention.

The above concerns distill to rather simple yet challenging questions. Who or what is responsible for securing the needs and rights of those subjected to family violence? How are those needs and rights to be secured? What are these needs and rights? All these issues remain largely unresolved and highly contested. I propose that, even though international human rights law necessarily does not (and should not) offer clear answers to what constitutes some forms of human rights violations, international mandates do offer a clear approach to determine and respond to family violence, which still tends to be construed as unequivocally private and immune from human rights analyses.

Terminology and Disciplinary Approach

What constitutes family violence remains problematic for any investigation. Many thoughtful discussions about the numerous definitions of family violence highlight how debates continue, and potential consensus remains far from reach.[58] Even the types of violence that have been the subject of extensive inquiry remain problematic in that what constitutes certain forms of violence and the terms themselves frequently vary from one study to another; for example, child sexual abuse may be identified and investigated as sexual harm, incest, exploitation, abuse, maltreatment, misuse, mistreatment, harassment, molestation, assault, violence, and rape.[59] Examining family violence across cultures exacerbates definitional problems even more. Investigators who examine family violence within cultural groups have been inclined to define and describe events and practices in terms of the investigated cultures themselves, with a resulting tendency to explain many violent actions as essentially not violent because they were pervasively culturally condoned.[60] Although investigators increasingly reject culturally condoned practices,[61] the labeling of certain actions or inactions as violent still remains a controversial issue.

Given the continued controversy, I address violence in terms of both the *emic* ("insider's") view (from the highlighted cultures themselves and frequently in terms of different groups within cultures) and an *etic* ("outsider's") view (i.e., from the view of activists, researchers, and commentators from outside the specific cultures).[62] This approach undoubtedly complicates the discussion and leads to a very broad use of the term *family violence*. For this investigation, family violence includes family members' acts of omission or commission resulting in physical abuse, sexual abuse, emotional abuse, neglect, or other forms of maltreatment that hamper individuals' healthy development. To assess the full ramifications of family life, the following discussion accepts that practices are violent when viewed as such from inside the relevant culture; it also (for the purposes of investigation) tends to accept as violent practices that may be viewed as violent from outside the culture, from specific groups within the culture, or from the perspective of international human rights law. Thus, unless explicitly stated otherwise, the practices presented herein constitute or relate to some form of violence.

Although numerous examples may be offered to illustrate the significance of a broad approach, two recent anthropological investigations of wife battering reveal the need to take a broad view of violence. Domestic relations in Wape, a New Guinea society, are marked by lack of physical violence between husbands and wives.[63] A closer look at domestic relations, however, reveals that violence may be more subtle but actually more lethal. "Unhappy" wives deal with overly critical and abusive men through suicide attempts and suicide rather than fighting back, escalating disputes, and ensuring that abusive events are recognized and responded to by neighbors—a way of dealing with domestic problems reported in many societies, including those in which women use suicide attempts to deter violence (as in Kaiai of Papua New Guinea cultures)[64] or to actually escape violence through death (as in many Asian cultures).[65]

The Ujelang of the Marshall Islands also exhibit low rates of wife battering.[66] Yet talk of violence and threats of abuse are a communal preoccupation and are used to control others. Violence generally takes two forms described in similar ways: supernatural and physical violence. Young male individuals typically exhibit physical violence, and individuals within the society attempt to control the violence. Women, especially older women, use magical or supernatural violence, a form of violence viewed as more threatening because it is lethal, its parameters cannot be easily delimited or contained, it may even impact the entire clan, and it can only be countered effectively by outsiders who may have more powerful sources of magic. The potential and actual violence controlled by women is viewed as necessary to reimpose a morally just order to social relationships that they believe are out of balance. Again, other cultures use supernatural forces to stop or impose violence, such as Kaliai wives who threaten spouses with sorcery or, because they are deemed polluting during menstruation, instill life-threatening fear of contamination.[67] Violence, then, takes many forms, and cross-cultural investigations must remain open to various possibilities.

The above terms and definitions highlight the need to delineate more precisely the parameters of culture. As with family violence, precisely what constitutes a culture remains a highly controversial issue.[68] Many now even argue that the traditional conception of culture—as independent, coherent, and stable entities—rapidly becomes irrelevant, especially in an increasingly interconnected global society[69] and particularly when approached from different members' perspectives.[70] Although the text actually highlights local realities and the place of distinct cultural identities in international and national politics as well as in everyday lives of people and recognizes the need for investigations to do so,[71] the text adopts a much more permeable view of cultures. The reasons for this approach are explained most directly in chapter 4 but also are argued throughout.

To simplify the presentation of issues related to cultures, I use the following terms. I use *culture* rather broadly to refer to a geographically localized group or society; the same broad reference to culture is meant by use of the phrase "cultural life." The terms *cultural practices*, *cultural forces*, or *cultural factors* denote derivatives of cultures that help explain individuals' actions, thoughts, and emotions. The term *cultural location* is used to highlight how specific individuals or groups are situated in the relevant culture and are influenced differently by cultural practices, factors, and forces. Thus, depending on one's cultural location, cultural practices, factors, or forces may cause violence to individuals; however, from the view of the culture or even the individual, the events and outcomes may not be perceived as violent.

The challenges associated with defining and discussing family violence and culture find parallels in efforts to define and accept human rights. Human rights clearly have different sources, and cultures place different emphases on different aspects of those rights.[72] Those differences make it difficult to evaluate the extent to which human rights are recognized and respected. To address those difficulties, I adopt an empiricist approach to human rights. That is, I define human rights mainly according to international instruments—treaties, customary international law, declarations of human rights, and judicial opinions and scholarly commentaries regarding those instruments. This approach embraces the notion that human rights exist only to the extent that they are recognized as such by public international law and policy or that they are suggested as outcomes of international human rights principles.[73] The approach does not deny that cultures and nations have their own conceptions and sources of human rights; indeed, all cultures exhibit some respect for international human rights and, arguably, all cultures recognize most of the enumerated international human rights as critical (that is why they can legitimately be called "human" rights). The distinction between the rights are for analytical purposes in that they allow for comparing the more localized rights and local emphases placed on those rights with international human rights standards.

I demonstrate that human rights law pervasively involves laws regulating nations and as such focuses on societies more than individual cultures. The actual language of treaties and human rights documents, however, makes use of the term *culture* instead of *society*, which reflects a concern for cultural practices regardless of the society or nation in which the practices are found (see chapter 4). Because human rights law focuses on cultures and their practices rather than societies, the analysis seeks to make limited use of the term *society*. When used, *society* refers to groups of cultures (as in "American society") or to the cultural group as a whole (as is commonly done when referring to "indigenous societies").

In analyzing the recognition, observance, and implementation of human rights, the text undoubtedly calls for taking culture seriously. To do so, I take an interdisciplinary approach that does not fall neatly into existing disciplines that investigate cross-cultural and cultural materials. Thus, experts in cross-cultural psychology,[74] comparative anthropology,[75] cultural psychology,[76] psychological anthropology,[77] comparative criminology,[78] cultural criminology,[79] and cross-cultural criminology[80] find that the text does not remain faithful to their methodological and interpretive approaches. Unlike the works emerging from those disciplines, the present analysis does not compare one culture with another in the specifics of certain practices or compare practices with statistical or scientific rigor, as Levinson[81] has done with family violence and Finkelhor[82] has done with child sexual abuse. Nor do analyses present how a specific culture's numerous cultural forces impact one form of violence, as exemplified by the works of numerous anthropologists.[83] Nor do I seek universal manifestations of aggression or universal explanations for crime by men or women, as done by researchers interested in cross-cultural psychology.[84] Rather, I interpret and synthesize existing research from different cultures to understand how cultural practices relate to various forms of family violence. In addition, I take what we know about cultures to enhance the recognition and implementation of human rights.

The analysis that follows does not deny the significance of existing approaches and recognizes that operating outside of disciplinary boundaries has important limits. Existing approaches identified above certainly occupy an important place in the analysis that follows. For example, close analysis and evaluations of cultural practices in the contexts of acculturation and immigration (see chapter 7) relies on contributions from cross-cultural psychologists. However, reliance on already accumulated materials necessarily leaves analyses incomplete. This is especially true for the many forms of family violence that remain hidden because of cultural forces that foster victims' shame, embarrassment, fear, and compliance. As the chapters that follow make more obvious, however, reliance on an admittedly flawed approach currently remains necessary given the understanding of family violence and cultural forces impacting violence. The same is true for human rights law. International conceptions of human rights remain incomplete; but the incompleteness serves as an important point of reference to develop protections against violence associated with families.

An Overview of the Chapters

In the chapters that follow, I examine important issues of definitions, legitimacy of standards, and methods for intervention to address family violence. Chapter 1 introduces readers to international law and its human rights movement. This foundational chapter details institutional structures that have become responsible for defining human rights and how the international community now accepts universal principles and rudimentary human rights standards. To do so, the discussion begins by highlighting traditional precepts and some radical developments in international human rights law and concludes with an analysis of several human rights documents that aim to regulate family structures, dynamics, and social conditions that support them. The analysis emphasizes how shifts in global dynamics and social conditions greatly influence the international community's human rights agenda, and how those shifts now aim to develop a human rights agenda addressing family life and the cultural forces that sustain it.

Part I consists of two chapters that explore the numerous intersections between cultural life and family violence. Chapter 2 surveys the nature of family violence from a cross-cultural perspective. The thematic investigation examines family violence manifested throughout the life span, an approach that remains absent from cross-cultural and human rights analyses. The approach emphasizes the manner in which individuals who maltreat others are influenced by their cultural location. That emphasis results in the need to understand how cultures define violence, create climates conducive to violence, serve as buffers from violence, and influence intervention efforts. This cultural view of family violence tempers more polarized conceptions that focus either on individuals or their social surroundings to understand the causes, nature, and consequences of violence.

Chapter 3 then examines how cultural forces stifle legal reforms that seek to respond to family violence. The discussion provides examples of five different yet interrelated cultural forces that challenge responses to family violence. These forces include the following: ingrained discrimination against vulnerable individuals, limited economic and social resources, customary law and customs, religious traditions, and prejudice against entire groups of people within societies. These cultural forces underscore the need for a human rights perspective, the need to proceed cautiously in urging reform, and the difference a human rights approach can make.

In Part II, I return to the analysis to human rights law and address the second goal of this inquiry: how transformations in human rights law now require responses to family violence. The argument proceeds in two parts—one concerns the manner in which human rights affect cultures and another concerns the manner in which human rights affect familial relationships associated with violence. Chapter 4 begins with an analysis of polarized debates and conceptions of cultures in human rights law, of the manner in which human rights law approaches cultures and cultural practices, and reasons to rethink fears of cultural imperialism. The discussion then details important developments in modern human rights law that directly aim to affect cultural practices. That analysis leads to the need to emphasize two points: (a) the significant role cultural forces play in interpreting, applying, and enforcing human rights and (b) the need to recognize the place of human rights law in the context of rapid cultural and global changes. Chapter 5 moves the analysis toward the approach of human rights law to issues related to family violence. The chapter underscores how both domestic and international legal systems increasingly do not distinguish between public and private behavior in attempts to deal with harms. The merging of private and public boundaries makes legitimate intervention in violent families and moves human rights analyses toward efforts to understand how national and international behaviors and regulations may be molded to respond more appropriately to family issues. The analysis enumerates several bundles of human rights that may serve to insulate individuals from family violence. These rights are examined at three levels: (a) internation levels (e.g., right to development and rights of aliens); (b) intranation levels (e.g., rights to life and health; protection from torture and inhuman treatment; freedom from discrimination; right to education, liberty, and security of the person); and (c) interpersonal levels (e.g., right to protection from "private" forms of violence). The analysis emphasizes the need to recognize how these rights and levels of analysis are inseparable and to transform how the international community, nations, societies, and individuals treat each other.

Part III brings the analysis to the United States. The analysis necessarily proceeds in two important directions: (a) how the United States approaches human rights law and (b) how the United States makes use of cultural information in its responses to family violence. Chapters 6 and 7 address these topics. Chapter 6 details how international human rights law works in U.S. law and suggests how human rights principles can make, and do make, a difference. To do so, the analysis highlights two different approaches to the application of human rights law in domestic contexts: a narrow approach (espoused by most commentators) and a broad approach. These two perspectives are used to highlight the potential impact of human rights law on current approaches to family violence. Taken together, the perspectives suggest that human rights principles offer three challenges: (a) individuals must become subjects of their own rights, (b) individuals must gain rights against their own families, and (c) States must actively support individuals within families. These three principles differ dramatically from current approaches to family violence policy making in the United States. To highlight the difference, reference is made to the United States' approaches to the numerous human rights detailed in chapters 1 and 5.

Chapter 7 explores the various ways that U.S. law makes use of cultural evidence in responses to family violence. A discussion of the controversial and peculiar manner in which cultural evidence is used (and not used) serves as a basis to explore alternative responses to cultural information. The proposed responses draw from human rights principles and highlight parallels between the manner in which human rights law requires countries to approach each other's cultural practices and the manner in which countries may approach cultural practices within their own borders. The chapter suggests concrete steps to interrogate cultural evidence, including the need to (a) determine its relevance and reliability, (b) consider dissenting voices to such evidence, (c) weigh the harms and benefits of the cultural practices, and (d) seek alternative responses to existing cultural practices. Although seemingly reasonable, the approach differs considerably from the formal use of cultural information in U.S. law relating to family violence. The chapter ends with ways to counter objections to the use of cultural information in a manner that respects human rights mandates.

Chapter 8 revisits themes and details how attention to human rights principles and cultural forces can help re-envision approaches to family violence. The chapter then explores the implications for the United States of four basic developments in human rights law: (a) providing individual family members with rights, (b) having the rights adhere to individuals and allowing the individuals to control the exercise of these rights, (c) recognizing that families are inseparable from their cultural location, and (d) recognizing how human rights seek to transform individual relationships and cultural forces. The chapter ends with a delineation of how modern conceptions of human rights may (and increasingly must) help people move away from practices and assumptions that condone, encourage, and improperly respond to family violence.

Conclusion

Reality and human rights law defy the ideal of nurturing, care-taking families. Most human suffering around the globe tends to occur by family members or because of families. Although it is critical not to place blame on families alone—they simply constitute one institution and respond to other cultural forces—their paradoxical position in societies offers hope for efforts to alleviate violence. Human rights law seeks to uncover and respond to the reality that individual members within "families" may enjoy few rights while still protecting families so that they perform their traditional functions. In exploring intersections between family violence and human rights and the implications of those intersections, this text offers four fundamental contributions. The text applies a cross-cultural approach to challenge current psychological and sociological conceptions of family violence; expands conceptions of international and human rights law to reveal that they reach private, violent behavior; applies emerging conceptions of culture to legal systems and their development to highlight how human rights legitimately affect cultural forces and personal life; and details how modern conceptions of human rights can (and increasingly do) transform U.S. policy responses to family violence.

Endnotes

1. *See* N. Scheper-Hughes and C. Sargent, Eds., *Small Wars: The Cultural Politics of Childhood* (Berkeley: University of California Press, 1998).
2. *See* J. I. Kosberg and J. L. Garcia, Eds., *Elder Abuse: International and Cross-Cultural Perspectives* (New York: Haworth Press, 1995).
3. *See, e.g.,* L. L. Heise, "Violence Against Women: An Integrated, Ecological Framework," *Violence Against Women* 4 (1998):262–290.
4. *See* R. J. R. Levesque, *Child Sexual Abuse: A Human Rights Perspective* (Bloomington: Indiana University Press, 1999); Roger J. R. Levesque, *Adolescents, Sex, and the Law: Preparing Adolescents for Responsible Citizenship* (Washington, DC: American Psychological Association, 2000).
5. R. J. R. Levesque, "Piercing the Family's Private Veil: Family Violence, International Human Rights, and the Cross-Cultural Record," *Law & Policy* 21 (1999):161–187.
6. J. E. Durrant, "Evaluating the Success of Sweden's Corporal Punishment Ban," *Child Abuse & Neglect* 23 (1999):435–448; M. Straus, *Beating the Devil Out of Them: Corporal Punishment in American Families* (New York: Lexington Books, 1994).
7. L. Simmons, "Ageing in Primitive Societies: A Comparative Survey of Family Life and Relationships," in *Handbook of Social Gerontology: Societal Aspects of Ageing*, C. Tibbets, Ed. (Chicago: University of Chicago Press, 1960).
8. *See* L. M. Morgan, "Ambiguities Lost: Fashioning the Fetus Into a Child in Ecuador and the United States," in *Small Wars: The Cultural Politics of Childhood*, N. Scheper-Hughes and C. Sargent, Eds. (Berkeley: University of California Press, 1998); N. Scheper-Hughes, *Death Without Weeping: The Violence of Everyday Life in Brazil* (Berkeley: University of California Press, 1992).
9. A. Krugman, "Being Female Can Be Fatal: An Examination of India's Ban on Pre-Natal Gender Testing," *Cardozo Journal of International & Comparative Law* 6 (1998):215–237.
10. R. J. R. Levesque, "International Children's Rights: Can They Make a Difference in American Family Policy?" *American Psychologist* 51 (1996):1251–1256.
11. M. Bograd, "Strengthening Domestic Violence Theories: Intersections of Race, Class, Sexual Orientation, and Gender," *Journal of Marital and Family Therapy* 25 (1999):275–289.
12. G. Zdenkowski, "The International Covenant on Civil and Political Rights and Euthanasia," *UNSW Law Journal* 20 (1997):170–194.
13. A. P. Glascock, "By Any Other Name, It Is Still Killing: A Comparison of the Treatment of the Elderly in America and Other Societies," in *The Cultural Context of Aging: Worldwide Perspectives*, J. Sokolovsky, Ed. (New York: Bergin & Garvey, 1990).

14. Levesque, *Adolescents, Sex, and the Law*.

15. K. Silbaugh, "Turning Labor Into Love: Housework and the Law," *Northwestern University Law Review* 91 (1996): 1–86.

16. L. Aitken and G. Griffin, *Gender Issues in Elder Abuse* (Thousand Oaks, CA: Sage, 1996).

17. C. S. Tang, "The Rate of Physical Child Abuse in Chinese Families: A Community Survey in Hong Kong," *Child Abuse & Neglect* 22 (1999):381–391.

18. M. Smithey, "Infant Homicide: Victim/Offender Relationship and Causes of Death," *Journal of Family Violence* 13 (1998):285–297.

19. P. Chmielewski, "The Public and the Private in Primitive Societies," *International Political Science Review* 12 (1991):267–280.

20. M. A. Fineman, *The Neutered Mother, the Sexual Family and Other Twentieth Century Tragedies* (New York: Routledge, 1995); M. A. Fineman and R. Mykitiuk (Eds.), *The Public Nature of Private Violence: The Discovery of Domestic Abuse* (New York: Routledge, 1995).

21. D. L. Wardle, "Legal Claims for Same Sex Marriage: Efforts to Legitimate a Retreat From Marriage by Redefining Marriage," *South Texas Law Review* 39 (1998):735–768.

22. U.N. General Assembly, 44th Sess., Official Records, Suppl. 49 at 166, Resolution 44/25, A/44/49; 28 ILM 1448 (1989).

23. *Id.*, Article 19.

24. *Id.*, Article 35.

25. *Id.,* Article 36.

26. *Id.,* Article 4.

27. *See, e.g.,* Articles 3, 5, 7, and 8.

28. U.N. General Assembly, 48th Sess., Official Records, Resolution 104, Agenda Item 11, A/RES/48/104.

29. *Id.,* Article 1 (Preamble).

30. *Id.,* Article 4 (Preamble).

31. 1993 World Conference on Human Rights, A/Conf. 157/24.

32. U.N. Doc A/Conf. 177-20 (1995) (draft Platform); DPI/1766/Wom (1996) (final).

33. *See* J. L. Charney, "Universal International Law," *American Journal of International Law* 87 (1993):529–551.

34. G. H. Fox, "New Approaches to International Human Rights: The Sovereign State Revisited," in *State Sovereignty: Change and Persistence in International Relations*, S. H. Hashmi, Ed. (University Park: Pennsylvania State University Press, 1997),

35. C. Henderson, *International Relations: Conflict and Cooperation at the Turn of the 21st Century* (Boston: McGraw-Hill, 1997).

36. M. Akehurst, *A Modern Introduction to International Law* (New York: Routledge, 1993); O. Schachter, *International Law in Theory and Practice* (Boston: Marinus Nijhoff, 1991).

37. P. R. Baehr and L. Gordenker, *The United Nations at the End of the 1990s* 3rd ed. (New York: St. Martin's Press, 1999).

38. J. J. Paust et al., Eds., *International Criminal Law: Cases and Materials* (Durham, NC: Carolina Academic Press, 1997).

39. *See, e.g.,* M. J. Perry, *The Constitution, the Court, and Human Rights* (New Haven, CT: Yale University Press, 1982); *cf.* D. Q. Thomas, "Advancing Rights Protection in the United States: An Internationalized Advocacy Strategy," *Harvard Human Rights Journal* 9 (1996):15–26.

40. U.N. General Assembly, 34th Sess., Official Records, Suppl. 46 at 193, GA Resolution 34/180, Doc A/34/46, 1979.

41. *See* Thomas, "Advancing Rights Protection in the United States."

42. U.N. General Assembly, 21st Sess., Official Records, Suppl. 16 at 49, GA Resolution 2200 Annex, A/6316; 993 UNTS 3; 6 ILM 360, 1966.

43. *See also* R. J. R. Levesque, "Child Advocacy and the Power of Human Rights Law," in *Children as Equals? Exploring the Rights of the Child*, B. Klug and K. Alaimo, Eds. (Chicago: St. Xavier University, in press-a).

44. S. M. Schneebaum, "Human Rights in the United States Courts: The Role of Lawyers," *Washington & Lee Law Review* 55 (1998):737–756.

45. J. Quigley, "Human Rights Defenses in U.S. Courts," *Human Rights Quarterly* 20 (1998): 555–591.

46. H. Blackmun, "The Supreme Court and the Law of Nations," *Yale Law Journal* 104 (1994):40.

47. Stanford v. Kentucky, 492 U.S. 361, 369 (1989).

48. *See* C. A. Bradley, "Breard, Our Dualist Constitution, and the Internationalist Conception," *Stanford Law Review* 51 (1999):529–566.

49. *See, e.g.,* Breard v. Greene, 118 S.Ct. 1352 (1998); *see also* chapter 6.

50. R. J. R. Levesque, "Piercing the Family's Private Veil."

51. *Cf.* Fineman and Mykitiuk, *The Public Nature of Private Violence*.

52. *See, e.g.,* M. Schuler, Ed., *Freedom From Violence: Women's Strategies From Around the World* (New York: UNIFEM, 1992); L. E. Walker, "Psychology and Domestic Violence Around the World," *American Psychologist* 54 (1999):21–29.

53. *See, e.g.,* Kosberg and Garcia, *Elder Abuse*.

54. *See, e.g.,* D. A. Counts, J. K. Brown, and J. C. Campbell, "Introduction," in *Sanctions and Sanctuary: Cultural Perspectives on the Beating of Wives* 2nd ed., D. A. Counts, J. K. Brown, and J. C. Campbell, Eds. (Urbana: University of Illinois Press, 1999); Heise, "Violence Against Women."

55. *See, e.g.,* A. S. Bilyeu, "Trokosi—The Practice of Sexual Slavery in Ghana: Religious and Cultural Freedom vs. Human Rights," *Indiana International and Comparative Law Review* 9 (1999):457–504.

56. *See* A. Jamrozik and L. Nocella, *The Sociology of Social Problems: Theoretical Perspectives and Methods of Intervention* (New York: Cambridge University Press, 1998).

57. *See, e.g.,* Heise, "Violence Against Women"; Levesque, *Child Sexual Abuse*.

58. R. E. Emery and L. Laumann-Billings, "An Overview of the Nature, Causes, and Consequences of Abusive Family Relationships: Toward Differentiating Maltreatment and Violence," *American Psychologist* 53 (1998):121–135.

59. *See* Levesque, *Child Sexual Abuse*.

60. *Cf.* L. deMause, "Childhood and Cultural Evolution," *Journal of Psychohistory* 26 (1999):642–723.

61. *See* R. B. Edgerton, *Sick Societies: Challenging the Myth of Primitive Harmony* (New York: Free Press, 1992).

62. For differences between these methodological approaches, *see* C. Kagitçibasi, *Family and Human Development Across Cultures: A View From the Other Side* (Mahwah, NJ: Erlbaum, 1996); H. C. Triandis, *Culture and Social Behavior* (New York: McGraw Hill, 1994).

63. W. E. Mitchell, "Why Wape Men Don't Beat Their Wives: Constraints Toward Domestic Tranquility in a New Guinea Society," in *To Have and To Hit: Cultural Perspectives on Wife Beating* 2nd ed., D. A. Counts, J. K. Brown, and J. C. Campbell, Eds. (Urbana: University of Illinois Press, 1999).

64. *See* D. A. Counts, "'All Men Do It': Wife Beating in Kaliai, Papua New Guinea," in *To Have and To Hit: Cultural Perspectives on Wife Beating* 2nd ed., D. A. Counts, J. K. Brown, and J. C. Campbell, Eds. (Urbana: University of Illinois Press, 1999).

65. *See* S. Lateef, "Wife Abuse Among Indo-Fijians," in *To Have and To Hit: Cultural Perspectives on Wife Beating* 2nd ed., D. A. Counts, J. K. Brown, and J. C. Campbell, Eds. (Urbana: University of Illinois Press, 1999); B. D. Miller, "Wife Beating in India: Variations on a Theme," in *To Have and To Hit: Cultural Perspectives on Wife Beating* 2nd

ed., D. A. Counts, J. K. Brown, and J. C. Campbell, Eds. (Urbana: University of Illinois Press, 1999).

66. L. M. Carucci, "Nudging Her Harshly and Killing Him Softly: Displays of Disenfranchisement on Ujelang Atoll," in *To Have and To Hit: Cultural Perspectives on Wife Beating* 2nd ed., D. A. Counts, J. K. Brown, and J. C. Campbell, Eds. (Urbana: University of Illinois Press, 1999).

67. Counts, "All Men Do It."

68. A. Kuper, *Culture: The Anthropologists' Account* (Cambridge, MA: Harvard University Press, 1999); C. W. Nuckolls, *Culture: A Problem That Cannot Be Solved* (Madison: University of Wisconsin Press, 1998).

69. *See, e.g.,* H. J. M. Hermans and H. J. G. Kempen, "Moving Cultures: The Perilous Problems of Cultural Dichotomies in a Globalizing Society," *American Psychologist* 53 (1998):1111–1120.

70. Nuckolls, *Culture*.

71. *Cf.* T. L. Holdstock, "The Perilous Problem of Neglecting Cultural Realities," *American Psychologist* 10 (1999):838–839.

72. *See, e.g.,* P. Van Ness, Ed., *Debating Human Rights: Critical Essays From the United States and Asia* (New York: Routledge, 1999).

73. For a similar use, *see* D. P. Forsythe, *The Internationalization of Human Rights* (Lexington, MA: Lexington Books, 1991).

74. M. H. Segall, W. J. Lonner, and J. W. Berry, "Cross-Cultural Psychology as a Scholarly Discipline: On the Flowering of Culture in Behavioral Research," *American Psychologist* 53 (1998):1101–1110.

75. R. L. Monroe and R. H. Monroe, "A Comparative Anthropological Perspective," in *Handbook of Cross-Cultural Psychology: Theory and Method* Vol. 1., J. W. Berry, Y. H. Poortinga, and J. Pandey, Eds. (Boston: Allyn & Bacon, 1997).

76. M. Cole, *Cultural Psychology: A Once and Future Discipline* (Cambridge, MA: Harvard University Press, 1996).

77. R. A. LeVine, *Culture, Behavior, and Personality* 2nd ed. (Chicago: Aldine, 1982).

78. P. Bierne and J. Hill, *Comparative Criminology: An Annotated Bibliography* (New York: Greenwood Press, 1991).

79. J. Ferrell and C. Sanders, *Cultural Criminology* (Boston: Northeastern University Press, 1995).

80. R. Heiner, *Criminology: A Cross-Cultural Perspective* (Minneapolis–St. Paul: West, 1996).

81. D. Levinson, *Family Violence in Cross-Cultural Perspective* (Newbury Park, CA: Sage, 1989).

82. D. Finkelhor, "The International Epidemiology of Child Sexual Abuse," *Child Abuse & Neglect* 18 (1994):409–417.

83. *See, e.g.,* J. Gregor, "Male Dominance and Sexual Coercion," in *Cultural Psychology: Essays on Comparative Human Development*, J. W. Stigler, R. A. Shweder, and G. Herdt, Eds. (New York: Cambridge University Press, 1990); N. Scheper-Hughes, "Mother Love and Child Death in Northeast Brazil," in *Cultural Psychology: Essays on Comparative Human Development*, J. W. Stigler and R. A. Shweder, and G. Herdt, Eds. (New York: Cambridge University Press, 1990).

84. *See* D. L. Best and J. E. Williams, "Sex, Gender, and Culture," in *Handbook of Cross-Cultural Psychology: Theory and Method* Vol. 3., J. W. Berry, M. H. Segall, and J. Kagitcibasi, Eds. (Boston: Allyn & Bacon, 1997); M. H. Segall, C. R. Ember, and M. Ember, "Aggression, Crime, and Warfare," in *Handbook of Cross-Cultural Psychology: Theory and Method* Vol. 1., J. W. Berry, M. H. Segall, and J. Kagitcibasi, Eds. (Boston: Allyn & Bacon, 1997).

Chapter 1
TRADITIONS AND INNOVATIONS IN
HUMAN RIGHTS LAW

For centuries, the field of international law was concerned with legal relationships between sovereign States. Sovereignty, which was based on political independence and territorial impermeability, helped define international law by a simple maxim: Only States (what people commonly understand as nations or countries) possess international legal rights and duties; no other entities are capable of possessing international legal rights and obligations.[1] International law essentially involved how nations dealt with one another, particularly how nations respected or failed to respect other nations' borders. Thus, cultural groups, corporations, religious groups, families, individuals, and any other entity that today may be viewed as legal subjects or objects possessed neither rights nor obligations under international law. Matters within particular State jurisdictions were matters of State, not international issues.

The international community's *laissez-faire* approach to domestic issues effected important consequences. The manner in which nations treated their own inhabitants and legal entities was not a subject of international concern. States resisted all criticisms of their domestic actions with the simple but dispositive claim that human rights were matters of domestic jurisdiction and the responsibility of each State alone. Government officials essentially were free to oppress, maim, kill, and heap other abuses on their citizens. Governments were free to embark on repressive social policies that would lead to strife, struggle, and rampant discrimination against entire groups of individuals. Governments were free to ignore ingrained social problems, such as poverty, that were linked to numerous rights violations. Under the traditional rules of international law, then, States retained considerable power to dictate their domestic affairs.

Times have changed. Since the middle of the 1900s but especially since that century's last decades, how nations behave within and beyond their own borders has become a matter of international concern, of international politics, and of international law. International law no longer posits that national governments have unfettered control over what happens within their own territories. Nor does international law posit that only States can be the subject of regulation or that other entities (e.g., corporations) do not perform State functions. International law has evolved and adapted to the emergence of radically different roles and functions of States and of other social entities. As a result, international law has broadened to include much more than legal relationships between States. International law now includes legal relationships between and among international organizations, individuals, multinational corporations, and other entities that may possess characteristics of international personality.

Transformations in the reach of international law spurred, supported, and complemented the development of modern human rights law. As a result, international human rights law now applies both to international and domestic concerns. The modern human rights movement has ushered a moral *lingua franca* available for such diverse contexts as global politics and interpersonal relationships. Heads of State, grassroots associations and nongovernmental organizations, religious communities, rebel movements, and even children argue their causes in the parlance of human rights. The language is not just available to those deemed victims of human rights violations. Even oppressors and tyrants invoke human rights and the need to protect fundamental ideals acceded to by the international community. Human rights issues are raised in political, economic, social, cultural, and individual interactions across the world.

The transformation of human rights law finds clear expression in a host of recent events that have riveted the attention of human rights activists. The dramatic arrest and attempt to extradite Augusto Pinochet for trial presents an unprecedented development in human rights law. While recovering from back surgery in a London clinic in the fall of 1998, Pinochet (a leader of a military dictatorship that had ruled Chile from 1973 to 1991), was arrested by British police acting on an Interpol warrant from Spain. Spain sought extradition for trial for alleged violations of most serious of international crimes: genocide, terrorism, torture, and the various crimes that constitute the practice of forced disappearance. Spain gained jurisdiction for the charges by invoking the traditional jurisdictional concept of *passive personality*, which permits a country to prosecute defendants who victimize its citizens in any place outside of the home country.

As originally filed, the charges named seven victims of Spanish descent who had been murdered or who had "disappeared" in Chile during Pinochet's dictatorship. Although Pinochet avoided trial because of ill health, the extradition proceedings against him were successful in establishing legal precedent that was hailed by human rights activists and academic commentators as a major advance for international human rights law.[2] That the arrest of General Pinochet so took the world by surprise reveals not only how rarely countries avail themselves of existing legal tools to address the most serious crimes against humanity but also the immensely precedential value of the proceedings against Pinochet. Having one country judge the human rights practices of another nation, through criminal prosecution of that country's former leader, undoubtedly stands as a radical departure from accepted models of international law.[3]

The unprecedented efforts to gain Pinochet's extradition drew on a rapidly expanding human rights foundation that increasingly responds aggressively to abuses by instituting tribunals even for violations that heretofore remained essentially invisible and unaddressed by human rights law. Prior to the 1990s and despite decades of active campaigns by various international organizations to draw attention to violence against women, for example, the international community all but ignored reports of rape, sexual assault, and sexual slavery as a facet of war.[4] The 1990s, however, witnessed a remarkable reversal. The responses to the rapes and other forms of violence against women in Yugoslavia and Rwanda in the 1990s drew unusual attention. In fact, widespread reports of violence committed against women in the former Yugoslavia played a key role in the U.N. decision to establish an ad hoc international tribunal to prosecute those responsible for war crimes.[5]

The need to respond to such crises was so powerful that, soon after the establishment of the Yugoslav Tribunal, a similar tribunal was established to address atrocities committed during Rwanda's internal armed conflict.[6] Although few prosecutions actually have occurred, it is difficult to discount these tribunals' singular achievements. At the end of 1998, the Yugoslav Tribunal handed down a series of judgments that, for the first time, found a defendant guilty of rape and classified it as a war crime.[7] Similarly, decisions from the Rwandan tribunal authoritatively affirmed the intricate linkage of sexual violence to the genocide committed during the Rwandan conflict.[8] These judgments constitute the most progressive case law on gender ever pronounced by an international judicial body. Although unusually progressive in light of traditional human rights law, the existence of the tribunals and their findings provide the international community with important precedents likely to have enduring and widespread implications.

The international human rights community also responds to leaders who are not deemed at war but who are alleged to have committed flagrant human rights violations. Responses to the Taliban in Afghanistan provide an important case in point. When the Taliban took power in the mid-1990s, one of its first edicts removed girls from schools, forbade women from employment outside the home, and required women to cover themselves completely when they appeared in public. This measure clearly abrogated numerous principles set forth in human rights standards, particularly prohibitions against discrimination against women and minority religions.[9] The international community responded by rejecting the Taliban as legitimate rulers; it refused to provide them with representation at the United Nations and urged economic sanctions. The rejection is significant, especially because the Taliban actually do control the country, and at least some commentators justify their actions as consistent with human rights standards and principles, such as the right to protect religious and cultural beliefs and the traditional right of sovereign countries to direct their domestic policies.[10]

The international community's responses to behaviors that challenge respect for fundamental human rights highlight the legitimacy gained by human rights law. Human rights may be used to scrutinize behaviors within resisting nations' borders and to challenge the actions of leaders once deemed immune from international sanctions. Regardless of the legitimacy of the Taliban's claim or of Pinochet's attempts to avoid accountability, it is now clear that the international community can respond to alleged abuses. The aggressive responses to war crimes illustrate even more clearly the human rights community's power; commentators do not argue against the need to hold those charged with war crimes accountable, despite the numerous political considerations that are generally raised and that work to protect those who perpetrate such atrocities.[11] The power of the international community's responses increasingly overwhelms dissenting voices. International human rights advocacy certainly has come far and increasingly gains power when it converges in response to human rights abuses.

Few would question the rapid advance of human rights ideals; nor would they question the need for such advances. Although recent advances may be right and further justice, the progression may remain troubling. For example, by all accounts Pinochet's regime involved numerous human rights violations. Yet placing criminal enforcement in the hands of self-selected third-party governments presents numerous dangers. The danger of politically motivated prosecutions of U.S. officials already has caused the United States to withhold its support for the proposed International Criminal Court, an institution that would provide far more criminal process protections than the method involved in this case.[12] Likewise, conducting prosecutions without the consent of the country where the abuses occurred runs the risk of undermining the choices made by the very communities most affected by the human rights abuses. Nations may have rejected prosecution to facilitate transitions to democracy or opted for alternative processes to prosecution, such as the truth and reconciliation process developed in South Africa.[13] It is unclear why the executive official in one country—in this instance, Spain—should determine how international human rights law should be structured or enforced. Recognition of atrocities and of the need to respond does not dictate the proper course of events, and any course of events likely remains inadequate to respond to massive and sustained human rights violations.

Even the most recent achievement of the human rights movement, the ad hoc international tribunal, exhibits numerous shortcomings. Although there may be room for efforts to hold individuals accountable, the focus on individual adjudication can neither capture the nature of atrocities nor fully redress them. Rationales for establishing these tribunals range broadly: from educating people about human rights, deterring future atrocities, punishing those who committed the atrocities, and incapacitating offenders to restoring peace and ending cycles of violence by reconciling communities.[14] These numerous objectives clearly cannot be achieved through the institution of tribunals—the achievement of human rights entails a much more complex process than the establishment of a court. Effective responses must address the root causes of genocide and the creation of a society that fosters the entire spectrum of human rights. Not surprisingly, some argue that nongovernmental organizations, which mobilize efforts and help cultivate a consciousness about human rights, are the most likely candidates to accomplish proper responses to human rights conflicts involving mass atrocities.[15] Others propose that truth and reconciliation commissions can best address past massive human rights violations of genocide in instances of ongoing animosity and retributive violence between former and current governments and their respective followers.[16] These criticisms are significant. Criticisms reflect the concern that the international community's response necessarily sets precedents that become part of the human rights machinery that could narrow responses to problems that require a much more expansive approach.

Although the above examples of massive human rights violations do not evoke much sympathy toward perpetrators, the cases highlight well how, even though protecting human rights and responding to human rights violations may be a good idea, realities complicate efforts to determine and respond to violations. Despite impressive and substantial progress, international human rights law still struggles with basic concerns: Who determines what constitutes human rights violations? Who should determine whether rights were violated? Who should respond to violations? What should be the nature of the response? These questions affirm how images of human rights that encourage quick resolutions mask deep ambiguities in the nature of human rights. The normative authority of human rights claims stands against a widely shared confusion regarding the relationship between the popular, moral, and imagined views of human rights' ideals and the more mundane legal dimensions of human rights that require deliberate action and principled responses. The above human rights crises emerging from complex sociopolitical processes—much like the human rights violations I examine in the chapters that follow—require much more than prosecution of criminal violations or economic sanctions against rogue governments.

Given the massive expansion of human rights law and its attendant challenges,

I begin this investigation with an examination of the content of international human rights law and its sources. This discussion remains necessarily general as it focuses on how the international community has negotiated and accepted rudimentary standards and universal principles and how those principles now reach so far into countries that they affect (and actually seek to regulate) family life. The analysis emphasizes how shifts in global dynamics and social conditions greatly influence the international community's human rights agenda, and how those shifts now include an aggressive and expansive human rights arsenal that provides an unprecedented statement on the numerous ways human rights law implicates family life and the cultural structures that sustain it.

Formal Sources of International Human Rights Law

Over the past half-century, the globalization of human rights has emerged from several sources and numerous human rights regimes. The most precedent-setting, expansive, universal, and revolutionary human rights system, however, clearly derives from the work of the United Nations. Under the leadership of the United Nations, the global community has elaborated on and established a now massive body of international law, which serves as a foundation for human rights law. The United Nations clearly is the only governmental body with the most global reach consisting of Nation States (countries or States vs. states within a country) that belong to it and States Parties that agree to specific treaties. Although that transformation of human rights has taken several turns, its primary source continues to be the International Bill of Rights. The cornerstone of the International Bill of Rights, which continues to spur the human rights movement, is the Universal Declaration of Human Rights of 1948.[17] The Universal Declaration has been viewed as one of the greatest steps forward in the process of creating and ensuring modern human rights.[18] It proclaims that all people everywhere possess certain basic and identifiable rights, that universal standards exist for the world as a whole, and that human rights are matters of legitimate international concern and are no longer within the exclusive jurisdiction of Nation States. To transform the Universal Declaration's standards into enforceable principles, the treaty was supplemented by two additional international covenants: the Covenant on Civil and Political Rights of 1966 (Political Covenant)[19] and the Covenant on Economic, Social and Cultural Rights of 1966 (Economic and Social Covenant).[20] Taken together, these three documents constitute the International Bill of Rights.

Since the promulgation of the International Bill of Rights, other important extensions have been made to strengthen and expand the reach of international human rights law. Two of the most notable additions include the almost universal ratification of the Convention on the Elimination of All Forms of Discrimination Against Women of 1979[21] (Women's Convention) and the Convention on the Rights of the Child of 1989 (Children's Convention).[22] The United Nations has adopted other important human rights treaties, such as the Convention on the Elimination of All Forms of Racial Discrimination of 1969 (Racial Discrimination Convention).[23] In addition, the United Nations has adopted other precedent-setting mandates in the form of numerous declarations of human rights. Such efforts most significantly include the recent Vienna Declaration of Human Rights of 1993,[24] which directly addresses attempts to deal with conflicts between different rights and seeks to promote all human rights as indivisible and necessary parts of the global human rights revolution.

The substance of the rights protected in the International Bill of Rights and of the ensuing international mandates reflects the entire range of rights that have evolved over the past 50 years. Despite their recent formal appearance, these rights have evolved at such a rapid pace that there now exists four distinct but related generations of rights. These generations have been influenced by changing concerns about global issues relating to the power of nations and their roles in recognizing and ensuring basic human rights.

The *first generation of rights* concerns primarily protections of the basic security of people against State power. These first rights include civil and political protections for individuals from governmental interference and encroachment. That is, they represent "freedoms from" State powers. The Universal Declaration of Human Rights of 1948 exemplifies these first generation human rights through (for example) protections from certain forms of punishments undertaken by governments. These protections reflect what had fueled the development of human rights standards: the atrocities of State power and violations of basic standards of humanity by Nazi Germany. Indeed, it was recognition of these atrocities at the aftermath of World War II that focused world attention on the need for international promotion and protection of human rights and led to the founding of the United Nations and the virtual domination of Western nations and Western political concepts in the drafting of the Universal Declaration of Human Rights.

The Universal Declaration of Human Rights simply declared rights and promulgated broad principles; it remained to be determined how nations could be held accountable and what kinds of specific rights nations could be required to uphold. To the extent practicable, nations agreed to delineate further substantive rights and also to establish monitoring and enforcement mechanisms. That process remained so contentious that Nation States abandoned the concept of a single, all-encompassing covenant. Instead, the human rights enumerated in the Universal Declaration of Human Rights were segmented into two Covenants containing the "first" generation of civil and political rights (the Political Covenant) and the "second" generation of social, economic, and cultural rights (Economic and Social Covenant).

Although first-generation rights may have dominated the foundational document, the covenants that followed included what have become known as *second-generation rights*, which take the form of socioeconomic rights. These rights, championed by socialist and welfare states, involve "positive rights to" as opposed to "freedoms from" State actions. Although recognized as fundamental, the rights were considerably expansive. This generation of rights encompasses such broadly stated rights as those to employment and fair working conditions, to a standard of living that ensures health and well-being, to social security, to education, and to participation in the cultural life of the community.

Further expansion of the United Nations, particularly by the inclusion of countries from Africa and Asia in the 1950s and 1960s, fueled efforts for even greater human rights protections. Although the impact of Third World nations arguably was not explicitly felt in the two covenants, the new parties to the United Nations instrumentally promoted *third-generation rights*; these rights have become known as the right to "solidarity" or "development" and focus on the need for a more equitable social and economic order and a sustainable environment. The efforts culminated in the U.N. General Assembly's adoption of the Declaration of the Right to Development[25] in 1986. As cold war political and ideological confrontations subside and global tensions polarize the North (industrialized countries) and the South (developing countries), the human rights machinery increasingly seeks to recognize and address the impact of the different resources and general outlook of new member nations on international problems and human rights.

The rights of previously unrepresented groups expanded with their increased representation to the United Nations. Indigenous peoples constitute the most recent group to emerge and become powerful enough to succeed in their efforts to place their needs onto the global human rights agenda. Their claims that existing traditional State frameworks threaten their group rights fueled the propagation of *fourth-generation rights*, which roughly coincided with the final years of the cold war. These rights aim to protect peoples' rights to political self-determination, to grant them control over socioeconomic development, and to preserve group cultures, languages, cultural property, and natural resources.

Although the expansion of the human rights corpus certainly can be applauded, the development of several generations of rights has not eradicated disagreements. Profound disagreements revolve around the fundamentally different values and visions of governmental involvement in everyday life. As explained in chapter 4, commentators remain especially critical of Western conceptions of universal human rights and challenge prevailing notions of human rights as ethnocentric. Others insist that the rights of individuals cannot be separated from their collective context. The schisms and failure to embrace different conceptions of rights is important to note because it continues to influence (and especially to hinder) the furtherance of human rights. The hierarchical arrangement of categories of rights has resulted in the tendency to impute a questionable universality to the later generational categories. That tendency results in the human rights community's tendency to accept the earlier generation of rights as legitimate, universal rights and their concomitant tendency to legitimize less respect and concern for succeeding generations. Thus, Western states and nongovernmental organizations, in particular, have tended to treat economic, social, and cultural rights as if they were less important than civil and political rights, a difference in treatment that translates into the design of several complaint mechanisms to protect civil and political rights at the international level whereas the other rights often are considered as generally unenforceable directives for States.

Despite disagreements and continued conflicts, five conclusions may be made regarding the emergence and shifts of human rights law. First, although nations may not officially adopt the concept of indivisibility of rights, they increasingly do so in practice. The United Nations officially holds the position that human rights are indivisible and that to protect human rights, all visions or generations of rights must be respected. As I discuss in the last section of this chapter, the application of human rights obscures their "negative" or "positive" nature: When applied, rights necessarily involve both positive and negative dimensions. Second, the visions of human rights tend to be polarized and overdrawn. Those who champion civil and political rights generally recognize how they affect social and cultural rights and vice versa. Indeed, the general argument of those who champion specific generations of rights is that their approach recognizes the necessary prerequisite to the eventual recognition of the other rights (e.g., political rights are necessary to ensure economic rights).

Third, even though nations may subscribe more to some generations of rights

than to others, and even though those rights receive strong endorsement in the constitutional and legal systems of those countries, activist groups, nongovernmental
organizations, and even governmental organizations continue to charge those very
countries with involvement or complicity in violating those rights. Individuals and
communities increasingly call on human rights arguments to advance their social and
political claims; and the extent to which this occurs globally, irrespective of culture
or polity, expresses an emerging international civil society and the universal appeal
of human rights. Fourth, the foundational documents arguably contain all four generations of rights. The most highly ratified and accepted documents—the Universal
Declaration of Human Rights of 1948 and the Children's Convention of 1989—
actually contain all generations of rights; and the other documents may be interpreted
as affecting all rights. Last, it remains unclear why debates about approaches to
human rights and about which rights should retain precedence continue at the abstract
level as opposed to addressing basic issues, such as the plight of families, and how
nations can press forward and ensure greater respect for human rights. When addressing practical human rights issues, it becomes clear that enumerated human rights
are indivisible, that all forms of rights must be respected to ensure protection, and
that no society ensures fully the rights it champions.

Extending Human Rights Law to Family Members

The shifts in human rights law, which have led to distinct generations of human
rights, now include the regulation of families and, more importantly, an effort to
transform family life. Human rights law now focuses on the importance of recognizing the centrality of every individual in every family and every society. It also
recognizes the importance of family life for individual fulfillment. Thus, the international approach views family life in terms of individual rights and personal fulfillment. This conception of family life may seem paradoxical, especially when applied to an institution historically viewed in terms of obligation and of the need to
erase most of its members' individuality. Yet international human rights law now
clearly recognizes the significance of families for individuals and even views family
life as a necessary source for individual fulfillment.

Advances in the awareness and acceptance of human rights promise to revolutionize the way the world views family life. The slogan of the 1994 International
Year of the Family, "Building the Smallest Democracy at the Heart of Society,"
reflects the prevailing theme regarding how family life should operate and how
societies should approach families.[26] The slogan reflects the growing recognition of
the need to recognize each individual family member's rights, within every family
and every society. The objectives of the year were to increase awareness of the
importance of the family and family issues among governments and the private
sector; to enhance understandings of the functions and problems of families; to focus
attention on the rights and responsibilities of all family members; and to strengthen
national institutions to more effectively formulate, implement, and monitor family-
related policies and programs.[27] The year placed family life on the international and
national human rights agenda.

As with all other instances in which the United Nations institutes international
themes, the themes reflect an important, achieved status. The themes result not only

from the need to further recognize certain rights but also from recognition that an established body of international law supports them, that societies increasingly do recognize the themes as a worthy aspiration, and that the approach actually results in progress toward fulfilling human rights. The manner in which family life is approached, then, necessarily reflects the fundamental promises of human rights law. Family life is now a recognized subject of human rights.

Extent of Protection

Human rights documents reveal that respect for human dignity and equality guides international human rights law, and human rights approaches to families provide no exception. Although the International Year of the Family sought to catalyze efforts, numerous international documents already show the significance of families and of individuals within families. For example, the preambular paragraphs of the Universal Declaration of Human Rights of 1948, the Political Covenant of 1966, and the Economic and Social Covenant of 1966 all find "the inherent dignity and equality of *all members of the human family* as the foundation of freedom, justice and peace in the world" (emphasis added). Through these documents, the international community reaffirms the belief (expressed in the Preamble of the Universal Declaration of Human Rights) in "fundamental human rights, in the dignity and worth of the human person and in the equal rights of men and women." That is, the fundamental essence of human rights is that they are the entitlement of every human being by virtue of being human, regardless of domestic frontiers, be they familial or national.

International human rights law geared toward family life recognizes the fundamental need to respect all individuals within families even as the human rights protections also recognize the need to protect families. Perhaps the most oft-cited international provision concerning families is Article 23(1) of the Political Covenant of 1966, which states that "the family is the natural and fundamental group unit of society and is entitled to protection by society and the State." That provision is echoed by Article 10(1) of the Economic and Social Covenant of 1966, which also recognizes that "the widest possible protection and assistance should be accorded to the family, which is the natural and fundamental unit of society, particularly for its establishment and while it is responsible for the care and education of dependent children."

The foundational documents of the modern human rights movement, then, seek to recognize the inherent dignity and equality of inalienable rights of all, and that recognition forms the basis of all international human rights law. All civil and political rights as well as economic, social, and cultural rights recognized by these and all other international documents derive as necessary implications or practical manifestations from the inherent dignity and integrity of every human person. Moreover, those fundamental rights of the human person are recognized as operating within families.

The enumerated rights of women enshrined in the Women's Convention of 1979 also aim to ensure respect for women's inherent dignity and equality to others, particularly as those rights relate to familial obligations and affect gendered roles. These human rights standards reflect a new awareness and greater protection for the domains of gender, language, work, and educational rights. For example, to ensure women the "effective right to work," States Parties assume the obligation to prevent discrimination against women "on the grounds of marriage or maternity" and the obligation to take measures to "prohibit discrimination" against women on grounds of pregnancy, maternity leave, or marital status.[28] States further pledge to eliminate discrimination against women in the exercise of their right to family benefits, bank loans, mortgages, and other forms of financial credit.[29] In addition, Article 16 of the Women's Convention confers on women, on the basis of equality with men, the same rights to enter freely into marriage; to decide freely on the number and spacing of their children; and to have access to information, education, and other means to enable them to exercise these rights. It also assures women equal rights and responsibilities, regardless of marital status, in matters relating to children.[30] Women also are given educational rights, and Article 10 requires the elimination of gender stereotypes affecting all levels and forms of education. The Women's Convention clearly aspires to transform the place of women in society as well as in their families.

Although recognition of the need to move toward equality between men and women may be radical, it remains far less radical than the aspirations of the international children's rights movement. The Children's Convention of 1989 centers on the need to respect all children's individual dignity and the need to treat children with the respect granted others (including adults). This recognition constitutes one of the most important developments in human rights law. As a whole, the Children's Convention acknowledges the family's leading role in preparing children for participation in society and the assumption of adult responsibilities. This is reinforced by Article 12(1):

> States Parties shall assure to the child who is capable of forming his or her own views the right to express those views freely in all matters affecting the child, the views of the child being given due weight in accordance with the age and maturity of the child.

The convention does not necessarily grant children equal rights as those possessed by parents or others acting *parens patriae* (those empowered by law to act as parents would). Instead, it specifies that children's basic human dignity is to be respected by considering their own interests,[31] giving them voice in matters affecting them,[32] and offering them special protections.[33] What is significant, and to a large extent historically radical, about this move is that rights are bestowed on children, as opposed to being conferred on parents or the State. Indeed, what the Children's Convention does confer on parents, the State, and every individual is the duty to ensure that children's rights are respected. The Children's Convention champions the need to consider children's independent interests, respect their dignity, and ensure their development into citizens who respect the principles established by the United Nations.

Existing human rights documents, however, do not capture the rights of all vulnerable groups. For example, the International Bill of Rights and the Women's Convention of 1979 relate explicitly to adults, yet no convention delineates the rights of elderly people. Indeed, the international protections to family life focus on families as care-taking units for young people, not as units that care for elderly people. Although the Economic and Social Covenant of 1966 does not contain express references to the rights of older people, in 1995 the U.N. Committee on Economic, Social and Cultural Rights adopted General Comment No. 6 on the rights of older people.[34] Through Comment No. 6, the Committee emphasized the need to monitor more closely the rights of elderly people that are enshrined in the treaty and also sought to increase the strength of the Vienna International Plan of Action on Ageing.[35] Through these efforts, the Committee is seeking to "make all the necessary efforts to protect and strengthen the family" and respond to the needs of its dependent aging members. The latest recognition of the need to develop and ensure the rights of potentially vulnerable family members reflects much more than the need to protect and foster families; it confirms the continued recognition that the rights of potentially vulnerable individuals within families matters most to human rights law.

Nature of Protection

The precise manner in which the international community, individual nations, and other parties that may fall under the jurisdiction of human rights law are to offer protection and assistance to families and individuals within them remains to be clarified. In drafting international instruments, governments generally have attempted to avoid ideological confrontation and have preferred to strike a balance between two opposing postulates. Solutions range from a *laissez-faire* approach that emphasizes individual and familial autonomy to a more socialist perception of States as beneficial agencies against which certain claims may be made to promote the common welfare of all the community's constituents.

Although the extent to which States are to assume an active role in regulating family life remains contentious, international statements place emphasis both on protection from governmental intrusion in family life and on governmental assistance. On one hand, several of the instruments affirm the principle that no one shall be subjected to arbitrary or unlawful interference with his or her family, as found in Article 12 of the Universal Declaration of Human Rights, Article 17 of the Political Covenant, and Article 16 of the Children's Convention. From this perspective, families receive protection by governmental restraint from intervening in family life. On the other hand, numerous international instruments recognize the principle that States are obligated to take measures to assist the family or some of its individual members. Most notably, the Universal Declaration of Human Right's Article 25(2) affirms that "motherhood and childhood are entitled to special care and assistance." The Economic and Social Covenant's (1966) Article 10(3) proclaims that "special measures of . . . assistance should be taken on behalf of all children and young persons without any discrimination." The Preamble of the Children's Convention recites the conviction that "the family . . . should be afforded the necessary . . . assistance so that it can fully assume its responsibilities within the community." That treaty further recognizes the right even more explicitly in Article 18(2), which obliges States Parties to "render appropriate assistance to parents and legal guardians in the performance of their child-rearing responsibilities and . . . ensure the development of institutions, facilities and services for the care of children." In summary, the international treaties directly address the manner in which States Parties protect families, although the precise way nations do so remains to be balanced and determined.

Although the different approaches to regulating family life seemingly take opposing stances, it is important to emphasize that their oppositions are far from polar. First, both approaches are necessary to protect families. States tend to adopt both approaches when regulating family life. For example, even the United States, which officially adopts a clear noninterventionist stance, actually offers considerable assistance to families, particularly those trapped in family violence.[36] Indeed, some responses to violence even remove adults' control over the extent of the States' intervention, as revealed most recently in the rise of mandatory arrest policies for instances of family violence involving adults.[37]

Second, even mandates that do not necessarily mention families apply to family life. For example, the International Bill of Rights, the two conventions directly affecting families, and numerous other treaties affect family life by protecting individuals' right to life and ensuring efforts to diminish racial discrimination. Likewise, the general human rights movement to ensure respect and equality for all provides an environment that could be conducive to healthy family life. Such measures ensure, for example, that individuals within families have equal access to resources and that societies' resources could be distributed more equitably both within and across families.

Third, the right to found a family figures prominently in human rights instruments, and that right involves both nonintervention and special assistance. For example, several conventions recognize the "right of men and women of marriageable age to marry and to found a family,"[38] and the Women's Convention of 1979 further amplifies the content of this right and obligates States Parties to ensure men and women the "same right to decide freely and responsibly on the number and spacing of their children and to have access to the information, education and means to enable them to exercise these rights."[39] The right is rather expansive and embraces not simply the right to conceive, bear, and rear children; the provision arguably even includes the right to sex education.[40]

Fourth, formal treaties have been supplemented by numerous plans of action that relate to family life. These efforts adopt comprehensive stances.[41] Most notably (and as discussed in greater depth in chapter 5), the new human rights agreements address violence against women and children. The human rights machinery continues to expand as it recognizes the need to protect families from unnecessary intervention and the need to offer formal protections to those vulnerable to familial harms.

Last, and most critically for my purposes here, there now exists several visions of how international human rights law works (and should work). As demonstrated especially in chapters 4 and 5, the extent to which human rights law can reach across and within nations to ensure the protection of basic human rights continues to change, develop, and allow for greater "intervention" in nations and families. Although efforts to reach within each State's frontier necessarily involves contentious issues, it can no longer be doubted that human rights law may address relationships that serve as any society's foundations.

Conclusion

The notion of international human rights increasingly gains currency. This is a remarkably radical achievement. Although the subject of impressive developments, conceptions of human rights law continue to change and adapt to a rapidly changing world. Despite resistance, criticisms, and concern, the world in which human rights operates already has changed and renders increasingly obsolete the radical developments challenged by those who fear recriminations for violating rights conceived by international legal machinery. Since its inception, the concept of international human rights law has meant law relating to sovereign nations and has involved the challenges that sovereignty posed. Human rights law now infiltrates what heretofore have been considered relationships unfettered by social concerns and outside the purview of international law. Today's political, legal, and cultural geography presents opportunities and challenges not faced by the drafters of the most fundamental human rights documents. Yet current global conditions and advances in the understanding of family violence make more urgent the need to recognize, embrace, develop, and foster human rights that may seem radical today but which lay the foundation for ensuring human rights protections in contexts that evince the most rampant abuses that currently go ignored.

Endnotes

1. *See* M. Akehurst, *A Modern Introduction to International Law* (New York: Routledge, 1993).
2. R. J. Wilson, "Prosecuting Pinochet: International Crimes in Spanish Domestic Law," *Human Rights Quarterly* 21 (1999):927–979.
3. *See* C. A. Bradley, "The 'Pinochet Method' & Political Accountability," *Green Bag 2d* 3 (1999):5–10.
4. B. Stephens, "Humanitarian Law and Gender Violence: An End to Centuries of Neglect?" *Hofstra Law and Policy Symposium* 3 (1999):87–109.
5. *Id.*
6. M. C. Bassiouni, "Combating Impunity for International Crimes," *University of Colorado Law Review* 71 (2000):409–422.
7. A. B. Ching, "Evolution of the Command Responsibility Doctrine in Light of the Celebeci Decision of the International Court Tribunal for the Former Yugoslavia," *North Carolina Journal of International Law and Commercial Regulations* 25 (1999):167–205.
8. *See* K. D. Askin, "Sexual Violence in Decisions and Indictments of the Yugoslav and Rwandan Tribunals: Current Status," *American Journal of International Law* 93 (1999): 97–123.
9. A. S. Fraser, "Becoming Human: The Origins and Development of Women's Human Rights," *Human Rights Quarterly* 21 (1999):853–906.
10. *See* M. E. Ghasemi, "Islam, International Human Rights & Women's Equality: Afghan Women Under Taliban Rule," *Southern California Review of Law & Women's Studies* 8 (1999):445–467.
11. Bassiouni, "Combating Impunity for International Crimes."
12. *See* M. David, "Grotius Repudiated: The American Objections to the International Criminal Court and the Commitment to International Law," *Michigan Journal of International Law* 20 (1999):337–412.
13. Bradley, "The 'Pinochet Method' & Political Accountability."
14. T. Howland and W. Calathes, "The U.N.'s International Criminal Tribunal, Is It Justice or Jingoism for Rwanda? A Call for Transformation," *Virginia Journal of International Law* 39 (1998):135–167.
15. *See* M. Minow, "The Work of Re-Membering: After Genocide and Mass Atrocity," *Fordham International Law Journal* 23 (1999):429–439.
16. J. Sarkin, "The Necessity and Challenges of Establishing a Truth and Reconciliation Commission in Rwanda," *Human Rights Quarterly* 21 (1999):767–823.
17. U.N. General Assembly, 3rd Sess., Official Records, *Pt. I. Resolutions*, Resolution 217A, A/810, 1948.

18. See P. G. Lauren, *The Evolution of International Human Rights: Visions Seen* (Philadelphia: University of Pennsylvania Press, 1998).
19. U.N. General Assembly, 21st Sess., Official Records, Suppl. 16 at 49, GA Resolution 2200, A/6316; 999 UNTS 171; 6 ILM 368, 1966.
20. U.N. General Assembly, 21st Sess., Official Records, Suppl. 16 at 49, GA Resolution 2200 Annex, A/6316; 993 UNTS 3; 6 ILM 360, 1966.
21. U.N. General Assembly, 34th Sess., Official Records, Suppl. 46 at 193, GA Resolution 34/180, Doc A/34/46, 1979.
22. U.N. General Assembly, 44th Sess., Official Records, Suppl. 49 at 166, Resolution 44/25, A/44/49; 28 ILM 1448, 1989.
23. International Convention on the Elimination of All Forms of Racial Discrimination (1965), *opened for signature* Mar. 7, 1966, 600 U.N.T.S. 195.
24. Vienna Declaration of Human Rights, A/CONF. 157/23 (1993).
25. Declaration of the Right to Development, U.N. Gen. Assembly Res. 41/128, 41 U.N. GAOR, Supp. No. 53, U.N. Doc. A/41/925 (Dec. 4, 1986).
26. *See* J. Boyden, *Families: A Celebration and Hope for World Change* (London: Faine & UNESCO, 1993).
27. See R. J. R. Levesque, "The Internationalization of Children's Rights: Too Radical for American Adolescence?" *Connecticut International Law Review* 9 (1994):237–293.
28. Women's Convention, Article 11.
29. *Id.,* Article 13.
30. *Id.,* Articles 5 and 16.
31. Children's Convention; *see, e.g.,* Article 5.
32. *Id., see, e.g.,* Articles 12 and 13.
33. *Id.,* Articles 19, 20, and 32–36.
34. United Nations, U.N. Committee on Economic, Social and Cultural Rights, Comment No. 6. UN Doc E/C.12/1995/16/Rev.1.
35. Vienna International Plan of Action on Ageing, G.A. Res. 46/91 (Dec. 16, 1991).
36. For a review, *see* R. J. R. Levesque, "The Failures of Foster Care Reform: Revolutionizing the Most Radical Blueprint," *Maryland Journal of Contemporary Legal Issues* 6 (1995):1–35.
37. *See* L. Mills, *The Heart of Intimate Abuse* (New York: Springer, 1998).
38. Political Covenant of 1966, Article 2.
39. Women's Convention of 1979, Article 16(1)(e).
40. See R. J. Cook, "International Human Rights and Women's Reproductive Health," *Studies in Family Planning* 24 (1993):73–86.
41. *See, e.g.,* Vienna Declaration on Human Rights (1993).

Part I

Culture's Role in Family Violence

Chapter 2
FAMILY VIOLENCE AND CULTURAL LIFE

The field of inquiry that falls under the general rubric of family violence remains rather broad. As currently conceived, the study of family violence involves essentially all maltreating behaviors perpetrated by related individuals. Interest in various forms of child abuse, spousal battering, and maltreatment of elderly people exemplifies the vastness of the field of inquiry as much as it does the pervasiveness of violence.[1] In addition to interest in numerous forms of family violence and different groups of victims, researchers, policy makers, and those on the front line of service delivery continue to make immense progress in identifying and responding to family violence. Progress is so great that it no longer seems radical to suggest that families are not necessarily the safe havens they once were thought to be. Few question the scale and importance of family violence uncovered by research.

Although progress continues to be made in efforts to recognize, document, and respond to a broad range of abusive situations, this area of research remains limited in its investigation of the various ecological contexts in which violence occurs. The role of cultural forces in family violence and the cross-cultural manifestations of such violence continue to be neglected in the study of family violence.[2] The United States, for example, contributes to the pool of "authoritative knowledge" exported to countries around the world. Even though the United States is multicultural, exported concepts and research generally draw from the "mainstream" population (typically White with European descent) or fail to delineate cultural variations.[3] More problematically, even empirical investigators who acknowledge the need to recognize heterogeneity in cultural groups migrating to the United States still use measures that homogenize the "American" culture and use those measures to determine risks of family violence without determining whether the measures have the same functional meanings outside the host culture.[4] Health and social services professionals continue to transfer accepted concepts from one culture to others and generally ignore the need to develop theoretical and empirical evaluations of the phenomenon within culture-specific contexts. Indeed, cross-cultural analyses now increasingly take Western conceptions of abuse as guides, as revealed in the most comprehensive empirical reports of international rates of child sexual abuse culled by leading researchers[5] and general child abuse compiled by the International Society for the Prevention of Child Abuse and Neglect.[6]

Investigations that do recognize and explore the significance of cultural experiences remain limited in significant ways. They tend to be limited to certain forms of maltreatment or groups of victims. The trend finds expression in the most recent cross-cultural analyses of child maltreatment,[7] elder abuse,[8] and wife beating.[9] Moreover, investigations that adopt a cultural perspective generally focus on manifestations of maltreatment within one society and entangle status, poverty, ethnicity, race, or other group variables. Studies pervasively fail to tease out, for example, how poverty manifests itself differently among different cultural groups and how those differences may affect family violence.[10] Just as with analyses of culture, those who conduct culturally sensitive investigations also tend to confuse ethnicity, culture, and social class as they examine variations within particular societies.[11] A final shortcoming of many cross-cultural analyses of policy making and legal responses to family violence is that they remain limited to legal analyses and do not consider how to reconceptualize violence by making use of other cultures' experiences with violence.[12] Legal analyses and suggestions for reform draw primarily from empirical studies conducted in the United States and pervasively place central concern on individuals as the source of violence and as the site for intervention.[13] Thus, instead of drawing insights about the nature of family violence found in other cultures, recent cross-cultural researchers generally aim to find whether Western forms of abuse exist and how legal systems respond to such violence.

These narrow conceptions of family violence and cross-cultural investigations are significant because they (a) reinforce the belief that individuals act alone and perpetuate the belief that family violence involves solely private events, (b) dictate that responses and suggestions for reform adopt narrow approaches to deal with violence, (c) increasingly win out in efforts to reform legal and welfare systems that deal with family violence, and (d) generally concern themselves more with comparative than cultural analyses, which do not highlight the cultural roots of maltreatment.[14] Thus, although broad in scope, the study of family violence generally remains limited in its concern for cultural contexts and cultural forces, which in turn limits conceptions of family violence and responses to such violence. This emphasis on the manner in which cultural forces affect family violence (frequently perceived as private acts) serves as a necessary prelude to the discussion of human rights responses to family violence, which places significance on the need to address cultural forces to affect violence deemed private.

This chapter explores the extent to which cultural forces necessarily influence family violence, thereby highlighting the need to respond to public, sociocultural forces if family violence is to be addressed properly. To do so, I survey the nature of family violence from a cross-cultural perspective and focus on the different manifestations and forms of violence that individuals may experience as they develop. The approach emphasizes the cultural moorings of private violence—the manner in which cultural location influences individuals who maltreat family members.

Why and How Culture Matters

It remains difficult to move beyond thinking in terms of individual behavior when conceptualizing violence among family members. It is easier to conceive of violence as committed by individuals rather than by some amorphous and invisible force called society or culture. Yet any individual's violence is only understandable in light of that individual's cultural milieu. Researchers have shown well how different cultures respond differently to acts deemed abusive.[15] However, cultures do much more than influence the types of systems in place to deal with issues of family violence. Cultural forces actually define the experience of maltreatment, create climates conducive to maltreatment, provide important buffers against maltreatment, and affect intervention efforts. To a large extent, then, it seems fair to propose that individual acts of violence and individual victimization experiences remain largely culturally determined. This section explores these cultural influences.

How Cultures Define Maltreatment

Cultural analyses of family violence underscore the remarkable extent to which societies provide the experiential and interpretive context for violence. Although cultures do so in several ways, a most notable example involves how cultures provide rationales and justifications for violence. Cultures can make violent practices healthy and central to normal human development and social processes. The manner in which societies prepare children for full participation in society and the manner in which some adults' participation in society moderates their perceptions of violence reveal the culturally determined nature of violence.

A cursory examination of cross-cultural analyses of children's sexual development uncovers numerous practices that many reasonable individuals would deem abusive. Yet societies do not subject these "abusive" practices to sanctions or censure. In some societies, family members permanently disfigure and dismember their children's sexual organs—a practice affecting up to 18 million girls and millions more boys.[16] In other societies, families predetermine their daughter's husbands and allow them to engage in prepubertal sexual relations.[17] In some cultures, parents, with the assistance of prospective bridegrooms, school officials, and a variety of State actors, routinely submit girls to virginity exams, an invasive practice meant to control sexual activity.[18] In yet other societies, parents require boys to engage in oral or anal sexual activities with adults.[19] In some Indian, Chinese, Japanese, Middle Eastern, Latin American, and Native American societies, parents may routinely massage their children's genitals, a practice meant to help children sleep.[20]

The examples from the existing cross-cultural record reveal the immense diversity in children's socialization and the range of behavior that would be considered acceptable treatment of children. It is important to emphasize that these practices are not necessarily perceived as problematic, are not necessarily practiced by the majority of individuals in those societies, and are not necessarily linked to disruptive outcomes in the societies that practice them. That is, most of the practices described above would be construed as problematic in the West, as revealed by a growing list of commentators who view the above behaviors as abusive and champion reform and abolition.[21] Taken out of their cultural contexts, these practices tend to be viewed as repressive and inappropriately torturous, degrading, and inhumane acts. Even the apparently least abusive and damaging behaviors, the maternal–neonatal genital touching, have been shown to have powerful sexualizing effects on boys' behavior at a very young age, which then may set boys on different paths of sexual development.[22] Viewed in appropriate cultural context, however, the above practices may not even be seen as sexual in nature, let alone as abusive or inappropriate. Indeed, cultures may deem some of the practices necessary. The cultural practices may remain pervasively condoned, encouraged, and viewed as necessary for a fulfilling life and successful community membership, even to the extent that leading cross-cultural investigations of sexual and child development note that parent–child sexual contact in many cultures is neither abusive nor incestual because it is normative.[23]

The cross-cultural record of how children develop and socialize into adult roles reveals how cultures recognize only some harms as violent and render some forms of violence invisible. The principle applies not only to exotic societies but also to those in the West. For example, some Western researchers and societies now grapple with the extent to which the legal system should recognize the significance of sexual harassment, rape, and sexual assault committed by very young perpetrators.[24] Some harms are not necessarily invisible but are nevertheless condoned simply because they are viewed by some sectors of society as culturally appropriate: Faith healing exemptions from prosecutions for child maltreatment[25] and the continued corporal punishment of children by schools and parents[26] serve as prime examples of the extent to which societies do not provide children with uniform protection.

Although many may find the failure to protect children a powerful example of the failure to recognize the need to protect vulnerable individuals, adults also experience their own abuse differently when in different cultural contexts. Research that compares the experience of different cultural groups within the United States presents numerous examples of the manner in which cultural beliefs and values moderate adult victims' appraisals of family violence. Direct comparisons between Mexican American women and mainstream women reveal that the former have a more tolerant attitude toward partner abuse and minimize the seriousness of physically assaultive incidents.[27] Unlike mainstream women, Mexican American women are less likely to consider numerous acts as abusive, including being constrained against their will, having things thrown at them, and being slapped, punched, shoved, or grabbed. Even within societies, then, cultural forces affect assessments of violence.

Research also indicates that different groups perceive abuse in forms that do not necessarily abide by more mainstream conceptions of violence. Studies of immigrant women, for example, report very different abuses that would not fall under the rubric of domestic violence if the operative legal definition of assault is at work. Indigenous understandings of wife abuse reported to service providers include forcing wives to engage in activities against their will, forcing them into lifestyles against their values, not allowing them to visit relatives, using them as labor to care for in-laws, and requiring them to ask permission to go out. In many instances, the husband's family or the wife's own family committed the abuse, not the husband.[28] Although violent and controlling, these actions do not necessarily constitute battering. As currently envisioned by the law and mainstream activists, determinations of what constitutes "domestic violence" focuses on the type, extent, and frequency of physical abuse.[29]

Research on elder abuse also reveals important cultural patterns in perceptions. For example, a sense of suspicion, fatalism, detachment, and fear of the outside world characteristic of Appalachian culture fosters acceptance of elder abuse and encourages elderly people to remain in abusive situations.[30] Equally illustrative are direct cultural comparisons of the older population's perceptions of abuse. Compared with older African American and mainstream women, older Korean American women perceive several situations as not abusive and not worthy of official intervention.[31] Commentators attribute the lower incidence of labeling situations as mistreatment or help seeking among Korean Americans as rooted in cultural expectations. Korean culture's emphasis on family harmony over individuals' needs and the belief that suffering and enduring are to be expected as part of normal family life contribute to perceptions of family violence that differ from other cultures' understandings and experiences. For example, traditional Korean culture emphasizes obedience to rules, reliance on the family, and the dominance of male over female individuals. The family is expected to work through problems; sharing them with outsiders would bring shame to the family.[32] These beliefs contribute support for a finding that emerges from an unusually large study of battered Korean immigrant women: Battered women reported that their own abusive husbands serve as their primary resource person they could turn to for help.[33] Cultural backgrounds, then, contribute to the meaning an individual attaches to violence.

The power of culture also finds clear expression in the impact of its available vocabulary on the social response to violence. It can be argued that the most pervasive obstacle to protecting family members is victims' lack of understanding that what is happening to them constitutes violence. Before a problem becomes a problem, it is necessary to identify it as a problem. The failure to do so helps explain, for example, how countries that explicitly aimed toward egalitarian gender relations essentially ignored violence against women. In Russia, for example, the hope that communism would redefine women and men's roles spurred support for that ideology. Yet the country was unable to recognize the violence women endured within their families. It was only after the collapse of the Soviet system that thousands of Russian women were reported as murdered in their homes.[34] Russian women are 2.5 times more likely to be murdered by their partners than are their American counterparts, and American women are twice as likely as women in comparable Westernized countries to be victims of spousal homicide.[35] Although Russian women now are the most vulnerable in industrialized countries, even the rapid social changes and increased interest in women's rights have yet to affect those who experience battering, simply because no language exists to describe their experience—the Russian language has no term for "battering," "batterer," and "battered women."[36]

Examples of the impact of cultural forces on individuals' definition of violence connected to family life highlight four points: (a) the lack of censure some societies place on practices others would deem violent; (b) the effect of cultural beliefs on the perception of violence individuals receive; (c) the substantial obstacles to reform, simply because some societies do not view some practices as problematic, let alone as worthy of intervention; and (d) the extent to which otherwise private acts of violence essentially are deeply ingrained cultural practices.

How Cultures Create Climates Conducive to Violence

Cultural analyses of family violence also highlight the extent to which cultural forces create climates that lead to maltreatment. Societies target certain groups of individuals when faced by ecological stresses. When societies experience precarious ecologies, three groups generally become more susceptible to family violence: children, women, and elderly people. The manner and extent to which these groups generally remain at risk is important to explore because it reveals how societies contribute to "private" family violence, a point that will gain increasing significance in terms of the extent to which the legal system may respond legitimately to various forms of family violence in the future.

Studies that focus on child maltreatment reveal how cultural attitudes and structural forces foster family climates that may contribute to child maltreatment. For example, in a worldwide study of malnutrition, Cassidy[37] found that many parents concentrate their resources on only a few children when they are unable to give all their children full care. More recently, Creighton's[38] international comparative analysis of infant mortality and child deaths expanded the research and demonstrated links between increased infant homicide rates and family stress, available resources, and cultural variables related to the low status of women. These findings comport with a ground-breaking study conducted in the 1970s that reveals how cultural factors are more important than personal factors in determining child abuse.[39] The findings of that study show that worldwide, children are more likely to be abused and neglected in cultures that resist family planning and have an abundance of unwanted children, where the child's parents are the only caretakers, where there is lack of father involvement in child rearing, and where families are not connected to their community.[40] Although these findings do not mean that situations with the reverse conditions are free from child abuse, they do highlight the point that the relative degree to which child abuse occurs depends on the cultural context.

These findings relating to cultural forces that place children at risk for abuse essentially reinforce results from numerous cultural analyses of child abuse that highlight how children who are targets of abuse become so because of different cultural values placed on children. The finding has been reported in numerous studies, including several in the United States and Europe[41] and in Africa,[42] which reveal how death and malnourishment disproportionately fall on certain groups of children. The most extensive and revealing reports derive from India. Commentators reveal that infant Indian girls are more likely to be weaned prematurely and neglected by parents who wish to try for sons. When a girl's health suffers, she is less likely to receive medical care. Female fetuses also are more likely to be aborted, as revealed by studies of abortion clinic fetuses that find over 99% of aborted fetuses to be females.[43] Several reasons account for the greater likelihood that Indians abort female fetuses; murder female infants; and favor sons in terms of food, medical treatment, and education. These reasons fundamentally relate to cultural expectations and practices. Most notably, for example, Indian society pervasively considers young girls burdensome. Her family must expend valuable resources and receive fewer benefits for her care; when she marries, she becomes part of her husband's family, which makes her unavailable to support and care for her parents in their old age. Furthermore, when she is old enough to marry, her parents must amass large quantities of money and other goods to induce her new family to take on the burden of her maintenance.[44] The cross-cultural record, then, supports well the notion that cultural forces may foster climates conducive to family violence and place individuals at greater risk of violence.

Although the most frequently discussed correlate of maltreatment continues to be biological sex, other categories relate to risks of maltreatment. Considerable research highlights how disabled children suffer higher risks of family violence and how family violence contributes to disability.[45] For example, the apathetic, anorexic, and unresponsive behaviors of a malnourished child may not foster the parental solicitousness necessary to improve the child's health status and alleviate malnourishment. Solicitousness to less healthy children varies considerably with culture. In areas of Mexico and Central America, children who display behaviors indicative of malnourishment may be perceived as *chipil*, as angry at a new sibling or at the mother for weaning. The result is that the child is punished or ignored for behavior perceived as bad rather than being fed to ameliorate the underlying cause of the problem.[46] In Israel, a study of 1,450 families in which parents had an abnormal or ill child reveals that the majority of parents referred to the child in stigmatic terms, such as a "monster," a "devil," "Satan," and by other names that cast the child both as a nonperson and as morally contaminated, which allowed the family to seclude the child.[47] Even when parents professed to love their child, their actual behavior revealed a completely different attitude: rejection and violence. Many researchers have reported how attractive babies and good-looking children receive more positive attention and suffer lower rates of abuse.[48] Values placed on children and categories of vulnerable children affect the extent to which they are placed at higher risk for harm.

The process by which victims define themselves as having been assaulted has been the subject of important research dealing with gender roles and family formation. The process involves what victims undergo to ultimately recognize that they were victimized and how the process fits into the broader context of the relationship between the perpetrator and victim. A most notable and highly researched phenomenon involves the toleration of violent dating behavior.[49] Youth find coercive sexual intercourse permissible in a variety of courtship situations. A large body of research conducted in North America relating to "rape myths" reveals how youth adhere to rape myths even without understanding the meaning of rape. This research is supported by recent investigations that reveal how slightly over one quarter of rape victims fail to view their victimizations as rapes, even when their experiences fall under the legal category of rape, and how half of rape victims who are physically coerced blame themselves for the rape and do not define their experiences as rape.

Researchers attribute the silence about abuse, failure to recognize the actual experience of assault, and the broader culture of acceptance to social stereotypes that govern gendered social relationships. The major stereotype that arguably forms the basis of the abuse is one in which male individuals dominate, control, and use power whereas women do the opposite. Each gender expects disparate levels of aggressiveness and victimization and conditions those involved in violence to not even notice coercion. Although the most comprehensive research in this area involves sexual assaults in dating situations, similar beliefs are evident in other abusive relationships, particularly child sexual abuse and partner battering. For example, research from the United States and several other countries reveals how women support several justifications for battering by husbands, such as the wife's sexual infidelity and disobedience, and these beliefs are more held by those who adopt more traditional gender roles.[50] Cultural beliefs operate to place individuals at risk.

Cross-cultural investigations of spousal violence also reveal the importance of cultural values and the significant impact of structural forces. The leading comprehensive survey of spousal beatings illustrates the power of forces beyond the private family. Counts, Brown, and Campbell[51] revealed that the availability of supportive kin who provide a place of safety for women decreases the likelihood of wife beating. They also reported that cultures can defuse situations that otherwise might have escalated to violence when they allow either partner to return to the family of origin, temporarily and without shame. These conclusions receive support from numerous studies that examine the status of women and the extent to which they suffer numerous forms of violence, including those justified by traditional customs and rituals.[52]

The Counts, Brown, and Campbell[53] study extends another notable cross-cultural study on wife beating. Levinson[54] compared ethnographic data on 90 societies throughout the world and found wife beating present in 75 of them. Most significantly, the analysis yielded four cultural factors that seemingly predict this form of maltreatment: economic inequality between the sexes, a pattern of using physical violence for conflict resolution, male authority and decision making in the home, and women's inability to divorce. The general rule that emerged was that the more restricted and dependent women were on men, the more likely they were to be abused. Although the data certainly were limited, the analysis does suggest that cultural forces do play a powerful role in determining rates of wife beating. These studies pointed to the need to consider more than safe havens for victims, and they revealed how the exclusion of groups (in this case, women) from efforts to set social, religious, economic, and political agendas contributes to social stratification and higher rates of violence against those without voice.[55] Simply stated, the cultural perception of women's status, the extent to which women may participate in their cultural life, and the environment in which families find themselves all contribute to private family violence.

Studies of elder abuse are the subject of considerably fewer analyses. Yet cross-cultural gerontology equally illustrates the importance of cultural attitudes and practices in the creation of situations that place individuals at risk for family violence. These studies continue to dispel the myth that all societies venerate and invariably treat elderly people well.[56] Although the treatment of elderly people considerably varies across societies, researchers increasingly have noted that elderly people suffer from high levels of physical and emotional abuse as well as financial, nutritional, and medical neglect.[57] In their cross-cultural study of elder abuse, Kosberg and Garcia[58] emphasized the tremendous variety in treatment families provide their older relatives and the manner in which maltreatment of elderly people generally relates to perceptions of dependency. Other investigators supported their conclusions. Anthropologists, for example, often note that, in some societies subjected to precarious environments, elderly people may be required to commit suicide or wander away from the group to a certain death when they do not keep up or contribute to the group.[59]

In fact, societies need not be living precariously to create circumstances that allow elderly people to suffer. Current debates in the United States about Medicare and euthanasia reveal the extent to which cultures must deal with members of society in need of extensive care and the extent to which public resources dictate the risk of violence perpetrated on elderly people.[60] The extent to which society provides support is significant. In terms of assisted suicide, the majority of those who favor the right to die do so for fear of burdening their spouses and families with financial difficulties.[61] Researchers have noted that as a result, cases are more likely to involve women and will continue to do so because of gender differences in gender roles, suicidal behavior, depression, life expectancy and illness, health care access, and quality of physician–patient relationships.[62] These factors may create greater risk to the middle class, who may feel pressure to choose assisted suicide (poor people, however, are more likely to receive state supports).[63] In terms of recognized forms of abuse, researchers consistently find that family members who abuse their older relatives tend to have financial problems, feel isolated, and have little social support.[64] Policies are not helpful to the extent that they do not address the isolation of elderly people and their lack of resources to resolve or avoid abusive situations.[65] Instead, policies increasingly aim to place more burdens on private, individual families and, as several have argued, increasingly disempower the older population and increase risks of maltreatment.[66] Although victim–perpetrator dependency, care-giver stress, and other factors lead to different forms of elder abuse and comparative studies reveal distinct profiles of abuse, neglect, and exploitation,[67] cultural studies challenge the belief in the sanctity of the home and the inherent goodness of those who care for others.

Cross-cultural researchers often conclude that cultures may revere the well aged population while practicing "death-hastening behavior" on the decrepit aged population.[68] Although no solid research on the topic has been reported, it is widely acknowledged that elderly people with disabilities, compared with those without disabilities, suffer higher rates of maltreatment at the hands of those who care for them.[69] Yet anthropologists have long recognized the categorization of the aged population. Societies often distinguish between the socially and physically functioning and those who are not. For the latter, the terms for their social status varies from culture to culture, and include "senility," "the overaged," "the useless state," the "sleeping period," "the age grade of the dying," and even "the already dead."[70] These categories make problematic an approach to abuse that would not recognize the individual "victim's" social role. Those who fall in the more decrepit category of abuse continue to be subjected to socially sanctioned death-hastening behavior.

The finding that different societies treat certain individuals differently has considerable consequences for conceptualizing family violence. Given trends that certain groups are systematically at risk for violence within the family, it is difficult to argue that individuals act alone. To an extent, then, individuals simply are the "weapons" cultures use in their efforts to control and respond to their ecologies. Cultural forces affect personal relationships that lead to maltreatment. Social influences affect the extent to which individuals engage in family violence. This perspective differs considerably from the continuing conceptualization of family violence as acts of violence perpetrated by people who knowingly act on free will. Although it would be inappropriate to argue that individuals cannot control their actions, the approach does note how different cultures and pervasive social forces contribute to family violence.

How Cultures Buffer Individuals From Violence

Cultural analyses of maltreatment reveal that cultural beliefs buffer groups from maltreatment when ecological conditions would otherwise encourage violence. The finding receives considerable support from research in the United States that focuses on fostering community development and involving communities in child protection.[71] The policies derive from extensive research that finds important roles played by supportive networks in preventing harm, alleviating harm's negative consequences, and reintegrating offenders.[72] Although numerous factors contribute to the occasional failure of such networks, a major reason for success derives from recognition of certain individuals as people in their own right. Thus, although these most vulnerable groups identified above may be at somewhat higher risk, cultural beliefs and practices may buffer some of them from conditions that would increase their risk for maltreatment. The general rule that often emerges and is worthy of our attention hypothesizes that recognition of an individual's worth and dignity decreases the extent to which he or she is a victim of family violence.

Numerous examples illustrate the simple rule and highlight the need to consider the inclusion of individuals into their societies based on their dignity and worth as human beings. Considerable research supports the claim that considerations of worth, dignity, and equality affect how partners and spouses treat one another. In Western societies, for example, volumes of research support the finding that the extent to which spouses have a say in decision making and share domestic responsibilities relates to their individual psychological well-being, career satisfaction, and marital satisfaction.[73] In general, research reveals the ways in which men benefit most from marital arrangements and women tend to suffer from them.[74] The more visible forms of violence also relate to considerations of worth, as illustrated best by extensive cross-cultural research. That literature suggests that societies in which husbands and wives have egalitarian relationships in terms of resources and decision making create the least likely conditions for spousal violence. For example, research consistently reveals that asymmetry in resources, power, or recourse contributes to the beating of wives.[75] A highly cited example involves dowry-related violence in India that stems from women's dependency on husbands (and in-laws) and lack of educational opportunities.[76] The literature receives additional support from cross-cultural research, which consistently reveals that attitudes toward women's sexual victimization mirror attitudes toward women which in turn are linked to women's relative social status, such as their participation in the labor force and educational opportunities.[77]

Although human rights commentators frequently focus on visible, cross-cultural examples, the general rule also applies to overt family violence in Western societies. In the United States, for example, battered women who attempt to change power dynamics in their intimate relationships encounter severe difficulties: Studies reveal that 70% of the reported injuries from domestic violence occur after the separation of the couple,[78] and the women's likelihood of being killed dramatically increases by more than 30-fold when she seeks independence or attempts to gain independent resources.[79] Separation does not guarantee the termination of violence, a finding explained by the unrivaled insight offered by feminists who propose that violence begins or escalates in situations of external or internal, real or imagined threats to the abuser's power and control of women viewed as unworthy of self-determination.[80]

In addition to findings relating to separation and violence, the exclusion of several types of romantic relationships (e.g., young adolescents, those living with their parents) from protections deriving from the domestic violence reform movement also highlights the need for individuals to be recognized as worthy of protection. Reviews of domestic violence laws reveal that adolescent victims of relationship violence generally are not offered access to services.[81] This reflects the failure to recognize adolescents' legal personhood and to recognize that they may be in abusive relationships worthy of concern.[82] The robustness of these findings is reflected in efforts by researchers and policy makers to change societal views of women as people worthy of protection and as potentially independent individuals, which serves as the necessary precursor to an increased availability of services and assistance.[83]

The treatment of elderly people also is related to the extent to which they are seen as equal members of society. Anthropologists highlight how even cultures marked by strong values of filial piety do not necessarily protect elderly people, particularly those who do not have control over resources.[84] For example, cross-cultural research reveals that the treatment elderly people receive depends on their ability to control resources and to contribute to the economic needs of their household or communities.[85] That research emphasizes that cultural values, particularly those about human development and family responsibility, place elderly people in vulnerable positions. For example, Indian customs such as giving away one's property in preparation for the next world, viewed as a last stage of life, increase the likelihood of financial and related forms of exploitation.[86] In addition, cross-cultural research reveals how societies that rely on informal care systems, such as the ubiquitous reliance on families for support and care of their members, place elderly people at increased risk for violence and general exploitation.[87] Likewise, customs practiced in many Asian societies (as well as many others) that involve rigid inheritance rights to certain family members, generally sons, may promote adult sons' financial dependence on their older parents and their neglect of responsibility for their parents' physical, emotional, and financial well-being; even when inheritance laws change, elderly people continue to consider adult sons and their wives who are unwilling to provide living and caretaking arrangements as abusive.[88] Cultural forces help determine who is abused.

Societal perceptions of certain children's relative worth also illustrate the extent to which cultures buffer some children from family violence. The expectation that some children will contribute more to family status and subsistence leads families to treat them preferentially: The cross-cultural record is virtually unanimous in reports that families more readily place girls at risk. Research reveals that families respond to societal pressures to subject girls more readily to abortions and deferred infanticide. Human rights organizations document well how the practice of warehousing children in orphanages overtly leads to the death of more girls "by default."[89] Male individuals almost universally benefit from more parental attention and receive more scarce societal resources such as food, education, and medicine.[90] For example, in several Asian communities, the female child is disadvantaged by the priority accorded to boys in their access to schooling, which decreases girls' choices and increases their risk of involvement in prostitution.[91] Two-thirds of the children in the global South (developing countries) who do not attend primary school are girls.[92] Such discrimination between boys and girls appears to be attributed to factors such as family size, birth order, and ratio of sons to daughters, all of which determine children's differential economic value to parents. These forces similarly lead to the denial of girls' opportunities in the global North (industrialized countries): Impressive studies document the extent to which girls suffer from the lack of certain educational opportunities.[93] More dramatic, however, is the estimate by a recent Nobel Prize winner in economics that as many as 100 million women worldwide are currently "missing" and that a "great many more than a hundred million women are simply not there because women are neglected compared to men."[94] Thus, in societies perceived as repressive for women, the female:male ratios dip as low as 48:100 (United Arab Emirates), 60:100 (Qatar), and 84:100 (Saudi Arabia) when the typical female: male ratio at birth is 100:106.[95] Cultural practices that favor some groups of individuals over others effect predictable consequences.

Although cultural practices may lead to disadvantaging groups, it is important to understand that the apparently advantaged group may also suffer consequences. Recent research from China illustrates the point.[96] The abuse of girls does tend to be overrepresented in social and health service settings. Yet community surveys reveal that boys are more likely to be victims of severe physical violence. Commentators attribute this violence to preferences for sons. The argument is that sons are expected to continue the family line, care for elderly parents, and thus have higher demands placed on them, and families may turn to strict discipline to ensure their sons' satisfactory performances in school and to train their filial behavior at home.[97] Note that these studies find parallels in countries that place less focus on filial piety; in the United States, for example, boys are most vulnerable to both moderate and severe violence at the hands of their parents.[98]

Ecological and cultural forces determine a person's worth. The greater the recognition of their equality, the less likely they are to be maltreated. The rule, of course, also reveals that the greater the inequality, the greater the need to address ecological and cultural conditions to alleviate maltreatment rates. Although it would be inappropriate to equate access to and availability of resources as the sole buffer against maltreatment (as revealed by the abuse of boys), the above examples explicitly highlight the significance of considering how cultures help determine who suffers most when faced with difficult circumstances simply because cultures dictate who is worthy of protection and assistance when facing different ecological conditions.

How Cultures Affect Intervention Efforts

Cultures obviously do considerably more than define, buffer, and place certain individuals at risk for maltreatment by their families. Most notably, cultures affect intervention efforts in three significant ways: They prohibit or hinder disclosure of abusive acts and play a role in seeking legal or social services assistance, they affect the nature of systems in place to respond to family violence, and they affect the extent to which interventions gain acceptance by those identified for intervention.

Seeking Assistance

Intervention to alleviate and stop violence in families requires specificity to cultural beliefs and practices. Mental health professionals, for example, are increasingly concerned over their own failure to meet the needs of pluralistic societies.[99] As several have noted, however, cultural issues associated with clinical service delivery (and even basic family services) have not assumed prime consideration,[100] although a growing body of knowledge and innovative technologies have resulted in useful guidelines and starting points for addressing cultural diversity but not the cultural diversity of violent families.[101] Other forms of services offered to violent families remain generally devoid of discussions of cultural issues. Yet cultural issues are significant in that they determine the extent to which services are viewed as needed, affect the way services are provided, limit the relative success of service provisions, and influence the extent to which clients take advantage of services.

Cultural issues affect the nature of the maltreating behavior, which in turn affect the extent to which services are viewed as needed. One of the most interesting examples deals with the experience of wife assault. The dominant explanation, conceptualized as the "battered women syndrome" and originally proposed by Walker,[102] continues to guide intervention efforts and to enjoy predominance in criminal law. Descriptions of the syndrome involve both the experiences felt by women and the phases of battering. Women who experience the syndrome typically reveal learned helplessness, lowered self-esteem, impaired functioning, fear or terror, anger or rage, hypervigilance, and perceptions of diminished alternatives. In terms of phases, the syndrome includes what has become known as a cycle of violence, including a tension-building phase, acute battering incidents, and a contrition phase in which the batterer uses promises and gifts to increase the woman's hope that violence will stop.

Although Walker's model is complex and she herself noted, for example, that not all battered women report the general pattern of abuse, many theorists and activists continue to challenge her general propositions. For example, researchers especially have challenged the syndrome's tendency to play down women's active participation in the definition of their relationship and their more accurate description as survivors who do try to escape relationships but lack support to do so;[103] critics have argued that the use of the syndrome may lead to injustice in the courts.[104] More important for my analyses is that the syndrome may lead to perceiving women's positions in violent relationships as essentially alike, a point worthy of emphasis even though Walker herself explicitly recognizes differences that may arise in different situations.[105] Those potential differences are illustrated by cross-cultural analyses that suggest the dynamics found in U.S. studies may not apply to other groups. An important study of 200 Jewish battered wives in the United States reports caution in generalizing findings on family violence from mainstream culture to other cultures.[106] Compared with non-Jewish battered women, the study shows that Jewish battered women had not been exposed to family violence in childhood, had been engaged for a relatively long time, and had parental support for marriage. In addition, abusive husbands had a history of sexual dysfunctions. Likewise, abused women begged for forgiveness and made every effort to ensure that the attention of children and neighbors were not made aware of abuse by (for example) not screaming. These experiences contrast sharply from the stages of battering described by Walker,[107] which typically involves tension building, acute battering, and contrition. The Jewish women reported that abusive episodes were unprovoked and not preceded by arguments, that the husbands did not try to make up for the battering episodes, and that they themselves sought forgiveness. Thus, different groups may experience maltreating events differently, which may exacerbate the difficulties others face in situations that happen to garner the same label.

The extent to which maltreated elderly people recognize their own maltreatment and seek assistance also varies by cultural group. In the United States, for example, research indicates that older African Americans show greater willingness than some Asian and Hispanic American cultural groups to contact agencies that serve elderly people. Compared with other groups, elderly African Americans are more likely to seek legal recourse against their abusive adult offspring.[108] Japanese Americans and Korean Americans, on the other hand, choose informal assistance for responding to elder mistreatment situations. For the latter groups, the family and community are the preferred sources of assistance, not outsiders such as police and helping professionals.[109] That finding derives partly from different perceptions of the need for intervention but also, and arguably more importantly, from the perceived worth of official intervention. Although early research found that Asian Americans hesitated to use official intervention,[110] recent research finds that the same cultural groups exhibit much higher rates of help-seeking behaviors and are indistinguishable from other groups when they are similarly integrated in communities and have better access to culturally appropriate services.[111] Again, the extent to which social responses to violence address cultural contexts determines their worth.

A most remarkable aspect of violence that occurs within intimate relationships is the pervasive failure to seek assistance even when systems are in place. Cultural forces affect victims' responses to maltreating experiences. Emerging literature suggests that the extent to which victims view themselves as assault victims depends on their personal network's reactions. Although the above findings relating to elder and domestic abuse support the proposition, the clearest empirical evidence derives from sexual assault in dating relationships. Whether or not victims have supportive friends who reassure them that they were not to blame and who help define the victimization as rape by intimate partners tends to be highly influential. Those whose close social networks interpret the experience as loving unanimously report that they were not victims of rape.[112] Social group's support of stereotypic attitudes and behaviors that may lead to rape may not only lead to victimization but also help define the victimization experience.

Even though individuals in need of assistance may have been identified and targeted for intervention, the extent to which they remain in intervention programs varies considerably according to cultural grouping. For example, sexually abused children from diverse cultures are less likely to remain in and sustain mental health service intervention. In the United States, African American and Hispanic American children who have experienced sexual abuse are significantly less likely than their White counterparts to sustain involvement in treatment after the first therapeutic contact.[113] The social and psychological consequences of penetration abuse and the meaning of virginity to the child, the family, and the cultural community provide important therapeutic themes. These themes relate closely to cultural perceptions, which are key in intervention efforts and help explain why culturally insensitive therapeutic intervention results in no intervention.

The nature of the services offered, including whether they are offered at all, affects the extent to which individuals seek assistance to deal with violent relationships. The extent to which services adopt culturally sensitive approaches—including, for example, offering bilingual counselors, considering immigration status, mediating the experiences of minorities within legal systems and their family dynamics—determines the extent to which services are effective.

Forging Assistance

Analyses of comparative sociolegal systems reflect the extent to which broad cultural beliefs affect the nature of legal systems that respond to family violence.[114] Legal systems largely constrain societal responses to issue resolution. Although there are several types of legal systems, they tend to operate between two extremes.[115] One extreme emphasizes and privileges the protection of innocent defendants and their individual freedoms. This adversarial model arrives at decision making through the presentation of evidence by adversarial parties and a decision maker who, largely constrained by the parties' presentations, eventually decides the dispute's outcome. The focus provides protections to the accused as he or she proceeds through the legal system. The other extreme emphasizes the common good and societal interests rather than privileging personal freedom. This inquisitorial approach emphasizes the more active role of the decision maker, the courts. These courts take considerable initiative: Inquisitorial courts gather information, question all involved in the matter, and then determine who prevails. Countries do not fit neatly into these two extremes, and countries often have various jurisdictions that adopt different approaches which themselves are in a state of flux and constant development.[116] Existing differences reflect the social framing of abuses, and legal systems attempt to accommodate.

The different methods of deciding disputes necessarily determine their response to family life. Inquisitorial systems tend to view abuse as a familial, not a societal or legal, problem. The result is that the systems are characterized as family support systems in which policy and practice emphasize partnership, participation, prevention, and family support.[117] The approach also focuses on helping parents and children in the community in a supportive manner that minimizes police, surveillance, and coercive intervention. Thus, mental health agencies rather than criminal justice agencies are most involved with abusive incidents. Rather than treating abuse as a criminal act, agencies adopt a therapeutic philosophy that focuses on a strong belief in families and their preservation. The focus on families is significant: It translates into a move that protects families more than vulnerable individuals within families.[118] It is the focus away from direct intervention, broader support of families, and their enactment of more family-friendly legal procedures that separates this approach to family welfare from the adversarial. To a large extent, the rights of vulnerable individuals within families (e.g., children) are coterminous with their familial rights.

Adversarial approaches to dispute resolution differ considerably from inquisitorial systems. Countries adopting this approach tend to minimize the role of the State in private life, restrain government spending, and encourage individual and family responsibility and solutions. Although it may be an oversimplification to interpret trends protecting vulnerable individuals within families along the lines of greater emphasis on the privacy of the family and the diminution of the role of the State, the factors do help illustrate the predominant features of this model of family welfare, which focuses on individual responsibility and individual failure. These systems perceive abuse foremost as a problem that demands protection from harm; when systems function according to plan, allegations result in rapid efforts to remove victims from contact with abusers, including family members.

Two aims characterize the adversarial model's protective efforts. The first aim involves efforts to uncover maltreatment through the use of aggressive mandatory reporting schemes that mainly encourage professionals to report suspicious signs of maltreatment. The second aim concerns the need to determine whether abuse has occurred and, in certain instances, to punish offenders. Both goals seek to tackle the silent ecology of family violence by sleuthing to uncover abuse and providing clear statements regarding its prohibition. Although this approach involves State intervention, the State generally seeks to limit intervention by focusing on more extreme cases of family failure and limiting intervention inside the family to protect the privacy of families rather than broadly providing supportive services.

Although it could be difficult to imagine that some legal systems simply ignore or do not recognize abusive incidents within families, the majority of the world's victims do not live in countries that could offer legal protection. For example, abuse in developing countries remains relatively undocumented, uninvestigated, and essentially outside of legal arenas.[119] The failed sociolegal recognition of child abuse in India is illustrative. The extent to which child abuse is a problem in India remains unknown. There are no accurate figures of the extent of child abuse simply "because incidents are neither reported nor punished."[120] Several beliefs play key roles in the failure to recognize and combat abuse. Traditional themes of the sanctity of the family, prerogatives of parents, and children as parental property have protected abusive families from societal inspection and intervention. To exacerbate matters, the failure to recognize the need for intervention makes the focus on intrafamily child abuse even seem somewhat futile in the absence of intervention services and failure to invest limited social services resources in preventive and parental education programs. Given the size of the child population in India (over 300 million below the age of 16),[121] the large majority of whom live in poverty, coupled by the country's limited financial resources, attempting to meet the needs of individuals in especially difficult circumstances is not a realistic goal. Most resources simply aim to address the basic survival needs of children and families.

Countries need not be poor to embrace lenient attitudes toward family violence. Japanese society, for example, commonly understands that private family life is free from legal intervention.[122] As a result, some forms of violence are not recognized and, when recognized, are not necessarily responded to appropriately. For example, in the case of child abuse, incest is not a criminal act, and no criminal laws exist to punish parents who sexually abuse their children.[123] Reviews of State intervention in child abuse cases report that the laws that do exist are virtually nonfunctional. The center that handles cases of child abuse nationwide reported nearly 2,000 cases, only 1 of which resulted in the parent's loss of custody, and only 3 of which resulted in restraining orders.[124] The failure to address children's needs makes less curious the otherwise striking sensationalization of family violence as a social problem through concern about victimizations of mothers by their children. The legal system, then, reflects one of the themes presented earlier: The rights of family members supersede the rights of the child, the child's welfare, and even the welfare of family members who care for them.[125]

Cultural forces, then, deeply affect the nature of offered social and legal services. The dominant legal mode generally dictates approaches to violence, which in turn limit attempts to adopt alternative modes to address family violence (and, when alternative modes arise, they must be integrated into existing legal frameworks). Moreover, perceptions of personhood affect intervention efforts to the extent that some are viewed as worthy of intervention. Cultures deal with different resources differently and allocate only specific amounts to certain forms of violence deemed worthy of intervention.

Accepting Assistance

A close relationship clearly exists between efforts to seek assistance and the extent and nature of assistance available. Related to those aspects of the cultural forces that help determine intervention efforts is the willingness of victims and perpetrators to accept assistance: Cultural forces, including notions of family privacy, gender roles, and discrimination, affect the extent to which individuals accept intervention efforts. Cultural forces also help dictate the impact of coerced intervention in family life.

Family privacy and allocation of familial responsibilities affect the acceptance of intervention. Examples of family violence involving young children illustrate the significance of cultural forces. In Arab cultures, as in numerous societies, only relatives and close friends are trusted with intervention in family life.[126] These differences suggest that interventions that do not respect traditional family relationships jeopardize the therapeutic relationship with the family. Culturally attuned approaches are required to attend to issues surrounding legitimacy of intrusion on family privacy in efforts to protect the welfare of children, an approach that differs sharply from

Western methods of child protection, which focus on protection of family members from harm through formal institutions.[127] Research within Chinese cultures reveals similar findings. Many Chinese cannot even name any form of child abuse, with the vast majority equating abuse with physical abuse.[128] Equally important, less than half (40%) of the surveyed adults would report abuses to State officials. In addition, they would be more likely to report abuses that occurred in their own homes rather than those occurring outside their homes. The researchers interpret the hesitancy to report as reflecting a firm belief that child abuse is a family matter not to be interfered in by others unless the family desires intervention,[129] resulting from family protectiveness about shameful matters, belief that outsiders have no right to intervene in private family matters, and the subordinate position of children.[130] Providing adequate intervention requires adapting to traditional values.

Examples of family violence involving women and elderly people also illustrate well how family privacy and allocation of familial responsibilities affect the acceptance of intervention. Cultural beliefs that place value on filial piety and avoidance of shame, as discussed above, lead those interested in service provision to champion the need to address those values in the context of elder abuse. For example, social services providers who seek to address elder abuse now look to therapeutic efforts that strengthen entire families without singling out individuals or assigning blame.[131] Similar efforts aim to protect women and children from battering fathers. Because it often is difficult to get batterers to attend treatment programs and such programs do not necessarily exist, a massive effort in Central America (involving Belize, Costa Rica, El Salvador, Guatemala, Honduras, Nicaragua, and Panama) adopts a public health approach as it seeks to move beyond narrow legal definitions of domestic violence recognized in those countries to provide women and children access to services based on victims' definitions of violence and needs.[132] That approach is significant. The effort seeks to shore up support services to reflect the reality that the vast majority of victims who do reach out for help actually turn to trusted family and friends rather than to formal, public systems (e.g., police, courts, hospitals).[133] Differences in the manner in which individuals approach family privacy and allocate familial responsibilities, then, are of considerable significance and directly affect the legitimacy and effectiveness of efforts to assist.

Perceptions of gender roles also exemplify the extent to which cultural forces affect the willingness to accept assistance. A primary example of such cultural influence involves the apparent underreporting of family violence against men and boys in the United States. In terms of elderly people, researchers in the United States have reported that suicide rates for older men far outnumber those of women. A recent review of the literature that takes into account cultural forces suggests that different rates relate to gender roles.[134] Differences appear to be related to older men's attempts to escape abuse perpetrated against them by others and their efforts to mask other physical, economic, social, and psychological problems. Researchers also suggest that older men do not have the social networks or friendships that older women generally have. An emerging theme in reviews of boys' victimization, especially in research conducted in the United States, is that their abuses tend to remain more hidden and that male individuals tend not to seek (or receive) appropriate services to deal with their victimizations. Researchers report, for example, that although boys are as adversely affected by sexual victimization as are girls, they do not disclose their abuses as readily as girls. They do not do so for various reasons: They do not define their experiences as abusive and view the consequences of disclosure as worse than consequences of nondisclosure. When they do disclose, evidence suggests that clinicians and other confidants are more likely to not believe that abuse occurred or, if they do believe, they are more likely to discount the damage and deny the impact of abuse.[135] Child protection professionals (and especially police and social workers) do not consider female-perpetrated sexual abuse to be as serious as male-perpetrated abuse.[136] Research on violent partner abuse against men reveals high levels of violence reported by women, that self-defense does not adequately explain these high levels, and that, when women do engage in violence against men, their violence actually tends to be more injurious.[137] These findings remain highly controversial and are often viewed as artifacts of what gets reported. The controversy, however, does highlight the difficulties faced by battered men, the lack of clear understanding of what may constitute abuse, and the challenges faced by efforts to understand men's tolerance of violence against them. In summary, those who would offer assistance and victims do not readily conceptualize male individuals as potential victims, for reasons relating to culture and gender roles.

Perceptions of discrimination affect how minorities experience interventions to alleviate violence. How women of nonmajority background experience intervention highlights how cultural forces factor into responses to family violence. The intersection of racism and sexism exacerbates many problems commonly faced by women in battering relationships.[138] For women in the United States, for example, racism operates in two significant ways. First, the racial bias in the housing market and disparities between Black and White women's earning power increase the difficulties confronting women of color who attempt to leave battering relationships. Second, violence perpetrated against minority communities places different burdens on minority victims, which may result in attempts to not involve law enforcement because of the desire to maintain community integrity and discourage the perception of Black male violence or the desire to not bring shame on the family.[139] When law enforcement intervention does occur, its effectiveness varies considerably across social groups: For example, one recent study reports that Black women who received protective orders against batterers were three times more likely than White women to report re-abuse, and poor Black women were 10 times more likely to report re-abuse than poor White women.[140] Thus, although violence may be a common issue for women, the violence occurs within a context that varies according to race, class, and other social characteristics of particular women. Other countries report similar findings. An important case study of Palestinian women in Israel reveals how laws designed to help women actually may revictimize them when they are from minority groups that have been oppressed and discriminated against and that hold different cultural values regarding the place of women within families, the community's role in protecting women, and the perceptions of governments' roles in dictating family life.[141] Minority status complicates interventions and responses assumed to be appropriate and necessary to address family violence.

How children of nonmajority backgrounds experience intervention also highlights how cultural forces factor into responses to family violence. For example, research in the United States continues to identify Black and Hispanic children as suffering from higher rates of maltreatment.[142] It does seem clear that children from poor and minority families are more vulnerable to receiving the label "abuse" than children from more affluent households.[143] The decision biases seemingly operate at several phases of intervention: in the acceptance of reports for investigations, disposition of allegations, and decisions to open cases.[144] Although numerous factors may account for disproportionate responses to maltreatment, it does seem clear that some disparities in maltreatment do exist and are nothing short of alarming: For example, more than 40% of all infant and toddler (under age 5) homicides by parents and caretakers are Black, yet only 15% of children under age 5 are Black.[145] Although it is difficult to imagine how differences in investigation and reporting can narrow or eliminate such a huge gap, structural forces, such as increasingly punitive responses to poverty and discrimination outside of family life, link to potential increases in family violence, affect certain groups disproportionately, and reveal how social services broadly affect family life.[146]

Research related to the above examples also reveals how cultural forces help dictate the impact of coerced intervention in family life. For example, the recognition of wife and partner battering led to efforts to arrest, jail, and incarcerate batterers as the most effective means to eradicate the violence, even to the unusual extent that the system increasingly ignores the victim's preference to avoid criminal intervention in her violent relationship.[147] The approach, adopted by the majority of states in the United States,[148] has been viewed as the most successful technique for stopping violence against women even though it actually garners little support from research. Early research that found arrests to be the most effective way to reduce violent recidivism[149] was not replicated by the vast majority of studies it inspired.[150] Research continues to show the effect of the batterer's social context on the effectiveness of the intervention, including the extent to which arrest may increase physical violence. Men who lack community ties and have a reduced need for social conformity do not respond to aggressive, criminal justice intervention.[151] It is significant that the only randomized study of mandatory prosecution shows that a battered woman is safest when she has the choice to drop charges and halt prosecutorial efforts but elects not to do so.[152] Despite the focus on the batterer, then, a focus on his surroundings, particularly his victim and the cultural forces that operate on her (her lack of readily marketable skills, economic resources, social support, and fears of violence), may actually lead to the most effective intervention.[153]

Cultural forces, then, affect the extent to which and the manner in which individuals seek assistance. How systems offer services is as important as whether the services are offered at all. Conceptions of who experiences victimization and the types of responses they need tend to generalize violence. The need to generalize may serve as an important strategy to gain legal recognition, reform, services, and assistance. However, generalizations do not capture certain facts, such as how violent events do not exist in the absence of abusive relationship patterns and the particularities of any individual's relationships and place in society. In summary, the failure to particularize responses to different needs of those affected differently by cultural forces reduces the likelihood that victims (as well as those who victimize them) not only fail to seek assistance but also reject the assistance offered.

Conclusion

Despite the notable absence of systematic, cross-cultural examinations of family violence, important trends in findings already emerge from existing examinations of cultural influences on certain forms of family violence. First, research that does examine family violence reveals that almost all cultures recognize the existence of family violence, even though some forms of intrafamilial violence may be rarer in certain societies and some forms may be ignored. Second, although family violence may occur in private relations and remain hidden, family violence is fundamentally cultural; that is, family violence is not isolated from cultural practices, and families are a major repository of cultural values. Third, attempts to transform private relationships and combat family violence must also aim to transform cultural forces.

Research that highlights the significance of culture in understanding and responding to family violence requires reframing conventional thinking about family violence. In the reframing, the results presented thus far highlight the fundamental point: The boundary between cultural forces and private life is fluid. Recognition of the public nature of private violence is critical to rethinking how family violence may be a subject of human rights law. The recognition suggests that to affect and address family violence, international law must not only reach individual, private behavior but also intervene in cultural practices and foster broad societal reform. Thus, to address family violence, international human rights law must affect the forces that define maltreatment, create climates conducive to violence, serve as buffers from violence, and influence intervention efforts.

Research reveals that the types of intervention needed to address family violence requires that international law address both "private" and "public" practices. Regrettably, the use of international human rights law for these interventions remains highly contentious and subject to considerable challenges. Traditional human rights law remains fundamentally concerned with "public" acts attributable to State actions and with protecting State and cultural sovereignty. However, the private–public distinction increasingly loses its power in international law and the international community increasingly intervenes to change cultures and influence private life. Despite the growing boldness of international law, cultural forces still pose obstacles to all forms of legal and social reform efforts. These obstacles are examined in the next chapter, and subsequent chapters highlight the human rights response to those obstacles and how human rights law may be used to alleviate family violence.

Endnotes

1. For a thorough review of research in the United States, *see* O. W. Barnett, C. L. Miller-Perrin, and R. D. Perrin, *Family Violence Across the Lifespan* (Thousand Oaks, CA: Sage, 1997).
2. *Cf.* J. Korbin, "Social Networks and Family Violence in Cross-Cultural Perspective," in *The Individual, the Family, and Social Good: Personal Fulfillment in Times of Change*, G. B. Melton, Ed. (Lincoln: University of Nebraska Press, 1995).
3. *See, e.g.,* D. J. Truscott, "Cross-Cultural Perspectives: Toward an Integrated Theory of Elder Abuse," *Policy Studies* 17 (1996):287–298.
4. *See, e.g.,* M. C. Acevedo, "The Role of Acculturation in Explaining Ethnic Differences in the Prenatal Health-Risk Behaviors, Mental Health, and Parenting Beliefs of Mexican American and European American At-Risk Women," *Child Abuse & Neglect* 24 (2000): 111–127.
5. D. Finkelhor, "The International Epidemiology of Child Sexual Abuse," *Child Abuse & Neglect* 18 (1994):409–417.

6. D. Daro, G. Migely, D. Wiese, and S. Salmon-Cox, *World Perspectives on Child Abuse: The Second International Resource Book* (Chicago: International Society for the Prevention of Child Abuse and Neglect, 1996).

7. J. Korbin, "Culture and Child Maltreatment," in *The Battered Child* 5th ed. rev., M. E. Helfer, R. S. Kempe, and R. D. Krugman, Eds. (Chicago: University of Chicago Press, 1997).

8. J. I. Kosberg and J. L. Garcia, Eds., *Elder Abuse: International and Cross-Cultural Perspectives* (New York: Haworth Press, 1995).

9. D. A. Counts, J. K. Brown, and J. C. Campbell, "Introduction," in *Sanctions and Sanctuary: Cultural Perspectives on the Beating of Wives,* D. A. Counts, J. K. Brown, and J. C. Campbell, Ed. (Boulder, CO: Westview, 1992).

10. *See* G. B. Melton and M. F. Flood, "Research Policy and Child Maltreatment: Developing the Scientific Foundation for Effective Protection of Children," *Child Abuse & Neglect* 18 (1994):1–28.

11. *See* I. A. Canino and J. Spurlock, *Culturally Diverse Children and Adolescents: Assessment, Diagnosis, and Treatment* (New York: Guilford Press, 1994).

12. *See, e.g.,* N. Gilbert, *Combatting Child Abuse: International Perspectives and Trends* (New York: Oxford University Press, 1997); B. L. Bottoms and G. S. Goodman, Eds., *International Perspectives on Child Abuse and Children's Testimony* (Thousand Oaks, CA: Sage, 1996).

13. *Cf.* R. J. R. Levesque, "The Failures of Foster Care Reform: Revolutionizing the Most Radical Blueprint," *Maryland Journal of Contemporary Legal Issues* 6 (1995):1–35.

14. *Id.*

15. R. B. Edgerton, *Sick Societies: Challenging the Myth of Primitive Harmony* (New York: Free Press, 1992).

16. G. C. Denniston and M. F. Milos, Eds., *Sexual Mutilations: A Human Tragedy* (New York: Plenum Press, 1997).

17. S. Y. Lai and R. E. Ralph, "Female Sexual Autonomy and Human Rights," *Harvard Human Rights Journal* 8 (1995):201–227.

18. Human Rights Watch/Women's Rights Project, *A Matter of Power: State Control of Women's Virginity in Turkey* (New York: Author, 1994).

19. G. H. Herdt, Ed., *Ritualized Homosexuality in Melanesia* (Berkeley: University of California Press, 1993).

20. L. DeMause, "The Universality of Incest," *Journal of Psychohistory* 19 (1991):123–164; S. G. Frayser, "Defining Normal Childhood Sexuality: An Anthropological Approach," *Annual Review of Sex Research* 5 (1994):173–217.

21. *See* R. J. R. Levesque, "Piercing the Family's Private Veil: Family Violence, International Human Rights, and the Cross-Cultural Record," *Law & Policy* 21 (1999):161–187.

22. *Id.*

23. *See, e.g.,* C. S. Ford and F. A. Beach, *Patterns of Sexual Behavior* (New York: Harper & Row, 1951); G. J. Broude, *Growing Up: A Cross-Cultural Encyclopedia* (Santa Barbara, CA: ABC-CLIO, 1995); W. H. Davenport, "Adult–Child Sexual Relations in Cross-Cultural Perspective," in *The Sexual Abuse of Children: Theory and Research* Vol. 1., W. O'Donohue and J. H. Greer, Eds. (Hillsdale, NJ: Erlbaum, 1992); C. Konker, "Rethinking Child Sexual Abuse: An Anthropological Perspective," *American Journal of Orthopsychiatry* 62 (1992):148–153; J. E. Korbin, "Child Sexual Abuse: Implications From the Cross-Cultural Record," in *Child Survival: Anthropological Perspectives on the Treatment and Maltreatment of Children,* N. Sheper-Hughes, Ed. (Boston: D. Reidel, 1987).

24. R. J. R. Levesque, *Adolescents, Sex, and the Law: Preparing Adolescents for Responsible Citizenship* (Washington, DC: American Psychological Association, 2000).

25. J. L. Rosato, "Putting Square Pegs in a Round Hole: Procedural Due Process and the Effect of Faith Healing Exemptions on the Prosecution of Faith Healing Parents," *University of San Francisco Law Review* 29 (1994):43–119.

26. V. I. Vieth, "Corporal Punishment in the United States: A Call for a New Approach to the Prosecution of Disciplinarians," *Journal of Juvenile Law* 15 (1994):22–56; J. E. Durrant, "Evaluating the Success of Sweden's Corporal Punishment Ban," *Child Abuse & Neglect* 23 (1999):435–448.

27. S. Torres, "A Comparison of Wife Abuse Between Two Cultures: Perceptions, Attitudes, Nature, and Extent," *Issues in Mental Health Nursing: Psychiatric Nursing for the 90's: New Concepts, New Therapies* 12 (1991):113–131.

28. B. Agnew, *In Search of a Safe Place: Abused Women and Culturally Sensitive Services* (Toronto: University of Toronto Press, 1998).

29. *Cf.* E. M. Schneider, "Particularity and Generality: Challenges of Feminist Theory and Practice in Work on Woman Abuse," *New York University Law Review* 67 (1992):520–568.

30. G. J. Anetzberger, "Elderly Survivors of Family Violence," *Violence Against Women* 3 (1997):499–515.

31. A. Moon and O. Williams, "Perceptions of Elder Abuse and Help-Seeking Patterns Among African American, Caucasian American and Korean American Elderly Women," *Gerontologist* 33 (1993):386–395.

32. M. S. Lee, K. S. Crittenden, and E. Yu, "Social Support and Depression Among Elderly Korean Immigrants in the United States," *International Journal of Aging and Human Development* 42 (1996):313–327.

33. Y. I. Song, *Battered Women in Korean Immigrant Families: The Silent Scream* (New York: Garland, 1996).

34. S. Horne, "Domestic Violence in Russia," *American Psychologist* 54 (1999):55–61.

35. E. W. Gondolf and D. Shestakov, "Spousal Homicide in Russia," *Violence Against Women* 3 (1997):533–547.

36. Horne, "Domestic Violence in Russia."

37. C. Cassidy, "World-View Conflict and Toddler Malnutrition: Change Against Dilemmas," in *Child Survival: Anthropological Perspectives on the Treatment and Maltreatment of Children*, N. Sheper-Hughes, Ed. (Boston: D. Reidel, 1987).

38. S. J. Creighton, "Fatal Child Abuse—How Preventable Is It?" *Child Abuse Review* 4 (1995):318–328.

39. R. P. Rohner and E. Rohner, "Antecedents and Consequences of Parental Rejection: A Theory of Emotional Abuse," *Child Abuse & Neglect* 4 (1980):189–198.

40. *Id.*

41. See O. D. Jones, "Evolutionary Analysis in Law: An Introduction and Application to Child Abuse," *North Carolina Law Review* 75 (1997):1117–1242.

42. S. LeVine and R. LeVine, "Child Abuse and Neglect in Sub-Saharan Africa," in *Child Abuse and Neglect: Cross-Cultural Perspectives*, J. E. Korbin, Ed. (Berkeley: University of California Press, 1981).

43. A. K. Carlson-Whitley, "Dowry Death: A Violation of the Right to Life Under Article Six of the International Covenant on Civil and Political Rights," *University of Puget Sound Law Review* 17 (1994):637–664.

44. E. Bumiller, *May You Be the Mother of a Hundred Sons: Journey Among the Women of India* (New York: Random House, 1990); B. D. Prasad, "Dowry-Related Violence: A Content Analysis of News in Selected Newspapers," *Journal of Comparative Family Studies* 25 (1994):71–89; *see also* chapter 3.

45. D. Sobsey, *Violence and Abuse in the Lives of People With Disabilities* (New York: Brooks, 1994); E. Goldson, "Children With Disabilities and Child Maltreatment," *Child Abuse & Neglect* 22 (1998):663–667.

46. Korbin, "Culture and Child Maltreatment."

47. M. Weiss, *Conditional Love: Parents' Attitudes Toward Handicapped Children* (Westport, CT: Bergin & Garvey, 1994).

48. For a review, *see* N. Etcoff, *Survival of the Prettiest: The Science of Beauty* (New York: Doubleday, 1999).

49. For a review, *see* Levesque, *Adolescents, Sex, and the Law.*

50. *See, e.g.,* H. N. Bui, "Domestic Violence in the Vietnamese Immigrant Community: An Exploratory Study," *Violence Against Women* 5 (1999):769–796; M. M. Haj-Yahia, "Belief About Wife Battering Among Palestinian Women," *Violence Against Women* 4 (1998):533–559.

51. D. A. Counts, J. K. Brown, and J. C. Campbell, "Introduction," in *Sanctions and Sanctuary: Cultural Perspectives on the Beating of Wives,* D. A. Counts, J. K. Brown, and J. C. Campbell, Eds. (Boulder, CO: Westview, 1992).

52. W. M. Holloway, "Trends in Women's Health—A Global View," *Scientific American* (August 1994):75–83; L. L. Heise, "Violence, Sexuality, and Women's Lives," in *Conceiving Sexuality: Approaches to Sex Research in a Postmodern World,* R. G. Parker and J. H. Gagnon, Eds. (New York: Routledge, 1995); R. Kapur and B. Cossman, *Subversive Sites: Feminist Engagements With Law in India* (New Delhi, India: Sage, 1996).

53. Counts, Brown, and Campbell, "Introduction."

54. D. Levinson, *Family Violence in Cross-Cultural Perspective* (Newbury Park, CA: Sage, 1989).

55. *See also* Edgerton, *Sick Societies.*

56. K. Tout, *Ageing in Developing Countries* (New York: Oxford University Press, 1989).

57. Peter Decalmer and Frank Glendenning, *Mistreatment of Elderly People* (Newbury Park, CA: Sage, 1993); F. A. Boudreau, "Elder Abuse," in *Family Violence: Prevention and Treatment,* R. L. Hampton, T. P. Gullotta, G. R. Adams, E. H. Potter III, and R. P. Weissberg, Eds. (Newbury Park, CA: Sage, 1993); S. Moskowtiz, "Saving Granny From the Wolf: Elder Abuse and Neglect—The Legal Framework," *Connecticut Law Review* 31 (1998):77–204.

58. J. I. Kosberg and J. L. Garcia, "Common and Unique Themes on Elder Abuse From a World-Wide Perspective," in *Elder Abuse: International and Cross-Cultural Perspectives,* J. I. Kosberg and J. L. Garcia, Eds. (New York: Haworth Press, 1995).

59. Korbin, "Social Networks and Family Violence."

60. J. E. Rein, "Preserving Dignity and Self-Determination of the Elderly in the Face of Competing Interests and Grim Alternatives: A Proposal for Statutory Refocus and Reform," *George Washington Law Review* 60 (1992):1818–1888.

61. Y. Goldfeder, "Assisted Suicide and the Illusory Poverty Component," *Georgetown Journal on Fighting Poverty* 5 (1998):335–348.

62. *See* C. A. Prado, "Effects of Gender Differences on Physician-Assisted Suicide: Practice and Regulation," *Southern California Review of Law and Women's Studies* 8 (1998): 101–144.

63. Goldfeder, "Assisted Suicide and the Illusory Poverty Component."

64. M. F. Bendik, "Reaching the Breaking Point: Dangers of Mistreatment in Elder Care-Giving Situations," *Journal of Elder Abuse & Neglect* 4(3) (1992):39–59; S. K. Steinmetz, "The Abused Elderly Are Dependent: Abuse Is Caused by the Perception of Stress Associated With Providing Care," in *Current Controversies in Family Violence,* R. J. Gelles and D. R. Loseke, Eds. (Newbury Park, CA: Sage, 1993).

65. Moskowitz, "Saving Granny From the Wolf."

66. Rein, "Preserving Dignity and Self-Determination of the Elderly in the Face of Competing Interests and Grim Alternatives."

67. P. O. Sijuwade, "Cross-Cultural Perspectives on Elder Abuse as a Family Dilemma," *Social Behavior and Personality* 23 (1995):247–252.

68. A. P. Glascock, "By Any Other Name, It Is Still Killing: A Comparison of the Treatment of the Elderly in America and Other Societies," in *The Cultural Context of Aging: Worldwide Perspectives*, J. Sokolovsky, Ed. (New York: Bergin & Garvey, 1990) at 43.

69. *See* N. J. Baladerian, "Recognizing Abuse and Neglect in People With Severe Cognitive and/or Communication Impairments," *Journal of Elder Abuse & Neglect* 9 (1997):93–104.

70. L. Simmons, "Ageing in Primitive Societies: A Comparative Survey of Family Life and Relationships," in *Handbook of Social Gerontology: Societal Aspects of Ageing*, C. Tibbets, Ed. (Chicago: University of Chicago Press, 1960) at 87.

71. U.S. Advisory Board on Child Abuse and Neglect, *Neighbors Helping Neighbors: A New National Strategy for the Protection of Children* (Washington, DC: U.S. Government Printing Office, 1993); J. Waldfogel, *The Future of Child Protection: How to Break the Cycle of Abuse & Neglect* (Cambridge, MA: Harvard University Press, 1998).

72. R. J. R. Levesque, "Prosecuting Sex Crimes Against Children: Time for 'Outrageous' Proposals?" *Law & Psychology Review* 19 (1995):59–91.

73. For a comprehensive review, *see* J. M. Steil, *Marital Equality: Its Relationship to the Well-Being of Husbands and Wives* (Thousand Oaks, CA: Sage, 1997).

74. *Id.*

75. Levinson, *Family Violence in Cross-Cultural Perspective*; J. K. Brown, "Introduction: Definitions, Assumptions, Themes, and Issues," in *Sanctions and Sanctuary: Cultural Perspectives on the Beating of Wives*, D. A. Counts, J. K. Brown, and J. C. Campbell, Eds. (Boulder, CO: Westview, 1992).

76. Prasad, "Dowry-Related Violence."

77. C. Ward, *Blaming Victims: Feminist and Social Psychological Perspectives on Rape* (London: Sage, 1995).

78. M. Liss and G. Stahly, "Domestic Violence and Child Custody," in *Battering and Family Therapy: A Feminist Perspective*, M. Hansen and M. Harway, Eds. (Newbury Park, CA: Sage, 1993).

79. W. W. Barnard, H. J. Vera, M. I. Vera, and G. Newman, "Till Death Do Us Part: A Study of Spouse Murder," *Bulletin of the American Academy of Psychiatry and the Law* 10 (1982):271–280.

80. *See* A. Sev'er, "Recent or Imminent Separation and Intimate Violence Against Women," *Violence Against Women* 3 (1997):566–590.

81. R. J. R. Levesque, "Dating Violence, Adolescents and the Law," *Virginia Journal of Social Policy and Law* 4 (1997):339–379.

82. R. J. R. Levesque, "Emotional Maltreatment in Adolescents' Everyday Lives: Furthering Sociolegal and Social Services Provisions," *Behavioral Sciences and the Law* 16 (1998): 237–263.

83. For a synopsis of this area of research and list of citations, *see* Levesque, "Dating Violence, Adolescents and the Law."

84. Korbin, "Social Networks and Family Violence."

85. Tout, *Ageing in Developing Countries*.

86. G. Shah, R. Veedon, and S. Vasi, "Elder Abuse in India," in *Elder Abuse: International and Cross-Cultural Perspectives*, J. I. Kosberg and J. L. Garcia, Eds. (New York: Haworth Press, 1995).

87. Kosberg and Garcia, *Elder Abuse*.

88. J. Chang and A. Moon, "Korean American Elderly's Knowledge and Perceptions of Elder Abuse: A Qualitative Analysis of Cultural Factors," *Journal of Multicultural Social Work* 6 (1997):139–154.

89. Human Rights Watch/Asia, *Death by Default: A Policy of Fatal Neglect in China's State Orphanages* (New Haven, CT: Yale University Press, 1996).

90. J. Boyden, *Families: A Celebration and Hope for World Change* (London: Faine & UNESCO, 1993).

91. V. Muntarbhorn, *United Nations Special Rapporteur on the Sale of Children, Child Prostitution and Child Pornography, Preliminary Report on the Sale of Children*, U.N. Doc. No. E/Cn.4/1991/51 (January 28, 1991), para. 34.

92. C. Colgough and K. Lewin, *Educating All the Children: Strategies for Primary Schooling in the South* (Oxford, England: Clarendon Press, 1993).

93. American Association of University Women (1992).

94. A. Sen, "More Than 100 Million Women Are Missing," *New York Review of Books* (Dec. 20, 1990) at 66.

95. M. C. Nussbaum, "Human Capabilities, Female Human Being," in *The Quality of Life*, M. C. Nussbaum and J. Glover, Eds. (New York: Oxford University Press, 1993) at 90.

96. C. S. Tang, "The Rate of Physical Child Abuse in Chinese Families: A Community Survey in Hong Kong," *Child Abuse & Neglect* 22 (1999):381–391.

97. C. S. Tang, "Frequency of Parental Violence Against Children in Chinese Families: Impact of Age and Gender," *Journal of Family Violence* 13 (1998): 13–130; Tang, "The Rate of Physical Child Abuse in Chinese Families"; D. Wu, "Chinese Childhood Socialization," in *The Handbook of Chinese Psychology*, M. H. Bond, Ed. (Hong Kong, China: Oxford University Press, 1996).

98. G. D. Wolfner and R. J. Gelles, "A Profile of Violence Toward Children: A National Study," *Child Abuse & Neglect* 17 (1993):197–212.

99. S. S. Kazarian and D. R. Evans, "Cultural Clinical Psychology," in *Cultural Clinical Psychology: Theory, Research, and Practice*, S. S. Kazaran and D. R. Evans, Eds. (New York: Oxford University Press, 1998).

100. R. Forehand and B. A. Kotchick, "Cultural Diversity: A Wake-Up Call for Parent Training," *Behavior Therapy* 27 (1996):187–206.

101. *See, e.g.,* J. Giordano and M. A. Giordano, "Ethnic Dimensions of Family Therapy," in *Integrating Family Therapy*, R. Mikesell, D. Lusterman, and S. McDaniel, Eds. (Washington, DC: American Psychological Association, 1995); M. McGoldrick and J. Giordano, "Overview: Ethnicity and Family Therapy," in *Ethnicity and Family Therapy* 2nd ed., M. McGoldrick, J. Giordano, and J. K. Pearce, Eds. (New York: Guilford Press, 1996).

102. L. E. Walker, *The Battered Woman* (New York: Harper, 1979).

103. C. M. Sullivan and D. I. Bybee, "Reducing Violence Using Community-Based Advocacy for Women With Abusive Partners," *Journal of Consulting and Clinical Psychology* 67 (1999):43–54.

104. *See* D. A. Downs, *More Than Victims: Battered Women, the Syndrome Society, and the Law* (Chicago: University of Chicago Press, 1996).

105. L. E. Walker, "Psychology and Domestic Violence Around the World," *American Psychologist* 54 (1999):21–29.

106. M. Scarf, *Battered Jewish Wives: Case Studies in the Response to Rage* (Lewiston, NY: Edwin Mellen Press, 1988).

107. Walker, *The Battered Woman*.

108. G. J. Anetzberger, J. E. Korbin, and S. K. Tomita, "Defining Elder Mistreatment in Four Ethnic Groups Across Two Generations," *Journal of Cross-Cultural Gerontology* 11 (1996):187–192.

109. *See, e.g.,* S. K. Tomita, "The Consideration of Cultural Factors in the Research of Elder Mistreatment With an In-depth Look at the Japanese," *Journal of Cross-Cultural Gerontology* 9 (1994):39–52.

110. *See* Moon and Williams, "Perceptions of Elder Abuse and Help-Seeking Patterns Among African American, Caucasian American and Korean American Elderly Women."

111. S. Pablo and K. L. Braun, "Perceptions of Elder Abuse and Neglect and Help-Seeking Patterns Among Filipino and Korean Elderly Women in Honolulu," *Journal of Elder Abuse & Neglect* 9 (1997):63–76.

112. Levesque, *Adolescents, Sex, and the Law*.
113. M. E. Haskett, N. P. Nowlan, J. S. Hutcheson, and J. M. Whitworth, "Factors Associated With Successful Entry in Child Sexual Abuse Cases," *Child Abuse & Neglect* 15 (1991): 467–476; K. D. Tingus, A. H. Heger, D. Foy, and G. A. Leskin, "Factors Associated With Entry Into Therapy in Children Evaluated for Sexual Abuse," *Child Abuse and Neglect* 20 (1995):63–68.
114. Bottoms and Goodman (1996); Gilbert, *Combatting Child Abuse*; D. J. Shoemaker, *International Handbook on Juvenile Justice* (Westport, CT: Greenwood Press, 1996).
115. J. R. Spencer and R. Flin, *The Evidence of Children: The Law and Psychology* 2nd ed. (London: Blackstone, 1993).
116. *See, e.g.,* K. J. Swift, "Canada: Trends and Issues in Child Welfare," in *Combatting Child Abuse: International Perspectives and Trends*, N. Gilbert, Ed. (New York: Oxford University Press, 1997).
117. N. Parton, "Child Protection and Family Support: Current Debates and Future Prospects," in *Child Protection and Family Support: Tensions, Contradictions and Possibilities*, N. Parton, Ed. (New York: Routledge, 1997).
118. *Id.*
119. *See, e.g.,* F. I. Omorodion, "Child Sexual Abuse in Benin City, Edo State, Nigeria: A Sociological Analysis," *Issues in Comprehensive Pediatric Nursing* 17 (1994):29–36.
120. U. A. Segal, "Children as Witness: India Is Not Ready," in *International Perspectives on Child Abuse and Children's Testimony*, B. L. Bottoms and G. S. Goodman, Eds. (Thousand Oaks, CA: Sage, 1996) at 274.
121. J. P. Grant, *The State of the World's Children* (New York: Oxford University Press, 1994).
122. J. Kozu, "Domestic Violence in Japan," *American Psychologist* 54 (1999):50–54.
123. Y. Ikeda, "Letter to the Editor," *Child Abuse and Neglect* 16 (1992):313–314.
124. Kozu, "Domestic Violence in Japan."
125. *Id.*
126. *See* M. M. Haj-Yahia and R. Shor, "Child Maltreatment as Perceived by Arab Students of Social Science in the West Bank," *Child Abuse and Neglect* 19 (1995):1209–1219.
127. *Id.*
128. J. T. F. Lau, J. L. Y. Liu, A. Yu, and C. K. Wong, "Conceptualizing, Reporting and Underreporting of Child Abuse in Hong Kong," *Child Abuse and Neglect* 23 (1999): 1159–1174.
129. *Id.*
130. *See* T. P. Ho and W. M. Kwok, "Child Sexual Abuse in Hong Kong," *Child Abuse & Neglect* 15 (1991):597–600; K. Y. C. Lai and C. K. Wong, "Critical Analysis of the Investigation of a Case of Physical Abuse," in *Responding to Child Abuse: Procedures and Practice for Child Protection in Hong Kong*, C. O'Brian, C. Y. L. Cheng, and N. Rhinds, Eds. (Hong Kong, China: Hong Kong University Press, 1997).
131. See D. S. Sanders, "Future Directions in Social Services: Asian and Pacific Islander Perspectives," in *Handbook of Social Services for Asian and Pacific Islanders*, N. Mokuau, Ed. (Westport, CT: Greenwood Press, 1991).
132. Walker, "Psychology and Domestic Violence Around the World."
133. L. Kelly, "Tensions and Possibilities: Enhancing Informal Responses to Domestic Violence," in *Future Interventions With Battered Women and Their Families*, J. L. Edleson and Z. C. Eiskovits, Eds. (Thousand Oaks, CA: Sage, 1996); G. A. Fawcett, L. L. Heise, L. Isita-Espejel, and S. Pick, "Changing Community Responses to Wife Abuse: A Research and Demonstration Project in Iztacaloco, Mexico," *American Psychologist* 54 (1999):41–49.
134. J. I. Kosberg, "The Abuse of Elderly Men," *Journal of Elder Abuse and Neglect* 9 (1998):69–88.

135. G. R. Holmes, L. Offen, and G. Waller, "See No Evil, Hear No Evil, Speak No Evil: Why Do Relatively Few Male Victims of Childhood Sexual Abuse Receive Help for Abuse-Related Issues in Adulthood?" *Clinical Psychology Review* 17 (1997):69–88.

136. J. Hetherton and L. Beardsall, "Decisions and Attitudes Concerning Child Sexual Abuse: Does the Gender of the Perpetrator Make a Difference to Child Protection Professionals?" *Child Abuse & Neglect* 22 (1998):1265–1283.

137. For a review, *see* P. W. Cook, *Abused Men: The Hidden Side of Domestic Violence* (Westport, CT: Praeger, 1997).

138. K. Crenshaw, "Race, Gender, and Violence Against Women: Convergences, Divergences and Other Black Feminist Conundrums," in *Family Matters: Readings on Family Lives and the Law*, M. Minow, Ed. (New York: Free Press, 1992); Schneider, "Particularity and Generality."

139. P. C. Johnson, "Danger in the Diaspora: Law Culture and Violence Against Women of African Descent in the United States and South Africa," *Journal of Gender, Race & Justice* 1 (1998):471–527.

140. M. J. Carlson, S. D. Harris, and G. W. Holden, "Protective Orders and Domestic Violence: Risk Factors for Re-Abuse," *Journal of Family Violence* 14 (1999):205–226.

141. N. Shalhoub-Kevorkian, "Law, Politics, and Violence Against Women: A Case Study of Palestinians in Israel," *Law & Policy* 21 (1999):189–211.

142. National Research Council, *Understanding Child Abuse & Neglect* (Washington, DC: National Academy Press, 1993).

143. G. L. Zellman, "The Impact of Case Characteristics on Child Abuse Reporting Decisions," *Child Abuse & Neglect* 16 (1992):57–74.

144. T. D. Morton, "Letter to the Editor," *Child Abuse & Neglect* 23 (1999):1209.

145. S. Ards, C. Chung, and S. L. Myers, Jr., "Letter to the Editor," *Child Abuse & Neglect* 23 (1999):1211–1214.

146. *Id.*

147. C. Hanna, "No Right to Choose: Mandated Victim Participation in Domestic Violence Prosecutions," *Harvard Law Review* 109 (1996):1850–1910.

148. *See* L. Mills, *The Heart of Intimate Abuse* (New York: Springer, 1998).

149. L. W. Sherman and R. A. Berk, "The Specific Deterrent Effects of Arrest for Domestic Assault," *American Sociological Review* 49 (1984):261–271.

150. Mills, *The Heart of Intimate Abuse.*

151. F. Dunford, D. Huizinga, and D. Elliot, "The Role of Arrest in Domestic Assault: The Omaha Police Experiment," *Criminology* 28 (1990):183–206.

152. D. Ford and M. Regoli, "The Criminal Prosecution of Wife Assaulters: Process, Problems, and Effects," in *Legal Responses to Wife Assault: Current Trends and Evaluation*, N. Z. Hilton, Ed. (Newbury Park, CA: Sage, 1993).

153. *Cf.* Mills, *The Heart of Intimate Abuse.*

Chapter 3
CULTURALLY ROOTED CHALLENGES
TO LAW REFORM

Cultural forces affect the extent, nature, and responses to family violence. Understanding how a human rights approach could affect the cultural features of family violence requires two analyses. The first analysis concerns the extent to which cultural practices stifle attempts to respond to family violence; the second involves how cultural forces may be enlisted in efforts to address family violence. This chapter addresses the first analysis and reserves for the next chapters the complicated issues relating to the harnessing of cultural forces to effect cultural change consistent with a human rights approach and enhanced protections from family violence.

The task of this chapter—understanding how cultural forces may hamper legal reforms—would benefit from comprehensive epidemiological and interpretive analyses of family violence as experienced throughout the world's societies. It is regrettable that no such analyses exist. The lack of such analyses is not surprising. As demonstrated in preceding chapters, the nature and experience of family violence differs within and among societies that differently define and respond to violence. Given how societies influence the nature of violence, purely epidemiological studies would not necessarily further the understanding of family violence. Studies of significance would be those that both report on the existence of violence and explore reasons such violence occurs and continues within particular societies and, to the extent practicable, across societies.

An interpretive reading of existing reports of family violence across numerous societies reveals five different yet interrelated sociocultural forces that challenge reform efforts to respond to family violence. First, ingrained discrimination against vulnerable individuals makes legal reform difficult, and laws often reflect the discrimination. Second, limited economic and social resources necessary to ensure greater social justice hamper the implementation of laws and unproductively skew the nature of laws themselves. Third, several societies have customary laws and customs that may be inconsistent with more formal, governmental laws of the modern State and that challenge the enforcement of laws deemed more progressive. Fourth, ingrained religious traditions make reforms difficult, especially when new laws directly confront established religious practices. Fifth, legal systems continue to have difficulty viewing certain groups of people as individuals worthy of protection in their own right: Legal systems reflect dominant cultural beliefs relating to who and what is worthy of protection. As a whole, these challenges reflect the extent to which profoundly cultural values inhibit the development of individuals' self-determination and their protection from violence which local, national, and international communities increasingly agree violate a host of fundamental human rights.

Although a cross-cultural perspective and analysis of family violence highlights the challenges to legal reforms, it is important to delineate more precisely the significance of a cultural approach to understanding the challenge to legal reforms that would offer greater protection to individuals victimized by their families. Establishing the cross-cultural existence of violence and the nature of responses serves as the necessary first step—it provides a factual record to evaluate whether a need for reform exists. Legal analysis necessitates understanding the differing cultural assumptions that underlie societal approaches to specific issues. Law itself is a culturally specific expression of traditions and norms of a particular society. Moreover, numerous practices present distinctive patterns of violence that reflect common themes that run through all forms of family violence; for example, practices such as *sati* (widow burning), bride burning, trafficking of women, genital circumcision, and infanticide may remain associated with particular cultures and regions of the world but they reflect (among other things) how cultures allocate certain resources along gendered distinctions. A cultural perspective on family violence also provides insights about ways to alter patterns of violence within families, insights that emerge from understanding the common threads that run through the exotic and ordinary forms of violence. Various forms of national and international intervention inevitably must affect numerous cultural forces to respond appropriately to family violence, and justifications for extending the protection of international law become more compelling only to the extent that family violence is not specific to a small number of countries and societies. By looking at cultural barriers to human rights intervention, one may discover ways to use culture to enhance human rights protections. A final reason in support of a cross-cultural perspective is that establishing the existence and nature of family violence is an empirical task that must serve as a necessary prelude to establishing the normative and legal task of ensuring that fundamental human rights of family members should not be abridged, that all family members are entitled to international law's frequently enumerated recognition that the human community must respect the inherent dignity and equal and inalienable rights of all.

Although the significance of the exercise is worth noting, it also is worth noting that the cultural forces in and of themselves may not be problematic and may not necessarily contribute to violence. Cultures may appropriately discriminate between individuals, cultures may hold religious beliefs, cultures may have customary laws, and cultures may struggle with the proper allocation of resources. How these forces contribute, as a whole or in part, to family violence makes them subject to challenges. Indeed, several of the problematic cultural forces may and must be harnessed to ensure greater human rights protections.

Discriminatory Laws

When examined from a cultural perspective, discrimination takes different forms and frequently intersects with issues of gender, economics, class, and group affiliation. Despite different manifestations, discrimination essentially takes two forms when viewed in terms of laws that would affect family violence: the failure to recognize the impact of laws and the failure to enact laws that appropriately redress discriminatory circumstances. Both forms of discrimination pervade legal systems' responses to family violence and stifle attempts to engage in law reform that would protect individuals from family violence. A single look at existing research that focuses on family violence makes obvious the discriminatory nature of laws, even progressive laws, that aim to combat family violence.

Failed Recognition

The manner in which some laws seek to protect women from violence reveals the extent to which laws may discriminate and fail to offer protection from abuse. The previous chapter demonstrated that cultures tend to select and protect some groups of people more than others; here the focus is on understanding how laws may factor into the failure to recognize how individuals may be discriminated against and how laws enforce and reflect those cultural beliefs.

A clear example of the failure of the law to recognize discrimination in the context of family violence involves several countries' responses to battering between spouses. Although evidence of discrimination may be culled from most countries that have enacted legal responses to battering, two South American countries (Brazil and Chile) have received the most attention in regard to the extent to which their legal systems fail to recognize the discriminatory impact of laws that allow battering to continue. Americas Watch, for example, reported that, between 1988 and 1990, women in the Brazilian State of Mranhio registered at the main police station more than 4,000 complaints of battery and sexual abuse in the home.[1] Of those complaints, less than 8% were forwarded to the court for processing. The court processes resulted in the conviction and imprisonment of only two men. Similar statistics have been reported for cases in Chile. Researchers report that 50% of all Chilean women have been subject to physical abuse by their male partners and that 25% of all women are consistently beaten by their partners.[2] Yet the Chilean prosecution rates remain low.

Commentators cite discriminatory laws as the major reason for the legal system's failure to protect women. Human rights reports note that Brazilian law accepts, either by judicial or legislative fiat, the murder of women involved in domestic disputes. For example, the "honor defense" allows men to murder, without legal rebuke, wives or girlfriends whom they suspect of infidelity.[3] Although the courts do not legally recognize the defense, they consistently permit this defense as a basis for acquittal.[4] Other defenses, such as the "privileged homicide" defense, are also available to men seeking to escape punishment for the murder of their partners.[5] The privileged homicide defense focuses on the proposition that unjust motivation led to violent emotions and to the murder, and courts liberally allow the defense in cases of premeditation of family violence. Unlike the honor defense, defenses like the privileged homicide defense are legislatively based doctrines. Although the defenses may be limited in scope, they run the danger of being used to excuse violence.

The Chilean response presents another variation in the discriminatory nature of laws. Although laws do address the battering of women by their husbands, the legal system implements the law in a manner that reduces its effectiveness. Reports reveal that the Chilean system functionally prevents women from successfully prosecuting their cases. Two examples are illustrative. First, the Chilean Penal Code sets forth a 14-day rule, which bars criminal penalties for abuse that results in less than 14 days of either hospitalization or loss of work.[6] Second, to press charges, women must be examined by the Instituti Medico-Legal, which determines whether abuses are severe enough to warrant prosecution. The process, however, makes it difficult to obtain examinations before physical wounds disappear.[7] Although the measures have been set in place to protect the rights of the accused and ensure responses to severe cases, the nature and implementation of laws reveal that they ultimately discriminate against victims. Although violence and murder may not be permitted by law, systems fail to

respond appropriately. The responses result in distrust of the court and law enforcement system, which exacerbates difficulties posed by reform efforts. The examples,
then, are particularly illustrative not only of failed recognition of problems by the
legal system, but also of the difficulty of reforming legal systems: Even though laws
have been reformed to address forms of family violence, their effectiveness may
remain questionable.

The country that has served as a model for aggressive reforms, the United States,
also exhibits continued discrimination in its laws. Domestic violence is the most
widespread form of violence in the United States and is the major cause of injury
to women.[8] Each year, approximately 3 to 4 million women are beaten in their homes
by their male partners. Twenty percent of hospital emergency visits by women result
from battering, and 50% of all women killed in the United States are killed by their
male partners. Although the rapid rise in laws responding to domestic violence reflects law enforcement's attempt to combat its discriminatory response to violence,[9]
the legal system's responses pervasively fail (a finding with parallels in other countries that have taken apparently aggressive approaches to sexual assault and domestic
violence).[10] The reason for continued failure, despite important progress, rests on the
failure to also address other forces of discrimination linked to battering. From this
perspective, addressing domestic violence requires addressing other forms of discrimination, such as women's subservient position within society and the family
structure, sex discrimination in the workplace, economic discrimination, lack of child
care, lack of access to divorce, inadequate child support, and lack of educational and
community support.[11]

Failed recognition, however, runs deep and plays an important role in family
violence. The example of child labor is illustrative, even though analyses of family
violence tend to ignore this form of familial violence. Laws directly provide protections for children engaged in child labor, yet they tend to allow the exploitation of
child labor by family members. For example, one of the most reported areas of study,
Guatemala, constitutionally guarantees the protection of minors and their right to an
education and contains a lengthy and specific list of minimal social rights of labor
legislation.[12] Likewise, the Guatemalan Labor Code provides a minimum age of
employment of 14 years. In addition, the government has taken several measures to
combat child labor more aggressively, such as the establishment of a department to
monitor the rights of children, a fund to combat poverty, a campaign to fight illit-
eracy, and an educational campaign to inform individuals of their rights under international law.[13] Yet lack of political will and resources have led to pervasive unen-
forcement.[14] Researchers have reported that inspectors fail to enforce laws, judicial
systems remain ineffective, and rulings are not enforced.[15] The implementation of
laws reflects the pervasive observation by commentators who have noted that the
most extreme forms of child labor are perpetrated by private actors with the acquiescence of public officials.[16] Most notably, the laws fail to protect children who work
with or for their families, which is the context in which the vast majority of exploited
children work.[17] The failed response contributes to a growing number of children
involved in exploitative child labor condoned by families, as revealed by numerous
other analyses that highlight how countries have laws that address child labor but
fail to address important cultural forces that ensure that the practice continues.[18] In
viewing child labor as a form of family violence, it is important to understand how
familial exploitation of child labor not only constitutes violence in itself—such as

the harm suffered by extended hours, unsafe working conditions, and conditions akin to slavery[19]—but also in terms of long-term consequences in the form of stifling educational and other future opportunities.[20] Although it is important to emphasize that not all family-related labor is harmful and labor actually may be beneficial to children,[21] the failure to realize harms and regulate risks reveals the extent to which laws fail to recognize areas in need of reform.

It is unnecessary to focus attention only on legal shortcomings in other countries; child labor in the United States provides a clear example of discriminatory laws as they relate to family life and violence. For example, it is commonly held that child labor in rural areas is unproblematic because it occurs within a family context: The family is seen as providing protection for its younger members and labor is seen as less harmful. Work within the family unit may be considered to be a duty, an honor, or an expression of family solidarity, which leads both children and their parents to accept laboring. Moreover, in rural areas, the family is the main unit of production and the child's labor is more naturally incorporated within it. However, the labor potential of rural children can be abused by their families, particularly poor families and those who migrate to find seasonal labor. A clear example derives from the educational difficulties facing migrant children—work replaces educational efforts and legal responses inadequately address their needs.[22] The circumstances are exacerbated by discrimination against migrant workers' families to the extent that federal farm policy provides exemptions from social, labor, health, and safety legislation.[23] The legal failures jeopardize the health of even the children who do not work but simply follow their families: Migrant children are at high risk for child maltreatment, numerous health hazards, and educational failure.[24] As a result, even though laws protect children from educational neglect, child labor, and other exploitative conditions, the children of migrant workers do not receive sufficient protection.[25]

Unintended Consequences

Discrimination in terms of the impact of laws has been well documented. Many human rights reports on the impact of discrimination involve laws that respond to children in difficult circumstances. In this context, laws discriminate in several ways: They discriminate against children as a whole, against children in particular societies, and against groups of children within certain societies. The discrimination finds expression in most common forms of abuse and highlights the difficulty of addressing family violence through law reform.

A most frequently cited form of discrimination involves female infanticide and selective abortions. Several human rights groups report that these practices are increasing, particularly in many parts of Asia. Sex-selective abortions are prevalent in countries such as China and India and, to a lesser extent, in Taiwan, South Korea, and Pakistan.[26] In China, for example, 97% of abortions are of female fetuses,[27] which has led to vastly unequal sex ratios that favor boys. The abortions reflect systems of laws that discriminate and affect familial and other pressures that override existing laws that seek equal protection. For example, laws that limit the number of children in families and that place preference on male children in societies that traditionally prefer boys to girls contribute to sex-selective abortions.[28] The most frequently cited example is China's "one-couple, one-child" policy, which mandates family planning for all couples, including obtaining permits before trying to conceive a child, using effective contraception, terminating pregnancies that are "out-of-plan," and undergoing sterilization.[29] Penalties for failing to comply with the policy include stiff fines, disqualification of "out-of-plan" children from benefits, and administrative demotion and dismissal from employment.[30] In addition to these formal sanctions, those who have children out of plan may suffer intimidation and violence to themselves and their property by co-workers and authorities.[31] Despite laws that may prohibit discrimination, then, other laws may factor in and foster discrimination. These laws and cultural beliefs are strong enough to render ineffective laws prohibiting sex-selective abortions. Thus, discrimination continues seemingly unabated even though several societies now have legislative enactments that prohibit the use of prenatal sex-determination tests and selective abortions to ensure that parents have male children.[32]

Although several would argue that abortions do not constitute child abuse, the findings reflect the disproportionate abuse girls suffer. Often discussed in the context of selective abortions are findings related to how girls disproportionately suffer infanticide or its frequent equivalent, abandonment. These forms of abuse directly reveal how laws may protect in some ways but actually create conditions that discriminate and lead to violence. China's laws are again illustrative. China's mandatory family planning policies discussed above have been reported as instrumental in fostering infanticide and abandonment of girls.[33] Despite laws that may prohibit discrimination, then, other laws may factor in and foster discrimination.

Reports from other parts of the world suggest that laws may be directly implicated in fostering forms of violence against girls even where they do not explicitly foster family planning. A recent study in Madras, India, found that more than half of 1,250 women surveyed had at some time killed a baby daughter.[34] Those high rates, however, relate to laws that fail to enforce the equal protection of girls and ensure that girls constitute a heavier burden on families through the use of dowry (among other factors).[35] Again, laws have a discriminatory impact; they simultaneously prohibit yet contribute to bringing about violence.

Other examples reveal the extent to which laws may explicitly mandate equal treatment yet allow discrimination to continue. Less explicit forms of violence resulting in death deal with denying girls access to education and medical services. Estimates show that female children are three times more likely to suffer from malnutrition than male children and receive less pediatric care because they are considered less important and less productive than their male counterparts.[36] That failure to protect girls continues despite mandates that they must be treated equally and that they must, for example, attend compulsory schooling until a designated age.[37] Parents may not actively dislike or actively compromise the well-being of their daughters, yet the marked cultural preference for sons fosters conditions that ensure families treat boys and girls differently.

India again provides a key example of how systems of laws discriminate despite the existence of specific laws that prohibit such discrimination. Reports from India reveal a higher death rate for girls in their teens. For example, a highly cited government report for the State of Gujarat found that over half of the women who committed suicide were younger than age 15.[38] The rates have been interpreted as attributable to early childbearing and to young girls' difficulties in adjusting to the extended families of in-laws. The police reports used in the government study indicate that in many cases of alleged suicide, the victim had actually been poisoned, beaten, drowned, burned, or hanged. Those who did commit suicide did so to escape their husband's or mothers-in-law's harsh treatment deliberately aimed to do away with them. Again, laws prohibit such acts, but the practices continue; moreover, even when societies have moved to eliminate discriminatory laws and practices that lead to violence, other parts of the legal systems may operate and lead to discriminatory consequences.

Ineffective legal systems that discriminate against those subjected to crimes within the family provide only a partial explanation for the failure to protect individuals from family violence. It is important to note that studies from other regions of the world also reveal how the social structure, in the form of economic, political, religious, and familial forces, takes a toll on groups of individuals. Many of these forces are regulated by customs and customary laws, which constitute a second theme of culturally rooted forces that stifle efforts to address family violence.

Customs and Customary Laws

The term *customary law* is often used in modern anthropological literature to denote nonlegislative law in a tribal society or law that existed prior to colonialism or modern legal reforms.[39] Traditional customs, which often take the form of customary laws, reinforce attitudes and beliefs that place individuals within families at risk for violence. Analyses of violence toward women and children most often focus on these customs and often argue that they serve as convenient pretexts for violence and subordination of individuals. Despite these views, customs and customary laws remain exceedingly complex, their analyses controversial, and their impact difficult to pinpoint. Regardless of these difficulties, customs and "laws" no longer in force often play a role in fostering violence against vulnerable family members and reflect and reinforce other cultural beliefs and practices.

The situation in South Africa illustrates the extent to which customs and customary law play a role in the violence individuals may suffer in their families. Under both Roman–Dutch law and English law, from which the principles of African law are derived, a "right" to batter a wife was recognized.[40] Similarly, the payment of *lobola*, or brideprice, is often viewed as giving an African man married under customary law the right to beat his wife, who is regarded as his property.[41] Although these principles no longer find formal endorsement in the law, the attitudes they reflect still remain. For example, the new Constitution makes clear that everyone has a right "to be free from all forms of violence from either public or private sources" as well as the right not to be tortured in any way,[42] and legislative mandates allow women to obtain restraining orders against abusive partners.[43] Yet magistrates and police remain unaware of extra protections and are unsympathetic or even hostile to abused women. Likewise, inadequate and uncoordinated governmental services hamper the effectiveness of legal reform that prohibits domestic violence; problems range from lack of legal representation to obtain redress to lack of health services, economic assistance, and emergency shelters. In addition, the formally abolished system continues to be used.[44] It is important to understand that the legal abolishment of the practice may not readily lead to protection. The practice of *lobola* provides women with a catch-22 type problem. Those for whom *lobola* is not paid, either by choice or inability to do so, may find themselves as much abused as those for whom *lobola* was paid. Lack of *lobola* payment deems the woman a worthless outcast unvalued by her family. The outcome of the perception, then, is more abuse; victims continue to view themselves as not having rights.[45]

As with other consequences of cultural forces, the continued negative effects of rejected laws finds expression in numerous societies. We already have seen, for example, how U.S. law fails to address woman battering. It is important to note at this juncture that much of the failure also has been linked to English common law's early influence. Under early American law, women belonged to their fathers until marriage and then became the property of their husbands. Part of men's rights included the use of physical force to discipline their wives under the "rule of thumb." That rule allowed men to beat their wives as long as the stick was "no thicker than a thumb" and, ironically, provided women protection from overzealous husbands.[46] Although law has abrogated the right of chastisement, its influence is still felt in the attitudes of the legal systems' response to domestic violence. The attitude persists in systems that minimize the significance of woman abuse, consider it a private matter, or blame the victim for her own abuse.

Although laws and public perceptions relating to battering have changed, the changes have been less than dramatic in efforts to acknowledge that such violence exists in particular relationships and in the legal systems' continued failure to respond so as to protect women who are under the control of abusive partners. Again, abused women are under the control of men, and the legal system has difficulty ensuring that abused women should be under their own control. Progress away from sanctioning woman abuse has not led to reforms of systems that operate to trap women in abusive relationships, such as customs regarding divorce and custody, restrictions on access to the legal system, and the economic impact of separation. Thus, for example, although "father preference" in custody cases has been abrogated, it operates at a less visible level, such as the award to men in contested custody cases, difficulties in modifying custody and child support awards, and the challenges battered women face when dealing with visitation, joint custody, and child abduction.[47]

The legal system's tolerance for the control of women finds expression beyond the challenges faced by battered women who attempt to leave abusive situations. Two examples illustrate how the legal system protects the husband's control on his wife's sexuality. The first example involves the traditional marital rape exemption, which exempted husbands from rape accusations.[48] Although pervasively abolished, some jurisdictions have replaced the rule with a marital rape allowance, which makes wife rape a lesser crime than other forms of rape;[49] where not replaced, prosecutors and juries continue to treat the parties' relationship so as to not find coercive sex in ongoing relationships.[50] The second example involves the law's tolerance for civil actions against third parties who interfere with the marital relationship. These laws, which originated to protect the wife's services as a servant to her husband, reflect the proprietal interest in their attempt to compensate for relational losses in another's emotional or physical being. Thus, for example, the alienation of affections doctrine allows a civil action against the party who alienates the affections of another's spouse, and the tort of criminal conversation allows compensation from the person who had sexual intercourse with the spouse.[51] The actions reflect the need to compensate the husband for violation of his exclusive right to marital intercourse (e.g., the shame brought to his honor and suspicion cast upon the legitimacy of his offspring).[52]

The extent to which customary laws affect family violence also finds reflection in efforts to respond to child abuse. Cross-culturally, the form of abuse children suffer and that continues to attract the most attention and controversy involves genital circumcision or, as more controversially known, genital mutilation, which semantically conveys a sense of horror and disgust about the practice and distinguishes it from male circumcision. Although the practice takes several forms, it generally requires the partial removal of girls' clitoral prepuce, labia minora, and sometimes parts of the labia majora. Girls typically undergo the procedure before or at puberty; and the type of circumcision and the age at which the practice is carried out varies.[53] Although small segments of Western societies do perform female circumcisions, the practice continues mostly in several societies across Africa, the Middle East, and to a lesser extent Asia, Australia, and Central and South America. World Health Organization[54] estimates reveal that more than 130 million women in the world have been subjected to some form of circumcision, and that, each year, 2 million girls are subject to the practice, a rate of 6,000 per day.

Despite the differences in practices and the percentage of girls affected, traditional grounds justify all forms of genital circumcision. Among the most often cited and culturally persuasive reasons are the need to ensure girls' virginity before marriage and chastity afterward as well as the need to undergo the rite of passage necessary for marriage.[55] These practices remain deeply embedded in cultural thinking, particularly the customary jurisprudence that still rules and clashes with the law of the modern State. The end of colonialism left a legacy of a peculiar set of plural legal systems in which family law derived from European law was applicable to non-Africans, whereas the majority of the African population remain subject to a legal regime labeled customary.[56] As a result of these plural systems, modern customary law derives from the interaction between African customary law and the colonial rule. The mixture of laws makes it difficult to invoke custom in opposition to reform. The disparity and possible conflict between different kinds of laws, those more customary and those of the modern State, are not unique to Africa or to colonialism. A more rapid pace of economic change and wider diversities between regions and classes ensure greater disparities between different laws. Disparity may be even greater in that keen differences often exist between formal laws, customary laws, and laws in practice.

A most striking aspect of this rite of passage that several view as abusive is that local laws prohibit female circumcision. For example, in an attempt to eradicate the practice, several African nations now legally prohibit the practice; if not explicitly illegal, nations seek to eradicate the practice through educational efforts.[57] These laws have not only been ineffective, but in some cases they further entrenched the practice, particularly when the societies perceived the laws as imperialistic and imposed by colonizers.[58] The failure of reform also reflects how the practice remains part of other customs and laws. Most notably, for example, the practice relates to marriage customs. In societies where marriage for a woman is her best means of survival and where circumcision is a prerequisite to marriage, convincing women to relinquish the practice for themselves or for their children is an exceedingly difficult task.[59] Marriage provides the exclusive opportunity for women to attain social acceptance and economic security.[60] As with the *lobola* practices presented above, legal attempts to eradicate the traditional practice may leave victims in a catch-22 situation.

Customary laws provide only partial explanations for the active embrace of these rites of passage. Numerous other rationales, however, also relate to customary laws. For example, related arguments propose that the practices are necessary to maintain gender roles that are seen as foundational to values relating to appearance, virginity, and economic values.[61] Other more controversial justifications include the need to continue these practices for religious purposes.[62] Likewise, other major justifications for the practice rest on tradition and heritage, rather than religious demand, health and hygiene, and the demands of marriage (virginity, virility, and sexual pleasure). All of these are regulated by customary laws.

Circumcision is implicated in the eventual validation of full adult standing and community membership because it prepares children for marriage and complete social personhood. The practices clearly relate to the roles social systems have defined and circumscribed. The extent of custom as an important force is revealed by the pervasive exclusion of boys from recent national bans on genital operations. Yet no cases of female circumcision exist without the concomitant practice of male circumcision.[63] In addition, five out of six children who are circumcised are boys.[64] Although several rightly have argued that some forms of female genital circumcision are considerably more intrusive than the male practice,[65] recent research reveals that the average removal of foreskin actually involves half of the skin of the penis,[66] and pediatric associations, most notably Canadian and Australian, recently have recognized that circumcision should not be routinely performed and may contravene human rights.[67] Yet the practice continues. One of the important ironies of failing to address male circumcision is that all genital circumcision practices remain integral parts of female and male existence and, as such, cannot be treated in isolation as a single issue destined for elimination.[68]

Other practices have received increased attention. A most frequently cited custom that defies legal intervention is the system of dowry as practiced in India. India's practice of arranged marriages, which involves the giving and receiving of dowry, is at the root of dowry violence. Dowry traditionally consisted of gifts given to the bride at the time of her marriage to ensure her financial security in her marriage into a new family.[69] Today, dowry involves the wealth that the bride's parents must pay the groom and family as part of the marriage arrangement. Payment, which now involves goods such as cars and televisions, lasts after the wedding.[70] The financial burden these gifts place on the bride's natal family leads to demands for more dowry that cannot be met. Human rights groups and researchers report that the demands often result in the husband's and mother-in-law's abuse and harassment of the young bride.[71] The violence frequently culminates in her murder or results in suicide to spare her family further hardship.[72] Thus, the violence women endure reflects the extent to which Indian society views female individuals as valueless burdens; and because Indian marriages are generally for profit, Indian society implicitly sanctions the practice of dowry murders. Although there are no accurate statistics on the number of dowry deaths per year, officially registered deaths have increased 10 times since the early 1980s, with reports finding that by 1991 more than 5,000 deaths had been registered and by 1993 more than 6,000 deaths.[73] These are remarkably high numbers, yet they do not even account for attempted killings, suicides, and failure to report simply because the bride's families prefer to avoid publicizing the shameful incident.[74]

Through a series of important laws, the Indian government has tried to combat the problem by enacting various laws to prevent such deaths from occurring and to punish those responsible when they do occur.[75] Currently, the Dowry Prohibition Act[76] prohibits the giving, taking, or demanding of dowry and makes violations punishable by imprisonment or fine. In addition, the law requires the police and a judicial magistrate to investigate every unnatural death of a woman married less than 7 years, and it provides for imprisonment between 7 years and life for dowry deaths. The law now presumes a dowry death whenever a woman is subjected to dowry-related cruelty or harassment soon before her death. Although laws seem to take dowry deaths seriously, those who report on the law's effectiveness report rampant failure. First, rather than preventing the practice, the practice of giving dowry actually now spreads from Hindu middle-class families in north India to different castes, provinces, religious groups, and economic classes.[77] Second, despite more stringent laws, very few convictions have been obtained.[78] Despite mandates, less than 10% of apparent dowry-related deaths are actually investigated; police and prosecutors dismiss such crimes as family disputes and report them as "kitchen accidents."[79] The dismissals result in a failure to investigate and prosecute the crimes vigorously and ensure that they receive a low priority.

Numerous factors account for the failure to protect women from dowry deaths. The conviction that women are their husband's property, as highlighted by the practice of dowries, pervades Indian society.[80] The gifts that families receive are not considered "dowry" simply because the gifts are expected.[81] The culture fails to recognize the nature of dowry; the law, too, focuses on property and money given at the wedding ceremony, not the gifts that are expected later. Moreover, attitudes toward women further impede efforts. Most notably, the deaths occur because of the focus on women's roles in families, the need to serve without complaint, the inability to return to her original family, their inability to divorce, and need to suffer harmful abuses in silence and without support. Again, these situations derive from customs.

Customs and customary laws, then, reinforce notions that it is permissible to discriminate against groups of individuals. It remains difficult to delineate clearly the influences of custom and colonialism and other forces on certain societies. Most problematically, the analysis also involves a complex intertwining of customary and religious heritages. The general process of legal development has been shaped fundamentally by the fusion of customary law and religious standards and precepts, which themselves have been influenced by colonial rule. The result, as several argue, is that vestiges of colonialism figure prominently in customs and religious beliefs that are seen as the primary source of traditions that allow violence to continue. Regardless of the source of the customary practice or customary law, they serve to hinder efforts for local reform that would address family violence. The frequent link between custom and religion, however, suggests that religion plays a dominant role as a cultural force. Although inseparable from customs, religious influences are worthy of a separate discussion, and they are addressed in the section that follows.

Religious Traditions

Human rights activists have become increasingly concerned with religious practices that have a tendency to result in violence against individuals. Although the brief analysis in this section on the power of religion focuses on how it may become enmeshed in violence, it is important to emphasize that the analysis is not offered as a broad indictment of religion. Religion may in fact serve to buffer groups of individuals from violence. Likewise, recent commentaries highlight how no society has become secular, that all major religions exhibit increases in fundamentalist movements, and that religious traditions greatly influence family life even in societies that seek to secularize laws and policies affecting families.[82] Equally importantly, religious organizations clearly provide important sources of familial support, including facilitation of social change reducing factors relating to family violence such as the status of women, and increasingly serve as dominant sources of support for families given new trends in the provision of social services.[83] The following simply aims to reveal how, as with other cultural beliefs and tendencies, religion cannot be extracted from other cultural forces and how cultural forces may work together and allow forms of violence to continue in the name of religion.

The relationship between religious traditions and child prostitution illustrates religions' ties to family violence. The United Nations' Special Rapporteur on the Sale of Children recently examined Nepalese customs and criticized practices in which girls are offered to temples to become goddesses or "married to God."[84] He concluded that these children inevitably fall prey to coercive sexual practices and ultimately prostitution, and he further noted that some communities have taken such traditional practices and "distorted [them] conveniently to legitimize prostitution as a cultural practice."[85] The potentially problematic effects of these forms of child marriages are well known and are even condoned despite local laws that prohibit the practices.

The *devadasi* system provides a powerful case in point of the power religion wields and the extent to which it may be implicated in violence. Although the practice is referred to by different names in different States, *devadasi* means offering and dedicating girls to the goddess or the god.[86] Although several commentaries actually ignore how the tradition leads children to prostitution, these child bride customs reveal how traditional, religious practices may provide a cover for legitimizing prostitution. Researchers indicate that the *devadasi* account for an average of 15% of the prostitution in India and up to 80% of those living in the southern regions of the country.[87] Those who examine the roots of child prostitution report that what leaves young children vulnerable to prostitution actually is not difficult to understand. After the child is devoted to her god, she leaves her parents. However, she lacks the means to support herself once outside the family environment. In addition, anyone marrying her is considered a social outcast because she is perceived as the property of the god. Because she is never offered any legitimate jobs, she is forced to work as a temple prostitute and become part of commercialized prostitution. Although these traditional practices are banned by the government, they continue.[88]

Other cultures practice similar customs that involve religious beliefs. In parts of Africa where women are viewed as mediums of exchange and their reproductive labor is viewed as belonging to the family, families give away young female virgins as "gifts" to oracles and shrines to pacify gods for offenses allegedly committed by other members of their families. For example, in Ghana, girls as young as 10 years old are left with the shrine's chief priest. The girls are known as *trokosi*, which blends "*tro*," meaning god, and "*kosi*," referring to "virgin, slave or wife."[89] Estimates reveal that at least 4,000 girls are bound to shrines and that they have an estimated 16,000 children.[90] The practice involves a mixture of religious beliefs and ways to deal with violations of proper social conduct. The practice stems from the philosophy that punishment is communal, that individuals with no connection to a crime may be punished to spare others, and that punishment is necessary to avoid vengeance on the entire community. Historically, the girls would have been killed as a sacrifice to appease angry gods, but they now are kept as slaves by priests who are believed to communicate with the gods and represent them. The shrine priest can decide whether and when the girls have atoned for the sin and free them. As a result, many children stay with priests from the age of 8 up to 15, although commentators suggest that most *trokosi* actually are condemned to a lifetime of hard labor and sexual servitude.[91] The *trokosi* know that no member of their families would take them back, which removes the option of running away and seeking familial protection. Likewise, they fear the wrath of gods if they do not fulfill their obligations.[92] Lack of alternatives leaves them trapped and unable to leave their priest−husband. Even once released, they tend to remain with their priests because they generally have poor health, no family ties, no education, no skills, and no hope of marriage.[93] Again, religious beliefs serve to reinforce practices that leave individuals at risk for violence.

Religion also plays a critical role in marriage and family formation that does not involve marriages to shrines or priests yet still involves violence. One of the most often cited examples involves arranged marriages. For example, Muslim family law assumes fathers to be "fond of their offspring" and as not having "sinister motives in arranging their [children's] marriages."[94] The assumption allows fathers to orchestrate their daughter's union with prospective husbands and their families. Fathers have the right to give their daughters in (first) marriage regardless of their daughter's age or consent.[95] Their power, however, is not absolute. After their first marriage, daughters are given the power to consent. Although divorce may be permissible and ostensibly provides child brides with some protections, it remains infrequent and does not necessarily protect the daughter's best interests. The nature (and lack) of the protections divorce offers is understandable by the impact of early marriages on girls' eventual health and the consequences of ill health on women.

Practices in Northern Nigerian towns have received increasing scrutiny, which challenges the role of religion in influencing violence through early marriage condoned by families and religious beliefs. In these towns, it is not uncommon for women to be married at age 10 to men three or four times older than themselves. According to one study, one-quarter of all women in Nigeria are married by the age of 14, one-half by the age of 16.[96] Not all are married voluntarily. For example, Hausa parents frequently give away their prepubescent and adolescent girls in arranged marriages, even though girls attempt to run away and express objections.

Commentators who report the negative consequences of child marriages that involve prepubescent girls to older men highlight how most child brides engage in sexual relations with their husbands immediately after marriage and how many give birth before they are physically mature. Pregnancies and births before mothers reach appropriate maturity may have potentially devastating consequences, including illness and death from childbirth. According to the World Health Organization, Nigerian girls aged 15 have a maternal mortality rate seven times higher than that of women ages 20−24.[97] Nigerian women younger than 15 years of age are four times more likely to die during pregnancy and childbirth than women ages 15−19.[98] Those who do survive are sometimes abandoned by their husbands when medical complications arise. Recent estimates reveal that more than 20,000 women who had been married and pregnant at an early age in predominantly Muslim Northern Nigeria suffer from vesicovaginal fistula, a disability resulting from ruptured uterus and accompanied by tearing of the intestine or bladder, caused by obstructed labor.[99] This often has long-term health, social, and economic consequences.[100] Young brides are then not only abandoned by their husbands but also ostracized by their natal families. The social and economic consequences are undoubtedly devastating.

The Nigerian example again illustrates how religious beliefs may provide rationales for the practices, but the practices are actually deeply embedded in cultural tradition. Gender role expectations clearly drive the institution of child marriage. In addition to concern with children's virginity, the practice reflects images of what girls are to be. For example, girls are expected to adopt the traditional domestic roles of child-bearer and family caretaker. This view of domesticity renders girls' formal education essentially unimportant. The belief helps explain why families frequently withdraw child brides from schools and let their brothers continue so they may assume the status of the head of their households.[101] Thus, although laws may proscribe a minimum age of marriage for either boys or girls, young boys are rarely married off, with or without their consent.

Again, religious beliefs do not operate only in foreign cultures with different legal and religious systems. Religious factors also play a role in some forms of family violence in the United States. The United States already is home to many forms of abuse that continue partly because of religious protections. A most notable example involves the corporal punishment of children. Although increasingly challenged, a main rationale that permits the corporal punishment of children is the religious conviction that directs parents to use force.[102] The rise in religious fundamentalism seeks legal reform, which not only would protect parents who inflict violence but also create environments that several researchers view as conducive to family violence. These efforts include the need to recognize the subservient role of women, foster obedience to men, restrict divorce, and implement other mechanisms that maintain women's chastity and control their sexuality.[103] These fundamentalist efforts are found in all of the world's dominant religions—Buddhism, Christianity, Hinduism, Islam, and Judaism. Howland's exhaustive review of fundamentalist texts reveals how the fundamentalist regimes of all major religions seek similar control of women throughout their life span.[104] Girls first learn obedience to their fathers and marriages may be arranged to protect their chastity; the marriage contract provides husbands control over modes of dress, economic, sexual, educational, and reproductive decisions. Although these lessons do not mean that cultures must move away from religion and toward more secular ways of life and do not deny the significant role religion plays in alleviating family violence, they do highlight how all religions constitute powerful forces that may have negative consequences as cultures change to adopt different views of people's roles in families and society.

The extent to which religious beliefs and customs may foster environments that place individuals at risk for family violence reveals the extent to which cultural practices would challenge law reform efforts. Although all cultural practices and beliefs reflect a society's views of what constitutes right, moral, and just behavior, none do so more deeply than religious tenets. As seen, however, such beliefs are inseparable from other cultural influences. The manner societies view some people as belonging to others constitutes the next cultural belief, related to those discussed above, that would challenge law reform efforts to combat family violence.

Images of People as Property

Ingrained beliefs regarding family relationships and ingrained views that some family members essentially are property constitute a pervasive theme in cross-cultural analyses of family violence and the challenges that face legal responses. The Brazilian defenses reported above, for example, are based on the belief that a wife is her husband's property and that her act of adultery offends her husband's honor and legitimizes his violence.[105] Other societies make even more explicit the belief that some individuals are or can become the property of others. Laws actually view individuals as property or allow individuals to be treated as exchangeable property. The image of some people as legitimate property leads to numerous consequences that affect efforts to offer assistance even when laws explicitly prohibit practices that view people as property.

A most common example of how images of people as property contribute to family violence involves servile marriages. Servile marriages include forced marriage —where the female child has no right to refuse the proposed union—as well as the sale of women into marriage by their families. These marriages take place primarily in societies where women have a low social status and cultural attitudes perpetuate the belief that wives are property controlled by husbands and families.[106] Although numerous reports find broad acceptance for the belief that brides become the property of their husbands, South Africa has received considerable commentary for its rates of family violence and discussion of how rationales related to women-as-property allow the violence to continue.

Several sources that report on violence against women in South Africa estimate that approximately one in four women is abused by her partner and that one in every six women is regularly assaulted by her partner; some report that nearly half have been subjected to marital rape or assault.[107] One recent study revealed that 70% of disabled women became disabled as a result of domestic violence.[108] Commentators and human rights groups convincingly suggest that because customary beliefs include the notion that women are the property of men, men believe they have the right to batter and that belief ensures that society does not respond effectively to the battering of women.

Effects of the notion that some individuals are the property of others reverberate. The traditional values reinforce the attitude that "wife beating" is a private affair, which renders complaints evidence of disloyalty which, in turn, invites ostracism.[109] Human Rights Watch concluded its report of domestic violence by noting that violence is seen as a necessary evil of having a boyfriend or husband, that husbands are necessary for economic security, and that "a degree of violence in male–female relationships is frequently accepted as normal and inevitable."[110] South Africa's culture marked by the outside violence of apartheid arguably contributes to more acceptance of domestic violence as a part of life.[111] Yet their experiences are far from peculiar. Recent analyses of family violence in Chile,[112] Russia,[113] Japan,[114] and Nicaragua,[115] for example, reveal that these cultures exhibit permissive views of violence and legitimize violence within the home, as reflected in the commonly accepted belief that men demonstrate love through violent acts and that women define themselves in terms of their relationships with their families and how they serve them.

In the above investigations and those from other countries, battered women consistently fail to seek help outside an informal network of friends and family. That failure tends to be explained by two major factors: (a) Women's fear of reprisals, shame, and self-blame lead to a reluctance to seek legal remedies; and (b) otherwise aggressive law enforcement and available social services fail to consider the obstacles to social service delivery, such as language-related barriers, immigration status, extreme gender roles, and distrust of police and authority. The belief that pervades these failures to seek assistance is that women belong with their husbands and families.

Although marriage may place some individuals at risk for violence because they are viewed as property, other more explicit and directly abusive practices result from such perceptions. In relation to children, the most often cited example involves societal beliefs that allow children to be treated as exchangeable commodities through sexual exploitation. One of the most consistent findings relating to sexual exploitation is its direct link to family breakdown and the belief that children belong to their families. In Thailand, for example, recruiting agents no longer need to apply much physical violence to lure children and youth into the sex trade.[116] Reduced need for overt, physical violence on the part of recruiters derives from parents' complicity in their children's exploitation. For example, the Centre of Protection of Children's Rights reports striking statistics related to procurement of child prostitutes.[117] Sixty-three percent of girls under age 16 in brothels were brought there by their parents; another 21% were brought by neighbors or friends who also were sending their children to the brothels; in contrast, only 16% were brought by agents.[118] The U.N. Special Rapporteur on Violence Against Women also notes parental complicity, such as the practice of *deukis* in Nepal where poor, rural Nepalese families sell their daughters to rich, childless families.[119] Rather than keeping the girls after they deliver their child, however, the rich families offer them to local temples, a practice similar to the *devadasi* and *trokosi* described earlier in the section on religious practices, which ultimately leads girls into forced prostitution. Studies of adult prostitutes report parallel findings in familial complicity; for example, research conducted in Taipei found that over one third mentioned a sense of filial obligation as the primary reason for entry into prostitution, and the majority reported good or very good relationships with their parents before they left home and continued to maintain such relationships.[120]

The notion that children are their parents' property also runs deep in legal institutions and even in societies that have developed an aggressive children's rights movement grounded in child protection. American family law illustrates the extent to which the belief continues to infiltrate family policy. Much of the children's rights movement has been exemplified as the move of children from the status of property to one of people. Yet even though children have gained considerable rights, the influence of history remains inescapable. Children remain under the legal control of their parents. Parents possess the right to control and even discipline them through physical and mental violence, and parents retain the right to refuse life-saving treatment.[121] The right to control even allows others, including state officials, to inflict punishment when no other group in society could be subjugated to such treatment.[122] By allowing family members to punish or refuse treatment in instances that would not be permissible if done by a nonfamily member, the legal system recognizes that the actions outside familial relationships would be harmful. The system further fails to recognize how these unaddressed outcomes of parental rights are harmful.[123] These laws reflect the status of children as belonging to someone else as opposed to themselves.[124] As the leading U.S. Supreme Court case put it, children are not the mere "creatures" of the state, they primarily *belong to* [not only with] their parents.[125] Although much commentary notes that children have moved from property to people status,[126] an equally persuasive host of commentaries suggests otherwise.[127] Thus, although corporal punishment and other results of a family's power over children may not be viewed as violent, the legal system views children as belonging to others, which permits violence to continue.

The notion that individuals belong to others, including to their own cultural group, allows for violence against them. The possibility for abuse arises regardless of whether the beliefs regarding ownership are explicit or implicit. The beliefs operate through the support of numerous cultural practices and social conditions. Most notably, for example, the belief relates to other customary laws, customs, and religious beliefs. These cultural forces are deeply related to economic concerns.

Economic Disparities

Undoubtedly the most pervasive theme to emerge from a cross-cultural survey of family violence relates to the difficulties societies experience in allocating scarce resources. Many reports highlight maltreatment as rooted in the underlying force of economic conditions and the intractable problems they pose. Just as it is impossible to extricate any cultural practice from the culture itself, it remains difficult to extricate and differentiate economic disparities that are due to policies that arise from within and across countries. Despite difficulties, several examples illustrate the role economic forces play in family violence.

The sex market illustrates well the power of economic forces. Over one million children a year are forced into the sex market, and families play a role in the eventual maltreatment of children involved in the market. The vast majority of these child prostitutes are concentrated in poor countries. For instance, it is estimated that there are 800,000 child prostitutes in Thailand, 400,000 in India, and 250,000 in Brazil.[128] Human rights groups estimate that such figures are actually underestimates and that many more children are involved in a lucrative, $10 billion-a-year industry.[129] In addition to the previously explored reasons for child prostitution, it is difficult to discount how broad economic policies play incremental roles in fostering conditions leading to the maltreatment of children.

Although the sex market has direct international dimensions, other abuses children suffer are much more diffuse and relate to economic programs within countries. China's policies that seemingly contribute to differential survival and maltreatment rates between girls and boys are presented as ways to achieve a higher standard of living; the alternatives are presented as leading to poverty, high infant mortality, and malnutrition.[130] Indeed, the need for developing countries to focus on economic and social rights often serves as the main rationale for playing down the need to accord greater respect for more civil and political rights.

Economic pressures also exacerbate cultural traditions relating to child marriage.

As discussed previously, child marriage clearly links to family violence. Child brides are at risk for maltreatment in their arranged relationships and from their natal families. Economic considerations play a key role. According to nongovernmental organizations and social services groups, for example, Nigeria's worsening economy under military rule has contributed to earlier and earlier girl-child marriages. Families simply want less children to feed. Even where the immediate impetus is economic necessity, however, underlying gender stereotypes create an environment where early marriages of daughters is considered an acceptable economic survival strategy.[131] Again, cultural forces intersect to place vulnerable individuals at risk for violence.

Another clear example of economic forces in family-related violence involves child labor. Child labor laws explicitly protect children from labor, yet economic conditions foster abuse. The International Labor Organization reports that at least 120 million children between the ages of 5 and 14 worldwide work full time.[132] When combined with the number of children who work in nonformal jobs, the number increases to 250 million. About 95% of these children live and work in developing countries. In addition to being concentrated in poor countries, they also are concentrated in poor rural sectors and work in the fields or in "sideline" jobs to help their families alleviate financial burdens. These circumstances offer children the least protection, mainly because it is assumed that families protect children from exploitation. Economic forces also ensure that girls are the ones who seemingly suffer and do the most. For example, in Malaysia, Nepal, and Java, girls work up to 75% more hours per day than boys do; yet parents view boy's work as more valuable.[133] The availability of fewer protections for girl children affects their economic situations. In addition to work outside the home, girls do domestic work, which legitimizes a social division of labor that reinforces their eventual "double burden" and subordination in society.[134] Girls are often sent by their families to work in the homes of other families and live in isolation from their families, which impedes their abilities to obtain an education and places them at risk for physical and sexual maltreatment.[135] Compared with boys, girls are seldom sent to school. Although economics play a factor, it is customary for even the poorest families from those societies to enroll male children in school.[136] Girls' chances of achieving occupational or societal mobility remain hampered.

Economics also figure prominently in reports of family violence endured by adults. Although violence against women occurs in all socioeconomic classes, research tends to link wife assault to low incomes and unemployed men,[137] a finding that receives support from societies around the world.[138] It remains to be determined how poverty increases the risk of violence and how poverty is influenced by other factors such as race, education, contact time between partners, and neighborhood rates of unemployment. Despite these unanswered questions, it does seem clear that increases in socioeconomic status do decrease the likelihood of assault.[139] In addition to that general finding, it is important to note how laws that regulate economic life often play a role in maltreatment. For example, laws that govern inheritance and employment prevent women from becoming economically independent and compel them to remain in abusive relationships.[140] The most explicit example involves dowry-related violence. Failure of brides to procure more resources for their in-laws contributes to their victimization. Attempts to prohibit dowries explicitly respond to economic issues and remain difficult to enforce without the government's attempt to also take preventive measures in the form of economic assistance. In addition to economic considerations of the entire family and laws that regulate employment and women's access to resources, women generally remain economically disadvantaged in relation to men; that disadvantageous economic status seriously impedes any strategy to protect women from domestic violence. The disadvantages are global: Women make up the great majority of the world poor. Much of women's work remains unpaid or low paying, in sectors of economies that are marginal and that lack benefits and job security.[141] Whether within families or separated from abusive husbands, battered woman tend to be in worse economic straits.

Although numerous other examples may be offered, the above examples typify the fluid causes and the intractable nature of problems grounded in economic issues. The abuses are a product of socioeconomic and cultural conditions. They result from poverty, social discrimination, prevailing attitudes, customs, and the inefficiency or inappropriateness of educational systems. All of these factors work together to place individuals at risk for victimization.

Conclusion

The accumulation of reports that document violence and the cultural challenges to reform reveal the intricate, interrelated nature of cultural forces that affect family violence. Existing reports, however, do much more than offer pictures of the tangled forces that contribute to family violence. The research also reveals pervasive failure. The general theme that emerges from these studies suggests that legal systems in particular and societies in general pervasively fail to protect individuals maltreated by family members. Violence continues and is endemic to all contemporary societies that have been investigated, even though rates may fluctuate markedly across societies. Lack of effective legal responses reflects the challenges violence poses for victims, families, communities, States, and those who respond to violence.

The analyses suggest that efforts to reform legal responses to family violence must confront the most unyielding forces that inhibit protections from family violence: traditional beliefs, economic conditions, existing laws, perceptions of individual worth, and prevailing views of what constitutes a moral life. The inextricable mesh of these cultural forces ensures that violence remains ingrained and intractable when laws simply prohibit practices. Thus, laws that simply prohibit dowry deaths, child labor, circumcision, and battering largely fail because they do not address appropriately the cultural practices and social forces that foster violence.

Support for laws, many of which already exist, is needed to reinforce protection. The law alone cannot fulfill its goals; it must be reinforced by various factions. Even the best law cannot play an important role if the level of legal consciousness in a society is low, both in terms of the understanding of law and of the relevant legal estimations and attitudes. To do so, laws must influence societal institutions that pervasively fail to respond appropriately to family violence they dismiss, condone, and accept. Several aspects of cultural life are necessary to consider in attempts to address family violence. Cultural forces that support family violence manifest themselves in discrimination, devaluation of self, views of proper roles in families and societies, notions of property, and perceptions that assaults are considered family affairs rather than a problem requiring social response. Most legal systems that have addressed the violence have not displayed an integrative approach; rather, they have addressed the various manifestations of family violence separately, without suggestions that they may have a uniform or even related structural cause. The failure to develop an integrative approach in legal remedies affects other areas, so that service provision and other strategies used to address the problem also remain fragmented. That fragmentation ensures that legal reforms essentially ignore root causes and correlates of violence. Addressing family violence in isolation from other forms of violence, including some forms of violence within families, results in characterizing family violence as a problem of families, rather than as a problem rooted in cultural structures. Thus, although countries may have laws that prohibit and punish the forms of violence that occur in family life, violence continues to occur, which suggests that efforts to combat family violence necessarily must change cultural forces.

Support for laws and legal reforms work best when the social value base agrees with the desired new norms. As long as existing regimes of values are in effect, the tasks of making the new norms operative, or activating the educative function of law to change values, are difficult and require action on numerous fronts. Laws must reach private life, foster culture change, and recognize connections in the treatment of individuals and their rights. Increased protection involves educational and informational activities that inform societies that violence will not be tolerated. Reforms require confronting issues of bias in legal systems and providing greater economic opportunities and opportunities in other institutions by removing impediments to the realization of rights. Reform requires citizens to examine, at a deeper level, the many diverse barriers to the enjoyment of basic rights. This ambitious and necessary feature of legal reform is precisely what human rights law seeks to institute. Those goals are the focus of the following chapters, which explore how the human rights movement offers hope: It addresses the many practices that contribute to family violence, seeks cultural reform, moves beyond simply prohibiting practices contributing to violence, and uses cultural forces to gain support for laws that foster conditions that alleviate violence.

Endnotes

1. Americas Watch, *Criminal Injustice: Violence Against Women in Brazil* (New York: Author, 1991).
2. K. M. Culliton, "Legal Remedies for Domestic Violence in Chile and the United States: Cultural Relativism, Myths and Realities," *Case Western Reserve Journal of International Law* 26 (1994):183–260.
3. U.S. Department of State, *Brazil Human Rights Practices 1993* (Washington, DC: Author, 1994).
4. Americas Watch, *Criminal Injustice.*
5. Culliton, "Legal Remedies for Domestic Violence in Chile and the United States."
6. *Id.*
7. H. Charlesworth, "What Are Women's International Human Rights?" in *Human Rights of Women: National and International Perspectives*, Rebecca Cook, Ed. (Philadelphia: University of Pennsylvania Press, 1994).
8. For a review of statistics, *see* A. Kosof, *Battered Women: Living With the Enemy* (Danbury, CT: Franklin Watts Press, 1994).
9. *See* R. J. R. Levesque, "Dating Violence, Adolescents and the Law," *Virginia Journal of Social Policy and Law* 4 (1997):339–379.

10. For an analysis of England's failed response, *see* J. Gregory and S. Lees, *Policing Sexual Assault* (New York: Routledge, 1999).

11. *See* E. M. Schneider, "Particularity and Generality: Challenges of Feminist Theory and Practice in Work on Woman Abuse," *New York University Law Review* 67 (1992):520–568.

12. J. Bol, "Using International Law to Fight Child Labor: A Case Study of Guatemala and the Inter-American System," *American University International Law Review* 13 (1998): 1135–1223.

13. *Id.*

14. T. A. Glut, "Changing the Approach to Ending Child Labor: An International Solution to an International Problem," *Vanderbilt Journal of Transnational Law* 28 (1994):1203–1244.

15. *Id.*

16. J. M. Diller and D. A. Levy, "Child Labor, Trade and Investment: Toward the Harmonization of International Law," *American Journal of International Law* 91 (1997): 663–696.

17. C. Grootaert and H. A. Patrinos, Eds., *The Policy Analysis of Child Labor: A Comparative Study* (New York: St. Martin's Press, 1999).

18. *See* K. Cox, "The Inevitability of Nimble Fingers? Law, Development, and Child Labor," *Vanderbilt Journal of Transnational Law* 32 (1999):114–165; Grootaert and Patrinos, *The Policy Analysis of Child Labor.*

19. A. Y. Rassam, "Contemporary Forms of Slavery and the Evolution of Slavery and the Slave Trade Under Customary International Law," *Virginia Journal of International Law* 39 (1999):303–352.

20. *See, e.g.,* N. Nieuwenhuys, *Children's Lifeworlds: Gender, Welfare and Labour in the Developing World* (New York: Routledge, 1994); Grootaert and Patrinos, *The Policy Analysis of Child Labor.*

21. D. M. Smolin, "Conflict and Ideology in the International Campaign Against Child Labor," *Hofstra Labor and Employment Law Journal* 16 (1999):383–451.

22. *See* R. J. R. Levesque, "Emotional Maltreatment in Adolescents' Everyday Lives: Furthering Sociolegal and Social Service Provisions," *Behavioral Sciences and the Law* 16 (1998):237–263.

23. E. M. Iglesias, "Structures of Subordination: Women of Color at the Intersection of Title VII and the NLRA. Not!" *Harvard Civil Rights–Civil Liberties Law Review* 28 (1993):395–503; G. T. Luna, "An Infinite Distance? Agricultural Exceptionalism and Agricultural Labor," *University of Pennsylvania Journal of Labor & Employment Law* 1 (1998):487–517.

24. J. B. Kupersmidt and S. L. Martin, "Mental Health Problems of Children of Migrant and Seasonal Farm Workers: A Pilot Study," *Journal of the American Academy of Child & Adolescent Psychiatry* 36 (1997):224–232.

25. J. M. Glader, "A Harvest of Shame: The Imposition of Independent Contractor Status on Migrant Farmworkers and Its Ramifications for Migrant Children," *Hastings Law Journal* 42 (1991):1455–1490; Luna, "An Infinite Distance?"

26. K. M. Backstrom, "The International Human Rights of the Child: Do They Protect the Female Child?" *George Washington Journal of International Law & Economics* 30 (1996):541–582.

27. *Id.*

28. G. Zhang, "U.S. Asylum Policy and Population Control in the People's Republic of China," *Houston Journal of International Law* 18 (1996):557–594.

29. *Id.*

30. X. Li, "License to Coerce: Violence Against Women, State Responsibility and Legal Failures in China's Family Planning Program," *Yale Journal of Law & Feminism* 8 (1996):145–191.

31. T. J. Fitzgibbon, "The United Nations Convention on the Rights of the Child: Are Children Really Protected? A Case Study of China's Implementation," *Loyola Los Angeles International & Comparative Law Journal* 20 (1998):325–359.

32. Backstrom, "The International Human Rights of the Child."

33. Zhang, "U.S. Asylum Policy and Population Control in the People's Republic of China"; Li, "License to Coerce"; Fitzgibbon, "The United Nations Convention on the Rights of the Child."

34. R. DesJarlais, L. Eisenberg, B. Good, and A. Kleinman, *World Mental Health: Problems and Priorities in Low-Income Countries* (New York: Oxford University Press, 1995).

35. A. K. Carlson-Whitley, "Dowry Death: A Violation of the Right to Life Under Article Six of the International Covenant on Civil and Political Rights," *University of Puget Sound Law Review* 17 (1994):637–664.

36. Backstrom, "The International Human Rights of the Child."

37. P. C. Littlewood, "Domestic Child Abuse Under the U.N. Convention of the Rights of the Child: Implications for Children in Four Asian Countries," *Pacific Rim Law & Policy Journal* 6 (1997):411–448.

38. T. Poffenberger, "Child Rearing and Social Structure in Rural India: Toward a Cross-Cultural Definition of Child Abuse and Neglect," in *Child Abuse and Neglect: Cross-Cultural Perspectives*, J. E. Korbin, Ed. (Berkeley: University of California Press, 1981).

39. L. Popisil, *Anthropology of Law: A Comparative Theory* (New York: Harper & Row, 1971).

40. A. Crump, "Wife Battering," *South African Journal of Criminal Law and Criminology* 11 (1987):231–241.

41. United Nations, *Strategies for Confronting Domestic Violence: A Resource Manual* (New York: Author, 1993).

42. A. K. Wing, "A Critical Race Feminist Conceptualization of Violence: South African and Palestinian Women," *Albany Law Review* 60 (1997):972.

43. Human Rights Watch, *Violence Against Women in South Africa: State Response to Domestic Violence and Rape* (New York: Author, 1995).

44. Z. Dangor, L. E. Hoff, and R. Scott, "Woman Abuse in South Africa," *Violence Against Women* 4 (1998):125–149.

45. *Id.*

46. *See* M. Griffith, "Battered Women Syndrome: A Tool for Batterers?" *Fordham Law Review* 64 (1995):141–198.

47. *See* J. Armatta, "Getting Beyond the Law's Complicity in Intimate Violence Against Women," *Willamette Law Review* 33 (1997):774–845.

48. J. Sitton, "Old Wine in New Bottles: The Marital Rape Allowance," *North Carolina Law Review* 72 (1993):261–289.

49. *Id.*

50. *See, e.g.*, S. McCooin, "Law and Sex Status: Implementing the Concept of Sexual Property," *Women's Rights Law Reporter* 19 (1998):237–245.

51. *Id.*

52. *Id.*

53. R. J. R. Levesque, *Child Sexual Abuse: A Human Rights Perspective* (Bloomington: Indiana University Press, 1999).

54. World Health Organization, *Female Genital Mutilation: A Joint WHO/UNICEF/UNFPA Statement* (Geneva: Author, 1997).

55. Levesque, *Child Sexual Abuse.*

56. *See* M. Chanock, "Neither Customary Nor Legal: African Customary Law in an Era of Family Law Reform," *International Journal of Law and the Family* 3 (1989):72–88.

57. E. Sussman, "Contending With Culture: An Analysis of the Female Genital Mutilation Act of 1996," *Cornell International Law Journal* 31 (1998):193–250.

58. *Id.*

59. A. D. Renteln, "Is the Cultural Defense Detrimental to the Health of Children?" *Law and Anthropology* 7 (1994):27–106.
60. F. N. Adjetey, "Reclaiming the African Woman's Individuality: The Struggle Between Women's Reproductive Autonomy and African Society and Culture," *American University Law Review* 44 (1995):1351–1381.
61. Levesque, *Child Sexual Abuse.*
62. Renteln, "Is the Cultural Defense Detrimental to the Health of Children?"
63. E. K. Hicks, *Infibulation: Female Mutilation in Islamic Northeastern Africa* (New Brunswick, NJ: Transaction, 1996).
64. J. S. Svoboda, "Routine Infant Male Circumcision: Examining the Human Rights and Constitutional Issues," in *Sexual Mutilations: A Human Tragedy*, G. C. Denniston and M. F. Milos, Eds. (New York: Plenum Press, 1997).
65. E. A. Gifford, " 'The Courage to Blaspheme': Confronting Barriers to Resisting Female Genital Mutilation," *UCLA Women's Law Journal* 4 (1994):329–364.
66. J. R. Taylor, A. P. Lockwood, and A. J. Taylor, "The Prepuce: Specialized Mucosa of the Penis and Its Loss to Circumcision," *British Journal of Urology* 77 (1996):291–295.
67. F. Hodges, "A Short History of the Institutionalization of Involuntary Sexual Mutilation in the United States," in *Sexual Mutilations: A Human Tragedy*, G. C. Denniston and M. F. Milos, Eds. (New York: Plenum, 1997); L. Haberfield, "The Law and Male Circumcision in Australia: Medical, Legal and Cultural Issues," *Monash University Law Review* 23 (1997):92–122.
68. Levesque, *Child Sexual Abuse.*
69. E. Bumiller, *May You Be the Mother of a Hundred Sons: Journey Among the Women of India* (New York: Random House, 1990).
70. A. Nangia, "The Tragedy of Bride Burning in India: How Should the Law Address It?" *Brooklyn Journal of International Law* 22 (1997):637–693.
71. M. Fernandez, "Domestic Violence by Extended Family Members in India: Interplay of Gender and Generation," *Journal of Interpersonal Violence* 12 (1997):433–455; Nangia, "The Tragedy of Bride Burning in India."
72. Carlson-Whitley, "Dowry Death."
73. U.S. Department of State, *Country Reports on Human Rights Practices for 1991* (Washington, DC: Author, 1992); Nangia, "The Tragedy of Bride Burning in India."
74. U.S. Department of State, *id.*; Nangia, *id.*
75. For a review, *see* M. Spatz, "A Lesser Crime: A Comparative Study of Legal Defenses for Men Who Kill Their Wives," *Columbia Journal of Law & Social Problems* 24 (1991):597–638.
76. Dowry Prohibition Act, No. 28, 6 INDIA CODE 40E (1961); the act and its recent amendments are reviewed in Spatz, "A Lesser Crime."
77. Carlson-Whitley, "Dowry Death."
78. Spatz, "A Lesser Crime."
79. Carlson-Whitley, "Dowry Death," at 647.
80. L. R. Pardee, "The Dilemma of Dowry Deaths: Domestic Disgrace or International Human Rights Catastrophe?" *Arizona Journal of International and Comparative Law* 13 (1996):491–521.
81. Spatz, "A Lesser Crime."
82. S. K. Houseknecht and J. G. Pankhurst, *Family, Religion, and Social Change in Diverse Societies* (New York: Oxford University Press, 2000).
83. R. A. Cnaan, R. J. Wineburge, and S. C. Boddie, *The Newer Deal: Social Work and Religion* (New York: Columbia University Press, 1999).
84. V. Muntarbhorn, *Sale of Children, Child Prostitution and Child Pornography.* E/CN. 4/1994/84, at 13.

85. *Id.*
86. J. Bapat, "Devadasi Rehabilitation Programme: An Empirical Study," *Journal of Indian Anthropology* 25 (1990):201–214.
87. K. Barry, Female Sexual Slavery (New York: New York University Press, 1984).
88. For a review, *see* Levesque, *Child Sexual Abuse.*
89. A. S. Bilyeu, *"Trokosi*—The Practice of Sexual Slavery in Ghana: Religious and Cultural Freedom vs. Human Rights," *Indiana International and Comparative Law Review* 9 (1999):466, note 62.
90. *Id.*
91. *Id.*
92. Adjetey, "Reclaiming the African Woman's Individuality."
93. Bilyeu, "Trokosi—The Practice of Sexual Slavery in Ghana."
94. J. L. Esposito, *Women in Muslim Family Law* (Syracuse, NY: Syracuse University Press, 1982) at 17.
95. S. Y. Lai and R. E. Ralph, "Female Sexual Autonomy and Human Rights," *Harvard Human Rights Journal* 8 (1995):201–227.
96. R. Cook, "Reducing Maternal Mortality: A Priority for Human Rights Law," in *Legal Issues in Human Rights Reproduction*, S. McLean, Ed. (Brookfield, VT: Gower, 1989).
97. E. Royston and S. Armstrong, Eds., *Preventing Maternal Deaths* (Geneva: World Health Organization, 1989).
98. Cook, "Reducing Maternal Mortality."
99. Levesque, *Child Sexual Abuse.*
100. Lai and Ralph, "Female Sexual Autonomy and Human Rights."
101. *Id.*
102. *See* K. K. Johnson, "Crime or Punishment: The Parental Corporal Punishment Defense —Reasonable and Necessary, or Excused Abuse?" *University of Illinois Law Review* 1998 (1998):413–487.
103. C. W. Howland, "The Challenge of Religious Fundamentalism to the Liberty and Equality Rights of Women: An Analysis Under the United Nations Charter," *Columbia Journal of Transnational Law* 35 (1997):271–377.
104. *Id.*
105. J. Rivera, "Domestic Violence Against Latinas by Latino Males: An Analysis of Race, National Origin, and Gender Differentials," *Boston College Third World Law Journal* 14 (1994):231–257.
106. Backstrom, "The International Human Rights of the Child."
107. Human Rights Watch, *Violence Against Women in South Africa.*
108. Wing, "A Critical Race Feminist Conceptualization of Violence."
109. Human Rights Watch, *Violence Against Women in South Africa.*
110. *Id.* at 47.
111. Wing, "A Critical Race Feminist Conceptualization of Violence."
112. P. T. McWhirter, *"La Violencia Privada*: Domestic Violence in Chile," *American Psychologist* 54 (1999):37–40.
113. S. Horne, "Domestic Violence in Russia," *American Psychologist* 54 (1999):55–61.
114. J. Kozu, "Domestic Violence in Japan," *American Psychologist* 54 (1999):50–54.
115. M. Ellsberg, T. Caldera, A. Herrera, A. Winkvist, and G. Kullgren, "Domestic Violence and Emotional Distress Among Nicaraguan Women," *American Psychologist* 54 (1999): 30–36.
116. R. J. R. Levesque, "The Sexual Use, Abuse and Exploitation of Children: Challenges in Implementing Children's Human Rights," *Brooklyn Law Review* 60 (1994):959–998.
117. *Id.*
118. *Id.*
119. B. C. Alexander, "Women in Nepal: Human Rights in Theory, Human Rights in Practice," *Human Rights Brief* 7 (Spring 2000):6–8.

120. C. H. McCaghy and C. Hou, "Familial Affiliation and Prostitution in a Cultural Context: Career Onsets of Taiwanese Prostitutes," *Archives of Sexual Behavior* 23 (1994):251– 265.
121. R. J. R. Levesque, *Adolescents, Society, and the Law: Interpretive Essays and Bibliographic Guide* (Chicago: American Bar Association, 1997).
122. *Id.*
123. M. Straus, *Beating the Devil Out of Them: Corporal Punishment in American Families* (New York: Lexington Books, 1994).
124. *See* Levesque, *Child Sexual Abuse.*
125. Pierce v. Society of Sisters, 268 U.S. 510, 535 (1925), emphasis added.
126. M. A. Mason, *From Father's Property to Children's Rights: The History of Child Custody in the United States* (New York: Columbia University Press, 1994).
127. *See, e.g.,* J. G. Dwyer, "Setting Standards for Parenting—By What Right?" *Child Psychiatry and Human Development* 27 (1997):165–177.
128. United Nations, *Report of the Working Group on Contemporary Forms of Slavery on Its Eighteenth Session,* E/CN.4/Sub.2/1993/30, at 7–8.
129. R. O'Grady, *The Child and the Tourist: The Story Behind the Escalation of Child Prostitution in Asia* (New York: ECPAT, 1992).
130. Fitzgibbon, "The United Nations Convention on the Rights of the Child."
131. Lai and Ralph, "Female Sexual Autonomy and Human Rights."
132. Bol, "Using International Law to Fight Child Labor."
133. J. Boyden, *Families: A Celebration and Hope for World Change* (London: Faine & UNESCO, 1993).
134. Nieuwenhuys, *Children's Lifeworlds.*
135. Backstrom, "The International Human Rights of the Child."
136. *Id.*
137. G. T. Hotaling and D. B. Sugarman, "An Analysis of Risk Markers in Husband to Wife Violence: The Current State of Knowledge," *Violence and Victims* 1 (1986):101–124.
138. *See* L. L. Heise, "Violence Against Women: An Integrated, Ecological Framework." *Violence Against Women* 4 (1998):262–290.
139. *Id.*
140. Pardee, "The Dilemma of Dowry Deaths."
141. Armatta, "Getting Beyond the Law's Complicity in Intimate Violence Against Women."

Part II

Human Rights Responses to Cultural Life and Family Violence

Chapter 4
WHY CULTURAL LIFE MATTERS TO HUMAN RIGHTS LAW

Having explained the significant role cultural forces play in family violence and in efforts to protect individuals from such violence, I now turn to the role of culture in human rights law. Human rights norms face fundamental challenges from conceptions of cultural life. Human rights law necessarily must balance the need to respect different cultural conceptions of humanity while still ensuring a minimal floor of universal respect for individuals' human rights. Ultimately, human rights law requires a balance between the rights of individuals and the cultural group within which they find themselves. That balance requires evaluating the nature and significance of cultural practices, their effects on vulnerable members of the group (e.g., those subjected to family violence), the degree to which the conflicting individual and group rights interfere with each other, the cumulative effects of potential restrictions on either form of rights, and the proportionality of restrictions. The evaluation necessarily involves numerous complexities, particularly as the increasingly pressing need to balance individual and group rights spurs renewed challenges and raises feverish resistance.

Human rights efforts aimed at the alleviation of family violence provide no exception to the need to balance and address debates enmeshed in complexities. Given that cultural life and its role in human rights law are of such significance to the development, respect, legitimacy, and effectiveness of human rights instruments, it is important to explore how cultural issues are central to conceptualizing human rights and ensuring their effectiveness. After examining the nature of debates surrounding the cross-cultural legitimacy of international human rights, I explore the different uses of the term *culture* in international law. I then examine the traditional methods used to enforce human rights standards and the need to reconsider enforcement methods in light of our understanding of the role cultural life plays in the implementation of human rights principles. That analysis lays the foundation for a discussion of how international law works and why apparently impotent protections from family violence actually have the power to transform cultures and interpersonal relationships. The chapter emphasizes the transformative power of human rights, a view of human rights that places significance on participatory models of individual, familial, and cultural development. The chapter ends by emphasizing why and how human rights principles and modern conceptions of human rights law should matter to those who respond to family violence in a rapidly changing world.

Debates About Cultural Life and Why They Matter

Human rights law faces challenges and resistance to the extent societies and individuals perceive it as imposing a foreign way of life. Positions that resist or promote international standards generally take the form of a contentious debate between universalism and relativism. That debate revolves around the source of standards that determine how countries should treat their citizens and how people should treat one another; also discussed is whether the standard has an absolute, minimal character or whether it is contingent and relative to different communities and cultures. This section examines the nature and consequences of the relativist–universalist debates and why they matter. The goal is to understand why the debates surrounding the cross-cultural applicability of international human rights norms hold significance for addressing cultural forces related to family violence.

Relativist–Universalist Debates

Both sides of the universalism–relativism debate generally adopt very different views of individuals, private life, human rights, and the legitimacy of international law. Universalists hold that an underlying human unity entitles all individuals, regardless of their cultural or regional location, to certain basic minimal rights. Relativists, on the other hand, argue that the promulgation of universal human rights law does not recognize the extreme diversity of cultural practices and that universal rights should be subsidiary to local cultural norms. These conceptions of rights and an individual's humanity frame the current debates regarding the legitimacy of modern human rights law.

Universalists argue that people are autonomous individuals whose rights are to be respected because of their individuality. Universalists, then, tend to take the position that the locus of human rights is most properly situated in an individual, and they recognize that the rights of groups are best protected through attention to individual rights. Relativists argue that people are understandable only in cultural contexts, and their contexts may require respect just as much as their alleged individuality. Thus, relativists adopt a group-centered view of the world. These views increasingly are framed in terms of the need for more respect for the dominant values espoused by the global North or the global South. The debate also continues in the form of a religious (West-Islam) framework or more broadly between developing (Third World) and developed (Western-Northern) countries. Regardless of the framework, the debates concern the place of individuals within their communities.

Given the different views of the place of individuals in community life, both sides also study human rights differently. Universalists generally examine how other societies already possess basic human rights that simply need further expression or reinterpretation. By doing so, universalists generally champion a positivist approach, which suggests that any biases found in the dominant human rights paradigm may be tempered by empirical research that confirms the universality of core human rights. Thus, the universalist view emphasizes comparability of cross-culturally or even globally applicable human rights dimensions or categories. From this perspective, human rights gain legitimacy to the extent they can be located and expressed in all cultures. Relativists, on the other hand, affirm that universal truths actually vary among societies and that positivistic, empirical paradigms do not uncover truths obvious to other societies. Relativist investigators eschew comparison and categorization and caution against the dangers of using categories derived from outside the culture. Relativists focus on the context of human rights within a culture and prize the ability to investigate and understand human rights within the culture's own frame of reference. At its most extreme, the relativist approach views cultures as the exclusive shaper of human experience, even to the extent that no unifying cross-cultural human characteristics exist.[1] The rise of this more epistemological relativism that finds no objective reality, truth, or reason coincides with the emergence of many new schools of thought, particularly deconstructionism and postmodernism, which profess that no one can know anything beyond one's direct experience and which reject the very concept of reality to the extent that language entirely defines and mediates reality. Their belief that human rights norms do not transcend cultural location and cannot be readily translated across cultures reflects the skepticism about the availability of universal norms. At the extreme, these commentators seek to deprive human rights advocates of the very foundation of human rights: The category "human" does not enable cross-cultural assessment of human practices or State actions. Universalists counter that the straitjacket of absolute respect for cultural behavior unnecessarily precludes the need to make cross-cultural judgments. They further counter that too much respect for cultural practices stifles meaningful comparisons necessary to address and verify the extent to which oppressive, self-serving, and cruel practices are actually culturally sanctioned and legitimate.

Universalists and relativists also view differently the extent to which human rights law demands changes in cultural practices. Universalists argue that human rights seek to transform specific, illegitimate cultural practices. They argue that a search will locate legitimate, indigenous beliefs that comport with universal human rights values and that claims of cultural relativism run the danger of being without cultural basis and, instead, derive from manipulations of repressive regimes and elites who have long since left traditional cultures behind. Relativists, on the other hand, argue that the structure of modern human rights recognizes the need to respect tradition and cultural practices. They also argue that differences in need of remedies have arisen from Western colonialism and exploitation, which require special measures and extra protections. Relativists also frequently champion the global benefits of diversity and warn that attempts to tinker with cultural life run the danger of inflicting irreparable cultural damage and even the destruction of cultures.

Both views also adopt different views of human rights' legitimacy. The relativists generally view international human rights as arbitrary, intrusive, elitist, and imperialist. Critics who espouse this view propose that international norms should not be the basis of value judgments in other cultural contexts. These commentators rebuke conceptions of international human rights on the grounds that the dominant Western discourse of rights is antithetical to the norms in non-Western societies.[2] The other side of the debate finds conceptions of human rights legitimate and similar to those found in all societies. These commentators view cultures as complex, contradictory, and diverse in conceptions of life. That diversity, for example, allows for questioning the purity of the "collectivism" said to be found in traditional cultures and highlights individualism. From this perspective, culture can be viewed as an uneasy compromise between conflicting needs and wants of various groups and classes within the society, where dominant group members seek to maintain perceptions and interpretations of cultural values and norms that support their own interests and contend that they possess the only valid view of that culture. Again, a search of cultural life reveals different conceptions of life, including aspirations for social change among those vulnerable to dominant beliefs and practices.

Universalists and relativists also disagree about the extent to which international human rights law transforms cultural life. Universalists propose that universalism deals with only a small core of violations and leaves intact legitimate cultural practices. In their view, the dilution of universalism allows oppressive regimes to continue violations of basic human dignities and to inappropriately justify their practices by claiming cultural rights. Relativists argue that leaving legitimate practices intact may require also leaving intact a small core of violations and, more importantly, that the core of violations are not necessarily violations of human rights as conceived by the host culture. Conceptions of the individual's place in cultural life necessarily play into the extent to which human rights law gains adherence and contributes to the transformation of cultural life.

Significance of the Universalist–Relativist Debates

The universalist–relativist debates are significant for several reasons. First, the explicitly global nature of international law requires that the effort to impose a global standard must address polarized views of cultural life. Second, attempts to intervene in cultural practices undoubtedly affect the entire culture and necessarily lead to cultural change. Third, polarized positioning allows violations to continue and ensures that significant developments in international human rights law remain ignored and unlikely to elicit commitment or compliance. Fourth, the debates suggest a need to rethink popular conceptions of how international law works and how it actually may lead to the alleviation of family violence and legitimately lead to reforming problematic cultural practices. Fifth, as human rights law continues to develop and extend its reach, the debates intensify and require renewed attention if human rights are to be further developed, respected, and practiced. Each of these reasons is worthy of further discussion.

Although debates continue, international human rights law demands a balance between universalism and relativism, between the rights of individuals and their cultures. The United Nations recognized the link between cultural rights and human dignity in its foundational human rights document: the Universal Declaration of Human Rights of 1945.[3] Article 22 of the Declaration provides that "everyone . . . is entitled to realization . . . of cultural rights indispensable for his dignity and free development of his personality." Human rights must recognize and protect the rights of individuals as well as the rights of groups. The centrality of cultural life is fundamental to human rights law. Human rights law protects cultural law by placing a high premium on individual sovereignty and cultural sovereignty. As the debates reveal, balancing the preservation of culture and individual rights remains fraught with difficulties, yet human rights law requires precisely such balancing.

The debates lead to the conclusion that attempts to address family violence must consider the impact of abolishing problematic customs and practices, even practices not perceived by the indigenous culture as overtly problematic. The significance of this concern cannot be overestimated. As relativists correctly suggest, ending certain practices may mean ending a practicing group's existing culture because cultures construct some of the questioned practices as central to cultural conceptions of human development, cultural participation, and cultural life. At the extreme, then, human rights hold the potential to erase cultural diversity. These potential consequences result in the need to proceed cautiously in efforts to determine which practices have the most legitimacy and which practices need transforming without compromising legitimacy.

Competing claims of universalism and relativism of human rights standards and continued debates about the nature of those standards allow violations to continue. Certain standards of human rights are frequently violated because they are not perceived as culturally legitimate in the context of the particular society. To the extent that political regimes and other dominant social forces can challenge the validity of human rights norms as alien or at least as sanctioned by the primary values of the dominant culture, they can dodge the negative consequences of their violation. This suggests a pressing need to address the relativist–universalist debates and to establish cultural legitimacy for human rights standards in the context of the particular society.

The manner in which the debates allow violations to continue suggests a need to rethink the dominant views of international law and how international law develops. International law continues to be viewed as a series of contracts between nations. Addressing the debate requires a modification of the concept of national sovereignty to enhance the principle of international accountability for violating human rights. Enforcement of human rights requires that the rights be recognized and adopted at several levels, including domestic, regional, and local levels. Such implementation remains necessary for human rights law to gain and maintain legitimacy. In addition, even though States may have official and formal participation in the development of human rights instruments, the lack of popular awareness of and support for accepted standards suggests that participation does not reflect genuine consensus of the targeted populations and does not reflect the needed re-evaluation of cultural traditions in terms of proposed universal and international human rights. That is, to be effective, human rights law must reach and relate to cultural and individual consciousness, an often ignored reality in the implementation and development of international legal principles.

Although the debate between the universal–relative positions is an old one, it takes on renewed vigor in light of the human rights movements' increasing progress. Notions of sovereignty, domestic jurisdiction, and cultural autonomy formerly enjoyed great strength, but they now suffer increasing deliberation as they are challenged by efforts to establish an international, universal human rights regime. On their face, human rights instruments surely fall on the "universalist" side of the debate—the founding, modern human rights document was the Universal Declaration of Human Rights of 1948. The most recent declaration regarding the balance of cultural and universal rights, the Vienna Declaration[4] also falls on the side of universalism; in Section I, paragraph 5, it bluntly provides that

> all human rights are universal, indivisible, and interdependent and interrelated. . . .
> While the significance of national and regional particularities and various historical,
> cultural and religious backgrounds must be born in mind, it is the duty of States,
> regardless of their political, economic and cultural systems, to promote and protect
> all human rights and fundamental freedoms.

As human rights law develops, it demands a universal approach that keeps in mind the need to respect some cultural traditions but nevertheless presses forward in the search for universals. As human rights law grinds forward, resistance accumulates. Yet much of the resistance comes from not understanding how international law conceives of cultures and how it only gains power and legitimacy through them.

The remainder of this chapter addresses these issues to emphasize why and how human rights principles and modern conceptions of human rights law should matter to those who respond to family violence rooted in cultural life.

Human Rights Law's Conceptions of Cultural Life

International law contains two conceptions of culture. The most dominant approach follows the popular conception of culture and accepts cultures as static, homogenous, and essentialized. The other approach follows the less dominant approach, now championed by anthropological theory, which conceives of cultures as fluid, dynamic, and often contradictory. Even though neither approach provides a neat, universal, and readily applicable approach to combating violence within certain cultures, both approaches provide important mechanisms that may be harnessed to address violence. This section examines these approaches with an eye toward understanding how conceptions of cultural life allow us to envision and respect individuals' right to protection from family violence.

Narrow

Human rights law adopts narrow approaches to cultural life that most legal systems adopt. These approaches use the term *culture* to identify fundamentally different, essentialized, and homogenous social groups. This use of the term *culture* fixes boundaries between groups in an absolute and artificial manner. From this perspective, international human rights law adopts two views. The first coincides with an attempt to protect minority and indigenous groups; the second relates to individual or groups' heritage manifested in the form of traditions and supporting historical materials, which require preservation.

The most recent and comprehensive human rights treaty, the Children's Convention of 1989,[5] illustrates the two approaches. Several protections adopt the view that culture is a reified entity that has definite substantive content, a view that culture involves a quality certain people possess or an entity to which people belong. For example, Article 30 protects the rights of individual children who belong to a minority group or one of the indigenous peoples and broadly bestows on children their individual right to enjoy their own culture. The approach also focuses on the preservation of cultures and often involves the accumulation of a particular group's material heritage, including monuments, artifacts, and various forms of information. In this form, the right to culture ensures access to this accumulated cultural capital: That right includes individuals' right to create their own cultures, without restrictions. International law adopts this approach, for example, when it recognizes the child's right to information and cultural activities as the law requires governments to "encourage the provision of appropriate and equal opportunities for cultural, artistic, recreational and leisure activity."[6]

Broad

For those who adopt a broad conception of cultural life, culture does not have a definite substantive content. Instead, culture involves contradiction as much as cohesion and perpetually changes meaning.[7] This approach provides a much more fluid and active view of culture. Cultures, then, constantly are constructed, reconstructed, invented, and reinvented by ever-changing individuals. The approach places emphasis on people's perception of their culture, on the discourse about culture rather than about culture itself, which (according to this approach) has no objective existence outside of the individual's subjectivity.[8] Culture, then, simply is a deliberate abstraction. This view of cultural life makes the term's use particularly problematic. Yet international human rights laws still manage to allow for and even embrace the approach.

Although the dominant approach to human rights law adopts a narrow view of cultural life, much evidence may be culled to support the claim that international human rights law also adopts a more expansive view of cultural life. Indeed, this broader, more expansive view of human rights arguably constitutes what modern human rights law is all about: a process that seeks to ensure cultural change so that societies protect the basic, fundamental rights of individuals within all cultures.

This forward-looking and expansive view of cultural life finds expression in numerous documents. Most notably, the approach is found in recent efforts to implement human rights. For example, human rights law now focuses on offering mechanisms that ensure publicity to effect compliance with international mandates. For example, Article 18 of the Women's Convention of 1979[9] binds States Parties to undertake submission of reports on the measures they have adopted to give effect to the convention and the difficulties they have encountered in implementing the convention. This allows each State and the international community to review the status of women's human rights and to suggest reform. In addition, human rights law focuses on interaction and voice in decision making, as revealed through the focus on providing human rights education and making universally recognized principles known to all citizens who constitute States Parties.[10] Likewise, human rights law also focuses on self-determination in a global community. The most notable example involves indigenous groups' rights to self-determination and the increasing significance and attention devoted to their rights. Commentators interpret this right as one that aims to protect peoples' rights to political self-determination and their rights against their own governments,[11] and it grants peoples control over their socioeconomic development.[12] Thus, although this broad view of culture remains considerably undeveloped as an approach to cultural issues in human rights law, it nevertheless finds expression in it.

The Narrow View Adopted in Human Rights Debates

The previous discussion of the two general approaches to culture and cultural rights suggests that the outline of debates between universality and relativism, or imperialism and cultural self-determination, remains limited. Modern human rights law's regime, in contrast to polarized debates, represents a thoughtful attempt to balance competing claims and to move societies toward efforts to protect those most at risk for human rights abuses. This view of modern human rights suggests that much of the current human rights discourse remains considerably problematic.

Results of the current, polarized debates are problematic because they do not consider and take better advantage of recent conceptions of culture. Debates about international law generally conceive of cultures as static and homogenous and accept a very narrow, restricted view of cultural life. Commentators all too frequently use culture as a static, readily observable collection of individuals who hold beliefs that explain and justify behaviors. This view of cultures and of cultural rights polarizes debates about the legitimacy of human rights law. Another problem of the debates is that they remain focused on intervention and the extent to which it destroys cultures. That focus does not capitalize on human rights law's potential contribution. By emphasizing stability and cultural continuity of customs or traditions, both sides discount the importance of social change. As currently conceived, the debates thus fail to take advantage of views that cultures are dynamic and ever-changing and to acknowledge the manner in which outside forces may gain legitimacy. These two reasons highlight a fundamental point about debates between imperialism and cultural self-determination: They do not consider recent developments in the understanding of imperialism, how human rights law works, and how human rights law has developed. The remainder of this chapter addresses these developments.

Culture's Place in Human Rights Law

Regardless of human rights law's approach to cultural life—an approach that is sometimes static and at other times dynamic—it is important to understand the weight human rights law actually gives to cultural practices that contribute to family violence. At least in the context of violence against family members, human rights law increasingly advocates a cultural pluralist perspective, which rejects the use of culture as an excuse for inflicting violence. International human rights law approaches cultures as institutions that serve the development of individuals and deserve protection only to the extent that they do not violate their constituents' human rights. Thus, human rights documents consistently address culture as a basis on which protections must be afforded; and when cultures fail to protect, they lose their protection from human rights law.

All three foundational human rights documents that constitute the International Bill of Rights address the need to respect different cultures' protective functions. Article 27 of the Political Covenant[13] recognizes the right of minorities "to enjoy their own culture." Article 1(1) of the Economic and Social Covenant[14] recognizes that "all peoples have the right to self determination . . . and freely pursue . . . their cultural development." The Universal Declaration of Human Rights mandates in Article 22 that "everyone . . . is entitled to realization . . . of . . . cultural rights indispensable for his dignity and the free development of his personality." Despite these apparently forceful recognitions of cultural rights, not one cites culture as a basis on which protections may be abridged. Rather than protecting culture at the expense of human rights, international documents reveal that culture necessarily must cede to universal rights. Indeed, as the above mandates suggest, cultures are protected so that they may enhance human rights, not lead to their derogation. That interpretation finds support from Article 1(3) of the U.N. Charter,[15] which seeks

> to achieve international cooperation in solving international problems of an economic, social, *cultural*, or humanitarian character and in promoting respect for human rights and for fundamental freedoms for all without distinction as to race, sex, language, or religion.

The language of the charter makes three things clear: Human rights are not dependent on specific cultures, no particular culture provides the source for human rights, and international cooperation is needed to resolve cultural disputes to promote human rights. Indeed, the charter states that human rights are to be respected "without distinction" as to the basic markers that influence different manifestations of cultural life: race, sex, language, and religion.

Several treaties that followed the charter and International Bill of Rights serve as examples of the approach that places the preservation of human rights as the most fundamental universal principle, even when human rights protections challenge cultural practices. Article 24(3) of the Children's Convention requires States Parties to "take all effective and appropriate measures with a view to abolishing traditional practices prejudicial to the health of children." The treaty stresses (in Article 29) the need for children to develop within the context of cultural identity and community practices and (in Article 19) the need to strengthen the family unit. These extra protections seemingly make it difficult to base human rights abuses on cultural tradition or bias. However, the Children's Convention clearly places a focus on the child's best interests,[16] the child's evolving capacities,[17] the principle of nondiscrimination,[18] and respect for the child's human dignity[19]—all of which recenter the focus of human rights back on children and require placing children's interests before those of their abusive cultural practices.

Likewise, the Women's Convention of 1979 confronts the possibility of misuse of culture as a pretext to support violence against women. The treaty's Article 5(a) mandates States Parties

> to modify the social and cultural patterns of conduct of men and women, with a view to achieving the elimination of prejudices and customary and all other practices which are based on the idea of the inferiority or superiority of either of the sexes or on stereotyped roles for men and women.

The Women's Convention seeks (in Article 5) to modify social and cultural conduct that discriminates against women and calls (in Articles 2, 4, 5, and 10) for modifications of existing laws, cultural practices, and even practices within the family unit. By emphasizing the need to change existing laws and judicial systems (in Article 2) and to receive education to teach the community to redefine the stereotypical societal roles of the sexes (in Article 10), the convention implicitly asserts the need to take far-reaching measures to combat cultural practices often ingrained in society. Again, cultures must serve to enhance human rights, not to abridge them.

In addition, the Declaration on the Elimination of Violence Against Women of 1994[20] makes an important statement. Article 4 firmly rejects cultural relativism as it prohibits States from invoking "any custom, tradition or religious consideration to avoid their obligations" in pursuing a policy of eliminating violence by all appropriate means and without delay. This recent recognition of the need to combat culturally ingrained violence reflects the increasingly accepted view that no other social groups have suffered greater violation of their human rights in the name of culture than women and children. That modern human rights law seeks to address the position of the most vulnerable individuals who would suffer from accepted cultural practices reveals an extraordinary development. Regardless of the need to protect cultural life, modern human rights law increasingly aims to reject cultural life as an excuse for violence within families.

The explicit sources are of considerable significance. As with any international treaty, analysis must be based squarely on the text.[21] Where the text provides standards and guidance for resolving conflicts, it is inappropriate to resort prematurely to a balancing approach (e.g., balancing cultural protection against certain forms of family violence). The balancing approach typically identifies factors of importance related to the text but not necessarily in the text, that are then weighed, in a process that is not itself guided by the text, to determine an outcome. The need to stay within the confines of the treaty itself is especially true in human rights law, where the parties already have identified and negotiated the factors that are important and have agreed to a final text that reflects the balance acceptable to the parties. In addition, a textual focus is particularly important in areas of cultural sensitivity, where the parties necessarily have compromised to resolve conflicts; such sensitivity requires acknowledgment that the agreed on language already represents the balance that nations desired to strike among themselves to harmonize their potentially conflicting cultures and acts of violence. Human rights protections of cultural life do not aim to insulate cultures and condone violence within families.

Justifying the New Cultural Imperialism of Human Rights Law

Efforts that aim to transform cultures, as the human rights movement undoubtedly aims to do, face the problem of losing legitimacy. Yet just as efforts to shield individuals from violence within families gain support, so do efforts to change cultures within the global community. These developments counter legitimate claims that the imperialistic efforts of colonial times inappropriately ignored indigenous conceptions of rights as they used Western, individualistic standards to judge and encourage social progress. Although the modern human rights law movement still remains imperialistic, the nature of its imperialism continues to change. Given these changes, several arguments may justify the apparent imperialism and highlight how debates about universalism and relativism unnecessarily hold to extremes.

First, Western norms of individuality and morality are as diverse as norms found in non-Western cultures. The commentators who most recently have popularized the role of individualism in modern American life and character point to "countervailing tendencies that pull people back from their isolation into social communion. . . . The habits and practices of religion and democratic participation educate the citizen to a larger view than his private world would allow."[22] Likewise, Western rights discourse does not focus solely on autonomy: The United States has extensive "programmatic rights" that were established after the two world wars and expanded dramatically during the Great Society years. Equally important, many in the West are critical of liberal individualism: Feminist writers have emphasized the prevalence and importance of communalism, both in interpersonal relations[23] and civil society.[24] Characterizations of the West as the bastion of unbridled individualism are somewhat misleading.

Second, Western precedents that contributed to modern human rights law represent early and incomplete conceptions of human rights, and these conceptions are undergoing evolution. Although revolutionary for their times, early human rights precedents focusing on the natural rights of man and the rights of men as citizens were not necessarily based on the principle of full equality of all human beings as recognized in current human rights law. Instead, the early Western human rights principles were based on a concept of personhood that elevated only certain categories (property-owning White men) to personhood and relegated others to the status of noncitizen. Thus, the history of human rights documents how, at various times and in various ways, slaves, heathens, barbarians, colonized peoples, indigenous populations, women, children, the insane, and the impoverished have been thought to be essentially nonhuman and unworthy of bearing human rights.[25] In addition, although the appeal was to universal truths, the concern was directed to internal law and laws within countries, not to international law. The modern concept of human rights moves toward more egalitarian principles, is less individualistic, and extends beyond its national legal precedents.[26]

The development of human rights law, then, suggests that even though human rights language may derive from Western sources, it no longer remains solely Western. No particular culture or political group can claim that it alone correctly understands and interprets human rights guarantees. In fact, from its very first meeting to develop human rights instruments, the United Nations consciously sought to discover universal principles by creating a discourse where no regional philosophy or single way of life was permitted to prevail. Efforts were made to address fundamental differences and resist cultural imperialism.[27] Although charges continue to be made that the human rights movement engaged in imperialist efforts,[28] numerous indicators suggest an emerging transnational legal culture. Leading commentators on law and society have noted that law is in the process of a globalization that converges several legal systems to create a modern legal culture.[29] That trend is witnessed in the new wave of national constitutions that incorporate international law into domestic law and judicial practice.[30] Thus, those who argue that human rights focus too much on individualistic or on collectivistic conceptions of rights ignore the evolving human rights legal culture that interprets rights to be interdependent and indivisible, disregard precedents and contributions from numerous cultures, and dismiss the growing realities of emerging global legal transformations. The human rights culture is no longer Western. All human rights are in a constant process of evolution, which relies on debate and contending claims.

Third, no society is an insular entity. A variety of external forces influence countries and societies. New conceptions of international relations focus on individuals, groups, institutions, and transnational actors that exert different pressures on local, national, and international governments.[31] The current international economic order ensures that political boundaries lose their former significance. The impact of these developments remains to be determined. It is clear, however, that economic and cultural forces do more than develop a universal body of legal norms that constitute a common worldwide legal consciousness. These forces inevitably affect interpersonal relations, thereby contributing to the transformation of human rights, as much as claims of cultural imperialism and the benefits of other approaches to human development are recognized and legitimized. Debates that ignore the necessary connections among societies and cultures do not reflect the realities of a changed world.

Fourth, modernity does more than bring cultures together—it renegotiates the role of the State and the content and meaning of State sovereignty. A central development in the human rights discipline shows that State sovereignty is not an unbending concept. Internationally recognized rights are suprasovereign and pierce States' territorial borders. As discussed above and in chapter 1, the reconceptualization of sovereignty consonant with evolving notions of human rights rejects the traditional shield of sovereignty and seeks to protect individuals and families from harmful governmental actions.

Fifth, static conceptions of cultural life that emphasize the continuity of customs and traditions inappropriately minimize the significance of social change. Every society inevitably changes, and some traditions are selectively discontinued whereas others persist. Sahlins revolutionized anthropology by demonstrating how cultures evolve.[32] Although controversial, the approach highlights well how some practices disappear and, indeed, how entire societies disappear. The major criticism of relativistic and postmodernist conceptions of culture is that it leaves unprotected disenfranchised individuals as it avoids the reality of system power imbalances, such as that existing between the sexes.[33] At any particular moment, cultural practices are not necessarily adaptive, optimal, or consented to by the majority of its adherents. The constant reinterpretation, reinvention, and modification of customs allow societies to survive. The abandonment of numerous erotic customs, such as Chinese foot binding, and customs that ensure the marketability of girls by reducing their erotic desires, such as some forms of female genital circumcision,[34] provide powerful examples of how societies may adapt and change, eliminating practices that exert heavy costs on groups of individuals.

Sixth, human rights challenge all cultures. Although critics of human rights law frequently view the movement as an effort by Western countries to impose their values on non-Western countries, several other critics also notice the failure of Western countries to take certain human rights more seriously. Industrialized countries resist rights that infringe on their own cultural values. For example, the United States, arguably the most "Western" and imperialistic country, remains formally and essentially hostile to the human rights movement as articulated by recent international developments.[35] The resistance, although couched in terms of State and national sovereignty, still deals with the domestic application of foreign principles and visions of humanity. Most notably, for example, the deep philosophical and political opposition of the United States to economic rights principles leads to rejections of social welfare guarantees. For example, the United States does not generally recognize homelessness and poverty as human rights violations, nor does it recognize the basic right to medical care or education.[36] In addition to its inadequate domestic rights performance, it faces allegations that it is a chief abuser of (economic) human rights abroad. The U.S. "free-market" trade and foreign aid policies allow debt and pursuit of profit to dictate priorities that often result in (economic and social) human rights abuses.[37] Disavowing economic and social rights allows the U.S. government to sidestep criticisms relating to its foreign and domestic social welfare policies, which, under human rights law, violate the rights of impoverished residents. Human rights, then, are intentionally imperialistic, and their ideals fundamentally challenge the internal workings of all cultures and demand a radical reformulation of how all cultures view and treat individuals. In addition, the expansive production of human rights standards and norms entails an immediate policy and resource overload that no government or regime, however conscientious, can bear. No country meets the current standards required by human rights law.

Seventh, even though the human rights movement seeks important changes, the main objective simply remains to set the minimum acceptable standard for the way in which a State can treat all of its citizens. All major documents set minimum standards and denote ways to achieve progress beyond minimal protections. Human rights law does not impose arbitrary and homogenizing jackets on diverse cultural traditions. Each State and culture retains sovereign power over its own cultural development, although the power remains within limits delineated by international law. Those minimal protections merely seek to protect individuals from being at the mercy of governments and powerful groups that would not otherwise be held accountable for their actions.

It continues to be politically difficult to recognize diversity in conceptions of rights and even more politically difficult to accept that universality is not a static concept but one that evolves and responds to changing configurations of interests and needs. Yet the new international regime only makes the following points: No State may be given absolute power over its citizens for fear that it will abuse that power; an international approach to human rights is needed to protect individuals against States and other supralevel organizations; every individual is entitled to a basic modicum of human dignity; certain human rights are universal, fundamental, and inalienable and thus may not be overridden by cultural and religious traditions; and participation in any social or cultural group has no bearing on that individual's intrinsic human worth or entitlement to be treated as a human being. In addition, and seen more explicitly in chapter 5, the actual language of international treaties leaves so much room for maneuvering that what is most universal about human rights is the aspiration, not immediate reality of attainment. That conception of universality, however, leaves considerable room for cultural diversity, which fuels the major debates.

The tensions and conceptions of cultural life and of cultural rights are only likely to increase in the future. The tensions make more pressing the need to consider ways in which ideals may be internalized and legitimized in various cultures. Indeed, they make manifest one important issue about the nature of debates. Although the debates takes place on the more general level of the status of rights and their universal application, the need to focus on that discussion is not self-evident. Presumably, the debate could also focus on the substance and interpretation of specific rights themselves, and the debate perhaps more fruitfully could address such issues as the right to protection from family violence.

Enforcing the Sources of International Human Rights Law

Although human rights may gain increasing legitimacy and its relative legitimacy may remain an important source of debates, the extent to which debates about legitimacy become meaningful in large part depends on the enforcement of international human rights principles and the power of the international community to ensure compliance with evolving, internationally negotiated principles. Given that the standards aim to be negotiated without privileging particular cultures, enforcing international standards seemingly would involve considerable resistance. The reality is that cultures do resist outside influence; that resistance, however, simply means that ensuring and enforcing human rights standards involves much more than the traditional modes of enforcement envisioned by either international or domestic law. Effective enforcement necessarily means infiltrating the roots of cultures. This section examines the traditional forms of enforcement and changes in the enforcement of human rights law, an analysis that lays the foundation for the next section's discussion of how human rights law gains legitimacy and reaches effectiveness only when it becomes culturally relevant.

As demonstrated in chapter 1, the evolving U.N. human rights legislative, monitoring, and judicial machinery has become a powerful source and reference point for modern notions of human rights. No single view of rights has prevailed, and humanity has currently organized itself into Nation States. These States obligate themselves, albeit to varying degrees, to protect rights internally and externally, individually and through international cooperation. Modes of enforcement take many forms, depending on their source, the relative weight given to particular rights, and the arena (international, domestic, or local) deemed responsible for enforcement. The following analysis examines mechanisms available to enforce international law.

Enforceable Sources

International law most typically derives from multilateral treaties that may be called "charters," "covenants," "conventions," or "protocols." A treaty is adopted by Nation States that become State Parties to the treaty once they have signed and appropriately ratified it. By adopting it, the States Parties agree to be bound by its provisions. In essence, the treaty serves as a contract among nations.

An international treaty imposes binding obligations on States Parties on how they treat their own citizens. Thus, even though individuals are not necessarily directly the subjects of international law, they are, in fact, the beneficiaries of international human rights law. International human rights law, then, merely provides a source of individual rights, which may be enforceable in domestic courts. Likewise, human rights law also is enforceable to the extent that Nation States take on themselves the obligations to ensure the rights, whether administratively, judicially, or by any other means. Through treaties, then, Nation States may be held accountable by other nations.

Other sources of international human rights law take the form of declarations authored by States' representatives issued at international conferences or meetings of international organizations, such as the U.N. General Assembly. These declarations and other international documents (e.g., "Platforms," "Plans of Action") do not create legal obligations for the States and are therefore not directly enforceable. Declarations and related instruments simply provide guidance as to how States themselves envision their responsibilities and how they interpret particular provisions of treaties and international documents. These documents, however, may become binding when incorporated into treaties or if they lead to the creation of customary international law. Thus, in addition to formal treaties, States are bound by what has become their customary behavior. With some exceptions, all nations generally become bound by customary law.

Human Rights in International Forums

Universal human rights rely on a growing number of international institutions and social movements to ensure protections. Generally, the international community uses five procedures to enforce State compliance with human rights treaties and other sources of international law. Efforts that focus on direct confrontation typically are not effective and (more importantly) generally are not used. Although they may be effective for some human rights violations, they are not necessarily effective for the forms of violations that would relate to family life and family violence. Instead, publicity and public scrutiny are used because they are viewed as more effective.

Informal diplomacy serves as the first avenue of international redress for violations of human rights. One State can influence the action of other States by exercising diplomatic pressure. Informal diplomacy in the form of consistent, continued condemnation by the global community may result in some changes. Although marked by some successes, when compared with other approaches the process has not been viewed as the most effective way to pursue claims against actions that violate international human rights norms. Two difficulties tend to arise: States must be ready to take the lead in advocating against the actions, and they must use diplomatic relations and pressure to effectuate the desired goal. Without resources, few States can exert sufficient power to alter other States' courses of action. Although informal diplomacy is an apparently weak method of ensuring human rights, it still remains important to not ignore its significance to the extent that several donor governments consider advances in human rights as a criteria influencing their aid-funding decisions.[38]

The second international forum in which to challenge practices is the International Court of Justice (ICJ), the body created by the U.N. Charter to be the principal judicial organ of the United Nations. The reach of the ICJ seems rather expansive. All member States of the United Nations are parties to the statute of the ICJ. In addition, the ICJ adopts, as its standards, international agreements and international customs as primary international law and recognizes secondary sources, mainly general principles of law, as recognized by civilized national and judicial decisions and the writings of prominent legal thinkers. Although seemingly powerful, the ICJ also has well-known limitations. States must be parties to the disputes. That means that individuals must rely on their State of nationality to bring the matter before the court. An obvious component of this problem is that States that violate individuals' rights are unlikely to bring the matter forward. In addition, jurisdiction of the ICJ is based on consent. A State cannot be forced to accept the jurisdiction of the ICJ to resolve allegations of human rights violations if brought to the ICJ. Despite these limitations, however, the ICJ has become an important source of human rights protections.

Charter-based organs provide the third forum that may be used to entertain complaints of human rights violations. The Commission on Human Rights is the primary and most important Charter-based organ for the enforcement of human rights violations.[39] The Commission has two procedures to adjudicate alleged human rights violations. Under Procedure 1503, individuals may allege gross violations of human rights through a private process. Procedure 1235 allows for public debate regarding complaints presented by governments and nongovernmental organizations about gross human rights violations. These mechanisms have been viewed as potentially effective. Even though the process is slow, secret, and vulnerable to political influences, the value of Procedure 1503 is the pressure it can place on governments engaged in human rights violations.[40] Although only governments and nongovernmental organizations may bring allegations through Procedure 1235, the public debates also hold considerable promise. The Commission has used working groups and special raporteurs to examine thematic problems and conditions in specific countries.

Several have viewed this approach as the most effective and objective way to monitor the international community.[41]

Treaty-based structures provide the fourth mechanism. The U.N. structure contains six organs that correspond to six human rights treaties: The Economic and Social Covenant (1966), Civil and Political Covenant (1966), Race Convention (1966),[42] Children's Convention (1989), Torture Convention (1984),[43] and Women's Convention (1979). These mechanisms work in three ways: Committees receive and evaluate the submission of periodic reports under the human rights system of key human rights treaties; the committees may function for interstate complaint procedures, whereby one State Party may bring a human rights violation complaint against another; and the committees may receive complaints filed by using the individual complaint process available under the Race Convention, Torture Convention, and the Civil and Political Covenant.

Despite the numerous ways of lodging complaints, several analysts question the effectiveness of this system. Interstate complaints actually are little used. Currently, only the Civil and Political Covenant allows for one State to file a claim that another State is not fulfilling its obligations. To date, however, no party has done so.[44] In terms of individual complaints, parties must affirmatively recognize the right of individuals to do so; and few States have exercised the option to be held accountable by claims made by individuals. The third approach, the focus on the public reports, remains equally criticized. Committees frequently deal with late reports, inadequate reports, uninformed State representatives, failures to disseminate reports, and failures to respond to examinations. In addition, many governments ignore their treaty obligation to file reports, they do not necessarily use reports to evaluate their policies and amend laws, and they tend to deny violations of international human rights standards.[45] The result of these criticisms is that constructive scrutiny by international bodies has been less than ideal.

Despite challenges and criticisms, the focus on treaty mechanisms also has been described as one of the most effective in the U.N. human rights system, as well as one of the most basic obligations under human rights treaties.[46] Self-reporting mechanisms actually serve a number of important objectives. First, self-reporting ensures that national legislation and administrative rules are reviewed so that they comply with the human rights treaty. Second, it ensures that the State Party regularly monitors specific human rights obligations. Third, it allows governments to demonstrate how they undertake policies designed to implement specific rights. Fourth, the reporting process allows scrutiny of governmental policies by domestic and international actors. Fifth, the reporting process gives the treaty body a means to evaluate State performance. This serves the State Party as it provides a means to identify goals and policy objectives. Sixth, by reviewing past policies and practices, States Parties can move toward a progressive realization of the full range of rights. Last, the process encourages a dialogue between States so that they (as well as activists and experts) may better understand common problems. Thus, even though fraught with potential problems, the focus on record keeping and reporting does advance human rights.

The strength of the treaty-based systems takes on renewed significance in light of the fifth mechanism at the disposal of human rights advocates: nongovernmental organizations. The formal U.N. legal framework of covenants and conventions provides a universal basis for appeal to human rights and an evolving set of mechanisms to track achievements and redress abuses. In enforcing those standards, nongovernmental organizations play an increasingly important role. Between the first World Conference on Human Rights in 1968 and the latest held in 1993, the number of organizations rose from 76 to nearly 2,500.[47] Under the umbrella of human rights law, nongovernmental organizations carry out human rights activities, especially human rights monitoring, human rights education, and grassroots appeals to redress specific instances of abuses, lobby governments, and build global networks. Actions of nongovernmental organizations have been critical in addressing gaps in enforcement and significant advocates in struggles that have not been priorities of governments.[48] Indeed, recent international treaties, such as the Children's Convention, formally allow for, and even rely on, nongovernmental organizations to be part of their enforcement machinery. The organizations have been enlisted for fact finding, reporting, and publicizing human rights abuses.[49] This development is of considerable significance. States are not the only parties responsible for the definition, implementation, and monitoring of human rights. Nongovernmental organizations have become major players in the national and international human rights systems, elevating themselves to a position from which to help enforce State's treaty obligations and actively negotiate with governments to formulate human rights.

In general, then, although international human rights standards have been proliferating, their enforcement mechanisms that would be seen as directly enforceable have tended to weaken. Shifts have been made toward other means to enforce human rights standards. Rather than relying on direct confrontation, human rights law relies on cooperative efforts and focuses on domestic activity.

Significance of Domestic Activity

Covenants and conventions become binding, contractual treaties with the authority of law when the necessary number of Nation States agree by their own free will to accept the international obligations. Such agreement typically first manifests itself by the signature of authorized representatives of States Parties to the agreement. Thereafter, ratification or accession in accordance with the basic law of each country is required, like the ratification required by two-thirds majority in the U.S. Senate. The second phase generally poses the most difficult and serious problems. At this stage, the influences of domestic politics play decisive roles. Struggles necessarily rage between competing interest groups. Likewise, some States do not ratify treaties unless or until their own laws already conform with the conditions of the international agreement, an approach that many accuse the United States of taking.[50]

Even though the international community plays an important role in reaching objectives, the rights are actually achieved through domestic activity, such as passing legislation and adopting policies that lead to the acceptance and enforcement of international standards. Definitions and terms for rights and freedoms are left purposefully vague so that national political culture can define actual standards to fit their own contexts. Several standards are left open to cultural interpretation and provide no precise prescriptions and proscriptions. Most notably, for example, numerous rights are left conditional; for example, human rights law conditions the fulfillment of economic rights on levels of national resources.[51] Indeed, the definition of *progress* to ensure human rights, an obligation that all Nations must accept, remains largely vague, uninterpreted, and difficult to enforce directly.

Although seemingly fatal to any legal enterprise, such vagueness actually advances modern human rights law making and progress toward fulfilling human rights goals. The most critical advantage of the focus on domestic activity to deal with vague wordings and minimal standards is that States can endorse human rights even when they lack consensus on some specific measures or values. For example, Article 1 of the Children's Convention defines *child* as "every human being below the age of 18 years unless, under the law applicable to the child, majority is attained earlier." This allows States freedom to define fetuses as children or nonchildren, which allows States to bypass controversial issues regarding abortion—a critical point given that religion, science, and the law have contradictory understandings of life's beginnings.[52] The definition further allows some children to be treated as adults, so long as the State law treats them as adults, which permits States to bypass controversial issues regarding the punishment of children by transferring them to adult court. States clearly are more likely to accept human rights institutions and to endorse treaties when the language of obligations are left imprecise and open to interpretation. It is at this critical juncture that cultural life gains relevance and significance to efforts to foster human rights—cultural values influence definitions of what constitutes human rights violations and the extent to which human rights law may be used to address human rights violations. The next section elaborates on the fundamental role cultures play in the definition, monitoring, and acceptance of human rights.

Culture's Role in Interpreting and Applying Human Rights Law

The above analysis proposes that respect for international human rights standards becomes most potent when standards relate directly to, and where possible are promoted through, local cultural institutions. Thus, although the subjects of international law are States and the U.N. apparatus of international treaties serves to implement human rights, the notion of human rights must appeal to every individual and organ of society. Emphasis on local applications holds special promise for efforts to address family violence. The analysis offered in chapters 2 and 3 reveals the need to consider the cultural roots of family violence, an analysis that parallels our understanding of human rights: Increases in protections from family violence and applications of basic human rights principles both depend on changes in cultural life. This section examines the role cultures play in interpreting and applying human rights law to reveal the relationships between local concepts and practices to international norms and the ways local actors may draw on the international framework to promote human rights in local contexts. At its core, the discussion emphasizes the need to recognize the transformative power of human rights law and the pivotal role that cultural factors alone can play in ensuring the relevancy and legitimacy of human rights laws.

Local Sources of Human Rights Law

Human rights emerge from local contexts. Although human rights law may derive from universal norms, universal norms still must be applied situationally. To be truly universal, human rights must be grounded in the moralities, ideas, and practices of human beings in cultural communities. Although human rights are often construed as top-down international legal efforts, advocates appropriately emphasize the dynamic nature of these rights. To be effective, human rights principles must relate to and address the concerns of local cultures and communities, be negotiable and flexible, and appeal to cultural rules and contexts at all social levels.

The focus on context and peculiar situations is not foreign to understandings of how laws become defined. Normative interpretation of any legal rule must be situational.[53] For example, practitioners necessarily balance formal legal rules with situations through their own acts of interpretation, a process highlighted by numerous commentaries concerned with the interpretations of statutes to find various meanings in law.[54] Differences in interpretations reveal how practitioners work in realms where all situational influences interweave. Interpreting the meaning of laws involves considering personal, legal, political, and other cultural domains. Norms come into existence only within these networks of factors and forces. The inherent localism of law even reflects itself at the international level. States and local jurisdictions actually make international law; for example, States engage in international policy making when they decide the terms to which they commit themselves.[55] Like any law, then, human rights law is and must be negotiated locally.

The common conception of how law functions provides only a limited view of local interpretations and applications of human rights. Human rights law operates at several critical yet related levels, all of which play crucial roles in the need to resolve deeply rooted cultural disputes. Rights need not be judicially or administratively enforceable, a point recognized by international treaties like the Children's Convention, which (in Article 4) bluntly requires States Parties to "undertake all appropriate legislative, administrative, and other measures, for the implementation of the rights recognized." In addition, rights may still be rights even though their violations may not be realistically redressable by judges and other State officials: Courts may lack the tools for successful implementation; judicial efforts may be futile or counterproductive; and courts can effect significant social reform only under a set of very narrow and special conditions.[56] Indeed, there are good reasons why courts should be modest in their interpretations of legal texts and the creation of new rights—most notably, courts are ill-suited policy makers and their roles involve interpreting, not making, laws.[57] In terms of international law, recognition of the need to look outside of the legal system is highlighted by the enforcement of treaties. In the enforcement of human rights, the United Nations created the position High Commissioner for Human Rights. The High Commissioner was not charged by the international community to play the role of chief prosecutor, but rather to use political and diplomatic channels to ensure a continuous dialogue to enhance human rights.[58] The Commissioner adopts a cooperative, inclusive, and comprehensive approach. This approach is critical because treaties frequently lack petitioning mechanisms. The Children's Convention relies on reports, record-keeping, and more cooperative approaches to ensuring that States follow the international community's mandates. Like the High Commissioner, conventions that follow the standard international law practice aim to be supportive and to provide educational efforts and information exchanges. Again, the focus is on local interpretation and local application.

The focus on local application of human rights principles also derives from the consent-based manner in which international law operates. With few exceptions, human rights law guarantees no direct enforceable mandates. In addition, States may withdraw from most rules of international law, and most international rules are intentionally written to allow for a maximum flexibility and relativity in interpretation. The flexibility and lack of enforcement is so pervasive that the international system often is described as international relations rather than international law because it lacks the main characteristics of legal systems—direct enforceability. Aside from extremes of military, trade, and political persuasion, the methods of enforcement reside in honor, public commitment, and accountability. States are autonomous and equal, and international laws are elastic.

Commentators often play down the significance of the cooperative and educational approach to enforcing international law. Although this reliance may seem to be a rather weak method of enforcement, it is a major weapon in struggles to ensure human rights. Human rights treaties seemingly function best indirectly—they offer norms that are comprehensive and flexible yet rigid enough to provide the international community some basis on which to constrain governments that circumvent internationally recognized standards. If nations fail to respect standards, the international community typically encourages, pushes, prods, and ultimately embarrasses States into taking steps to guarantee the proper implementation of rights.[59] In addition to foreign parties themselves, nongovernmental organizations increasingly grow in effectiveness. It is often through the expertise, recommendations, and lobbying of nongovernmental organizations that the United Nations and governments have become motivated to correct injustices, as exemplified by the movement to enact child labor laws and combat child sexual exploitation.[60] In addition, it remains difficult to underestimate the growing power of citizens to form local social movements that ultimately have global repercussions and even more difficult to ignore how charismatic individuals can play important roles at international policy-making levels, as exemplified by the former director of UNICEF and the current director of the Children's Defense Fund.[61] The extent to which human rights standards can influence States Parties' laws and policies depends on the extent to which governmental organizations, nongovernmental organizations, and individuals can be encouraged to support the human rights principles.

Local Application of Human Rights Law

Although human rights derive from local sources, human rights policy making, standard setting, and enforcement do not solely involve local endeavors. The application of human rights is best viewed as a *process* by which human rights law provides a common vocabulary that community members use to interpret and reinterpret their relationships with one another. Human rights, then, help people identify and resolve disputes as it provides mechanisms, and sometimes new languages, that seek to transform relationships. Such transformations begin with simple consciousness raising about alternatives. The human rights consciousness-raising vocabulary provides the base that helps mobilize cultural change, the already occurring processes that anthropological investigations so aptly have revealed in their conceptions of culture. Human rights law, then, can best be conceived and understood as a process, as part of the process through which cultures change. Like the cultures they imbue, the resolutions that human rights institute and reflect are never fixed. Law necessarily results from, and is on the edge of, a process of accommodation and competition among diverse interests, diverse groups, and diverse social needs and forces. This function allows individuals and groups to imagine and act in light of rights that have not been formally envisioned, recognized, or enforced. This level of rights formulation, the more transformative role of human rights law, plays a central role in the resolution of cultural disputes.

Human rights law progressively reforms the cultural structures in which it operates. That is what is meant, for example, when constitutions are referred to as *"living" documents* and when treaties are viewed as constitutional documents. That is, human rights consist largely of norms *de lege ferenda*, the law which ought to be made, as opposed to law which is already made (*lex lata*). Human rights law may be viewed as an autopoietic system that dynamically and imperceptibly spreads over interstices located between emerging social values and well-established legal rules. As a meaning-making and communicative system, the law produces norms of conduct both for its own operations and for society at large.[62]

The emergence of human rights law over local social values and local legal rules does not mean that modern human rights law does not contain universals. It is possible to acknowledge the impossibility of locating an objective source of justification while still arguing that efforts toward recognition and implementation should continue.[63] As currently conceived, for example, human rights focus on deliberation and the protection of deliberation.[64] This recognition necessarily serves as the foundation of human rights law: Given widespread social disagreements over what justice and rights require, human rights law must allow considerable scope for experimentation and debate. Human rights law seeks basic commitments to impartial deliberative principles that ensure the preconditions that allow for a process-perfecting, deliberative society. Through these commitments, societies help assure equal concern and respect for everyone alike. The law and its processes allow for deliberation about the justice of basic institutions and social policies and deliberation about how to live lives. Although the process historically concerned itself with political self-government,[65] it rests fundamentally on personal self-government (self-determination).[66]

The process of developing human rights necessarily deals with interpretive communities and places considerable faith in the power of discourse. Although international actors may bluntly demand rapid changes, such approaches contradict the principles that offer international law its legitimacy: respect for national, cultural, and personal sovereignty. That is the reason legitimate human rights law cannot operate counter to deeply held cultural values. (For example, the U.S. Supreme Court is necessarily "conservative" in that it tends to affirm and reflect pre-existing societal impulses, which provides a primary mechanism through which the court gains legitimacy.[67]) International law simply provides guiding principles that are used to rethink cultural values; it does not seek to directly supplant cultural forces. Concern for ensuring the consideration of children's interests provides a good example of how law aims to operate. The belief is that cultures change as they consider and reconsider children's interests.[68] In the transformation, the interpretations of law, the meaning that it develops, occurs inside and outside formal legal institutions.[69] Everyone engages in legal activity, not simply lawyers, judges, and those formally trained in law: Normative meanings are nurtured inside and outside of official legal culture. Through law and discourse about rights, people engage in meaning-making through communal narratives and summon a sense of potential community and transform personal relationships. That is the goal and operation of human rights law. Formal and informal human rights law flows into and filters the process of communication and meaning-making. Through this process of meaning-making, new rights emerge and gain legitimate authority. The law thus helps to create communities, to establish shared discourse, and to provide contexts for linking the past with the future, for bridging creativity and change with tradition. This conception of rights has been the one that has served as a motivational source of hope for the women's rights movement, as put by Williams: "It is the magic world of visibility and invisibility, of inclusion and exclusion, or power and no-power. The concept of rights, both positive and negative, is the marker of our citizenship, our 'participatoriness,' our relation to others."[70]

Human rights to a large extent involve visions that challenge the imagination, cause individuals to reexamine their assumptions, and often raise profound and disturbing questions about fundamental values. The ability of human rights to provoke discourse and pose difficult, thought- and conscience-provoking questions endows human rights with a power that encourages and enables; it forces people to test existing values, reexamine their assumptions, and sometimes change their minds. At their core, human rights are about consciousness-rising, stirring the conscience of humanity and changing patterns of thought. Human rights open for interrogation settled habits or representation of culture, humanity, and civilization; human rights make problematic that which was regarded as self-evident, natural, true, and just.

Significance of Local Interpretation and Application

Human rights law and the power of rights derive from the methods they provide for publicly resolving real and imagined (not yet publicly or privately accepted) injustices. Human rights simply allocate power to those who previously were ignored. Human rights aim to make interests visible, to include those who make claims into their communities, and to involve peoples' interests in communal debates; they assert and acknowledge membership. By doing so, human rights compel an equality of attention as they take aspirational language of society seriously and begin processes that promote and sustain change. Rights claims assert a right and thereby secure the attention of the community through transforming existing conflict. Because legal developments are processes by which meanings change, the critical role of participation again emerges as fundamental. Through participation, social actors may draw on law to claim self-determination and articulate new identities and knowledge. This is the most radical concept of international law ever imagined; it now even applies to children's rights that require the participation of children in determining their own lives.[71] In terms of violence and maltreatment, human rights law demands public debate about existing patterns of private power, aims to provide vulnerable individuals a public voice, and seeks to renegotiate relationships.

This resolution of the traditional dilemma facing universal laws and domestic application that rests on ensuring participation faces several challenges. The approach may be equally disturbing to champions of cultural diversity and cultural rights as well as to champions of universal rights. The former who resist change may find little solace in the proposition that all cultures are asked to adjust and accommodate, and they may find horror in the thought that ingrained social practices are doomed to disappear. The latter may reject the sluggish approach and argue for more immediate implementation. Yet international law necessarily mediates between the two extremes; it must work—deliberately, legitimately, and effectively. Participatory and cooperative transformation has become central to international law. Communities do not accept standards unless they have gained local legitimacy. Human rights gain their legitimacy from being rooted in the people, in humanity. The faith in discourse actually reflects what both historical and modern developments in international law are all about. The basic faith in human interactions characterized by visions of a humanity that champion equality, inclusion, and respect for human dignity forms the very foundation of human rights law. The democratic principles apply not only to what governments should strive for, but also to individuals in their everyday inter-actions.[72]

The focus on participation and voice gains considerable significance when jux-taposed to general understandings of family violence. Recall how cultures define, create, and prevent family violence. The public and private nature of violence can only be combated effectively by recognizing those who have been made vulnerable. That recognition only comes through deliberation and acceptance of an individual's worth—two fundamental principles of human rights laws. Although the human rights principles reflect what may be needed to address fundamentally cultural matters relating to family violence, it is important to understand why the human rights move-ment is of great significance to contemporary society and why it matters to modern cultural life.

Why Human Rights Law Must Matter to Changes in Cultural Life

Rapid global and cultural changes make pressing the recognition of human rights law. As demonstrated in previous chapters, family violence only can be alleviated through broad changes in cultural life that then impact personal relationships. The following highlights why human rights law must play a greater role in that trans-formation, regardless of the boundaries erected among nations, cultures, families, and individuals.

Human rights law must gain significance as the role of modern Nation States continues to decline. The declining power of modern States is marked by a concom-itant increase in roles for a new mix of actors, including international financial and development institutions, the private sector, regional and local governments, and individuals. In today's globalization, the actors involved are not only States but also transnational corporations and intergovernmental institutions. For example, more than half of the world's 100 biggest economies actually are corporations, not nations.[73] Thus, the heads of States may have much less impact on both individuals and on world events than those in charge of transnational corporations. These modern institutions differ in the scale and speed of their operations. The rush of products, ideas, people, and money transported and transformed with jet transportation, elec-tronic communication, extensive computerization, and massive decolonization offers a world that differs greatly from the flow of goods, capital, people, and ideas that existed even a decade ago. The result is that it is becoming increasingly difficult to identify the main actors responsible for policies and programs. This makes legal reformulations of protections more urgent so that individuals' fundamental needs are not at the mercy of changing programs and policies created and enforced by politically unaccountable actors.[74] The changes are significant: The right to participate in elections and influence decision makers gains recognition across the globe, but it provides rightsholders much less than it promises.

Human rights protections also become increasingly pressing as the breakdown of geographical and cultural ties that traditionally bound and protected individuals loosen traditional rights and attendant responsibilities. Research continues to indicate that rapid cultural changes exacerbate existing vulnerabilities and create the need to reconsider obligations. For example, migration patterns leave an ever-growing number of people alone with no family to offer care,[75] and once powerful institutions like religion can no longer be relied on to stay the process of disintegration of marriage and the family.[76] To be sure, cultural change does not necessarily lead to increases in family violence. Researchers note that social change has a variety of long- and short-term effects on family violence: It may increase or decrease its prevalence, alter its definitions, or change its forms.[77] Yet the possibility of contradictory consequences makes even more compelling human rights' activists admonitions that global societal transformations require a concept of human rights.

Increasing economic inequality, both across and within nations, further support the need to consider the role of human rights law. Two examples illustrate well how benefits of modernization do not accrue equally. Growing inequality between nations leads to the resurgence of "out-of-town brides" or "mail-order brides" from other countries.[78] Over the past two decades, the mail-order industry has served as a vehicle for marriage; Congress found that thousands of women are illegally transported to the United States facilitated by agencies that specialize in marketing available women to men.[79] Research reveals that such international marriages exacerbate gender inequalities and remove supports which, in turn, place women at a higher risk for spousal abuse and lack of recourse against abuses because they are married.[80] Growing inequality within States also has predictable outcomes. Research indicates that, despite increased general wealth in numerous nations, children within those nations increasingly suffer from poverty.[81] The phenomenon clearly affects family violence rates. Poverty of resources makes the development of programs difficult and exacerbates conditions that contribute to violence, such as lack of health and education programs.[82]

Human rights law also may alleviate the risks and opportunities for violence posed by new forms of technology. For example, research shows how modern transportation and advances in computer technology place children at greater risk for sexual maltreatment.[83] Research also suggests that even the most benign advances place certain individuals at greater risk for maltreatment. Medical breakthroughs lead to growth of an older population, which, in turn, places demands for family caregiving responsibilities that foster abusive environments.[84] Likewise, medical technology allows for saving the lives of fetuses that otherwise would not have survived, which places new groups of children at risk for maltreatment in their families and contributes to the foster care crisis.[85] Again, advances often have contradictory results that require new approaches to the protection of vulnerable groups.

The rapid transfer of capital, need to develop export markets, and search for inexpensive labor also play prominently in abuses that may only be controlled by international, global mechanisms. For example, child labor increases in many developing countries with the rising emphasis on the export market. The link remains especially troubling to the extent that it results from apparently benevolent efforts of the World Bank. Although the World Bank's development policies aim to further several economic and social rights such as health, education, housing, resettlement of peoples affected by development projects, gender issues, and environmental concerns,[86] evidence does suggest that structural adjustment programs mandated by the World Bank may have been partly responsible for increasing exploitative child labor.[87] Sweeping measures to curb inflation and encourage economic growth have caused new forms of poverty and new forms of labor, such as child sex tourism, which involves the travel of men from one country to another to benefit from unenforced laws and dire economic conditions, which allow them to engage in (and pay little for) sexual activity with minors.[88] Employers search for the cheapest, most docile workforce to stay competitive.[89] Child labor appropriately reveals how international causes cannot be immediately addressed by law and how the resulting abuses relate to numerous human rights violations. Prohibitive legislation, for example, has the ironic effect of making it more difficult to improve the working conditions of children who are not viewed by law as working: Children in informal sectors and on family-based subcontracting enterprises continue to work and do not legally exist to the extent that laws do not offer them as much protection as they would if they worked outside the direct supervision of their families.[90]

The examples above all reveal a need to consider how modern, global conditions affect the protection of individuals from violence. At this global level, human rights law has been most helpful as a model for developing effective strategies to deal with family violence. Arguably, the most important work in this area involves the need to recognize and respond to the limits of law because enforcement possibilities are limited in the context of international relations. Those who champion legal and legislative change realize that such change alone will not result in the necessary social change. The overall project of social change, that societal and individual internalization and understanding that family violence is not acceptable, is not achievable without greater consensus. This leads human rights organizations to focus on the need to monitor police officers, court cases, reporting of family violence, public and personal accountability, shaming, and other measures that move toward fundamental social changes. The recognition also leads human rights efforts to monitor and report outside of jurisdictions. The international community now recognizes some cultural practices of violence against vulnerable individuals as human rights violations and seeks to exert pressure on recalcitrant countries to ensure greater protection of the rights international law guarantees. Because cultural attitudes and norms are not merely superficial, but instead lie deep within the social fabric of a nation, change can occur only gradually. Only after cultural perspectives and values begin to change can any legal remedy make an impact. By fostering change, human rights efforts affect how all societies address family violence and move societies beyond cultural isolationism.

As societies consider, and are prodded to consider, the manner in which they must protect individuals from violence, they move toward universal protections from such violence. To move toward greater rights to awareness and respect, the human rights movement offers considerable force for change. Much of the power for reform derives from the transformative power of international tribunals, which have three interrelated advantages over other methods: pressure, publicity, and legitimacy. As discussed above, international law is frequently criticized as being unenforceable. However, the ability of international bodies to pressure States to uphold their inter-

national obligations should not be underestimated. Recommendations and judgments
from international bodies can apply much greater pressure than can be applied from
interest groups either within the State or internationally. This increased pressure is
due in large part to the greater publicity attached to an international forum. Tribunals
with the authority to deliver judgments have the greatest potential to pressure States
into compliance with international obligations. Several international human rights
treaties, for example, have monitoring bodies that require States Parties to write
regular reports detailing compliance, which places pressure on States to explain their
actions. Publicity of human rights issues increases pressure to comply with international obligations. Growing awareness legitimizes and popularizes human rights
issues. International human rights bodies have a high degree of legitimacy because
States have chosen to ratify these treaties that create bodies and the norms that they
apply. In contrast to unilaterally imposed sanctions, such as American trade legislation, the norms contained in widely ratified international instruments are associated
with a high degree of legitimacy, and States are more likely to comply with the
recommendations of judgments of such bodies if they have agreed to uphold such
norms. This is not to ignore the limitations of the international systems; it cannot
cure family violence, but it can legitimate human rights debates and provide tangible
examples of international human rights justice.

The example above reflects a final reason to consider the power of human rights
law. The notion of human rights gains new currency. Progress to recognize and
ensure human rights over the past half-century provides clear examples of the fundamental force of human rights. The notion of human rights spreads across the globe
with unprecedented velocity. Even the United States increasingly opens itself to
international human rights law. The United States recently ratified the Political Covenant and signed numerous human rights treaties including the most comprehensive
human rights treaty ever: the Children's Convention. These developments allow for
greater intrusion into what had been considered immune from outside intervention,
let alone formal international human rights intervention. Such developments are important to evaluate for two fundamental reasons. First, nations that ratify international
documents tend to take very narrow approaches that obfuscate the potential benefits
of ratification.[91] Second, commentaries play down the transformative role of human
rights law and also take narrow views of rights.[92] These reasons, coupled with those
enumerated above, support the view that a significant window of opportunity exists
to address problems associated with family life.

Conclusion

The sources of international human rights are broad, dynamic, and far reaching. Even
the most fundamental and directly enforceable sources of international law—treaties
—remain flexible. No general rule of international law requires treaties to have
specific legal effects in domestic law. The States Parties need only fulfill their obligations under the treaty by whatever means they choose. That flexibility is central
to developing local responses and fostering cultural change that would affect family
life.

In fostering cultural change through human rights, the dynamic, flexible view of
human rights suggests that attempts to conceive and enforce universal rights need

not inevitably be plagued by polarized debates between universalist and relativist resistance. Evolving conceptions of human rights and modern approaches to international human rights law now move toward resolution of potential cultural clashes and help resolve contentious issues that arise when efforts are made to implement universal human rights. Just as it would be erroneous to argue that international conceptions of human rights are not imperialistic, it is equally incorrect to propose that international law aims to inappropriately and decisively usurp cultural values. The nature of imperialism continues to change. Human rights law now allows for domestic or cultural differences in how individuals could be treated. To understand this point, it is important to recognize the diverse levels on which human rights operate. These levels have significant implications for the nature of respect accorded to cultural life. The different levels reveal how human rights must be interpreted and eventually applied and enforced locally, a point that highlights the significance of the more expansive, dynamic view of cultural life and human rights law.

In addition to how human rights law works, several other factors suggest a need to take human rights law seriously. The following factors all serve to highlight the need for a more global, universal approach to fostering human rights protections: breakdowns in geographical and cultural ties that traditionally bonded and protected individuals; increasing economic inequality, both across and within nations; intensifying debates about multiculturalism and the place of pluralism in multiethnic societies; increasing risks for violence posed by new forms of technology; spiraling migrations of culturally diverse peoples; and the increasing currency of human rights notions and the powerful insights and mandates they provide for societal transformation. The next chapter details the protection human rights law offers to address family violence.

Endnotes

1. *See* C. Geertz, "Distinguished Lecture: Anti-Anti-Relativism," *American Anthropologist* 86 (1984):263–278.
2. J. A. M. Cobbah, "African Values and the Human Rights Debate: An African Perspective," *Human Rights Quarterly* 9 (1987):309–331.
3. Universal Declaration of Human Rights, U.N. General Assembly, 3rd Sess., Official Records, *Part I. Resolutions,* Resolution 217A, U.N. Doc A/810, 1948.
4. Vienna Declaration and Programme of Action, 1993 World Conference on Human Rights, U.S. Doc. A/Conf. 157/24, 1993.
5. Children's Convention, U.N. General Assembly, 44th Sess., Official Records, Supp. 49 at 166, Resolution 44/25, A/44/49; 28 ILM 1448, 1989.
6. *Id.,* Article 31.
7. *See* A. Dirlik, "Culturalism as Hegemonic Ideology and Liberating Practice," *Culture Critique: The Nature & Context of Minority Discourse* 6 (1987):13–50.
8. E. Hobsbawn and T. Ranger, Eds., *The Invention of Tradition* (New York: Cambridge University Press, 1992).
9. Women's Convention, U.N. General Assembly, 34th Sess., Official Records, Supp. 46 at 193, GA Resolution 34/180, A/34/46, 1979.
10. *See* Universal Declaration of Human Rights, Preamble; Children's Convention, Article 42.
11. C. Tomuschat, Ed., *Modern Law of Self-Determination* (Boston: Martinus Nijhoff, 1993).
12. J. Crawford, *The Rights of People* (New York: Oxford University Press, 1992); S. J.

Anaya, *Indigenous Peoples in International Law* (New York: Oxford University Press, 1996).

13. Political Covenant, U.N. General Assembly, 21st Sess., Official Records, Supp. 16 at 49, GA Resolution 2200, A/6316; 999 UNTS 171; 6 ILM 368, 1966.

14. Economic and Social Covenant, U.N. General Assembly, 21st Sess., Official Records, Supp. 16 at 49, GA Resolution 2200 Annex, A/6316; 993 UNTS 3; 6 ILM 360, 1966.

15. United Nations Charter, 1 UNTS xvi, 1945 (emphasis added).

16. Children's Convention, Articles 3, 9, 20, 21, and 40.

17. *Id.*, Articles 5, 12, 14, and 40.

18. *Id.*, Article 2 and Preamble.

19. *Id.*, Articles 21, 28, 39, 40, and Preamble.

20. Declaration on the Elimination of Violence Against Women, U.N. General Assembly, 48th Sess., Official Records, GA Resolution 04, Agenda Item 11, A/RES/48/104, 1994.

21. For a review, *see* D. J. Sullivan, "Gender Equality and Religious Freedom: Toward a Framework for Conflict Resolution," *New York University International Journal of Law & Policy* 24 (1992):795–856.

22. R. H. Bellah, W. M. Sullivan, A. Swindler, and S. M. Tipton, *Habits of the Heart: Individualism and Commitment in American Life* (New York: Harper & Row, 1985) at 65.

23. C. Gilligan, *In a Different Voice* (Cambridge, MA: Harvard University Press, 1982).

24. S. H. Williams, "A Feminist Reassessment of Civil Society," *Indiana Law Journal* 72 (1997):416–447.

25. U. Baxi, "Voices of Suffering and the Future of Human Rights," *Transnational Law & Contemporary Problems* 8 (1998):125–169.

26. *See* J. W. Nickel, *Making Sense of Human Rights: Philosophical Reflection on the Universal Declaration of Human Rights* (Berkeley: University of California Press, 1987).

27. For a review, *see* P. G. Lauren, *The Evolution of International Human Rights: Visions Seen* (Philadelphia: University of Pennsylvania Press, 1998).

28. *See, e.g.*, A. D. Renteln, *International Human Rights: Universalism Versus Relativism* (Newbury Park, CA: Sage, 1990).

29. L. M. Friedman, "Borders: On the Emerging Sociology of Transnational Law," *Stanford Journal of International Law* 32 (1996):65–90.

30. V. S. Vereshchetin, "New Constitutions and the Old Problem of the Relationship Between International and National Law," *European Journal of International Law* 7 (1996):29–41.

31. A. Slaughter, "International Law in a World of Liberal States," *European Journal of International Law* 6 (1995):503–538.

32. M. D. Sahlins, "Evolution: Specific and General," in *Evolution and Culture*, M. D. Sahlins and E. R. Service, Eds. (Ann Arbor: University of Michigan Press, 1960).

33. *See* Edgerton (1992).

34. R. J. R. Levesque, "Prosecuting Sex Crimes Against Children: Time for 'Outrageous' Proposals?" *Law & Psychology Review* 19 (1995):59–91.

35. R. J. R. Levesque, "International Children's Rights: Can They Make a Difference in American Family Policy?" *American Psychologist* 51 (1996):1251–1256.

36. *See, e.g.*, C. J. Black, Jr., *A New Birth of Freedom: Human Rights, Named and Unnamed* (New York: Grosset/Putnam, 1997).

37. S. George, "The Structure of Dominance in the International Geo-Economic System and the Prospects for Human Rights Realization," in *Human Rights in Perspective: A Global Assessment*, A Eide and B. Hagtvet, Eds. (Oxford, England: Blackwell, 1992).

38. D. Gillies, *Between Principle and Practice: Human Rights in North–South Relations* (Montreal, Quebec, Canada: McGill–Queen's University Press, 1996); *see* also chapter 4.

39. H. J. Steiner and P. Alston, *International Human Rights in Context* (New York: Oxford University Press, 1996).
40. *See* F. Newman & D. Weissbrodt, *International Human Rights: Law, Policy and Process* (Cincinnati, OH: Anderson, 1996).
41. *See* P. Parker and D. Weissbrodt, "Major Developments at the UN Commission on Human Rights in 1991," *Human Rights Quarterly* 13 (1991):573–626.
42. Convention on the Elimination of All Forms of Racial Discrimination (*opened for signature* Mar. 7, 1966), 600 U.N.T.S. 195.
43. Convention Against Torture and Other Cruel, Inhuman or Degrading Treatment or Punishment, *opened for signature* Dec. 10, 1984, Annex G.A. Res. 46, *as modified,* 24 I.L.M. 535 (1985)
44. *See* Steiner and Alston, *International Human Rights in Context.*
45. A. F. Bayefsky, "Implementing Human Rights Treaties," *Proceedings of the American Society of International Law* 88 (1994):428–436.
46. Y. Dinsten, "Human Rights: Implementation Through the U.N. System," *Proceedings of the American Society of International Law* 89 (1995):242–247.
47. Gillies, *Between Principle and Practice.*
48. *See* A. Afsharipour, "Empowering Ourselves: The Role of Women's NGOs in the Enforcement of the Women's Convention," *Columbia Law Review* 99 (1999):129–172.
49. Children's Convention, Article 45.
50. *See* chapter 6.
51. *See* P. Alston, "U.S. Ratification of the Covenant on Economic, Social and Cultural Rights: The Need for an Entirely New Strategy," *American Journal of International Law* 84 (1990):365–393.
52. For an insightful review, *see* E. Spahn and B. Andrade, "Mis-Conceptions: The Moment of Conception in Religion, Science, and the Law," *University of San Francisco Law Review* 32 (1998):261–333.
53. O. Korhonen, "New International Law: Silence, Defense, or Deliverance?' *European Journal of International Law* 7 (1996):1–28.
54. *See, e.g.,* R. Colinvaux, "What Is Law? A Search for Legal Meaning and Good Judging Under a Textualist Lens," *Indiana Law Journal* 72 (1997):1133–1163.
55. J. Frankel, *International Relations in a Changing World* 4th ed. (New York: Oxford University Press, 1988).
56. G. N. Rosenberg, *The Hollow Hope: Can Courts Bring About Social Change?* (Chicago: University of Chicago Press, 1992).
57. *See, e.g.,* R. George, "Law, Democracy, and Moral Disagreement," *Harvard Law Review* 110 (1997):1388–1406.
58. *See* J. Ayala-Lasso, "Making Human Rights a Reality in the Twenty-First Century," *Emory International Law Review* 10 (1996):497–508.
59. J. W. Nickel, "How Human Rights Generate Duties to Protect and Provide," *Human Rights Quarterly* 15 (1993):77–86.
60. Levesque, "International Children's Rights"; P. Willetts, Ed., *The Conscience of the World: The Influence of Non-Governmental Organizations in the UN System* (Washington, DC: Brookings, 1996).
61. Levesque, "International Children's Rights."
62. *See* G. Teubner, *Law as an Autopoietic System* (Cambridge, MA: Blackwell, 1993).
63. *See* J. Goerecki, *Justifying Ethics: Human Rights and Human Nature* (New Brunswick, NJ: Transaction, 1996).
64. R. J. R. Levesque, "Piercing the Family's Private Veil: Family Violence, International Human Rights, and the Cross-Cultural Record," *Law & Policy* 21 (1999):161–187.
65. M. Sellers, "Republican Principles in International Law," *Connecticut Journal of International Law* 11 (1994):403–432.

66. Levesque, "Piercing the Family's Private Veil."
67. *See, e.g.*, Thomas R. Marshall, "Public Opinion, Representation, and the Moderate Supreme Court," *American Politics Quarterly* 16 (1988):296–316.
68. R. J. R. Levesque, "The Failures of Foster Care Reform: Revolutionizing the Most Radical Blueprint," *Maryland Journal of Contemporary Legal Issues* 6 (1995):1–35.
69. For a parallel analysis, *see* R. Cover, "The Supreme Court, 1982 Term—Forward: Nomos and Narrative," *Harvard Law Review* 97 (1983):44–68.
70. P. J. Williams, "Alchemical Notes: Reconstructing Ideals From Deconstructed Rights," *Harvard Civil Rights–Civil Liberties Law Review* 22 (1987):431.
71. Levesque, "International Children's Rights."
72. Levesque, "Piercing the Family's Private Veil."
73. R. McCorquodale and R. Fairborther, "Globalization and Human Rights," *Human Rights Law Quarterly* 21 (1999):735–766.
74. *See* E. Bevenisti, "Exit and Voice in the Age of Globalization," *Michigan Law Review* 98 (1999):167–213.
75. A. Y. Kwan, "Elder Abuse in Hong Kong: A New Family Problem for the Old East?" in *Elder Abuse: International and Cross-Cultural Perspectives*, J. I. Kosberg and Juanita L. Garcia, Eds. (New York: Haworth Press, 1995).
76. K. Tout, *Ageing in Developing Countries* (New York: Oxford University Press, 1989).
77. *Cf.* R. Morley, "Wife Beating and Modernization: The Case of Papua New Guinea," *Journal of Comparative Family Studies* 25 (1994):25–52.
78. D. R. Lee, "Mail Fantasy: Global Sexual Exploitation in the Mail-Order Bride Industry and Proposed Legal Solutions," *Asian Law Journal* 5 (1998):139–179.
79. *Id.*
80. K. L. Chin, "Out-of-Town Brides: International Marriage and Wife Abuse Among Chinese Immigrants," *Journal of Comparative Family Studies* 25 (1994):53–69; Lee, "Mail Fantasy."
81. G. B. Sgritta, "Inconsistencies: Childhood on the Economic and Political Agenda," *Childhood: A Global Journal of Child Research* 4 (1997):375–404.
82. J. Garbarino, "The Role of Economic Deprivation in the Social Context of Child Maltreatment," in *The Battered Child* 5th ed., M. E. Helfer, R. S. Kempe, and R. D. Krugman, Eds. (Chicago: University of Chicago Press, 1997).
83. R. J. R. Levesque, *Child Sexual Abuse: A Human Rights Perspective* (Bloomington: Indiana University Press, 1999).
84. J. I. Kosberg and J. L. Garcia, "Common and Unique Themes on Elder Abuse From a World-Wide Perspective," in *Elder Abuse: International and Cross-Cultural Perspectives*, J. I. Kosberg and J. L. Garcia, Eds. (New York: Haworth Press, 1995).
85. Levesque, "The Failures of Foster Care Reform."
86. *See* M. E. Wadrzyk, "Is It Appropriate for the World Bank to Promote Democratic Standards in a Borrower Country?" *Wisconsin International Law Journal* 17 (1999):553–578.
87. *See* C. Grootaert and H. A. Patrinos, Eds., *The Policy Analysis of Child Labor: A Comparative Study* (New York: St. Martin's Press, 1999).
88. V. Muntarbhorn, *Sale of Children, Child Prostitution and Child Pornography*. E/CN. 4/1994/84 (1994).
89. J. Bol, "Using International Law to Fight Child Labor: A Case Study of Guatemala and the Inter-American System," *American University International Law Review* 13 (1998): 1135–1223.
90. C. Grootaert and R. Kanbur, "Child Labor: An Economic Perspective," *International Labor Review* 134 (1995):187–203.
91. Levesque, "International Children's Rights."
92. *Id.*

Chapter 5
REACHING FAMILY VIOLENCE THROUGH
HUMAN RIGHTS LAW

Human rights law now includes mandates that reach family life, seek to regulate family relationships, and even seek to reform cultural practices that contribute to human rights violations. Still undetermined, however, is the way in which international law actually will reach into societies and affect human rights violations. Considerable debate surrounds the legitimate role international law can play in alleviating human rights violations. Commentators adopt rather different visions of the nature of human rights law—what it is and what it can do—and the extent to which human rights law legitimately may affect the internal workings of societies, cultures, and families. These visions are important to understand because they suggest different implications for addressing family violence, even though most commentators who theorize about the role of international law completely ignore family violence.

Although the numerous visions of the nature of modern human rights law defy strict categorization, for purposes of exposition it makes sense to view these visions as espousing three fundamentally different perspectives of who and what falls under the control of international law and the nature of their obligations. The traditional model envisions international law as regulating interstate behavior; the focus centers on how nations treat one another. This narrow approach tightly restricts the ambit of possible violations of international law and places obligations on States.[1] Another model proposes that international law holds nations accountable for violations within their own borders.[2] This model is exemplified most notably by international developments in human rights law that focus on the extent to which States respect the fundamental rights of its prisoners and political dissidents.[3] A more recent model— undoubtedly the most radical of the three—focuses on the extent to which any State may be accountable to the international community for its own citizens' actions, regardless of whether the citizens act on behalf of the particular State.[4] The approach also focuses on the extent to which social institutions other than the State's political subdivisions and individuals may be held accountable under human rights law.[5]

The three models pose different implications for the extent to which family life, regardless of whether it is viewed as primarily private or public, falls under international standards. The point is significant and challenges the reasons for ignoring human rights law in analyses of family violence. It is rather important to note that none of the models necessarily supports the claim that human rights law must stay out of family violence. On the contrary, each provides different methods to approach family violence and offers different human rights standards that may be used to address family violence.

Protection From and Right to Internation Actions

The classical approach to international law, which predates the foundation of the United Nations, holds that international law functions between Nation States.[6] This "statist" approach conceives of international law as primarily concerned with inter-nation actions conceived as public international law, not necessarily intranational actions and the actions of individuals within those nations, which fall under the jurisdiction of domestic or municipal law.

Even a cursory look at international documents reveals considerable continued support for this approach to international human rights law. Interventions in the domestic affairs of a nation, whether forcible or nonforcible, violate the mandate set forth in the document that serves to bind the international community together, the United Nations Charter of 1945.[7] The charter distinguishes between the public do-main of international law and the private sphere of domestic jurisdiction for the purpose of protecting the latter from international intrusion. Article 2(7) of the charter finds that

> nothing contained in the present Charter shall authorize the United Nations to inter-vene in matters which are essentially within the domestic jurisdiction of any States or shall require the Members to submit such matters to settlement under the present Charter.

The United Nations later codified the Nation States' and their peoples' right of self-determination as a human right in Article 1 of both the Political Covenant of 1966[8] and the Economic and Social Covenant of 1966.[9] Article 1 states, "all peoples have the right of self-determination. By virtue of that right they freely determine their political status and freely pursue their economic, social, and cultural develop-ment." In addition, the Declaration on Friendly Relations of 1970 provides that "by virtue of the principle of equal rights and self-determination. . . . All peoples have the right to determine, without external interference, their political status. . . . And every state has the duty to respect this right."[10] The general rule, then, is that States remain free to determine their internal political structures and pursue their own social, economic, and cultural life. The extent to which the general rule continues finds clear expression in modern international law's practice of treaty making that aims to bind nations as States Parties and not as non-State entities.

The approach that views States as subjects of international law and individuals as merely its objects has not been associated with human rights protections.[11] Under this approach, the limited extent to which individuals enjoy international law's ben-efits depends on whether they belong to a particular State. Although the noninter-ventionist approach undoubtedly continues in full force, evidence may be marshaled against the doctrine that international law is exclusively a law between States. The extent to which human rights protections within countries constitute international matters generally rests on three arguments.

The first argument suggests that domestic human rights practices actually are international matters because the U.N. Charter mandates progress toward human rights protections. Among the purposes of the United Nations, the charter's Article 1 lists the promotion of respect for human rights. Article 55 similarly provides that "the United Nations shall promote . . . universal respect for, and observance of, human rights and fundamental freedoms." Furthermore, Article 56 calls on all mem-ber States to support the United Nations in achieving these goals. Consequently, human rights are not a matter of domestic jurisdiction; they are matters governed by international law. Thus, efforts to bring about compliance with human rights obli-gations are not improper interferences in domestic affairs. In fact, the Article 56 pledge constitutes an affirmative obligation to promote human rights, an obligation that does not leave a State free to suppress or even remain indifferent to those rights. Member States, then, must not put themselves in the position of being incapable of cooperating because this would undermine the object and purpose of the charter. Although the language is at once directly binding and aspirational, both qualities demand that member States take no action to prevent or undermine the development and understanding of human rights in accordance with the charter. A twofold duty —to cooperate and not undermine—exists for each U.N. member, regardless of whether it is a party to any other human rights treaty and regardless of whether the rights in question deal with a State's internal affairs.[12]

A second argument proposes that at the time the U.N. Charter was ratified, concepts that were governed by international law were recognized to be *ipso facto* and by definition outside of the realm of domestic jurisdiction. This argument suggests that human rights were part of the charter's focus and thus remain an appropriate area to intervene in any other country's domestic domain.[13] The growing number of treaties devoted to human rights reinforces the point that the international community's interest in human rights goes beyond State jurisdiction.

The third and equally persuasive argument holds that, even if traditional law considered human rights a domestic issue and even if the human rights documents focused only on international concerns, recent actions by the United Nations and its member States recognize that compliance with basic human rights standards no longer can be considered a matter of domestic jurisdiction. This argument rests on the practice of nations since the adoption of the charter. Countries have acted in manners that, in effect, have nullified the edict of Article 2(7). Although such deviations from the charter do not alter its legal character, the persistent pattern inconsistent with the norm undermines the hypothesis that nations consider themselves under a legal obligation to comply with its article's directive.[14] Thus, for example, small and large countries do not follow the principle of nonintervention: Political and financial intervention, overt and covert, has been used to affect the domestic policies of other countries, including that of the superpowers.[15] Other interventions, described in greater detail below, involve direct attempts to combat human rights violations, such as resolutions to assist the oppressed Kurdish and Shiite populations in Iraq and to protect food distribution in Somalia.[16] In general, then, the international community may formally limit itself to a *droit de regard*: a right to monitor and encourage from the outside the protection of those rights within nonconsenting States. Despite that tendency, State practices actually reveal support for intervention in the internal affairs of rogue nations.

Despite arguments that allow for intervention in domestic matters, the traditional model of international human rights law has not offered much hope to those who champion a human right to protection from family violence. The traditional model of international law remains ignored in discussions of protections from family violence for reasons that are understandable. It remains difficult to argue that international law provides directly enforceable mandates that broadly regulate behaviors of those who engage in or respond to family violence. Yet given the insight gained from the cross-cultural record relating to family violence, it becomes difficult to underestimate the significance of international law's concern with State actions. International law, even narrowly conceived as applicable only to interstate actions, can alleviate family violence generally construed as being out of the reach of traditional international law. A close look at existing internation actions and international legal developments reveals numerous examples of international law's effect on family violence. The most notable examples undoubtedly involve international law's influence on broad sociopolitical forces that involve direct intervention to protect citizens in other countries and humanitarian efforts to admit individuals to countries that protect resident aliens.

Right to Development

Although one may argue that international law does not forcefully affect the internal dynamics of other countries, a most prominent and far-reaching example of such intrusions involves the obligations of countries to foster the right to development. From its inception, the United Nations has placed a high degree of importance on international economic regulations and the promotion of economic development of its member States. Article 55 of the U.N. Charter states that the United Nations shall promote "higher standards of living, full employment, and conditions of economic and social progress and development . . . [and] solutions of international economic . . . problems." Although the United Nations conceived this function as part of the responsibility of the Economic and Social Council (as stated in Article 60), pressure from developing countries resulted in transferring power to other agencies and institutions and to creating institutions with sizable capital bases to assist developing countries.[17] The effort resulted in the now well-recognized power of the International Monetary Fund (IMF) and World Bank as well as treaties that govern international trade (e.g., General Agreement on Tariffs and Trade) in certain spheres of activity.

The result of these activities now means that the United Nations occupies two important and interrelated roles. The first, more operational, role involves the U.N.'s direct impact on economic affairs through loans, technical assistance, donor consortia, and information dissemination. The second role, one of rule-making, involves the establishment of regimes to regulate economic behavior. Recipient countries must often change, for example, from communal approaches to dealing with property to using a property, individual-based approach to rights. The effects of that transformation reverberate. Both roles affect how nations contribute or respond to family violence.

The creation of institutions and treaties that govern trade affects cultural life—and thus, may affect family violence—in numerous and far-reaching ways. The pervasive effect is reflected in the numerous and extended criticisms related to the development policies adopted by specialized agencies that determine basic governmental policies of the States that make use of its resources.[18] The criticisms reflect more than the extent to which international efforts may be justified to the degree that they impose "shock therapy" on several societies.[19] The concerns also reflect how international mandates powerfully affect levels of poverty.[20] For example, the IMF and World Bank encourage recipient States to adopt certain policies regarding the extent to which nations provide educational and other social services to its citizens. The power to determine what citizens receive from their own social institutions results in the power to determine responses to family violence.

Poverty places stresses on societies that in turn place individuals at risk for maltreatment. For example, the policies of the World Bank, which encourage rapid development, have been implicated in sex tourism and the extent to which poor families place their children into the sex trade, especially in South American and Asia.[21] Likewise, poverty also has been implicated in the extent to which family members willingly "consent" to be involved in the sex trade or other forms of hazardous labors so as to support their families. In addition, the resources available to women trapped in violence relate directly to economic conditions. Reduced economic opportunities limit women's access to (or the option for) gainful employment, which affects their risk for victimization inside the home. Victimization then, in turn, affects women's ability to access social support and material resources needed to seek gainful employment; even attempts to gain those supports and resources increase the likelihood of domestic violence.[22]

The policies not only place individuals at risk for maltreatment but also relate to the availability of resources for services. As discussed in chapters 1 and 2, lack of social services for victims of maltreatment figures prominently in discussions of developing countries' failure to develop child protective systems and protect children from violence in their homes. International economic policies, however, do much more than affect available social services; they affect levels of unemployment, underemployment, malnutrition, and child survival. Responses to IMF recommendations for structural adjustments, for example, have led to food shortages and increased health risks for women and children.[23] Thus, by affecting poverty and broad social conditions, international law affects the nature, causes, and consequences of family violence.

Rights of Aliens

Another significant example of how international law may affect violence involves how the international community responds to wars, famines, and other domestic crises that place stresses on families.[24] The most frequently cited example involves the international standards of justice that make States responsible for the treatment of aliens within their borders, such as how countries treat refugees and those involved in asylum and extradition efforts.[25] Concern with foreigners reflects the traditional international law's focus on ensuring that governments' respect the rights of nonnational subjects and that they appropriately deal with the possessions of other countries.

Since 1951, the Office of the United Nations High Commissioner for Refugees has been responsible for protecting refugees and promoting lasting solutions to their problems. The commission derives this mandate from the convention relating to the Status of Refugees of 1950[26] (Refugee Convention), which provides the governing legal standard to define and enforce the legal status, rights, and obligations of refugees. The convention reflects traditional concerns as it calls on nations to prevent refugee crises from becoming a cause of international tension and to seek solutions through international cooperation.

To achieve its goals, the Refugee Convention (and later interpretations and additions to its mandates by Nation States) takes two stances. The first stance involves the treatment of individuals outside of their countries of origin. Once individuals are outside the country of their nationalities, the convention seeks to ensure that host countries address the particular needs and situations of those who qualify for refugee status. The convention then proceeds to define who is (and who is not) a refugee and to define the legal status of refugees and their rights and duties in their country of refuge. The treaty seeks to protect any person who "owing to a well-founded fear of being persecuted for reasons of race, religion, nationality, membership of a particular social group or political opinion . . . is unwilling to avail himself of the protection of that country . . . or return to it."[27] The second stance involves prevention of migration movements and the root causes of refugee crises. This latter approach, often ignored in analyses of refugee law, adopts a rather significant stance that aims to prevent refugee migrations in the first instance.

These two positions considerably affect the levels of violence families may encounter. When the convention was adopted, migration was considered as a given, so international law focused on actions and obligations of receiving States and international institutions. It was only in the 1970s and 1980s that the world community began to deal with early warnings of refugee flows and other possible humanitarian crises.[28] The most notable and swiftly implemented examples involved the protection of Kurds through special protected zones in Iraq and the creation of "safe areas" to protect Bosnian refugees inside Bosnia rather than resettlement in other countries. Although these provide important examples of intervention in other countries' domestic activities, it is important not to ignore that the humanitarian efforts were adopted in an atmosphere of caution and governmental concern about the prerogatives of sovereignty. Yet the efforts clearly do represent persistent and creative interpretations and implementation of international instruments beyond the scope originally envisioned by the international community and its treaties. A more controversial example of human rights protections under this model involves the international community's reservation of the right to humanitarian intervention if a State "shocks the conscience of mankind" in the way it treats its own nationals. Although the principle may seem to be an obvious part of international law, it still meets considerable opposition. Resistance to the principle finds support in part through the U.N. Charter, which prohibits the unilateral use of force in Article 2(4), and through international law's continued emphasis on respect for State sovereignty.

Although the focus on preventing refugee crises is gaining new momentum, concerns for refugees still predominantly involve the extent to which aliens may qualify for refugee status and may be allowed to remain in host countries. In this regard, the most notable example of how international law may affect family violence involves female genital circumcision and the extent to which it can serve as a grounds to obtain asylum.[29] The traditional definition of *refugee* adopted by the Refugee Convention did not include women as a protected class when it described qualifying refugees. Under this approach, claimants must satisfy two criteria. First, claimants must have a well-founded fear of persecution. Second, the fear must be based on membership in a particular social group. In cases of genital circumcision, a finding of refugee status would depend on the characterization or recognition of the circumcision as a form of gender-based persecution, which the United Nations recently recognized. The recognition has come in two parts that address the two components of the traditional definition of refugee. Claims of gender-based plight gained legitimacy in 1985 when the High Commission of Refugees commented that "women who face harsh or inhuman treatment due to their having transgressed the social mores of the society in which they live may be considered as a 'particular social group'" within the meaning of the convention.[30] Recognition that genital operations could lead to persecution of the "particular social group" came in 1993, when the High Commission for Refugees recognized sexual violence, including "female genital mutilation," as persecution.[31] Although the commission has not gone beyond making recommendations, these recent developments reflect a change in immigration regulation that permits some women to gain asylum to protect themselves or their children from persecution that would ensue from practices involving female circumcision.

Although developments have been rapid, they should not lead to the conclusion that human rights efforts have reached effectiveness. Efforts since the initial definition have aimed to include protections from genital operations, but protections have been difficult to obtain. Few asylum cases actually have been granted on the grounds of genital circumcision.[32] Reviewers report that no petitioner has been granted asylum in France, which was the first country to establish that the threat of genital mutilation was sufficient grounds to grant women refugee status; Canada, which pioneered guidelines expanding the basis of refugee claims to include gender-based persecution, granted asylum to one petitioner; and the United States, which only recently reformed its laws, granted asylum to two petitioners.[33]

Those seeking asylum encounter two difficulties. They must produce evidence to prove persecution or fears of persecution. Claimants may not want to discuss the topic in public forums; physical evidence may not be obtained if the claimant has not undergone the procedure; evidence of similarly situated and persecuted women from the country of origin may be difficult to obtain yet required to comply with the "particular social group" requirement.[34] The second difficulty, which has been made somewhat less difficult with recent developments, involves the inability of claimants to avail themselves of protections in their own countries. This difficulty arises from the need to show a State connection and demonstrate that authorities tolerate the conduct in question or that they refuse or are unable to offer effective protection.[35] The two limitations illustrate how laws aimed to condemn cultural practices remain difficult to implement.

Preliminary Conclusion

International law's impact on broad political, economic, and social forces in other countries serves as an example of several key points in efforts to combat family violence through the use of international law construed in the most narrow, traditional sense. First, the understanding of international human rights narrowly conceived as laws that concern mainly State interactions reveals how broad forces actually affect family life. Second, the approach reveals how international law evolves, how mandates originally meant to be applied narrowly increasingly expand to respond to global forces. Third, it reveals a salutary incremental growth in not only the reach but also the actual effectiveness of international law. Last, the approach reveals how several opportunities to affect family violence exist merely because the more traditional approach to international law continues to have the most legitimacy and may have the broadest repercussions on cultural forces.

Protection From and Right to Intranation Actions

The concept of State responsibility defines the limits of a government's accountability for human rights abuses under international law. In traditional human rights practices,

States are held accountable only for what they do directly or through an agent, rendering acts of purely private individuals outside the scope of State responsibility. Traditionally, the notion of vicarious responsibility for acts was acceptable: Such responsibility flows from the authorized acts of agents of the State or from people acting with the apparent authority of the State. Responsibility thus arises when an act is imputable to the State.

Modern international human rights law also replicates the division between public and private, most notably in its attempt to target State sanctioned or public actions that affect private life. Simply stated, human rights law and norms assume imputability for public acts; that is, violations of human rights law occur in the public arena and involve state action. For example, commentators generally view the right to life and bodily integrity mainly as a protection of individuals from arbitrary deprivation of life by execution or arbitrary torture by government officials.[36] This approach to private actions focuses on theories of government agency and finds State responsibility for violating explicit international duties.

Although the development remains limited to state action, the redefinition allows for a much more expansive view of the role of the international community in fostering human rights. The works of a leading commentator of international law, Louis Henkin, underscores the development. In the late 1970s, Henkin argued that human rights "are rights against society as represented by government officials."[37] In the late 1980s, Henkin continued and proposed that State Parties were obligated "to ensure" the recognized rights and that "that seems to imply that rights recognized are not merely rights against governments (as are rights under the U.S. Constitution for example), but also against other persons."[38] In the late 1990s, Henkin commented on how "international law is now holding States responsible for what we used to call private. We will not let the State hide even behind the generally laudable notion of rights of individual privacy; we have begun to penetrate even the veils of domesticity . . . but international law will have to insist on State responsibility to address even private violence."[39] This section analyzes these rapid developments in human rights that relate directly to protections from family violence and that require all States to make progress toward ensuring those rights. Before doing so, however, it is important to understand recent jurisprudential developments that move human rights law toward recognizing States' responsibilities to all their citizens.

Jurisprudential Developments

The test of the State's responsibility for an act depends on whether the actor is the State or a private individual. To hold a State accountable for the actions of State actors, one of two facts must be addressed. First, it must be shown that the State explicitly authorized the act, such as whether a senior official authorized or committed the act. Second, in the alternative, it must be demonstrated that the State systematically failed to address abuses committed by its agent, whether or not the acts were ordered by senior officials. When actors are private, the test is different. Nonprosecution or nonresponse by States to acts committed by private individuals becomes a human rights issue only if the reasons for the State's failure to respond can be shown to be rooted in a violation of an international obligation, such as the failure to address the Political Covenant's prohibition (in Article 26) of discrimination on "any grounds such as race, color, sex, language, religion, political or other opinion, national or social origin, property, birth or other status." From this perspective, the expansion of State responsibility to include accountability for some acts of private individuals is a critical factor in the analysis of family violence as a human rights violation.

A focus on formal government actions that involves the extent to which States fail to act and protect rights recognized by their international obligations has important implications and may reach family violence. An appropriate starting point to understand these developments is to examine a series of human rights cases decided by regional human rights courts, including the highly cited *Velasquez-Rodriguez v. Honduras*[40] and *X and Y v. Netherlands*[41] and two whose impact remains to be seen, *Osman v. The United Kingdom*[42] and *Case of A. v. The United Kingdom*.[43] In addition, *W. Delgado Paez v. Columbia*[44] remains virtually ignored yet is directly relevant to this analysis because it actually involves an important U.N. treaty. These cases exemplify how international human rights forums now develop jurisprudence that obliges States to put in place effective legal systems that address both public and private violence.

In *Velasquez-Rodriguez v. Honduras*,[45] the Inter-American Court commented on State tolerance of human rights violations in the form of torture and stressed that illegal acts that breach human rights laws can lead to a State's international responsibility. The case involved the disappearance of a student who was allegedly kidnapped, interrogated, and tortured by agents of Honduras's Office of Investigation. Because the student, Manfredo Velasquez-Rodriguez, was never found, the court heard testimony on the systematic and selective practices of disappearances carried out with the assistance or tolerance of the Honduran government.[46] The Inter-American Commission of Human Rights provided evidence that domestic judicial remedies were ineffective in protecting human rights, especially those of disappeared people.[47] The Honduran government argued that no evidence linked it or its officials in the disappearance of Velasquez-Rodriguez.[48] In rejecting the government's arguments, the court held that the kidnappings were carried out by military personnel, the police, or people acting under their guidance. The court further held that the government was responsible, even if the disappearance was not carried out by an agent acting under the color of public authority, because the State's apparatus failed to prevent the disappearances or to punish those responsible. Thus, by carrying out or acquiescing to the kidnapping, the government was liable for failing to guarantee Velasquez-Rodriguez his human rights as identified in the American Convention on Human Rights.[49] According to the court, the treaty imposed on ratifying States Parties two distinct obligations beyond abstention from violating guaranteed human rights: (a) prevention of violations by State and non-State actors and (b) investigation and punishment of both State and private human rights infringements.[50] Such obligations derived from the text of the ratified treaty that required parties "to respect" the rights guaranteed in the document and to "ensure" to all people their full and free exercise. However, a precondition that must be met before the *Velasquez-Rodriguez* principles can begin to bite involves the attribution to the State of conduct that implies nonperformance or active violation of an international duty (in this instance, an international treaty to which the country was a ratifying party).[51]

It would seem imprudent to venture that *Velasquez-Rodriguez* sets a clear and broad principle that leads to the ready assumption of State responsibility for private acts. The case clearly differs and is legally distinguishable from others that deal with purely domestic issues—the case involved the torture of a citizen from another country. Yet it would be equally hazardous to conclude that the narrow approach to State action is inherent to international law and that governments cannot be held accountable for their failure to act. International human rights jurisprudence does support the idea that States hold an affirmative obligation to address at least some forms of violence that occurs between "private" parties, as would be the case in family violence.

A leading and highly referenced case from the European Court of Human Rights, under the European Convention for the Protection of Human Rights and Fundamental Freedoms[52] (the European Convention), confirms that international law allows for holding States responsible for failing to address private violence. That case, *X and Y v. Netherlands*,[53] found that a country may be held accountable if it develops a legal system that ignores violence against children. The case involved litigation that arose from an unintended gap in Dutch criminal procedure that left a 16-year-old with mental retardation who was a victim of rape unable to initiate criminal proceedings. Dutch law required victims older than 12 to file rape proceedings and lacked any provision whereby a parent could file proceedings for child victims who were mentally incompetent. The applicant claimed that the loophole in Dutch law amounted to a failure to protect the mentally handicapped woman's right to privacy (in this case, against sexual assault). The Dutch government argued that the European Convention's relevant article, Article 8 relating to privacy protections, could not be interpreted to require a State to legislate specific rules of criminal procedure in cases where the applicant has been victimized not by State officials but by a private individual and where civil remedies are available; it also argued that the European Convention allowed States to determine the appropriate mix of civil and criminal penalties for wrongful acts.[54] The court ruled that Dutch criminal law was inadequate and held that respect for privacy includes positive obligations on States and may require the adoption of measures designed to secure respect for private life, even in the sphere of individual relations. The court was explicit: Rights found in the European Convention create obligations for States that involve "the adoption of measures designed to secure respect for private life *even in the sphere of the relations of individuals between themselves.*"[55] The court interpreted Article 8's mandate (that "everyone has the right to respect his private and family life, his home and his correspondence") as entailing positive and negative obligations on the part of the State. Although the loophole in protections was unintentional, it still amounted to a State omission that violated the applicant's right to privacy, a breach for which the Netherlands had to pay reparation.

Other more recent cases by the European Court of Human Rights confirm a jurisprudential move that obliges States to take positive steps to ensure that human rights can be protected from private individuals' violations. In *Osman v. the United Kingdom*,[56] the court addressed the nature of a State's obligations to protect individuals whose right to life are at risk by unlawful conduct of private parties.

The case involved a teacher's obsessive attachment to his student, so much so that he stalked and eventually even assumed the boy's name. The relationship between the student and teacher (Paget-Lewis) had alarmed another teacher, which led to Paget-Lewis's dismissal from his teaching position. The teacher then allegedly was involved in a series of incidents leading to damage against the school and family's property. The police never arrested the teacher, and they allegedly did not respond to some of the family's calls for assistance. In the end, Paget-Lewis shot and killed the student's father, wounded the student, wounded the other teacher, and killed the other teacher's son. The family filed suit on grounds that, although the police allegedly had acted negligently, the courts in the United Kingdom had held that the police were immune from liability on grounds that public policy required immunity from suits based on negligence.[57]

Although claiming numerous violations of the European Convention, the most important violation alleged by the applicants involved Article 2, which states that "everyone's right to life shall be protected by law." The European Court of Human Rights ruled that a

> State's obligation [to protect the right to life] . . . extends beyond its primary duty to secure the right to life by putting in place effective criminal law provisions to deter the commission of offenses against the person backed up by law-enforcement machinery for the prevention, suppression and sanctioning of breaches of such provisions. . . . [It] may also imply in certain well-defined circumstances a positive obligation on the authorities to take preventative operational measures to protect an individual whose life is at risk from the criminal acts of another individual.[58]

The court continued and set out the limits to the scope of this obligation in the following manner:

> it must be established . . . that the authorities know or ought to have known at the time of the existence of a real and immediate risk to the life of an identified individual or individuals from the criminal acts of a third party and that they failed to take measures within the scope of their powers which, judged reasonably, might have been expected to avoid that risk.[59]

On that standard, the court ruled against the family. A determining factor in their decision was that there actually had never been any independent judicial determination at the domestic level of the facts of the case.[60] Although the applicant did not succeed, the ruling remains groundbreaking to the extent that it actually establishes that a cause of action can exist. The Court had ruled against the family because it had not shown that the police did have the knowledge or ought to have had the knowledge of Paget-Lewis's murderous intentions or could have prevented the result.[61] Thus, the applicants to the Court failed on the facts, not the law.

In addition to the above cases seeking to hold States Parties responsible for the actions of private individuals, another important case actually confronted the issue of family violence: *Case of A. v. United Kingdom*.[62] That case involved the application by a 9-year-old boy who had been beaten by his stepfather within his home. The father was tried by a jury for repeatedly beating the child with a garden cane and for leaving visible bruises. Although charged for assault, the stepfather was found not guilty because the actions were deemed reasonable. On appeal to the European Court of Human Rights, the applicants on behalf of the boy argued that Articles 3 (that no one shall be subjected to torture or inhuman or degrading treatment or punishment) and 8 (everyone has the right to respect for his private . . . life) of the European Convention had been violated.[63] The court found that the domestic law that allowed for reasonable chastisement of children did not provide adequate protection against torture and punishment contrary to Article 3 and that the law should be amended.[64] The court then found it unnecessary to rule on other violations.[65] Thus, although the State Party could not be held directly responsible for the acts of the stepfather, it could be held responsible when the law failed to provide adequate protection against treatment or punishment contrary to Article 3.

Although the facts and principles of these leading cases may limit their utility, these decisions by the oldest and most effective international human rights court provide important support for the rule that States can be held responsible for protecting individuals from each other, which may include protections from family members. Their significance becomes even more apparent when the human rights that were supported find similar language in important U.N. human rights documents.

An arguably even more compelling case involves the United Nations Human Rights Committee's decision regarding the security of the person and the need for States to provide protection to individuals from even private parties. In *W. Delgado Paez v. Columbia*,[66] the committee held that anonymous threats and attacks on a school teacher, following harassment by ecclesiastical and educational authorities, constituted violation of the Political Covenant's Article 9. The Committee explicitly rejected the argument that the right to security of the person found in the first sentence of Article 9(1) was limited to circumstances of the second sentence found in Article 9(1) referring to arrest and detention. Because the threats and attacks were by unknown people, Delgado did not allege State action. According to the committee, the State violated Delgado's human rights when it failed to protect, regardless of the source of violence (private or public). The State could not avoid its obligations to the international treaty by simply having a system in place. In this case, Delgado could have used the Columbian court system or could have reported the threats and attacks to the police. The committee found that the State should have done more than have a system in place to garner responses and theoretically address claims. It seems difficult to find a more straightforward instance in which human rights law finds a nation accountable for failing to prevent or punish private acts. Under this approach, States possess an affirmative duty to take action. As with the other cases described in this section, the committee adopted a remarkably broad doctrine. The finding again reflected the equally broad treaty mandate that sought to bind nations with international obligations so that all people subject to their jurisdictions (aliens and citizens) enjoy the full exercise of rights and freedoms detailed in human rights law.

This approach to international law and human rights undoubtedly remains far from universally accepted as legitimate use of international law, particularly as the approach continues to evolve and seeks to hold nations accountable for actions not directly and previously imputable to State practices. Although radically different from the classical approach to international law, mounting evidence suggests acceptance of this move from concern with restraints on the exercise of State power, with limited affirmative duties for the protections, to a more generalized obligation to ensure respect for human rights. From this perspective, governments that tolerate private individuals' violations of the rights of others cannot hide behind the claim that such conduct remains outside the purview of the international law of human rights.

The preceding discussion suggests that States may have three levels of obligations. They may have a duty (a) to respect rights, such as the duty to refrain from carrying out direct violations; (b) to protect rights, such as the duty to prevent certain forms of violence carried out by non-State actors; and (c) to fulfill rights, such as the duty to take measures necessary to ensure the realization of the rights concerned. These duties, then, entail obligations to create the societal preconditions for the effective exercise of enumerated rights and to provide the means for realizing particular rights. It is through these approaches, for example, that international law can identify violations in duties, including discrimination or failure to take such minimal steps as formulating a national policy in the concerned area—even when the obligation requires only that States implement those rights progressively.

To identify potential violations and State obligations that relate to family violence, this approach suggests that the first step to hold States responsible for some forms of family violence involves identification of specific, enforceable human rights related to family violence. Current human rights developments suggest that numerous bundles of rights may function to protect individuals from private violence if the rights are approached in a comprehensive fashion. From this perspective, then, the right to protection from family violence may be viewed as an aggregate of rights that derives from a series of obligations that flow from particular rights within that aggregate. The remainder of this section reviews and provides examples of established rights that may constitute significant parts of the aggregate protection against family violence.

Right to Life

Among the numerous protections offered by the Universal Declaration of Human Rights[67] is its recognition that "everyone has the right to life, liberty and the security of the person."[68] Although the Universal Declaration is not intended to be formally binding, commentators view the document as a basic component of international customary law, binding on all States, not only members of the United Nations.[69] In addition, Article 6(1) of the Political Covenant finds that "every human being has the inherent right to life. The right shall be protected by law. No one shall be arbitrarily deprived of his life." Under Article 2(1), the Political Covenant requires States "to ensure" the rights expressed in the treaty, including the right to life. The Children's Convention[70] uses more succinct language [in Article 6 (1)] to express the same idea that "States Parties recognize that every child has the inherent right to life." The Political Covenant uses subsequent sections of Article 6 to address what is commonly viewed as prohibitions on State actions, as negative rights, whereas Article 6(2) of the Children's Convention expresses the duty of States to "ensure to the maximum extent possible the survival and development of the child." Without doubt, then, the right to life exists in human rights law. The remaining issue involves the extent to which nations actually must ensure the right.

In enforcing the right to life, consideration necessarily must address whether State action is required to violate the rights to life. Arguably, treaty provisions limit the concept of the right to life to protection against arbitrary deprivation of human life by the government and its agents. Reviews of the drafting process reveal, however, that the consensus was that direct State actions were not required. The right to life under Article 6(1) was interpreted to include the right of individuals to be protected by the State against arbitrary deprivations of life by other people within society.[71] Likewise, the Human Rights Committee,[72] through its General Comment 6, proposes that the right to life should be interpreted broadly, to include, for example,

issues of infant mortality and State's affirmative rights. Both approaches differ significantly from the original intent of Article 6(1) of the Political Covenant, which
sought to limit State action that would deny an individual the right to life. Although
controversies persist, nations must at least recognize the approach that restricts the
ambit of the right and frames it in essentially negative terms—the right not to be
deprived of life without due process of law (e.g., a State's terminating an offender's
life) rather than with the absolute preservation of life itself. Yet even this narrow
approach may offer assistance to those challenging State responses to practices that
lead to the deaths of individuals caught in family violence. By providing that "no
one shall be *arbitrarily* deprived of his life"[73] international provisions suggest that
programs should not be terminated, withheld, or terminated capriciously. Again, the
margin between negative rights and positive rights remains all but clear—basic rights
often entail both approaches to rights. Regardless of the approach, the right to life
finds clear expression in and supports the general right to protection from family
violence.

Several examples illustrate the impact that even a narrowly defined right to life
could have on efforts to alleviate family violence. Child-marriage often ends in
avoidable maternal death, which leads the practice to questions of whether legal
responses to the practice violate the right to life itself.[74] Likewise, dowry deaths,
because of their unwarranted, illegal, and arbitrary nature, arguably constitute arbitrary deprivations of life within the meaning of international law.[75] From this line of
reasoning, a human rights response to their violation could impose, for example, a
requirement that existing programs, such as family planning, not be depleted of
resources without a conscientious procedure.

A more expansive approach would suggest that international practice supports
the proposition that the right to life encompasses positive features. These obligations
impose affirmative duties on States to take any measures necessary to enable individuals to enjoy and exercise their right to life under the Political Covenant and
Children's Convention, including taking all possible measures to prevent violations
of this right by others. In addition, the treaties require that measures be "adequate"
and "effective," which at the very least require States to exercise due diligence to
prevent international deprivations of life by individuals and to respond to those who
take lives. For example, research indicates that 12 million children die before reaching their 8th birthday.[76] The World Health Organization (WHO) attributes these
deaths to a combination of measles, malaria, malnutrition, diarrhea, and pneumonia.[77]
Simply listing the primary causes, however, does not describe adequately the causes
of these childhood illnesses or the problems that create them. Observers propose
both direct and indirect causes of child mortality. The most primary cause includes
the major illnesses noted by WHO. The intermediate tier relates to general levels of
child care, such as nutrition and access to safe drinking water. Those elements do
not directly cause childhood death, but they significantly affect conditions that contribute to child mortality. The third level includes the social, economic, and cultural
processes that inform the other two tiers. When considering child mortality from this
level, the focus of analysis is on cultural beliefs, which affect who gets assistance
(e.g., boys more than girls) and the infrastructure's ability to deliver health care as
well as factors of parental literacy, socioeconomic resources, and even where the
parents live in parts of different countries.[78] Properly addressing these issues requires
taking a comprehensive approach, regardless of whether the right to life is protected

through narrow mandates such as protections from State actions or expansive mandates that would derive from more affirmative State obligations.

Right to Health

The permeability of rights and their impact on and inclusion of others find reflection in an important extension of the right to life: the right to health. Although the right to health has been an important source of recent debate, the international view of the right seems considerably settled. The right to health holds independent content in international law. Like the right to life, however, recognition of the right does not erase enduring controversies about its actual content and States' obligations. In addition, it includes other rights. Health is thus a free-standing right intertwined with other rights—to be ensured as one that should be recognized and treated on an equal footing with other rights.

The constitution of the WHO[79] contains the earliest delineation of health as a human right in the modern era. WHO defines *health* as "a state of complete physical, mental and social well-being and not merely the absence of disease or infirmities."[80] According to the WHO, "the enjoyment of the highest attainable standard of health is one of the fundamental rights of every human being without distinction of race, religion, political belief, economic or social condition."[81] This view of health finds direct expression in the Universal Declaration of Human Rights. The Universal Declaration states, in Article 25, that everyone has "the right to the standard of living adequate for the health and well-being of himself and his family, including . . . medical care." The article reiterates the view that health links overall well-being and concerns not merely with the absence of disease but also with the presence of a number of positive factors in the conditions of one's life.

These two documents are not alone in framing health in its broader context and asserting that health is a protected human right. The Economic and Social Covenant offers the most definitive and expansive conception of the right to health. The treaty recognizes (in Article 12) "the right of everyone to the enjoyment of the highest attainable standard of physical and mental health" and further identifies some steps to be taken for its achievement, including "those necessary for . . . the reduction of the still-birth rate and of infant mortality and for the healthy development of the child." The treaty mandates improvements of environmental and industrial hygiene, prevention, treatment, and control of epidemic, endemic, and other diseases and seeks to create conditions that would assure to all medical service and medical attention in the event of sickness. In both its detail and its scope, the expression of this right discloses the intensity with which it is to be pursued and its interconnection with other rights relevant to highest attainable standards. This approach seems strikingly consonant with the Children's Convention, which not only recognizes that "every child has the *inherent* right to life" but also that States Parties "shall ensure to the *maximum* extent possible the survival and development of the child."[82] By focusing on the inherency of the right, especially in light of its being the only right expressed in terms of inherency and one which binds States to exert maximum efforts to fulfill the right, the Children's Convention comports with proposals that the right to health inheres to children not by operation of law, but by the very fact of the child's human existence.[83] The Children's Convention further extends the right to health through Article 24, which provides that

> States Parties recognize the right of the child to the enjoyment of the highest attainable standard of health and to facilities for the treatment of illness and rehabilitation of health. States Parties shall strive to ensure that no child is deprived of his or her right to access to such health care services. . . . States Parties shall pursue full implementation of this right.

The Women's Convention[84] also protects the right to health, and it does so in an expansive manner. Its provision in Article 12 holds that "States Parties shall take all appropriate measures to eliminate discrimination against women in the field of health care to ensure, on a basis of equality of men and women, access to health care services." This language expressly deems unequal access to health care as a discrimination that must be addressed and eliminated. In 1992, the Committee on the Elimination of Discrimination Against Women issued Recommendation 19, which recognized that violence is a form of discrimination and that such violence violated the "right to the highest attainable standard of physical and mental health."[85] Additionally, under Article 5 of the Racial Discrimination Convention (1965),[86] States Parties agree to take measures to prohibit racial discrimination in all its forms, including as applied to the enjoyment of the right to public health and medical care. These documents highlight that the right to health must be situated in the human rights context and must be viewed broadly and holistically. The international treaties place health firmly in the human rights framework and treat it in the context of overall well-being—indeed, it even includes violence as a violation of the right to health. The language has been borrowed and used repeatedly since then and developed through international agreements, such as in the Beijing Declaration and Platform for Action,[87] which view health in an expansive manner so as to place health in social and political contexts.

Thus, from its very origins, international developments portray the right to health as a universal human right that must be viewed in the context of people's daily lives and living conditions. Likewise, protections of the right include not only access to medical care, but also access to services related to overall social, mental, and physical well-being. The international documents also solidify the notion that health is a right that logically must include more than an individual's right to personal health. The right to health also encompasses a family's health and their community's health because preventable communicable diseases go unchecked and affect the community as a whole if people are denied immunization and medical care.

Yet the notion of health as a human rights issue remains fraught with ambiguity and imprecision. Understandings of health reflect cultural, social, and economic circumstances, as well as individual and medical perceptions of what is normal, habitual, and attainable.[88] To acquire substance, the right to highest attainable standard of health requires refinement. The right is potentially expansive. For example, the right prescribed in Article 15 of the Economic and Social Covenant "to enjoy the benefits of scientific progress and its applications" could be coupled with the right to health. The right, then, could include protection for and access to scientific research on physical and mental health, health service delivery systems, and preventive health care, undertaken through biological, pharmaceutical, and related medical sciences as well as through psychological and sociological analyses of service delivery.

The current expansive view of the right to health arguably builds on both positive and negative rights. This comprehensive concept accommodates rights of self-care and access to necessary services, the benefits of scientific progress, the education necessary to understand the benefits of health protection, and information that others, bound by duties to render treatment, are obliged to provide. The health model transcends the medical model of service delivery and embraces a health promotion model. Either model, however, would greatly affect family violence.

Again, numerous examples could be offered to highlight the significance of the right to health for attempts to ensure the general right to protection from family violence. Wife battering, for example, directly implicates the right to health. Several commentaries and leading medical organizations, including the American Medical Association, now present violence against women as a health concern.[89] Cross-culturally, the practice that has received the most attention from this perspective is female genital circumcision. Descriptions used to show the extent to which practices may be unhealthy certainly seem to encapsulate what Article 24(3) of the Children's Convention seeks to eradicate: "traditional practice prejudicial to the health of children." Considerable support exists for this approach; indeed, the convention's *Travaux Preparatoires* reveals that this may have been the intent of the article.[90] This argument finds support from the person who chaired the Working Group during the entire period the Children Convention was drafted and who bluntly stated that the treaty explicitly prohibits the practice through this provision.[91]

In addition to finding support from numerous human rights instruments, the health argument, as a strategic move applied across several cultures, offers several advantages. First, a focus on observable health hazards provides a compelling reason for intervention—practices that do not seem dangerous are more readily tolerable. Second, campaigns for health are less likely to raise fears of Western cultural imperialism than are notions of children's or women's rights. Third, the approach provides a cross-cultural language that is neither inflammatory nor accusatory. Despite possible limits to this argument, such as the limited duty to implement the right progressively, the approach does take on increasing urgency and has become central to attempts to address related forms of violence. It is no surprise that commentators who advocate adopting a cautious and culturally sensitive approach accept the health argument and herald the low-key approach aimed at gradual change as an important example of how human rights bodies may appropriately address cultural practices.[92]

Right to Protection From Inhuman Treatment and Torture

Protections from torture and inhuman treatment are enshrined in a wide variety of human rights instruments. Article 5 of the Universal Declaration of Human Rights and Article 7 of the Political Covenant both bluntly provide, without modification, that "No one shall be subjected to torture or to cruel, inhuman or degrading treatment or punishment." Likewise, Article 37 of the Children's Convention reiterates that "No child shall be subjected to torture or to other cruel, inhuman or degrading treatment or punishment." In addition to these provisions, torture and inhuman treatment are governed by the United Nations Torture Convention,[93] which offers explicit protection. The prohibitions and protections are arguably part of international customary law and have attained the status of *jus cogens*, which makes the standard binding on all nations regardless of their commitments or persistent objection.[94] This is rather significant in that torture or inhuman and degrading treatment is viewed as a peremptory norm of international law, reaches both public and private violence, and as a violation, provides for universal criminal jurisdiction.

The extent to which these prohibitions have developed reflects an unusually rapid move in international law. Traditionally, to be considered torture, the State had to perpetrate, or at least tolerate, an act.[95] That perspective posed a major limitation of the torture argument for protection from family violence in that protections arose only with forms of torture that involved State action. Historically, the human rights community focused on State punishment and political torture, and the Torture Convention emphasizes this form of torture. However, other documents draft the prohibition not as a freedom from State-inflicted torture but as a positive right applicable to a particular form of violence. Analysts of the Torture Convention itself also have interpreted the treaty as extending to non-State transgressions[96] and, equally important, as not permitting private crimes to go unpunished simply because the treaty may concern itself with official (i.e., State-sanctioned) torture.[97] The treaty is more specific about State responsibility in that it compromised between those who wanted to include private torture and those who wanted to include only State-inflicted torture. Article 16 of the Torture Convention includes private acts of torture or ill-treatment when carried out with the "consent or acquiescence of a public official." The distinction is significant. Whereas *consent* suggests some form of affirmative encouragement, *acquiescence* describes passive acceptance or inaction. The difference has led the Human Rights Committee to affirm that States must ensure individuals' protection against acts of torture whether inflicted by people in their official capacity, outside their official capacity, or in a private capacity.[98]

Despite these momentous developments, ambiguities and difficulties remain in defining and urging responses to inhuman, degrading treatment. For example, although what constitutes torture may now be somewhat well established, especially in light of the focus on State action or inaction, controversy still surrounds what constitutes inhuman or degrading treatment: Some argue that it only involves inhuman or degrading treatment of political or other prisoners, whereas others argue that it involves other systematic acts of violence that are inhuman, such as violence against children that goes unaddressed.[99] Difficulties arise in terms of what international law demands of States. International law's demands for State responses to inhuman or degrading treatment remain unclear because it is difficult to define precisely what that treatment may be and the Torture Convention avoids providing definitions. However, the demands may be increasingly explicit in terms of responses to torture. Article 1 of the Torture Convention defines *torture*, albeit narrowly, to essentially involve inflicting pain or suffering by State officials or their representatives to obtain information or confessions. Under the convention, States must investigate and prosecute or extradite for torture,[100] avert torture through training and review of law enforcement personnel,[101] and investigate complaints and provide legal remedies and compensation.[102] These existing definitions and obligations placed on States challenge efforts to adopt a more expansive view of torture or inhuman or degrading treatment.

Regardless of the controversies, however, developments in the understanding of torture and its related forms of violence now affect family violence. Commentators now propose that wife battering, and other forms of ill treatment including dowry torture and dowry deaths, may involve violations of international human rights law under the prohibition against torture and inhuman or degrading treatment.[103] The argument is two-pronged. First, the experience of wife battering parallels torture and inhuman and degrading treatment. The current understanding of battering makes appropriate the comparison between domestic violence and torture. It illustrates what renders violence exceptional and heinous. Domestic violence usually involves some form of physical brutality that results in physical and mental pain, suffering, disfigurement, miscarriage, maiming, and death. Indeed, violence by intimate partners ranks as a leading cause of death for women.[104] Likewise, it involves threats to kill, mutilate, or torture even peers and family members or to create terror. Batterers also use subtle methods to break the person's will, such as isolation and arbitrary and unpredictable punishments. The batterer's expectations are illegitimate and deal with the partner's failure or suspected failure to properly carry out her role, to produce, to serve, or to be properly subservient. Domestic violence not only undermines victims' basic sense of security but also undermines their possibilities for independence, their exercise of human rights, their self-development, and their ability to pursue options outside their homes.[105]

Second, the Torture Convention still applies, despite the narrow approach it takes to torture (with its insistence on some form of State involvement, whether through passive acceptance or inaction). Both concepts are broad enough to embrace the failure of governments to redress domestic violence. The purpose was to include situations in which State machinery failed to protect. Domestic violence undoubtedly provides a case in point of this failure. Thus, laws and customs that exempt domestic aggressors from sanction, such as marital rape exceptions or the defense of honor, reflect active encouragement and consent of the State and discrimination against victims. Similarly, law enforcement practices that implicitly condone or minimize the seriousness of this form of violence also conflict with international law. Thus, where domestic violence is a matter of common knowledge, and law enforcement and affirmative prevention measures are inadequate, or where complaints are made and not properly responded to, the State may be held to have acquiesced in the continued infliction of violence.

In addition to wife battering, a more controversial example involves the corporal punishment of children. Controversy involves only the extent to which countries follow international mandates, rather than the clarity of those mandates. The Committee on the Rights of the Child[106]—the committee entrusted with interpreting the Children's Convention and which serves as the authoritative source with respect to the interpretation of children's international rights—interprets the physical chastisement of children by their parents as incompatible with the Children Convention's Article 37, which, *inter alia*, prohibits cruel and degrading treatment or punishment. In reviews of State's protections against violence inflicted against children, the committee recommended prohibition of physical punishment of children by family members. The European Court of Human Rights decision in *Case of A. v. United Kingdom*[107] made clear that this approach is gaining momentum.

The cumulative significance of these developments is straightforward. The developments have been rapid and far reaching. International human rights forums increasingly develop jurisprudence that obliges States to enact effective legal systems that do not tolerate torture and cruel, inhuman, degrading treatment or punishment. Moreover, the developments suggest that the protections exist regardless of whether the inflicted violence results from State responsibility in the public or in the private sphere. The protections fundamentally relate to other rights as well: Regardless of whether States adopt a negative or positive rights approach to human rights, the rights that serve to buttress the right to protection from family violence undoubtedly include both approaches to ensuring rights recognition and protection.

Right to Education

Human rights law expresses the universality of the right to education. The Universal Declaration of Human Rights initiated the significance of the right when it dedicated one of its articles to its enumeration. In Article 26(1), the Universal Declaration bluntly states that "everyone has the right to education." In addition to recognizing the right, the Universal Declaration took the unusual step of declaring the minimal extent to which the rights must be recognized; it found that at least primary education must be free and compulsory. As with other rights, the right to education also appears in a series of documents that further recognize and emphasize the right. Among the most important documents is the Convention Against Discrimination in Education of 1960,[108] which concerns itself with ensuring that States not discriminate and ensure equal educational access and opportunity. Section (a) of the convention expanded the right beyond primary education to include, for example, the State's obligation to "make secondary education in its different forms generally available and accessible to all." In addition, the convention expanded the right through its attempt to encourage nations to prescribe comprehensive national standards for public education. The aim was to encourage States to formulate, develop, and apply national policies in the hopes that they would further promote educational equality of opportunity and treatment.

The right to education also finds expression in leading human rights documents. The leading documents include the Economic and Social Covenant, which in Article 14 urges countries "to work out and adopt a detailed plan of action for the progressive implementation . . . of the principle of compulsory education free of charge for all." Perhaps more importantly, the Children's Convention recognizes and dramatically expands the right in Article 28. That Article reemphasizes the right to free and compulsory education, reiterates the need for access to be free of discrimination, and emphasizes that the right be implemented progressively. In addition to affirming preexisting formulations of the human right to education, the convention presents two new mandates. First, States must do more than simply provide access to compulsory education; they must take steps to ensure that children actually attend schools. Second, the convention demands that Parties to the convention encourage international cooperation in education, particularly in efforts to eliminate ignorance, facilitate access to scientific knowledge, and share modern teaching methods. Thus, the latest developments focus on ensuring that youth actually attend schools and, although the right can be fulfilled progressively, that resources be provided to make access more than merely theoretically available.

In addition to enumerating the extent of the right, international human rights law also details the basic nature of education. Again, the Universal Declaration sets the basic foundation for conceptions of the nature of educational rights. Article 26(2) of the Declaration forcefully states that

> education shall be directed to the full development of the human personality and to the strengthening of respect for human rights and fundamental freedoms. It shall promote understanding, tolerance and friendship among all nations, racial or religious

groups, and shall further the activities of the United Nations for the maintenance of peace.

The Economic and Social Covenant provides language similar to the one located in the Universal Declaration. The treaty finds that "education shall enable all persons to participate effectively in a free society, promote understanding, tolerance, . . . and further the activities of the United Nations for the maintenance of peace."[109] The nature of civic participation indelibly means more than a focus on contributing to society as a capital resource; individuals participate by promoting tolerance, understanding, and peace. Whereas the treaty aims to ensure a civic responsibility attuned to democratic principles, Article 13 seeks to ensure that education focus on "the full development of the human personality and the sense of its dignity." The Universal Declaration and the Economic and Social Covenant, then, articulate a dual purpose for education. Education functions for full personal development and for civic, democratic responsibility.

International law does more than recognize the nature and significance of the right—it also addresses the important question of who should control the right. Early documents, such as the Universal Declaration and the Economic and Social Covenant, made an unprecedented move when they declared who actually would control the content of education. Presumably, Nation States would hold considerable power because they need to ensure that educational programs strive to promote principles consonant with international human rights and States must set minimal standards. However, the documents actually bestow the right onto *parents*. Article 26(3) of the Universal Declaration provides that "parents have a prior right to choose the kind of education that shall be given to their children." The Economic and Social Covenant delineates the right even more. The treaty respects not only the liberty of parents to choose their children's schools but also the parental right to "ensure [that] the religious and moral education of their children [is] in conformity with their own convictions."[110] The treaty also seemingly exempts schools "established by the public authorities" from its reach; the treaty mandates conformity with "minimum educational standards" laid down by the individual State.[111] These documents, then, emphasize parental rights and leave considerable discretion to ratifying Nation States.

These important developments regarding the actual control of rights have undergone even more significant transformations. The Children's Convention develops educational rights considerably further. The treaty actually places enormous significance on education; it devotes two of its substantive articles (Articles 28 and 29) to educational rights and uses the right in conjunction with other articles. The articles that explicitly deal with education do not mention parental interests and rights. This omission significantly departs from previous enumerations. The omission suggests that children should control their own education because the convention recognizes the rights of individual children. Although the suggestion is consistent with interpretations of other rights and the guiding principles the Children's Convention attempts to follow,[112] this proposition is undoubtedly a radical departure from traditional conceptions of educational rights and thus necessitates a turn to the Children's Convention's other articles to determine parental interests in controlling their children's education.

Other articles found in the Children's Convention confirm that the treaty does aim to bestow educational rights on children. Several points support this assertion.

First, the child's level of development limits the power of parental rights. For example, the article that enumerates parental rights, Article 5, explicitly limits the right in that it requires parents to provide *"in a manner consistent with the evolving capacities of the child,* appropriate direction and guidance in the exercise by the child of the rights recognized" in the convention. As commentators have noted, the provision bestows on youth greater control in exercising their rights as the youth develop.[113] Second, the Children's Convention bestows recognized rights related to educational rights on youth themselves. For example, the convention recognizes the child's right to freedom of expression, which includes (in Article 13) the "freedom to seek, receive and impart information and ideas of all kinds." The only limitation to such an expansive right may derive from respect for the rights or reputations of others or for the protection of national security, public order, public health, or morals.[114] Article 17 of the convention also ensures a child access to materials especially "aimed at the promotion of his or her social, spiritual and moral well-being and physical and mental health"; and Article 14 recognizes the child's right to "freedom of thought, conscience and religion," a right where the parent's rights and duties are only "to provide direction in the exercise of his or her right in a manner consistent with the evolving capacities of the child." The child's right to "freedom of association and to freedom of peaceful assembly" also focuses on the child and remains consistent with the convention's focus on ensuring children's rights.[115] Note that these rights all find limitations not necessarily in parental rights but in the need to protect national security, public safety, and health or morals.[116] Given the focus on children's own rights and their own self-determination, it at least remains arguable that the convention bestows considerable control of education onto children themselves and that educational rights actually serve to ensure other rights.

Given rampant misunderstandings of positions taken by those who seek to enhance children's rights, it is important to highlight that providing children with increasing control over their own rights does not result in bestowing absolute control. As discussed at the beginning of this section, international documents essentially view education as necessary to ensure effective participation in society as well as full development of the individual's personality. Likewise, the Children's Convention recognizes the need to protect youth from their own vulnerabilities and to protect the rights of others. For example, it bestows on children their rights as they increasingly become capable of exercising control; the document also seeks to ensure (in Article 17) children's mental health and, perhaps even more limiting, the document ensures that youth be brought up to support the U.N. principles. However, the Children's Convention still radically departs from other documents and allows for an interpretation that the rights have been bestowed on children and, consistent with their evolving capacities, they may contribute and participate in matters that aim to ensure their right to an education devoted to their own personhood and citizenship.

Existing documents make it difficult to deny that the community of nations recognizes a right to education. Indeed, the instruments have created an impressive right. International treaties reaffirm the commitment to the principle of nondiscrimination and the right of every person to an education. More recently, the international movement seeks to ensure youth greater control over the nature of the general right to education.

The right to education and its central proposition that education must be provided are of critical importance to the protection from violence.[117] For example, including sexual violence information in school curricula can be a matter of profound contro-versy because teachers may explain sexual functions, gender relations, and family life in ways parents oppose; teachers may address questions about protections from violence that make parents and abusers feel uncomfortable; or teachers may bring up issues of gender equality that conflict with parental or community values. The human rights protections help confront narrow forces that resist sex and violence prevention education for the young, a protection that requires educating older gen-erations so that they understand that some programs reinforce rather than challenge basic human rights.

In addition to educational approaches in schools, educational campaigns provide a major strategy for preventing family violence. Efforts have been made to educate the general public and those directly involved in family violence by linking, for example, violence against women and children with other health and social prob-lems.[118] These educational campaigns serve as necessary starting points. For example, McWhirter's research in Chile reveals the importance of education that labels do-mestic violence as *la violencia privada* (the private violence) to underscore the need to make it public so that the underlying beliefs that maintain family violence in the family can be challenged openly.[119] Understanding the existence of violence and the beliefs that sustain it provides the foundation for prevention and intervention.

The human right to education addresses family violence in ways that go beyond specific programs targeted to violence prevention. Education opens opportunities for self-advancement in economic and other regards and for promotion of self-protection. Literacy, comprehension, and awareness of the broader implications and contexts of the choices one has to make also are of central importance to gaining protection from violence.[120] Having access to health information, understanding which systems require examination, following medical advice given in written instructions, and correctly using health products available without prescriptions all depend on the educated skill to read and comprehend. Under human rights law, all individuals have a right to be made aware of opportunities for personal development and achievement that derive from real educational opportunities.

Right to Freedom From Discrimination

Although the previously enumerated rights may seem integral to human rights law, the right to be free from discrimination arguably is the most fundamental and runs through all other human rights protections. The right to protection from discrimi-nation serves as the foundation of human rights. As the Preamble of the Universal Declaration of Human Rights states in its opening paragraph, "recognition of the inherent dignity and of the equal and inalienable rights of all" serves as the foun-dation for human rights. The Universal Declaration's first article similarly recognizes that "all human beings are born free and equal in dignity and rights." The Universal Declaration continues and begins most of its series of articles by stating either that everyone enjoys certain rights or that no one is deprived of certain protections. The exceptions to the way every substantive article begins relate specifically to equality: Article 7 begins with "all are equal before the law and are entitled without any discrimination to equal protection of the law," and Article 16 begins its recognition that men and women hold the same familial rights with "men and women of full age, without any limitation due to race, nationality or religion." The document provides no instances or circumstances under which to abridge the right to equal treatment without discrimination. It is difficult to find more explicit language recognizing the right to equal treatment and freedom from invidious discrimination.

As with all other rights, the other two foundational human rights documents contain an equal protection clause. Article 2(1) of the Political Covenant is worded similarly to Article 2(2) of the Economic and Social Covenant, which declares that

> States Parties to the present Covenant undertake to guarantee that the rights enunciated in the present Covenant will be exercised without discrimination of any kind as to race, colour, sex, language, religion, political or other opinion, national or social origin, property, birth or other status.

Both documents also devote themselves to ensuring equality through, for example, protections against discrimination in education, employment, family life, and other social institutions.

The three other often reported conventions also directly seek to ensure equality. Article 2 of the Children's Convention affords a similar protection to each child within the States Parties' jurisdiction. The entire convention aims to design conditions that allow societies to recognize and ensure, where possible, equal treatment of children by those who have attained adult status, including the children's own parents. Likewise, the Women's Convention and the Convention on the Elimination of All Forms of Racial Discrimination of 1966 also explicitly and by their very nature aim to prevent discrimination and ensure progress toward greater equal rights.

As discussed in chapter 3, issues of discrimination run rampant in responses to family violence and efforts to prevent violence. A most obvious example relates to gender discrimination. For example, a State that adopts adequate measures for the prevention, investigation, punishment, and reparation of private acts of violence against men, but not for private acts of violence against women, would violate human rights provisions against nondiscrimination. Under this scheme, cases involving noninvestigation and failed responses to killings against women would breach the duty to investigate and ensure the right to life in a nondiscriminatory manner. For example, Moroccan law excuses the murder or physical injury of a woman discovered while committing adultery. Yet a woman who discovers her husband committing adultery and who kills or injures him as a result is not similarly excused.[121] These discriminatory responses suggest that States that do not adopt reasonable measures to investigate and respond to "honor" killings fail to ensure human rights equally under human rights law.

Preliminary Conclusion

The clustering of rights around family issues is not static, and the rights are interrelated. The right to protection from family violence implicates an array of rights, each of which has gained distinctive normative content and may include a range of legal obligations. The content of these norms, however, has not been uniformly detailed, and in numerous cases the content of different rights overlaps. These rights may be enabling rights, which create the preconditions for the realization of protection, such as the right to information or the right to equality before law. They also may be constituent elements of the right, such as the right to health services. Although the rights are intertwined, their deep connectedness does not mean that specific obligations cannot be identified with particular rights for the purposes of whether States have not fulfilled their international duties. Obligations must be examined in the context of the specific rights concerned. Ensuring respect for the rights necessarily involve addressing the roots and consequences of family violence.

Protection From Interpersonal Actions

Although international law does remain concerned mostly with interstate actions and modern international law has expanded to include official State actions that may affect certain private acts, a third development expands human rights obligations even further. Rather than needing to attribute private actions to a State's actions or failure to act, this approach proposes that international law recognizes that individuals or private parties are capable of committing violations of human rights and that they can be held accountable. These proposals generally come in two forms.

Reaching "Private" Actions

Even the most traditionally recognized international human rights treaties note the duty of private individuals. Although international law was not meant to internationalize the relation between individual and society, the international human rights movement seeks to persuade every State to recognize a threshold human right standard and guarantee it within its own constitutional and legal system. Thus, States are to ensure that individuals are not only protected but also that individuals do not violate the rights of others. From this perspective, human rights law, through State enactment of its standards, reaches private actions. International law requires States to bind themselves and recognize their obligations within their national systems.

Despite the above general rule, some recent developments recognize individuals' direct obligations to international law. A State's international obligations create legal obligations also to its individual inhabitants. Much of the progress in this area involves actions conceived as international crimes. Although somewhat in its infancy, this development moves beyond traditional humanitarian law, discussed above, in that it may view people acting as agents of non-State entities as criminally accountable if they have perpetrated serious violations. The International Law Commission, for example, continues in its efforts to create an international criminal court that would prosecute individuals who breach not only treaty crimes of an "exceptionally serious" and international nature but also such crimes as drug trafficking and other organized crimes.[122] These attempts to hold individuals accountable face enormous challenges; still to be resolved, for example, are issues involving the identification, arrest, and detention of accused people; the collection and presentation of evidence; and the rules of evidence and procedures to be followed.[123] Yet the international community continues attempts to expand the number of crimes that would fall under international jurisdiction, such as the effort to develop systems of universal jurisdiction to address sexual violence against children.[124] These efforts reflect an emerging

pattern—individuals who commit gross atrocities may be held accountable to international law.

Ignoring Distinctions Between the Private and the Public

The second approach to recognizing protections from private (non-State) parties also
deals with the distinction between the private and the public. However, it focuses
less on the need to challenge the traditional conceptions of international human rights
law and more on the contention that it no longer remains viable to cling to the
traditional view that human rights violations only exist in terms of public, State
action. This approach suggests that human rights problems require "private" intervention and mandate holding individuals accountable. The suggestion gains support
from international documents that explicitly state the need to reach private action.
Four recent internationally negotiated documents that relate directly to family violence reveal the important trend.

First, the Children's Convention reinforces the duty on States for responsibility
for child abuse. The international approach aims to protect children from maltreatment by remedying familial and other problems that may contribute to abuse. To
accomplish this goal, Article 19 places a duty on States Parties to establish, as appropriate, social programs that aim to prevent, identify, report, refer, and investigate
cases of child sexual abuse, and it also specifies that the programs for dealing with
offenders are to be neither predominantly punitive nor the responsibility of any one
State agency; judicial involvement is to be resorted to only "as appropriate." Other
important articles supplement Article 19. Most particularly, the Children's Convention's Articles 34 and 35 mandate that States Parties "shall take all appropriate
national, bilateral and multilateral measures to prevent" the inducement or coercion
of a child to engage in any unlawful sexual activity and child abduction. Equally
important, Article 39 mandates States Parties to take all appropriate measures to
promote the physical and psychological recovery and social reintegration of child
victims. The convention, then, clearly brings abuse into the public sphere and extends
the State's duty beyond prevention, investigation, and prosecution to prevention. The
extent to which these developments can affect private relationships has been noted
by a leading commentator who proposes that international law now moves into "un-
familiar areas in which the effect of a human rights tribunal decision is tantamount
to deciding the role of family members."[125]

Second, the Women's Convention also makes room for reaching private actions.
For example, the expert committee responsible for the convention found that it covers
public and private acts, especially in Articles 5 and 16, which focus on familial roles
and relationships. Under Article 4, an effective policy of eliminating violence requires that the State use due diligence to prevent, investigate, and punish acts of
violence against women. The expert committee recommended examination of private
activity such as family violence, forced marriages, and female circumcision.[126] For
example, despite difficulty in locating explicit, usable language that relates directly
to child marriages, several important documents do relate to marriage. Article 23(3)
of the Women's Convention recognizes women's "right freely to choose a spouse
and to enter into marriage only with their free and full consent." Likewise, Article
16(2) calls on States Parties to set an "appropriate" minimum marriageable age. In

addition, the Political Covenant requires Parties to "undertake to respect and en-sure"[127] that "no marriage shall be entered into without the free and full consent of the intending spouses."[128]

Third, the Racial Discrimination Convention[129] directly reaches private life and family violence. Through Article 5(b), the convention guarantees the right to "se-curity of the person . . . against violence . . . whether inflicted by government officials or by any individual, group or institution." Although this may not be the traditional arena for international law, commentators find that the convention clearly extends prohibitions of discrimination to private life.[130]

Fourth, recent declarations that formally deal with violence make even more explicit developments in efforts to reach private violence. For example, the recently adopted Declaration on the Elimination of Violence Against Women[131] (Declaration Against Violence) defines *violence against women* in Article 1 as "any act of gender-based violence that results in, or is likely to result in, physical, sexual, or psycho-logical harm or suffering to women, including threats of such acts, coercion or ar-bitrary deprivation of liberty, whether occurring in public or in private life." The definition reaches family violence directly in the private sphere. Article 2 enumerates possible acts of violence that must be addressed, including

> physical, sexual and psychological violence occurring in the family, including batter-ing, sexual abuse of female children in the household, dowry-related violence, marital rape, female genital mutilation and other traditional practices harmful to women, non-spousal violence and violence related to exploitation.

In addition to that article, Article 3 links the rights of women to be free from violence to the previous U.N. human rights documents. Article 4 calls for State condemnation of violence against women, regardless of custom, tradition, or religious considerations and finds that States must punish acts of violence against women whether perpetrated by the State or by private people. These new, expansive protec-tions clearly aim to reach all forms of family violence, regardless of their source.

Although the Declaration Against Violence may not be formally enforceable, the General Assembly's adoption of the Declaration indicates U.N. commitment to pre-venting violence against women. That indication even more forcefully was made when the United Nations Commission on Human Rights appointed the first Special Rapporteur on Violence Against Women. The Special Rapporteur seeks to recom-mend ways to eliminate violence against women as part of global investigations of the causes and consequences of violence. The Rapporteur's first report set forth the international legal framework condemning domestic violence and detailed actions that some governments pursue to reduce domestic assault. With regard to State re-sponsibility, the Special Rapporteur found that

> in the context of norms recently established by the international community, a State that does not act against crimes of violence against women is as guilty as the per-petrators. States are under a positive duty to prevent, investigate and punish crimes associated with violence against women.[132]

The report continued and asserted that countries should not use tradition or custom to excuse their responsibilities to prevent violence against women.

All of these developments provide evidence for current recognition of the need to address family violence and of the future direction of international law, and they require countries to take such steps as examining and adapting their policies in all levels, such as legislation, case law, and policy directives within the public and private sectors, educational curricula, and media representations. These developments reveal the need to collapse the private and public boundaries in human rights law.[133]

This approach recognizes the changes in conceptions of "State" and addresses private threats from individuals and private structures. In addition, the approach recognizes the climates private actors create and how private actors can help facilitate the fulfillment of human rights. These developments parallel our more recent social science understanding of family violence. For example, the approach clearly coincides with our understanding of the public nature of violence; it includes considerations of broad social forces and how they affect individuals. The approach moves away from the search for State actors and toward protection and reparation for those who suffer human rights violations; it recognizes that various approaches must be taken to prevent, punish, or compensate for these violations; and it also underscores the need to deal with discrimination, a necessary aspect of human rights law that can address how cultures must confront fundamental notions of worth to combat certain forms of family violence. Simply stated, just as States have a duty to put in place effective legal systems that do not tolerate family violence, so do individuals have an obligation to alleviate family violence. Taken at face value, the provisions provide very forceful statements that demand countries address family violence.

Preliminary Conclusion

The developments described above are nothing short of radical. Human rights law increasingly aims to reach individuals who violate internationally recognized human rights. Likewise, human rights law increasingly does not distinguish between public and private behavior. The developments reflect a practical need to address family violence. Note, however, that international law does not necessarily aim to internationalize the relationship between individuals and society. Instead, the international community seeks to ensure that mechanisms and institutions are in place that further respect for human rights, including the right to protection from family violence.

Why Transformations in Human Rights Law
Matter to Family Violence Law

The expansion of human rights law clearly includes increased protection for rights that relate directly to family violence. Yet as detailed in the book's Introduction, the rights have not attracted commentaries that could serve to guide how countries, local communities, and the global, civil society are to piece together human rights provisions, interpret them in light of human rights principles, and ensure greater recognition of and protections from family violence. Although human rights law remains flexible and somewhat vague and sometimes apparently does not reach family violence, international human rights law still addresses important concerns and makes significant demands. The significance of the demands bears emphasis, especially because they remain generally invisible to public consciousness and even to experts in international law.

Human rights law's first demand involves an explicit move beyond the focus on public, internation action. The human rights mandates related to family violence involve a move into more private intrastate action and seeks to influence the State's treatment of individuals who maltreat others. The importance placed on every individual family member and the significance of family life to every individual's personal fulfillment found in universal standards are not just recognized and accepted by a small number of nations. A record number of countries now accept this conviction because they have ratified international human rights standards. Through ratification, these countries obligate themselves to monitoring these human rights and encouraging their implementation. The new documents are not toothless tigers.

The second demand involves the need to recognize the indivisibility of human rights. As discussed in the preceding chapters, nations typically adopt collectivist or individualist approaches to rights protection. Human rights law's efforts to protect individuals from family violence reflect the reality that either approach results in the need to address family violence. Several protections come in the form of direct family life regulations. Other protections are much more circuitous, such as rights that emerge from nations' approaches to economic development.

The third demand involves the creation of legal and social systems to address family violence. Although the international documents leave much to the discretion of States Parties, all nevertheless must make progress toward ensuring basic human rights, which include protections from family violence. Thus, States may do so in the form of legal systems that seek to support families so they do not inflict violence or provide punitive sanctions to deter violence (in this regard, see the discussion of adversarial and inquisitorial models to family violence in chapter 2). Regardless of the approach, nations must respond and seek to respect and ensure the rights of individuals subjected to family violence. Even though systems may be in place, their mere existence may not suffice to ensure progress and effective human rights protections.

Fourth, the human rights protections demand cultural change. As discussed in chapter 3, laws become effective only to the extent they infuse cultural life. Nations, then, must address the most profound challenge to international attempts to protect individuals from family violence: claims of cultural protection and cultural sovereignty. The delineation of international protections undoubtedly constitutes one of the greatest social transformations ever imagined and requires even more transformations. The principles of how family life must operate and of how individuals require protections from family violence are part of a larger, unparalleled effort to establish and maintain a global community on the basis of universal but evolving standards of human decency, morality, and dignity. Regardless of criticisms, evidence indicates a move toward greater human rights protection and a concomitant need to recognize that need and further the right to protection from family violence.

Fifth, the developments matter simply because they legitimate a broader debate of human rights as they raise the prospect that at least in the future, vulnerable individuals and those subjected to family violence will become legitimate foci of concern. Again, high hopes and lofty goals have not eradicated familiar difficulties. Commentators continue to decry the unacceptably expanding divergence between espoused and actual standards. In regards to family life, the distance between practice and theory is unsurprising. The global community has defined minimally acceptable gender and generational relations in a way that diverges from the realities of everyday life virtually everywhere in the world. Yet the discrepancy between reality and theory is important: It constitutes the challenge faced by all societies. All societies need to recognize where they have fallen short and to examine how to meet the prospects of realizing human rights ideals. These documents provide an important standard of comparison by which societies may be assessed, a process that holds the potential to increase respect for human rights.

Conclusion

This chapter has reviewed the various approaches to international law that may be taken to determine the extent to which human rights law recognizes private violence, mandates intervention, and thus may allow for the alleviation of family violence. Families and family life no longer are the subject of exclusive domestic jurisdiction by States. Global and regional intergovernmental organizations now place the family within their diplomatic agendas. International law, under its most traditional and most recent approaches, offers protections from family violence. States have a duty to protect those subjected to family violence, are under a duty to prevent such violations, and are obligated to investigate and respond appropriately when such violations occur. Such conclusions certainly are foreign to popular commentaries of human rights and international law. Yet the diverse approaches to international law confirm the legitimacy of these conclusions and do find human rights obligations that involve family violence.

Endnotes

1. *See* L. Henkin, "The International Bill of Rights," in *International Enforcement of Human Rights*, R. Bernhardt and J. A. Jolowicz, Eds. (Berlin: Springer-Verlag, 1987); O. Schachter, *International Law in Theory and Practice* (Boston: Martinus Nijhoff, 1991).
2. A. Clapham, *Human Rights in the Private Sphere* (New York: Oxford University Press, 1993).
3. *Id.*
4. R. J. R. Levesque, "Piercing the Family's Private Veil: Family Violence, International Human Rights, and the Cross-Cultural Record," *Law & Policy* 21 (1999):161–187.
5. *Id.*
6. R. J. R. Levesque, "The Sexual Use, Abuse and Exploitation of Children: Challenges in Implementing Children's Human Rights," *Brooklyn Law Review* 60 (1994):959–998.
7. U.N. Charter, 1 UNTS xvi, 1945.
8. Political Covenant, U.N. General Assembly, 21st Sess., Official Records, Supplement 16 at 49, GA Resolution 2200, A/6316; 999 UNTS 171; 6 ILM 368, 1966.
9. Economic and Social Covenant, U.N. General Assembly, 21st Sess., Official Records, Supplement 16 at 49, GA Resolution 2200 Annex, A/6316; 993 UNTS 3; 6 ILM 360, 1966.
10. Declaration on Principles of International Law Concerning Friendly Relations and Co-Operation Among States in Accordance With the Charter of United Nations, G.A. Res. 2625, U.N. GAOR 25th Sess., Supp. 18, U.N. Doc. 1/8018 (1970).

11. R. J. Vincent, *Human Rights and International Relations* (New York: Cambridge University Press, 1991).
12. For a similar argument, *see* C. W. Howland, "The Challenge of Religious Fundamentalism to the Liberty and Equality Rights of Women: An Analysis Under the United Nations Charter," *Columbia Journal of Transnational Law* 35 (1997):271–377.
13. S. G. Simon, "The Contemporary Legality of Unilateral Humanitarian Intervention," *California Western International Law Journal* 24 (1993):117–153.
14. *Cf.* L. F. Damrosch, "Politics Across Borders: Nonintervention and Nonenforceable Influence Over Domestic Affairs," *American Journal of International Law* 83 (1989):1–50.
15. B. F. Burmester "On Humanitarian Intervention: The New World Order and Wars to Preserve Human Rights," *Utah Law Review* 1994 (1994):269–323.
16. *See, e.g., id.*
17. S. Zamora, "Economic Relations and Development," in *United Nations Legal Order*, O. Schacter and C. C. Joyner, Eds. (New York: Cambridge University Press, 1995).
18. A. Orford and J. Beard, "Making the State Safe for the Market: The World Bank's World Development Report of 1997," *Melbourne University Law Review* 22 (1998): 195–216.
19. *Id.*
20. G. B. Sgritta, "Inconsistencies: Childhood on the Economic and Political Agenda," *Childhood: A Global Journal of Child Research* 4 (1997):375–404.
21. R. J. R. Levesque, "The Failures of Foster Care Reform: Revolutionizing the Most Radical Blueprint," *Maryland Journal of Contemporary Legal Issues* 6 (1995):1–35.
22. A. M. Oberhauser, "Households, Violence and Women's Economic Rights: A Case Study of Women and Work in Appalachia," in *Gender, Planning and Human Rights*, T. Fenster, Ed. (New York: Routledge, 1999).
23. For a discussion of the IMF's impact on the Dominican Republic, *see, e.g.,* L. M. Whiteford, "Child and Maternal Health and International Economic Policies," *Social Science & Medicine* 37 (1993):1391–1400.
24. I. Cohn, *Child Soldiers: The Role of Children in Armed Conflict* (New York: Oxford University Press, 1994).
25. *See, e.g.,* L. N. Schulze, Jr., "The United States' Detention of Refugees: Evidence of the Senate's Flawed Ratification of the International Covenant on Civil and Political Rights," *New England Journal on Criminal and Civil Confinement* 23 (1997):641–679.
26. Refugee Convention, 189 U.N.T.S. 137 (entered into force Apr. 22, 1954).
27. *Id.,* Article 1(A)(2).
28. D. Martin, "Refugees and Migration," in *United Nations Legal Order*, O. Schachter and C. C. Joyner, Eds. (New York: Cambridge University Press, 1995).
29. *See* V. Oosterveld, "Refugee Status for Female Circumcision Fugitives: Building a Canadian Precedent," *University of Toronto Faculty of Law Review* 51 (1993):277–303.
30. U.N. High Commissioner, *Report of the 39th Session,* General Assembly Official Records, 39th Sess., A/AC.96/673, para. 115(4) at (k), 1985.
31. U.N. High Commissioner's Program, *Report of the Forty-Fifth Session of the Executive Committee of the High Commissioner's Program*, 45th Sess., Agenda Item 21, A/AC/96/821, 1993.
32. For a review of cases, *see* G. A. Kelson, "Granting Political Asylum to Potential Victims of Female Circumcision," *Michigan Journal of Gender and Law* 3 (1995):257–298.
33. *See* L. A. Obiorn, "Bridges and Barricades: Rethinking Polemics and Intransigence in the Campaign Against Female Circumcision," *Case Western Law Review* 47 (1997): 275–378; M. M. Sheridan, "*In Re Fauziya Kasinga*: The United States Has Opened Its Doors to Victims of Female Genital Mutilation," *St. John's Law Review* 71 (1997):433–463.
34. Oosterveld, "Refugee Status for Female Circumcision Fugitives."

35. *Id.*
36. D. McGoldrick, *The Human Rights Committee* (New York: Oxford University Press, 1991).
37. L. Henkin, *The Rights of Man Today* (London: Stevens & Sons, 1979) at 2.
38. L. Henkin, "The International Bill of Rights" at 10.
39. L. Henkin, "Conceptualizing Violence: Present and Future Developments in International Law," *Albany Law Review* 60 (1997):576.
40. Velasquez-Rodriguez v. Honduras, Inter-American Court of Human Rights (Cer C) No. 4; 35 OEA/ser./L/v/III 19, Doc. 13, App. VI (1988).
41. X and Y v. Netherlands, 91 Eur. Ct. H.R. (Ser A) (1985).
42. Osman v. The United Kingdom, App. No. 23452/94 (1998), available at http://www.dhcour.coe.fr/
43. Case of A. v. The United Kingdom, App. No. 25599/94 (1998), available at http://www.dhcour.coe.fr/.
44. W. Delgado Paez v. Columbia, Comm. No. 195/1985 (adopted July 12, 1990, 39th Sess.), Report of the Human Rights Committee, Vol. II, Comm. No. 195/1985, Official Records, 45th Sess., Supplement 40, A/45/40, 1990.
45. *Velasquez-Rodriguez* (Cer C), no. 4 (1988).
46. *Id.* at 295, 298, 309–313.
47. *Id.* at 326.
48. *Id.* at 314.
49. *Id.* at 323.
50. *Id.*, para. 172, 175.
51. For further analyses, *see* D. Shelton, "Private Violence, Public Wrongs and the Responsibility of States," *Fordham Journal of International Law* 13 (1990):1–34; G. Van Bueren, "Deconstructing the Mythologies of International Human Rights Law," in *Understanding Human Rights*, C. Gearty and A. Tomkins, Eds. (London: Mansell, 1996).
52. European Convention for the Protection of Human Rights and Fundamental Freedoms, 213 UNTS 222 (Nov. 4, 1950).
53. *X and Y*, Vol. 19, para. 23 (1985).
54. *Id.* at 11–12.
55. *Id.*, para. 23 (emphasis added).
56. *Osman*, App. No. 23452/94 (1998), available at http://www.dhcour.coe.fr/.
57. *Id.* at para. 64.
58. *Id.* at para. 115.
59. *Id.* at para. 116.
60. *Id.* at para. 113.
61. *Id.* at para. 116–122.
62. *Case of A.*, App. No. 25599/94 (1998), available at http://www.dhcour.coe.fr/.
63. *Id.* at para. 18.
64. *Id.* at para. 24.
65. *Id.*
66. *W. Delgado Paez*, Communication No. 195/1985 (adopted July 12, 1990, 39th Sess.), Report of the Human Rights Committee, Vol. II, Comm. No. 195/1985, Official Records, 45th Sess., Supplement 40, A/45/40, 1990.
67. Universal Declaration of Human Rights, U.N. General Assembly, 3rd Sess., Official Records, *Part I. Resolutions*, Resolution 217A, UN Doc A/810, 1948.
68. *Id.*, Article 4.
69. T. Meron, *Human Rights and Humanitarian Norms as Customary Law* (Oxford, England: Clarendon Press, 1989).
70. Children's Convention, U.N. General Assembly, 44th Sess., Official Records, Supplement 49 at 166, Resolution 44/25, A/44/49; 28 ILM 1448, 1989.

71. *See* B. G. Ramcharan, Ed., *The Right to Life in International Law* (Boston: M. Nijhoff, 1985).
72. Human Rights Committee, *General Comment 6, Compilation of General Comments and General Recommendations Adopted by Human Rights Treaties*, HRI/GEN/1/Rev, 1982.
73. Political Covenant, Article 6 (emphasis added).
74. R. J. R. Levesque, *Child Sexual Abuse: A Human Rights Perspective* (Bloomington: Indiana University Press, 1999).
75. L. R. Pardee, "The Dilemma of Dowry Deaths: Domestic Disgrace or International Human Rights Catastrophe?" *Arizona Journal of International and Comparative Law* 13 (1997):491–521.
76. World Bank, *World Development Report 1993: Investing in Health* (New York: Author, 1993).
77. For a review, *see* J. S. Ovsiovitch, "Reporting Infant and Child Mortality Under the United Nations Human Rights Conventions," *Buffalo Law Review* 46 (1998):543–587.
78. K. Kim and P. M. Moody, "More Resources Better Health? A Cross-National Perspective," *Social Science and Medicine* 34 (1992):837–842; A. V. Millard, "A Causal Model of High Rates of Child Mortality," *Social Science and Medicine* 38 (1994):253–268.
79. Constitution of the World Health Organization (July 22, 1946; entered into force April 7, 1948), basic documents (Geneva, Switzerland: Author, 1993).
80. *Id.*, at Preamble.
81. *Id.*
82. Children's Convention, Article 6(1)–(2) (emphasis added).
83. Ramcharan, *The Right to Life in International Law.*
84. Women's Convention, U.N. General Assembly, 34th Sess., Official Records, Supplement 46 at 193, GA Resolution 34/180, A/34/46, 1979.
85. Committee on the Elimination of Discrimination Against Women, General Record 19, CEDAW/C/1992/L.1/Add.15 (Jan. 19 1992).
86. Convention on the Elimination of All Forms of Racial Discrimination (1966, *opened for signature* Mar. 7, 1966), 600 U.N.T.S. 195.
87. Beijing Declaration and Platform for Action, U.N. Doc. A/CONF. 177-20 (1995) (draft Platform); DPI/1766/Wom (1996) (final).
88. F. M. Willis, "Economic Development, Environmental Protection, and the Right to Life," *Georgetown International Environmental Law Review* 9 (1996):195–220.
89. M. M. Conway, D. W. Ahern, and G. A. Steuernagel, *Women & Public Policy: A Revolution in Progress* 2nd ed. (Washington, DC: Congressional Quarterly, Inc., 1999).
90. K. Brennan, "The Influence of Cultural Relativism on International Human Rights Law: Female Circumcision as a Case Study," *Law & Inequality* 7 (1989):367–398.
91. A. Lopatka, "An Introduction to the United Nations Convention on the Rights of the Child," *Transnational Law & Contemporary Problems* 6 (1996):251–262.
92. *See, e.g.*, Brennan, "The Influence of Cultural Relativism on International Human Rights Law."
93. Torture Convention, U.N. General Assembly, 30th Sess., Official Records, Supplement 34 at 91, GA Resolution 3452 (Dec. 10, 1984), 23 I.L.M. 1027, as modified, 24 I.L.M. 535.
94. P. Koojmans, Report of the U.N. Special Rapporteur on Torture, U.N. Doc. E/CN. 4/1991/17 para. 278, 1991.
95. R. Copelon, "Recognizing the Egregious in the Everyday: Domestic Violence as Torture," *Columbia Human Rights Law Review* 25 (1994):291–367.
96. *See* M. Lippman, "The Development and Drafting of the United Nations Convention Against Torture and Other Cruel, Inhuman, or Degrading Treatment or Punishment," *Boston College International & Comparative Law Review* 17 (1994):275–335.
97. F. R. Tesón, *A Philosophy of International Law* (Boulder, CO: Westview, 1998).

98. *See* McGoldrick, *The Human Rights Committee.*

99. G. Van Bueren, "Crossing the Frontier—The International Protection of Family Life in the 21st Century," in *Families Across Frontiers,* N. Lowe and G. Douglas, Eds. (Boston: Martinus Nijhoff, 1996).

100. Torture Convention, Article 4-9.

101. *Id.,* Articles 10–11.

102. *Id.,* Articles 12–14.

103. *See* Pardee, "The Dilemma of Dowry Deaths"; R. Carillo, *Battered Dreams: Violence Against Women as an Obstacle to Development* (New York: United Nations Development Fund for Women, 1992).

104. Human Rights Watch, *Violence Against Women in South Africa: State Response to Domestic Violence and Rape* (New York: Author, 1995).

105. Carillo, *Battered Dreams.*

106. Committee on the Rights of the Child, *Consideration of Reports Submitted by States Parties Under Article 44 of the Convention,* U.N. Doc. CRC/C/15 Add.34 (1995).

107. *Case of A.,* App. No. 25599/94 (1998), available at http://www.dhcour.coe.fr/.

108. Convention Against Discrimination in Education (Dec. 14, 1960), 429 U.N.T.S. 93.

109. Economic and Social Covenant, Article 13(1).

110. *Id.,* Article 13(3).

111. *Id.*

112. *See* R. J. R. Levesque, "The International Human Right to Education: Beyond the Limits of the Lore and Lure of Law," *Annual Survey of International and Comparative Law* 5 (1998):205–252.

113. *See* R. J. R. Levesque, "The Internationalization of Children's Rights: Too Radical for American Adolescence?" *Connecticut International Law Review* 9 (1994):237–293.

114. Children's Convention, Article 13(2)(a)(b).

115. *Id.,* Article 15(1).

116. *Id.,* Articles 14, 15, and 17.

117. *See* R. J. R. Levesque, "Sexuality Education: What Adolescents' Educational Rights Require," *Psychology, Public Policy, and Law* (in press).

118. L. E. Walker, "Psychology and Domestic Violence Around the World," *American Psychologist* 54 (1999):21–29.

119. P. T. McWhirter, "*La Violencia Privada*: Domestic Violence in Chile," *American Psychologist* 54 (1999):37–40.

120. *See, e.g.,* Oberhauser, "Households, Violence and Women's Economic Rights."

121. N. Kim, "Toward a Feminist Theory of Human Rights: Straddling the Fence Between Western Imperialism and Uncritical Absolutism," *Columbia Human Rights Law Review* 25 (1993):49–105.

122. For different developments in international criminal law, *see* B. Arnold, "Doctrinal Basis for the International Criminalization Process," *Temple International & Comparative Law Review* 8 (1994):85–115; T. L. H. McCormack and G. J. Simpson, "A New International Criminal Law Regime?" *Netherlands International Law Review* 42 (1995):177–206.

123. *See* J. Gurule, "Terrorism, Territorial Sovereignty, and the Forcible Apprehension of International Criminals Abroad," *Hastings International & Comparative Law Review* 17 (1994):457–495.

124. For a review, *see* Levesque, *Child Sexual Abuse.*

125. Van Bueren, "Crossing the Frontier" at 818.

126. *See* Committee on the Elimination of Discrimination Against Women, General Record 19, CEDAW/C/1992/L.1/Add.15 (Jan. 19 1992).

127. Political Covenant, Article 2(1).

128. *Id.,* Article 23(3).

129. Convention on the Elimination of All Forms of Racial Discrimination (1966, *opened for signature* Mar. 7, 1966), 600 U.N.T.S. 195.

130. *See* T. Meron, *Human Rights Law-Making in the United Nations* (Oxford, England: Clarendon Press, 1986).

131. Declaration Against Violence, U.N. General Assembly, 48th Sess., Official Records, GA Resolution 04, Agenda Item 11, A/RES/48/104, 1994.

132. Special Rapporteur on Violence Against Women, *Its Causes and Consequences,* U.N. Doc. E/CN.4/1995/42 (Nov. 22, 1994) at 18.

133. *Cf.* H. Charlesworth, "Worlds Apart: Public/Private Distinctions in International Law," in *Public and Private: Feminist Legal Debates*, M. Thornton, Ed. (New York: Oxford University Press, 1995).

Part III

Human Rights Law, Culture, and Family Violence in the United States

Chapter 6
HUMAN RIGHTS LAW AND U.S. LAW

Chapters 1, 4, and 5 enumerate the massive proliferation of human rights standards. The previous chapters reveal the enormous challenges human rights law faces in addressing family violence. The remaining issue involves the extent to which one may be optimistic about the impact of human rights law. As a general rule, human rights law does not offer much hope to those interested in immediate enforcement of basic, human rights values, even values most universally accepted by the international community. Nations' desire to expand the range of subjects covered by international law negatively correlates with their actual implementation of such mandates. The result of this maxim is that concern necessarily must shift to determine the extent to which agreed on standards can be implemented and contribute to appropriate reforms.

The paradoxical positions of Nation States—committing to human rights standards yet finding ways to avoid direct obligations to them—finds expression in commentaries of the U.S. approach to human rights law. The most frequent charge against the United States involves the way it develops human rights standards, foists them on others, and continues to ignore its own obligations.[1] Like many other nations, then, the generosity and eagerness exhibited in the recognition of human rights obligations dissipate when faced with issues of actual implementation. In terms of family policy, commentaries often take different stances when addressing issues of ratification and implementation. Although commentaries persistently challenge the United States to ratify more human rights documents, several commentators, including those who champion ratification, frequently argue that ratification of human rights standards is likely to result in little need for law reform.

Commentaries about the most radical and comprehensive human rights treaty, the Children's Convention of 1989,[2] provide the most recent and powerful example of the paradoxical views of the domestication of human rights standards. Legal analysts have suggested that the Children's Convention virtually mimics U.S. law.[3] They also have found that a small number of "reservations" (formal statements added to ratified treaties that clarify how countries do not accept some obligations) would ensure domestic compliance with international obligations.[4] These reservations would include, for example, statements that would allow the United States to continue capital punishment of juveniles, limit children's rights to education, protect the fundamental child-rearing rights of parents and their religious freedom, and only obligate the federal government (not individual states) to implement and abide by the treaty.[5] Even without these reservations, commentators generally doubt that ratification would present much improvement in current approaches to children's issues because the obligations states take on themselves tend to be aspirational and specific rights tend to be open to diverse interpretations that would allow states to continue current practices.[6]

Despite assertions that human rights' developments will have insignificant effects on U.S. law, activists and those interested in family policy making adopt a different stance. The Children's Convention's approach to children's rights continues to be hailed by children's advocacy groups, elicits policy commitments from international agencies, and prompts numerous conferences dedicated to implementing the convention's objectives.[7] Activists and those interested in family policy are not alone in championing ratification; even the legal analysts who perceive little inconsistency between the convention and U.S. law urge ratification.[8] The convention's potential power, though, is made most obvious by those who oppose its ratification. Parental rights advocates assail the convention and suggest that it would radically transform current approaches to children's rights. Rather than seeing reform as a positive step, however, they view ratification of the convention as supplanting the rights of parents and destroying traditional family units because states and local authorities allegedly would become powerless to control the nature of children's rights as they see fit.[9] As a result, those who seek ratification tend to argue that it would generally not affect U.S. law and would attach reservations to the treaty, so it most likely will not directly lead to radical changes, whereas those who oppose ratification tend to argue that the treaty will result in handing control over laws regulating children and families issues to an international, foreign, and unaccountable legislative body.

The paradoxical approach to ratification seemingly reflects the most frequent approach to the domestication of international standards into U.S. law. As a result, the United States has not ratified the Children's Convention. Even though few legal obstacles stand in the path of U.S. ratification, the public continues to oppose international treaties and to believe that the United States will lose its sovereignty over basic laws that regulate the upbringing of children.

Although paradoxical, the commentaries offer an important glimpse of the state of international human rights activity and discourse in the United States. Current discussions leave open two points of contention for those interested in understanding the potential role human rights law may play in family policy and efforts to address family violence in the United States. First, how does international law actually affect the laws of the United States? Second, how different is the international human rights approach from U.S. "human rights" laws? This chapter seeks to address these two questions.

Although seemingly straightforward, the two questions actually demand rather intricate and complex responses. This chapter approaches the issues in the following manner. The chapter first suggests two ways to view human rights law and the effect of international standards on domestic policy. That analysis reveals that commentators who find little potential impact from international human rights law take an unnecessarily and inappropriately narrow approach to human rights. Given the conclusion that human rights may affect U.S. law, the chapter then compares and contrasts the international and U.S. approaches to human rights that relate to family life. The analysis suggests a rather radical disjuncture between U.S. and international human rights law. Given the differences in approaches to rights relating to family policy, the chapter then explores the principal ways human rights may affect family policy. The analysis suggests that current commentators take an unnecessarily narrow approach to international law, that human rights law actually may have more power than currently envisioned by those who comment on human rights that affect family life, and that human rights law calls for change that may actually transform family policy making. That potential, as the chapter concludes, becomes jeopardized only when discussions play down human rights law's visions of family life and when such discussions essentially stifle the process of ratification and implementation that otherwise would set in motion revolutionary forces.

The "Domestication" of Human Rights Law Into U.S. Law

The ratification and implementation of human rights law allows for very different interpretations of the eventual impact international treaties may have on domestic law. Recent commentators[10] draw from traditional and modern jurisprudence to suggest that international law actually operates at two levels and that both must be considered when evaluating attempts to recognize the power of international mandates.

Before exploring the levels at which international human rights operate, it is important to address a potential misconception of the relation of international human rights law to national laws and legal systems. Rights recognized by international human rights law actually are "national" rights. Human rights generally are rights that individuals enjoy (or should enjoy) in their own society under its national law. International law, including the human rights movement, was not meant to internationalize the relation between individual and society. Instead, the movement simply seeks to establish a minimum, common, and global standard and to persuade States to recognize the threshold and to guarantee it within its own constitutional and legal system. States, then, assume obligations to other States when they undertake to respect and ensure the human rights of its inhabitants through its own legal system. Although some recent developments may recognize individuals' direct obligations to international law, the general rule remains: International law requires States to bind themselves and recognize their obligations within their national systems. This section examines how the human rights movement creates those obligations and how they contribute to reform through infiltration of not only legal systems but also social and individual consciousness.

Traditional Approaches to Human Rights Law

The traditional view focuses on two very narrow approaches to the domestication of international law: formal ratification and informal ratification. From this perspective, international human rights norms may be enforced in U.S. domestic legal systems to the extent that the United States recognizes international rules and standards.

Formal Ratification

The principal, direct means by which international human rights law becomes U.S. law is by ratification of a treaty. Through constitutional designation, the treaty then becomes the law of the land. Ratification simply involves signature of the President on the advice and consent of the Senate.[11] In principle, then, international treaty obligations are enforced as law in the United States. In practice, however, the principle is subject to important modifications. Thus, although the ratification process may seem unambiguous, several limitations may be placed on the treaties and narrow their eventual impact.

The treaty must be "self-executing." A *self-executing treaty* (or section of a treaty) is one that does not require further additional domestic legislative action to take force. In general, laws are not self-executing if they do not provide sufficient guidance to those charged with their implementation and would thus require more legislation to be implemented. In terms of international law, a treaty binds domestic courts only if Congress has passed legislation for the specific purpose of implementing the treaty provisions domestically.[12] Congress must pass enabling legislation to guide courts in their determination of the substance of the commitments the treaty entails. Consistent with this approach to self-execution, U.S. courts ordinarily abide by declarations attached to treaties that expressly find the treaties not self-executing and, absent such statements, the courts presume the treaty to be non-self-executing.[13] Thus, courts typically follow the legislative branch's lead.

Limitations arise to the extent that the treaty may conflict with existing law. For example, if the treaty conflicts with state law, then the treaty prevails;[14] if it conflicts with federal law, the most recent provision rules;[15] and if the treaty conflicts with the Constitution, the treaty does not control domestic obligations.[16] Therefore, the United States could undermine the domestic enforceability of international agreements by subsequently enacting conflicting federal legislation. Mitigating Congress's license to break international law is the standard canon of statutory construction that requires courts to interpret legislation as inconsistent with treaties only in the absence of other possible interpretation.[17] When violating international law, then, Congress must do so explicitly; and courts seek to prevent the political branches from heedlessly disregarding and abandoning international law.[18]

Potential limitations arise when the ratification process results in reservations and other devices that clarify the extent of the obligation the ratifying State views itself as undertaking. This process results in what Louis Henkin aptly has referred to as the "cluttering" of treaties with reservations and similar addenda, alternatively referred to as *understandings*, *declarations*, and *provisos*.[19] These mechanisms, however phrased or named, simply clarify the specific obligations ratifying Nation States actually view themselves as either adopting or rejecting.[20] For example, the United States routinely makes reservations regarding treaty self-execution, regardless of the actual need for such reservations.[21] These mechanisms ensure that ratification leaves as little ambiguity in terms of U.S. obligation to foreign parties, which clarifies obligations for both domestic and international legal systems.

Another important limit on the power of international law involves the accepted view that international treaties only bind the federal government. That the federal government has jurisdictional competence to implement treaty law is well understood.[22] Moreover, at a minimum, individual states cannot deny the permissibility assured under the treaties. Under the Supremacy Clause of the U.S. Constitution,[23] states must yield to actions assured in U.S. treaty law. The Supremacy Clause holds that

> this Constitution, and the laws of the United States . . . and all treaties made or which shall be made under the authority of the United States, shall be the supreme law of the land; and the judges in every state shall be bound thereby, any thing in the Constitution or laws of any state to the contrary notwithstanding.

Thus, the Supremacy Clause gives equal weight to federal laws and treaty laws, with both superseding state laws. A major issue that arises involves the extent to which substantive issues covered by the ratified treaty relate more to federal or state law and the general extent to which the issue remains within the jurisdiction of the states. If the issue remains within the general jurisdiction of the states, then the federal government, including the treaty, will have an attenuated impact. The approach is of considerable significance—despite the constitutional precept of federal pre-emption of state laws through treaty law, the treaty does not necessarily reach matters traditionally relegated to the states.

In summary, formal ratification actually involves specific rules that result in relatively clear outcomes. The clearest outcome is insulation from foreign mandates. From this perspective, then, U.S. law, which seemingly views international law as part of its laws, actually limits the extent to which international law can directly infiltrate domestic policy.

Informal Ratification

Traditional international law also involves the domestication of treaties through informal "ratification." That process makes use of a significant but often ignored form of law: law that has become customary. Unlike treaties, custom involves concordant practices repeated over time that eventually become backed by a general opinion that criticizes deviation, praises compliance, or both.[24] Custom essentially consists of two elements: State practice and *opinio juris*. The practice of States essentially is their diplomatic behavior; *opinio juris* is the belief that such behavior is legally required or permitted. Thus, customary law generally is viewed as standards Nation States (or other international legal entities) follow because of a sense of legal obligation to other countries, rather than out of a sense of kindness, courtesy, or convenience. To determine whether actions have become customary, nations generally find evidence that the practice is recognized through signed and ratified treaties, other international agreements, and practices of Nation States that may not even be embodied in treaties adopted by particular nations.

Those who comment on human rights law and its domestication into national systems often attach great significance to customary law. In theory, the impact of customary laws may be considerably powerful. In the United States, the legal rule regarding customary law is simple: If law is customary, it is "part of our law."[25] Under this approach, the United States can be held to standards it has not formally ratified. In addition, even if the United States has ratified documents but attached a non-self-executing reservation, the treaty still may be enforceable in U.S. courts through customary law. For example, some propose that because customary law is continually changed by actions and beliefs of the international community, it always is the latest statement and therefore supersedes federal statutes according to the latest-in-time rule (i.e., when treaties and federal statutes are inconsistent, the latest statement rules).[26] Others view customary law as having a stronger claim to supremacy than do treaties, which would make the customary principle rule over inconsistent federal and state mandates.[27] Thus, under this approach to international law and regardless of U.S. formal stance toward a particular human rights principle that has become customary, the United States generally cannot ignore its obligation to recognize, respect, and ensure the human rights mandate.

Although rules regulating the use of customary law seem rather expansive, several factors limit the use of such law when applied to U.S. domestic policy. The most important obstacle to the use of customary law derives from determinations of precisely what constitutes this form of law. The substance of customary law remains subject to considerable disputes. Although some of the more basic and long-recognized rights may be recognized as customary, even these rights might fail to meet the longevity standard (e.g., customs are not yet fully recognized and still developing) to be considered customary international law. This possibility may allow the United States to claim that it already recognizes the most basic rights enshrined in early human rights documents and that the more recently recognized rights simply fail to reach the level of customary law. Another important obstacle derives from the Supreme Court's approach to customary law, an approach that urges lower courts to turn to customary law "where there is no treaty, and no controlling executive or legislative act or judicial decision."[28] Although the court urges that courts turn to customary law and even that ambiguous federal statutes be construed so as to not conflict with international law,[29] it does not necessarily give supremacy to international law over U.S. domestic law.[30] Thus, U.S. jurisprudence views traditional customary international law as part of its laws, but precedent offers a preference against presuming that customary international human rights law is part of U.S. law without enactment or without alternative sources of law.

Yet another significant obstacle to the use of customary law is that the status of customary rights may depend on the significance the United States imputes to them through the reluctance to ratify the covenants containing those rights, the existence of U.S. laws expressly articulating the limitation of some rights, and the Supreme Court's readiness to find that these human rights are accepted by civilized nations. U.S. reluctance to ratify human rights treaties finds a parallel hesitation on the part of the Supreme Court to find customary law controlling. The court's use of customary international law remains inconsistent. In important children's rights cases, for example, the court turned to customary norms to interpret the 8th Amendment as prohibiting execution of a minor under the age of 16[31] only to ignore and aggressively reject such standards for a similar issue 1 year later.[32] Reviews of these and other cases that have addressed customary law suggest, as several have noted, that courts rest their decisions on some alternative source of values when they seek support from international law and that the United States remains reluctant to view customary law as binding international obligations.[33]

Preliminary Conclusion

In principle, the jurisprudential system of the United States remains congenial to international human rights. The "law of the land" includes both customary law and treaty law to which the United States is a party. Likewise, courts may sometimes refer to international human rights standards to define, refine, interpret, or illuminate domestic constitutional and legal standards. Indeed, the diverse U.S. jurisdictions regularly enforce human rights law when they enforce rights under the Constitution or under the laws that meet international standards and correspond to international norms. Yet in practice, judicial enforcement of international law has yet to flourish in the United States and even much heralded cases arguably do not hold great promise.[34] Even when jurisprudence may be conducive to giving effect to human rights mandates, the current system permits the political branches to impose obligations on judicial enforcement, as most obvious in the principle of non-self-execution. The weaknesses in U.S. enforcement of human rights, then, do not reside in its judicial system, but more in its weakness of political will and international cooperation to ensure that the rights become judicially enforceable. Many aspects of human rights law deal directly with these weaknesses; we now turn to mechanisms that help ensure greater respect for human rights.

Modern Approaches to Human Rights Law

U.S. reluctance to accommodate international standards and protect human rights more diligently than currently required by constitutional law or legislation should not deter efforts to enlist human rights law in reform efforts. Modern international law accepts limitations of ratification processes and finds ways around limits nations attempt to impose on their obligations to the international community and their own citizens. Commentators who write on the impact of international human rights law on domestic rights all too often fail to consider and report how these alternative methods actually may lead to changes in the U.S. approach to rights. Even a cursory glance at international law reveals four methods to circumvent traditional limitations placed on the ratification process and challenges the narrow views regarding the impact of international treaties.

Move Beyond the Judiciary

One method used to circumvent limits on ratification deals with executive and administrative discretion. The rule that deals with self-execution of treaties has been designed for judges. In theory, a non-self-execution declaration is a *non sequitur* as a matter of executive policy: The rule simply may not apply to the executive branch of government.[35] This leaves open the issue of whether executive and administrative officials whose work is affected by treaties must follow the judiciary's non-self-executing rule discussed above. It also leaves open the possibility that, when international laws are not viewed as applicable through the courts, other branches of government may press forward. Adverse Supreme Court decisions no longer are the final stops in the process of domesticating transnational norms.

Nonjudicial use of international standards gains increasing significance for four major reasons. The first reason to move beyond focusing solely on the judiciary as the sole means of enforcing human rights law is that the Executive Branch also holds considerable power. The Executive Branch may freely enter into agreements which, as federal law, prevail over inconsistent state law by reason of the Supremacy Clause.[36] Thus, both states and the federal government would be bound by the executive agreement unless the federal legislature or Executive Branch decided to enact new rules. Although seemingly unlikely, the method to circumvent limitations of traditional international law already has been evidenced. When the courts have failed to accept international rules, the Executive Branch has internalized international norms.

A recent representative example involves the response to the Supreme Court decision regarding the permissibility of transborder kidnapping to establish U.S. jurisdiction over foreign defendants.[37] Alvarez-Machain had allegedly administered stimulants to an American drug enforcement agent to keep him awake while being tortured by drug dealers who had captured and eventually murdered him. When informal negotiations for extraditing Alvarez-Machain to the United States failed, the Drug Enforcement Administration had him kidnapped. The Supreme Court ruled that federal courts have jurisdiction over a defendant abducted from abroad under the auspices of governmental authority. The court's analysis properly followed U.S. law as it simply held that the abduction did not violate an extradition treaty between Mexico and the United States and that, as a matter of principle, a U.S. court's exercise of jurisdiction is not defeated by a defendant's unlawful importation into the court's jurisdiction.[38] For example, bounty hunters in the United States can go out of state to retrieve fugitives and can act in ways considered illegal if done by police or federal agents; the practice is likely to continue given that attempts to reform only go to protecting innocent third parties and do not include efforts to provide more protection to the defendant's rights.[39] Because the Alvarez-Machain abduction involved internation actions, however, it contradicted established rules of international law. Although there were no domestic laws forcing the Executive Branch to change its position regarding abductions, it actually reversed its position rather quickly. Intense media criticism, protests from political leaders and the United Nations, and attempts to progress toward trade negotiations led the Executive Branch to reverse the U.S. position regarding the kidnapping of foreign nationals in other countries.[40]

The Executive Branch holds considerable power in other ways that provide it with immense discretion to follow or ignore international law. Where the Executive Branch refuses to endorse customary law, for example, courts refuse to find the Executive's actions improper. This legally unremarkable finding rests on the 1900 decision of the U.S. Supreme Court, *The Paquet Habana*,[41] which finds international customary law inapplicable in the presence of a "controlling action of the Executive." Whether the President must comply with (rather than terminate or suspend) international treaties remains unaddressed by the Supreme Court; the court has interpreted the issue to involve a "nonjusticiable" political question, which it cannot answer.[42] This long-standing rule essentially states that issues involving politics and policy making are better left to the political branches. As a result, this approach gives considerable freedom to the Executive Branch in its decisions to "execute" laws under its constitutional authority. For example, lower courts have allowed the lengthy and arbitrary detention of accused individuals in direct violation of customary human rights law.[43] Thus, the U.S. legal system allows the Executive Branch not only to enter into its own agreements when actions would be within the Executive Branch's independent constitutional authority but also to violate international law so long as the U.S. Constitution provides that the President may do so under independent constitutional authority. The Executive Branch, then, possesses considerable power. It can influence U.S. national and state policy and, often ignored, it can violate pre-existing customs and thereby contribute to the transformation of customary law.

The second reason to consider alternative sources of enforcement derives from the considerable discretion statutes and regulations grant to those entrusted with their implementation.[44] Laws necessarily are often vague to allow those who implement them freedom to use discretion and achieve the goals of particular mandates. The practical result of this view suggests that thousands of national and local decision makers who have discretion to enforce, interpret, and implement domestic laws could be encouraged to administer laws in a more progressive manner consistent with human rights mandates. From the perspective of laws relating to family issues, the potential impact of taking advantage of this method of recognizing and ensuring human rights can be enormous. This could affect prosecutors, welfare officials, principals, doctors, lawyers, teachers, psychologists, and those who directly interact with families.

The third rationale for moving beyond a singular focus on courts for implementing human rights standards stems from the treaties themselves. Human rights treaties generally hold that "States Parties shall undertake all appropriate legislative, *administrative, and other measures*, for the implementation of the rights recognized in this Convention."[45] According to the language of human rights treaties themselves, then, ratifying nations must undertake alternative methods to ensure human rights. This approach to rights moves away from the narrow view of rights as those directly and immediately enforceable through the courts. Human rights law recognizes that human rights are enforceable through several means, so long as States Parties end up recognizing, ensuring, and fostering basic human rights standards.

The last and equally powerful reason to focus beyond the judiciary to implement human rights standards stems from the previous discussion. Chapter 5 discussed how modern human rights documents place obligations on private parties, but the link between international treaties and private parties is not necessarily direct. However, international human rights law now places obligations on private parties, and modern international law increasingly creates methods to hold private parties accountable. For example, the Children's Convention obliges governments to recognize some of children's rights directly, plays down the traditional role caretakers have in controlling children's legal rights, and requires private parties to ensure children's rights. Likewise, similar approaches to addressing rights violations are found in recent approaches to dealing with violence within families and the need for States to recognize how private parties must be held accountable.

Focus on Monitoring and Publicity

Another attempt to circumvent narrow definitions of U.S. obligations involves recognizing an important development in human rights law: the focus on monitoring. The United States, like all other ratifying countries, cannot avoid the obligation to publicize, report on, and monitor the enforcement and failures of enforcement of all rights found in the documents it ratifies. In this regard, ratification necessarily opens the United States to domestic and international scrutiny on the basis of agreed international norms.

The U.N. structure contains several treaty-based committees that receive claims lodged for potential U.S. violations of human rights norms. Currently, six committees correspond to six treaties: Economic and Social Covenant of 1966,[46] Political Covenant of 1966,[47] Racial Discrimination Convention of 1965,[48] Women's Convention of 1979,[49] Children's Convention of 1989, and Torture Convention of 1984.[50] Although the treaty organs may differ, they primarily function to evaluate reports States Parties must submit pursuant to the particular treaty. The most recent treaties allow nongovernmental organizations and activist groups, including those clearly critical

of States Parties, to submit reports on progress and obstacles to human rights protections.

The United States, then, must submit reports on its compliance with the treaties
it has ratified: the Political Convenant, Racial Discrimination Convention, and the
Torture Convention. Although the treaties necessary limit their scope, the rights protected by the documents range widely and include health, education, special rights
accorded to children and minorities, and protections from inhuman and cruel treatment. The United States must report its progress in ensuring these rights in the
manner conceived by the international treaties.

Although the reporting mandates may be seen as ineffective compared with
directly enforceable measures, the weapon of international public opinion arguably
serves as the most powerful way to reach effectiveness in the implementation of
human rights. Because of the size, economic strength, and political influence of the
United States, traditional measures taken by the United Nations to compel the United
States to adopt a particular human rights position seem doomed. Yet collective criticisms and reproach from abroad and from within may lead to reforms. It is important
to keep in mind that the power of the global community derives from a surprisingly
broad base. Formal quasi-governmental organizations with a global reach, such as
the World Bank, have a tremendous affect on the lives of families and children.[51]
Likewise, nongovernmental organizations forcefully mobilize interest in children and
women's human rights.[52] International professional organizations also play important
roles in that they help discover, define, and influence the public reaction to social
issues.[53] Private citizens increasingly form local social movements that ultimately
have global repercussions.[54] Thus, although a cooperative and educational approach
to enforcing international law may seem to be a rather weak and unsophisticated
method of enforcement, it is a major weapon in the struggle to ensure human rights.
Human rights treaties seemingly function best indirectly, through pushing, prodding,
and even embarrassing States that fail to take steps to guarantee the proper implementation of rights.

Recognize International Obligations

The third method to circumvent limitations set in the ratification process deals more
directly with the nature of those limitations as applied to international obligations.
U.S. reservations and other limiting additions it places on treaties do not affect
obligations to foreign parties. Thus, human rights laws are also enforceable in international forums. This is critical for five reasons.

First, the United States becomes accountable for its obligations simply by signing
an agreement. Under international law, the United States can take no action inconsistent with the object and purpose of a treaty it has signed but has not yet ratified.[55]
Thus, just as the United States becomes directly domestically responsible for ratified
treaties or those that have become customary law, it also becomes responsible to
other nations for the treaties it has signed, such as the Economic and Social Covenant, the Children's Convention, and the Women's Convention.

Second, States Parties to any international treaty must operate in "good faith."[56]
Through ratifying and signing an international treaty, parties accept its core values
and standards. The obligation that arises from these is that States must seek to

implement the rights found therein. For example, States may not derogate rights, and they must not make reservations inconsistent with the treaty's basic principles and intent. The extent to which the obligation may hold significance is readily obvious from the titles of the major documents: the elimination of discrimination against women, the elimination of racial discrimination, and the rights of children. All of these are powerful obligations owed to other nations and the global community. For example, the United States may be violating its treaty obligations because it is a party to the Political Covenant and fails to respond to nonenforcement or the ineffective enforcement of positive laws aimed at protecting the right to life in cases of dowry deaths in India (which also signed the treaty). Equally important, the United States must also look within its own borders and move toward greater respect for the rights it has recognized, an obligation that stems from the need to act in good faith.

Third, human rights are *erga omnes*. All States, all world citizens, have an interest in recognizing and enforcing human rights.[57] This point is significant in that the interest goes beyond making rights judicially enforceable. Rights are to be enforced and recognized in other arenas of law making.[58] Thus, although the letter of the obligations set forth in the human rights documents may not impose direct obligations on the United States or subject it to foreign jurisdictions, the enumerated rights are, nonetheless, rights that Nation States now view every State and world citizen to have an interest in recognizing and enforcing. It would be unwise to discount the power of such rights, as reflected by calls to enact treaties with universal jurisdiction to reach rights violators essentially anywhere in the world.[59]

Fourth, the United States has obligations to the international community even if it has not signed or ratified human rights treaties at issue. The argument has two main threads.[60] First, by ratifying the U.N. Charter,[61] all member states accepted the general human rights obligations set out in Article 55(c), which focuses on the obligation to promote respect for and observance of human rights and fundamental freedoms, and Article 56, which finds that all members pledge to take action for achievement of the purposes set forth in Article 55. The argument asserts that human rights treaties subsequent to the charter simply have elaborated the charter-based obligations, not created new obligations in themselves. Second, the rules of customary law require such action. The rules require respect for specific rights and the jurisdiction of the international community to monitor, encourage respect for, and even enforce the implementation of those rights within the territory of nonconsenting States.

Last, how nations conduct their foreign affairs seeps into domestic relations. National interests are not givens, but rather socially constructed products subject to change. Even nations that resist the imposition of international mandates cannot insulate themselves forever from international law if they participate in the international community. Through a process of self-interest and norm internalization, international legal norms seep into and become entrenched in domestic and political processes. International law helps drive how national governments conduct their international relations. The most obvious and forceful example involves the prohibition of land mines. Even though the United States resisted the prohibition, the international community's outrage and persistent advocacy led to general acceptance of the ban.[62] International norms also contributed to the recent rise in advocacy related to child maltreatment. Children's rights advocates, armed with the Children's

Convention, pushed for legal reforms against the use of corporal punishment, and the same human rights laws are now being used to champion efforts in the United States.[63] Similarly, advocates followed the lead of other countries and also pushed for responses to genital circumcision of girls, which has resulted in federal and state legislation banning such practices as well as reform of immigration laws, which now recognize how the practice may reflect significant human rights violations.[64]

Reconsider Local Obligations

The international obligations of the United States are binding on individual states. Thus, both state and federal courts are required to enforce international obligations. Leading commentators suggest that the individual states may have greater obligations than the federal government does. For example, even if ratified treaties are not self-executing (i.e., the treaty requires additional domestic legislation, and Congress has not yet adopted implementing legislation), states still may be bound to implement international obligations because treaties represent national policy and national aspirations.[65]

The argument has been taken further by leading commentators on international law. Commentaries suggest that international law actually may pre-empt state authority or state practice to the contrary. The argument is that international law's pre-emptive power controls state authority.[66] State practices escape international law's scrutiny, given that constitutional law has been the favored vehicle for assessing the validity of exercise of state power with international law overtones. As noted by commentators, the problem is not that the state courts deciding cases reject the power of international law to invalidate a contrary state rule, it is simply that the argument escapes lawyers, judges, and scholars. Thus, because much international law concerns itself with how a government treats its own citizens, states cannot be considered exempt from international law on the grounds that what they do is not international law's concern. Although ultimate responsibility to ensure internationally recognized rights rests on the federal government, states do not necessarily enjoy automatic exemption. Even though the Constitution assigns to the federal government a virtual monopoly over international relations, it does not follow that states can ignore customary international law. The federal government simply conducts the foreign affairs of the states.

Although doctrinal areas of international law are numerous, the need to take the argument seriously particularly applies to the realm of human rights. In brief, the proposal is that Congress may be presumed to will that the states comply with international law (because international legal rules have the status of federal law and all federal law trumps state law) unless it has explicitly stated otherwise. State law inconsistent with international law, therefore, typically should be pre-empted. For example, the permissibility of certain state practices must be determined by consulting international legal norms themselves. It requires a look at international law's demands and, arguably, a move to find consistency with international standards.

Prospects of using international human rights law to inform state constitutional provisions appear more promising than their similar use at federal levels. As the federal courts move to narrow federal constitutional rights doctrines, state constitutions become a vanguard of civil liberties protection in many areas, including family law and criminal law. Human rights law may be particularly useful where a state's constitution or legislation contains no federal analog or where the state courts have construed a "mirror image" constitutional text to provide greater protections than its federal counterpart. Although human rights documents may only provide persuasive rather than directly binding authority, the impact may still be as potent. For example, to interpret the state constitution's preamble and "social compact" clause, a Connecticut court turned to international treaties to interpret and find a right to a minimum standard of subsistence[67]—an interpretation that radically departs from American law, as is demonstrated below.

A final reason to urge state activity involves the manner states shape their efforts to conform with human rights mandates and how those efforts effect U.S. understandings of federalism. With the adoption of the Political Covenant, for example, the United States explained that the treaty "shall be implemented by the Federal Government to the extent that it exercises legislative and judicial jurisdiction over the matters covered therein, and otherwise by state and local governments."[68] Thus, inasmuch as issues of criminal and family law are matters traditionally within the competence of states, state courts and legislatures not only can but must serve as the primary agents to give effect to treaties. The Senate's interpretation of U.S. legal obligations, then, encourages states to move forward.

Despite these arguments, Congress has yet to deploy the treaty power to compel states to conform with international human rights standards, and Congress's preemptive efforts to do so would violate federalist concerns, which leave states generally responsible for matters of criminal and family law. Recent U.S. Supreme Court cases reveal the limited extent to which the federal government can usurp the role of states in these matters. In one of the most sweeping of the justices' decisions in this area, *United States v. Morrison*,[69] the court applied a restrictive view of congressional power when it ruled unconstitutional the part of the federal Violence Against Women Act[70] that permits victims of rape, domestic violence, and other crimes "motivated by gender" to file federal civil charges against their attackers. The court rejected each of the two sources of constitutional authority that Congress had asserted as the basis for the legislation. The court concluded that the remedy provision was neither a valid regulation of interstate commerce nor a proper means of enforcing the equal protection guarantee of the 14th Amendment. The majority opinion viewed domestic violence, rape, and other gendered forms of violence as activities that did not substantially affect interstate commerce. The majority also viewed efforts to control the conduct of private individuals rather than state actors as insufficient to sustain an equal protection challenge because the 14th Amendment prohibits discrimination by states or public officials, not private actors. The task of protecting individuals from personal violence remains a distinctly state issue.[71]

Traditional approaches to international human rights reinforce the ability of states to avoid responsibility—the traditional rule of Nation States' responsibility absolves subnational entities such as state governments of any responsibility for violations of international law. Increasingly, however, newly emerging human rights implicate areas of law within the near exclusive authority of state governments in the United States. Scholars and activists propose that international law's focus on issues within the domain of particular Nation States (unlike the traditional international focus on interstate domains) should find a corresponding dilution of the doctrine of exclusively national responsibility. Spiro, for example, championed the notion of "condominium responsibility" with respect to individual states' violation of international human rights law's prohibition of the death penalty.[72] That approach would hold both Nation States and individual states within Nation States responsible for human rights violations. Thus, condominium responsibility allows for direct action against subnational units and precludes national governments from hiding behind their principle that they do not intervene and are not responsible for matters within state control.

The Supreme Court, however, flatly rejected the approach in *Breard v. Greene*.[73] *Breard* involved an appeal from a Paraguayan national who was sentenced to death as a result of a murder and rape conviction. Three years after his conviction, he filed a motion claiming a breach of the Vienna Convention on Consular Relations, which mandated that he be informed of his right to notify the Paraguayan consular authorities. The Supreme Court eventually denied his petition for habeas corpus and the petitions for certiorari on two grounds. First, the procedural rules of the forum state govern the implementation of a treaty in that state, unless the treaty prescribes otherwise. Second, recent federal laws precluded a habeas petitioner from raising alleged violations if those allegations had not been developed in state court proceedings. Under the second point, even if Breard had a right under the Vienna Convention, the subsequent act of legislation would have precluded his raising it at this phase. The court also noted that the outcome would have likely not have been any different had he been able to contact Paraguayan consular authorities.

However, the adverse Supreme Court ruling does not end the matter. In addition to legal challenges through the judicial system, the case also revealed massive efforts by the federal government, the International Court of Justice, other countries, and virtually all leading commentators on international law to prevent the state of Virginia from violating international law (even though the state had a legal right to do so).[74] Such activity reveals the extent to which the effort gains support and may actually lead to future reform. The future of the more modern position is not necessarily unimaginable. Its future is possible, especially given that nongovernmental organizations increasingly recognize the real-world significance of subnational authorities and increasingly target their efforts at such authorities and that states increasingly respond to foreign influence as they seek the rewards of the global marketplace and must subject themselves to its discipline.[75] In the face of federal inability to intervene in state-level action, the states have become, and will remain, key governmental players on important human rights issues. The potential swath of the "modern" position that contradicts current U.S. law sanctioned by the Supreme Court runs deep.

Preliminary Conclusion

A realistic evaluation of the ostensible inefficacy of the presently existing generous global rights reveals obstacles and avenues for progress. International human rights law faces considerable obstacles in its efforts to proscribe, prevent, punish, and otherwise respond appropriately to local wrongs. However, traditional weaknesses should not be viewed to indicate system failure or doomed aspirations. The human rights movement is still relatively young and, more importantly, evolving rapidly.

As demonstrated in chapters 3 and 4, much of the nature and evolution of human rights law deals with the addition by human rights of a new set of principles or views of how rights might work and, in essence, a new language to discuss and approach rights. Both international and domestic commitments become enmeshed with human rights norms. The commitments, especially when viewed through a more expansive view of human rights and its methods of enforcement, constitute a powerful way to bring basic human rights back home and engage in cultural and individual consciousness raising.

Human Rights Law's Radical Departures

In terms of laws that affect family policy development, three areas of fundamental difference exist between international law's regulation of family life and U.S. law. The differences are especially significant given that Supreme Court jurisprudence already speaks to the nature of U.S. obligations and provides the minimal obligations both federal and state governments have to meet to comply with the current domestic mandates. Existing constitutional doctrine reveals that the approach to human rights framed in international law does not receive much judicial solicitude. The divergence suggests that if taken seriously, international human rights law should dramatically transform U.S. family policy because human rights law departs from the minimalist approaches the United States adopts to protect and foster family life. This section examines the divergences; the section that follows addresses how the human rights approach may potentially affect U.S. responses to family violence.

Recognizing New Legal Individuals Within Families

The need to respect every individual's rights within families and their rights to relationships constitutes one of the most foundational developments in human rights. As discussed in chapters 1, 4, and 5, numerous documents reflect the view that families need special protection and that all individuals within those families have independent rights. The most notable and significant expansion involves children's rights. In terms of family life, for example, states must recognize that each child has separate rights and that these rights deserve consideration when approaching rights in particular relationships or groups that may be viewed as their family. For example, the Children's Convention places children's rights to relationships in the child rather than in the parent or state. Parties undertake the obligation to "respect the right of the child to preserve his or her ... family relations."[76] States further must respect the "right of the child ... to maintain personal relations and direct contact" with parents from whom the child has been separated.[77] These protections are consistent with the human rights principles of equality and nondiscrimination, regardless of any age, marital, economic, and social marker. Children have an independent, individual right to maintain relationships with family members. This approach to defining children's rights may seem a mere quibble in defining rights, but understanding how the United States approaches who controls the rights of children helps people realize the significance of the approach.

The Supreme Court's recent analysis of this issue represents a posture different from that of human rights law. Three areas of law are illustrative. The first area of law involves the permission granted by the Constitution to some individuals within families to control the rights of vulnerable individuals. Supreme Court case law, starting with *Meyer v. Nebraska*[78] and *Pierce v. Society of Sisters*,[79] has constitution-alized a vision of family relations that grants parents, and denies the state, primary control over their children's upbringing. Although both cases dealt with the power of states to control children's education, the court persistently highlighted the role and immense rights of parents. Indeed, it was in *Pierce* that the court noted the oft-cited phrase that "The child is not the mere creature of the State; those who nurture him and direct his destiny have the right, coupled with the high duty, to recognize and prepare him for additional obligations."[80] The rights of the child against the state, then, were rooted in the indirect right of parents to control and raise their children. Children did not have an independent constitutional right. In the most notable modern Supreme Court case adhering to this principle, *Wisconsin v. Yoder*,[81] the court again gave power to parents to determine their children's destinies. In *Yoder*, a case involving the rights of parents to prohibit their children from attending secondary schools, the court took the opportunity to expand on the rights of parents to conclude that parents have the right to raise their children as they see fit. Com-mentators have viewed this constitutionalized view of family life as one of a narrow, tradition-bound vision of the child as essentially private property.[82] That approach to family life finds further expression in the rise of the "parental rights" movement and attempts to confer on parents their traditional rights.[83]

The second area of law involves views of parent–child relationships and the extent to which either party possesses a right to relationships. The plurality opinion of *Michael H. v. Gerald D.*[84] provides the Supreme Court's most recent statement regarding the extent to which the existence of parent–child relations gains consti-tutional protection. In that case, the plurality ruled that a natural father did not have any constitutionally protected interest in maintaining his previously initiated rela-tionship with his child when the child's mother had been married to another man but had been cohabitating with the natural father at the time the child was conceived and born. The court also found that the child had no rights to such relationship either. The court viewed the U.S. Constitution as protecting "the unitary family." The con-clusion was rather simple: Neither natural parents nor their children have a consti-tutionally cognizable right to maintain relationships with each other when the type of family that asks protection has not received any legal support in U.S. history and traditions. Thus, the extent to which the court will recognize the entire panoply of families—including conditions that the court has called "extraordinary"—remains questionable.[85] For example, equally extraordinary is the rise in the number of chil-dren living with gay and lesbian parents. In those cases, the general pattern that has emerged has been to define *parent* in strictly biological terms; the result has been that children are denied the right to maintain relationships with people whom they have come to experience as parents.[86]

The third area of law involves the extent to which anyone from outside the family may petition the courts to recognize their relationship to the child and, for example, grant visitation rights. This was precisely the issue in *Troxel v. Ganville*.[87] In this case, the grandparents petitioned for the right to visit their deceased son's daughters. The grandparents had established a relationship with their granddaughters when the mother and father had separated and the father had moved into his parents' home where he had regularly brought his daughters for weekend visits. The girls' mother, who had since remarried and whose husband had officially adopted the girls, did not oppose all visitation; she simply challenged the amount of time the grandparents sought. The legal issue that emerged involved the Washington state statute on which the grandparents had sought visitation. The statute permits "any person" to petition for visitation rights "at any time" and authorizes the courts to grant such rights whenever visitation may serve "the best interests of the child."[88] The plurality found that the statute sweeps too broadly by allowing any person to petition at any time and, once the petition is filed, the visitation is granted without according deference to the parent's decision. By resting its decision on that statute's sweeping breadth, the plurality did not address the failure of the statute to require that the parent be shown unfit to make such a decision or that the parent had been unreasonable in deciding issues of visitation. Thus, the Supreme Court simply found that the statute impermissibly intruded into parental rights; the court did not address the extent to which the statute must clarify whether the parents were harming the child or not acting in the child's best interest.

The Supreme Court's ruling in *Troxel* is not surprising but nevertheless highlights how U.S. family law jurisprudence differs from the human rights approach. The plurality's holding is consistent with the heavy focus on parental rights and long-established precedent granting parents the fundamental constitutional right to rear their children, including the right to determine who shall educate and socialize them. Only one dissenting Supreme Court justice approached the statute in terms of the need to include children's rights to relationships outside the family as an issue potentially involving their rights as separate from those of their parents. Noting that the individuals seeking visitation would need to assert an established relationship and that state law already defines what constitutes the best-interest standard, the justice emphasized the need to recognize that there may be "circumstances in which a child has a stronger interest at stake than mere protection from serious harm caused by the termination of visitation by a 'person' other than a parent . . . and that [the U.S. Constitution] leaves room for States to consider the impact on a child of possibly arbitrary parental decisions that neither serve nor are motivated by the best interests of the child."[89] Rather than granting parents an isolated right that may be exercised arbitrarily then, an approach that focuses on including the rights of the child would at least allow for a statute that grants third parties the procedural right to ask the state to act as an arbiter between a parent's protected interests and the child's.

Under the human rights approach, the above cases may have led to different outcomes. The relationship outside of a married couple's family could deserve recognition at least to the extent that no harm would come to the parties (e.g., the parent who seeks a relationship is not likely to abuse the child). Human rights law protects the rights of children, regardless of their parents' status.[90] Likewise, children no longer are viewed as belonging to their parents. This could increase the opportunities for others to petition the courts to recognize their rights to relationships with children and, even more radical, allow children to petition the courts to recognize their relationships with third parties. As discussed, much control still may devolve to parents, but human rights law has recognized principles to ensure greater recognition of children's concerns and greater control over their own rights.

Guarding Rights Against Family Members

International law not only recognizes that individuals within families have rights and that those rights may conflict with the group considered their families but also recognizes that individuals retain rights against one another. The Children's Convention, for example, clearly aims (in Articles 16 and 12, respectively) to give children privacy rights and decision-making authority to exercise those rights, commensurate with the child's development. Likewise, the Women's Convention, which relates directly to family dynamics, recognizes (in Article 16) that women may have rights against their partners, children, and other family members. In addition, all human rights law seeks to offer individuals equal protection of laws recognized.[91] Likewise, numerous human rights treaties protect individuals from arbitrary or unlawful interference within their privacy, family, or home.[92]

Supreme Court jurisprudence has visited the issue and established important precedent contrary to human rights law. The court addressed the extent to which states protect the fundamental rights of those in families. In *Hodgson v. Minnesota*,[93] the court refused to intervene in family life and protect what would otherwise have been a child's right to obtain an abortion. This case suggests that, under U.S. law, children may have rights to privacy, but they have limited authority to exercise that right. The Constitution permits states to have children assert their claims only vicariously through parents.[94] Courts and legislatures continue to be reluctant to intervene in parent–child relations because parents' right to direct children's upbringing constitutes a right against state interference with family matters. Despite the general principle of noninterference in family relationships, however, states do routinely intrude into the family domain. States often justify the intrusion on the need to protect parental interests and to protect children from themselves on the theory that the parents know better than their children what is best for them. What has emerged in recent years is the trend that, even when children have a clear liberty interest, the court remains more faithful to parental interests.[95]

Once parents have abused their rights, however, those rights may be infringed, as was the case in *Prince v. Massachusetts*.[96] *Prince* involved the extent to which parental rights deserved protection when pitted against a state's child protection laws, in this instance protections against child labor being challenged by a guardian who had furnished religious pamphlets to her 9-year-old niece to sell on the streets. The court found that the state's interest in child protection could outweigh parental rights, finding that parents are free to become martyrs themselves but are not free to make martyrs of their children. *Prince*, then, stands for the proposition that the state's "parental authority" over children supersedes parental authority only when parents have failed to protect their child or have placed the child in jeopardy. This proposition more recently has been reaffirmed by the Supreme Court's view that it now is "made plain beyond the need for multiple citation" that the parental right deserves deference "absent a powerful countervailing interest."[97] However, in those instances, the court continues to maintain that state intervention directed toward the family should recognize that "parents retain a vital interest in preventing the irretrievable destruction of their family life."[98]

In addition to a development in children's rights to protection by the state, constitutional jurisprudence now grants similar rights to adults and arguably takes those rights much more seriously. Most notably, adults now have rights against other family members. Recent jurisprudence suggests that families are increasingly viewed as contractual, at least from the perspective of the parents. The legal system now views adult family members as individuals free to negotiate the terms of their relationships and the terms of their relationship's demise. The revolution emerged clearly in the

Supreme Court's *Eisenstadt v. Baird.*[99] The case involved the finding that prohibiting the distribution of contraceptives to unmarried adults violated the Constitution. Under this approach, the family could only be regulated through the protection of the autonomous individuality of each (adult) family member. Notably, it was only 7 years earlier, in *Griswold v. Connecticut,*[100] that the court found that the right to privacy inhered in the marital relationship and that the state cannot invade the "zone of privacy" that surrounds such relationships. The *Griswold* court espoused a rather traditional view of family relationships; the case offered factual disputes identical to *Eisenstadt* with the important exception that those denied contraceptives were married. *Eisenstadt* went much further in that it continued to define what a marital relationship actually is: "the marital couple is not an independent entity with a mind and heart of its own, but an association of two individuals . . . . If the right of privacy means anything, it is the right of the *individual,* married or single, to be free from unwarranted governmental intrusion."[101] Under this approach, the rights to privacy attaches to individuals, rather than to the whole, and allows for creating numerous versions of what constitutes "families" and protected relationships. This expanded view of relationships, however, remains limited. Most notably, the court more recently refused to extend the protection based on privacy to sodomy between consenting adults.[102] In summary, this new jurisprudence generally leaves states outside of family life and lets competent parties negotiate and even sever their relationships.

The vision of family life found in human rights law, then, differs from the family ideology espoused by the Supreme Court's interpretation of the U.S. Constitution. As can be gleaned from the above cases, taking human rights seriously could revolutionize family jurisprudence. Underlying human rights law is the belief that children's personhood should be respected, their views should be heard, and their liberties, including privacy, should not be taken capriciously. Individuals within families not only have rights; they also have the right to control those rights to a greater extent than current U.S. law seemingly allows. Likewise, under human rights law, individuals with relationships that are not viewed as traditionally sanctioned may garner protections. Indeed, the rights of those in nontraditional relationships already have been litigated in human rights arenas and have resulted in impressively expansive protections against discrimination.[103]

Expanding Visions of State Life

Even more radical than entitling individuals within families with their own rights is human rights law's vision of state involvement in family life. The human rights movement envisions a society that actively supports families. This expansive vision takes two forms. First, it involves the extent to which governments themselves may need to support individuals within families. Second, it involves a blurring between public and private boundaries both in terms of the obligations governments have toward private parties and in terms of obligations private individuals have toward each other.

In terms of the first expansive development, numerous examples arise from treaties concerned directly with family life. The Universal Declaration of Human Rights, for example, provides (in Article 25) that "everyone has a right to a standard of

living adequate for the health and well-being of himself and his family, including
. . . necessary social services." The most recent elaboration of that right, the Children's Convention, exponentially expands the state's obligations. That convention
devotes numerous articles to detail state obligations. For example, Articles 19 and
39, respectively, provide that states take all appropriate measures to protect the child
from all forms of abuse and to promote social reintegration to victims in a manner
that fosters health, self-respect, and dignity. From this perspective, human rights law
imposes duties of a positive nature as it moves away from simply imposing duties
that substantially can be fulfilled by government inaction. Admittedly, these "positive
rights" are to be achieved more progressively through programmatic implementation.[104] However, compliance with the human rights principles remains more than a
matter of establishing programs. Compliance means that steps have been taken to
implement effective programs. Again, human rights law requires Nation States to
respect and ensure all of the enumerated rights located in relevant documents. Individuals have a right to active governmental support. Although states need not
provide all services and benefits directly, they must provide ways to facilitate support
for individuals within families.

In terms of the second development, it has already been demonstrated (a) that
human rights law seeks to place duties on private parties and (b) that states' obligations considerably blur with those of private parties. The first duty takes the form,
for example, of requiring individuals to act in the best interests of others, such as
children.[105] The second obligation takes the form (as discussed in chapters 1 and 5)
of obligations described in the numerous platforms of action, which require states to
respond to both public and private violence, regardless of the violence's relationship
to the state. The violence itself creates state obligations.

The ideology of family life envisioned by those who interpret the U.S. Constitution diverges from the expansive view in four significant ways. First, without clear
"state action," governments generally are not held responsible for failing to protect
individuals from violence, as reflected in the major Supreme Court case directly on
point: *DeShaney v. Winnebago County Dept. of Soc. Services.*[106] In *DeShaney*, a
father beat his child into a coma approximately 1 year after the child protection
agency first received notice of the abusive relationship. After rejecting the claim that
the state must be responsible for the father's actions, the court noted that the U.S.
Constitution confers "no affirmative right to governmental aid, even where such aid
may be necessary to secure life, liberty, or property interest of which the government
itself may not deprive the individual."[107] The court ruled that the purpose of the due
process clause "was to protect the people from the State, not to ensure that the State
protected them from each other."[108] Simply put, the court found that the state was
not to be held responsible because, although the agency had released the child to
the father, the boy was not in the state's custody at the time of the injury. Thus,
although the court was sympathetic to the young boy's case, it found that "the most
that can be said about the state functionaries in this case is that they stood by and
did nothing when suspicious circumstances dictated a more active role for them."[109]
The ultimate result is that the court held that children have no constitutional right
to be protected against private violence, even when government officials have taken
steps to intervene and are aware or should be aware that child abuse is taking place.
Although one may dispute the genuineness of the court's characterization of the
government as having taken no affirmative action to thwart individual rights, the

result remains and the approach constitutes settled doctrine. The principle is rather straightforward: The Constitution limits the power of states, not private parties; it does not protect citizens against injury by private people.

Second, although *DeShaney* suggests that the state could have taken on itself an affirmative duty to act if the child had been in its custody, the court has now set a standard that effectively further narrows a state's affirmative duty to protect its children. It now appears that the converse of the "no custody–no duty" *DeShaney* rule may not hold. This was the result in another leading case, *Suter v. Artist M.*[110] *Suter* involved the issue of whether children supervised by a child welfare agency could compel state administration officials to provide federally mandated services. At issue was whether the Adoption Assistance and Child Welfare Act of 1980,[111] which partly aimed to reform states' responses to child welfare cases involving abuse and neglect, allowed aggrieved individuals to require states to perform their obligations under the act. The court flatly denied the children's claim. The court ruled that children under state administrative official's supervision, as well as children in foster care, lack adequate standing to bring suit to enforce the applicable statutory provisions. Thus, existing legislation that would protect individuals generally remains unenforceable. If appropriate legislation exists and statutes do not provide individuals the right to petition for redress to those who suffer for lack of enforcement, individuals do not have a right to enforcement and services. The practical impact of the *Suter* decision for families in violence is twofold. The case renders private parties unable to require government agencies to perform their statutory duties to make "reasonable efforts" to prevent removal of children from their homes and reunited families after these removals. Moreover, because the case relied on the federal statute, known as Section 1983, which provides a federal remedy for "the deprivation of any rights, privileges, or immunities secured by the Constitution and federal laws,"[112] the case indicates the extent to which that federal remedy may no longer be available to those whose rights have been denied when the legislature denies them rights to bring actions to enforce those rights.

A third difference between an expansive view of family life and an interpretation presented in the U.S. Constitution is that the latter protects family integrity by a principle of state noninterference. The Supreme Court has long interpreted the U.S. Constitution as creating a zone of privacy that insulates families from state intrusion. The constitutional rights to family integrity encompass the autonomy of adults in marriage and family matters, such as matters and rights relating to procreation and child rearing.[113] The court continues to maintain that state intervention directed toward the family should recognize that individuals retain the right to protection from the "irretrievable destruction of their family life."[114]

The fourth point involves the typical understanding of constitutional rights. Constitutional rights involve rights to be free from hostile government interference; the rights do not demand friendly governmental support. In a series of decisions beginning with *Dandridge v. Williams*,[115] Supreme Court majorities consistently have ruled that government officials have no constitutional obligations to ensure that all people in their jurisdictions are provided with certain basic necessities. That case upheld a state regulation that placed a ceiling on the amounts of benefits given under the Aid to Families With Dependent Children program, regardless of the size of the family receiving the benefits. The court made its position clear:

The Constitution may impose certain procedural safeguards upon systems of welfare administration. But, the Constitution does not empower this Court to second-guess state officials charged with the difficult responsibility of allocating limited public welfare funds among the myriad of potential recipients.[116]

Efforts to ensure that states do not infringe on people's rights, though, have led to important cases affecting welfare rights. Most notably, in *Saenz v. Roe,*[117] the U.S. Supreme Court linked the receipt of welfare benefits with the need for states to not infringe on the fundamental right of a person to travel. *Saenz* involves California's enactment of durational residency requirements to determine welfare benefits, a policy that limits the amount of benefits receivable by a new resident who has been in California for less than 12 months to the amount minus what he or she would have received in the state of his or her previous residence. The court found the statute unconstitutional by adopting a broad interpretation of the right of a person to travel. The court found that classification of residency imposes a penalty on a person's ability to exercise his or her right to travel. This penalty violates the Equal Protection Clause of the 14th Amendment, which includes the Privileges and Immunities Clause that was interpreted to protect a person's right to travel and establish residency in another state.[118] As a result, the Supreme Court limited the power of state legislatures to control and manage welfare assistance programs. It is important to note, however, that the court rarely examines how states allocate specific goods.

The only good that the Supreme Court confers constitutional right status to is found in the context of judicial proceedings, where, for example, the court held that a state cannot require poor people to pay a fee to appeal an adverse parental rights termination ruling.[119] Limiting "positive" rights to contexts that involve the deprivation of people's rights by the state highlights the focus on governmental noninterference rather than governmental assistance. Indeed, in the area of poverty law and access to services, the federal government actually has abolished "welfare as we know it" and requires states to follow its aggressive lead.[120]

Given the current U.S. stance of not according individuals within families affirmative rights, human rights principles would expand U.S. law. Although the human rights instruments may not require the United States to realize fully and immediately the affirmative rights enumerated, it seems clear that affirmative rights would become part of U.S. jurisprudence. Although economic and social rights are often seen as "goals" or rights of "progressive realization," they are nevertheless rights.

Preliminary Conclusion

The U.S. Supreme Court has long interpreted the U.S. Constitution as creating a zone of privacy that insulates families from state intrusion. The constitutional rights to family integrity encompass the autonomy of adults in marriage and family matters such as procreation and child rearing. It also protects the parental rights to the care and companionship of their children. The Constitution, however, has not been interpreted as to require the government to fund the exercise of those rights and privileges. Thus, implicit in the court's interpretation of family life is the notion that family integrity is best protected when laws shield the family from state interference, even when that interference is beneficent. Prevailing constitutional doctrine does not recognize a right of families to state assistance, even when such assistance may be necessary to protect and maintain family integrity. That doctrine essentially espouses the opposite view human rights law offers. Human rights law seeks to ensure active state support for families while still protecting families from improper governmental intrusion.

Potential Impact of Protections From Family Violence

Thus far, the discussion has led to two conclusions: that human rights law's current approaches to family life markedly depart from U.S. formal approach to family policy and that determining the potential impact of human rights law requires analyses of the two major ways human rights operate. As expected, the two approaches to understanding the domestication of international law offer fundamentally different conclusions about the potential impact of human rights law.

Traditional View of Human Rights Law

Although international law may become the law of the land, the narrow, traditional view of international law suggests otherwise. As reported by numerous commentators, the impact of international human rights instruments on U.S. law can be deemed negligible. Several points support this claim that the United States remains somewhat impermeable to human rights law as conceived by the international community.

The impact of ratified treaties remains to be determined. The United States has ratified several important treaties. The Convention on the Prevention and Punishment of the Crime of Genocide of 1948,[121] Political Covenant, Torture Convention, and the Racial Discrimination Convention have all become part of U.S. law and entered into force for U.S. law in 1989, 1992, and 1994.[122] Yet these treaties have had little formal impact on U.S. law, primarily because ratification efforts include documentation of how the United States already complies with human rights instruments, which creates considerable obstacles to efforts to find violations upon ratification. Moreover, the treaties have been subject to numerous reservations, declarations, or other understandings, which further limit their impact. The most frequent tactic to limit the use of treaties includes declarations that no treaty is self-executing. These obstacles to the implementation of treaties ensure that the United States complies with some of the treaties' mandates to the extent that the United States ratifies treaties, finds that it essentially complies with them, and thus escapes the charges that it has not made progress toward implementing human rights standards.

In addition to the failure of ratified treaties to affect policy and jurisprudence, their use as part of customary law is likely to be negligible if approached from a narrow view that focuses on judicial recognition. It has already been demonstrated that enforcement of such law faces numerous challenges. In addition, it is unclear which approach to protecting recognized customary rights would be mandated by international law. The narrow view of international law results in the conclusion that the United States already comports with human rights standards that provide protections from family violence. For example, both federal and state laws provide extensive, formal rights to protection from child abuse and neglect, elder abuse, spousal battering, and other forms of violence related to family life, such as exploitative child labor. Under this approach, the law already responds to protections that make the United States immune from challenges. In addition, the numerous other rights subsumable under the right to protection from family violence garner legal protection. For example, the rights to life, health, education, equality, and protection from inhuman treatment and torture all are subjects of impressive legislation. Equally important, the rights receive considerable state support in the form of financial backing. It would be difficult to argue that the United States fails to recognize these rights and has not taken steps to ensure their implementation.

In summary, international human rights implicated in efforts to protect individuals from family violence might not be enforceable in U.S. courts by either treaty or customary international law. Perhaps more importantly, if they were determined enforceable, much evidence could be marshaled to support claims that the United States already complies with its obligations. Domestic courts, and the U.S. legal system, however, may not be the only available avenue to pursue efforts to enact responses to family violence that respect human rights efforts.

Modern View of Human Rights Law

The broader approach to the domestication of international law suggests that international human rights may make a difference. The manner in which the human rights approach could reform current approaches to family violence is examined in chapter 8; it is important to examine at this point why the more expansive approach could affect U.S. law. The effect may come in four major ways, all of which are interrelated and seek to recognize the rights of individuals in families and the need to increase consciousness of rights.

International Obligations

The first benefit to derive from human rights law involves the extent to which the United States takes its international obligations seriously. Although few have argued that considering international obligations can benefit domestic responses to family violence, the obligations may play a powerful role. Most notably, the expansive view of human rights suggests that international obligations play a critical role: This view contributes to human rights consciousness and assists in mobilizing efforts.

An honest look at international protections from family violence, as enumerated in chapter 5, makes it difficult to conclude that U.S. law complies with the aspirations of human rights law. Every right, as enumerated in human rights law and viewed from an expansive view of such rights, fails to find full expression in the United States. The abuse and neglect of children offers a case in point. Even though some states in the United States arguably have moved toward ensuring children's rights in a manner consistent with a more expansive human rights approach, it would be difficult to conclude that current federal and state constitutional and legislative provisions actually comply with aspirations. For example, the right to an adequate standard of living[123] and health care[124] as well as the right to protection from child labor[125] and exploitation, abuse, and neglect[126] constitute the societal failures culminating in the current "national emergency" in child protection.[127] Likewise, the right to education constitutes a pervasively unfulfilled promise. The massive failure persists despite aggressive efforts in the form of millions of dollars per year spent on education, state recognition of the right to education as fundamental, and federal law's attempts to ensure access to education.[128] Rampant failure and disappointment in the state of American education would suggest that the United States fails to respect the right as envisioned in human rights law.[129]

Monitoring and Publicity

The human rights approach's second benefit emerges from the human rights law suggestion that there exists a need to focus on different levels of implementation. Among the most important aspects of implementation is the need to emphasize publicizing the nature and extent of family violence and monitoring those entrusted with implementing legal mandates. One reason to focus on monitoring and publicity derives from the current understanding of reforms. The major movements for greater protections have been triggered by persistent advocates. Much of the modern laws regulating child protection derive from the publication of "The Battered Child Syndrome," by Henry Kempe et al.[130] That article stimulated professional recognition of the full dimensions of the child maltreatment problem and helped bring the issue to the general public's attention. Likewise, the theoretical construct of the "battered women" was necessary to establish battered women as a legal and social construct.[131] These labels are strategically necessary for reform efforts. All reforms aimed at family violence emerged with record keeping, consciousness raising, and advocacy by professional groups. The extent of the power of such groups is marked by the growing criticisms against the professionalization and creation of social problems and "moral panics" that derive from efforts to enlist responses to recognized harms. Much of the furors relating to repressed memories and false accusations, for example, relate to the fabrication of memories by therapists.[132]

Moreover, the understanding of how reforms actually become and remain effective necessarily leads to a focus on publicizing and monitoring reforms. Sustained efforts come only through monitoring. For example, advocates use compliance monitoring to expose problem areas in the implementation of existing mandates, to prompt remedial action by agencies, and to educate the public about their rights. Compliance monitoring often takes the form of investigative studies and reports and direct legal assistance when laws permit. The child welfare system, for example, operates largely through compliance monitoring as it responds quickly to media exposes of failed efforts and, although less quickly, to children's rights advocates attempts to ensure that states comply with their basic mandates.[133]

Human rights law can contribute to the recognition and response to social problems by restructuring social consciousness. The major reason for failed legal reforms derives from the connection between consciousness and the law. As demonstrated in the closing chapter, the human rights movement both fosters discourse and charts responses.

Local Obligations

Another advantage of a more expansive human rights approach derives from the need to reconsider local obligations. Focusing on local obligations gains increasing significance because state laws largely control family law and criminal law. It can be argued that issues related to family policy remain formally within the province of states. The Supreme Court repeatedly assumes that family law is a matter for state law and argues for localism in family law.[134] Despite considerable evidence pointing to the existence of an exclusively local tradition in family law,[135] the Supreme Court officially adopts a localist approach to issues relating to family life.

A focus on state law also seems wise given that laws that do become federal percolate from state levels. For example, the federalization of laws relating to spousal and partner abuse has a long history. In the late 19th century, only two states (Alabama and Massachusetts) outlawed wife beating.[136] By the early 20th century, several other states took legislative action to classify wife beating as criminal assault. Yet prosecutions remained rare, and assaults were not considered "real" crimes.[137] The federal government responded at the end of the century, with the enactment of the Violence Against Women Act of 1994[138] and an effort to encourage more universal approaches to domestic violence.

Another reason to focus on state laws is that federal criminal laws and other laws relating to violence often have a state-level component. The federal–state interaction generally takes three forms. First, states remain free to move beyond minimal federal mandates. Second, federal criminal law has a "cooperative" component. Federalization of criminal laws results in cooperative jurisdiction, which places a focus on partnerships between federal and state officials.[139] Third, the federal government may grant funding on the condition that states enact specific laws. This last entanglement between federal and state arguably is the most powerful. Through the Child Abuse and Prevention Treatment and Adoption Reform Act of 1994,[140] for example, the federal government requires states to enact specific laws relating to child abuse and neglect. Likewise, the Violence Against Women Act provides $1.62 billion to battle violence against women. The bulk of the funding, however, only goes to states that submit plans to the U.S. Department of Justice, which evaluates the state's progress in enacting and enforcing legal reforms. For example, the statute authorizes the Attorney General to make grants to states if they certify that their laws have or encourage mandatory arrest procedures when dealing with domestic violence offenses.

A focus on state levels allows for a focus on reaching local consciousness. To reach effectiveness, reforms must affect local consciousness, and local consciousness must harness the power of reforms and seek further reform. Numerous effective responses to family violence provide strong examples of this need. Many groups and organizations, for example, have emerged to assist battered women. They have founded shelters and networks of "safe homes," set up hotlines, developed programs to work with battered women, and improved police and judicial responses.[141] In addition to advocacy, laws have created awareness. Likewise, much of the progress in response to child maltreatment derives from efforts to increase awareness about the nature and extent of such treatment as well as efforts to require individuals to respond by such measures as reporting instances of abuse.[142]

Move Beyond Judiciary

The modern human rights approach focuses beyond human rights as judicially enforceable. Proposals that argue the need to move beyond the judiciary may take two forms. First, judicial reforms continue to be far from effective in and of themselves, and several commentators have noted the limitations of the judicial expansion of rights. This is especially so with "programmatic" rights and those relating to discrimination. The educational reform efforts are illustrative of the challenge of judicial resolutions. Second, the problem with relying on judicial enforcement is that many existing laws remain ineffective. Although this is not to play down the need to rely on the judiciary to recognize basic human rights, it is important to emphasize that it is not the only approach to ensuring rights. Rather than focus on direct enforceability, the human rights movement focuses on ensuring rights through enabling conditions. From this perspective, states have only begun to enable the exercise of protections from family violence.

Four examples illustrate the need for reform that focuses beyond judicial involvement. The first example involves discrimination against those who are in need of services. Studies continue to identify concerns about differential treatment of minority families. Children of color are removed from their families more often than are White children and yet receive less comprehensive and possibly inferior services.[143] Interventions also vary by the color of victims of women battering and elder abuse. For example, certain minority populations receive less access to supportive services because multilingual services are not offered in shelters, hotlines, and counseling programs that target domestic violence victims.[144] The differential treatment continues into old age: Even though minorities are exposed to greater stressors, have fewer resources, and suffer from poorer health (both objectively and subjectively), they continue to have less access to in-home, community-based, and institutional services.[145] Other groups receive more intervention, as revealed by the disproportionate impact of mandatory arrests for domestic violence on non-White communities.[146]

The second example relates to research that concluded that poorer segments of the population do not have proper access to courts and services. Many of the problems faced by residents of low-income neighborhoods are legal problems or problems with legal components. Housing code violations, denials of public benefits, domestic violence, child custody, child support, health care coverage, and other issues suggest a distinctly legal solution.[147] Yet legal services for the poor have been cut dramatically and the funding that remains may limit the types of legal actions poverty lawyers could bring against governmental failures to fulfill legal obligations.

Third, children and adolescents continue to have limited access to the legal system. Adolescents, for example, are defined out of services available to those in similar situations, such as relationship violence, sexual harassment, and stalking.[148] Most notably, the law not only grants them less access to the services but also prohibits access to the legal system—children generally are viewed as legally incompetent and must rely on adults who may not recognize (or may be the ones doing) violence against them. Likewise, even though access may be available in theory, the children may not be aware of their rights or lack supportive services that would enable them to benefit from those recognized rights. In summary, the narrow focus on judicial enforcement of basic rights leaves the most vulnerable with human rights violations.

Fourth, child welfare systems continue to be in crisis. It is no secret that local child protection agencies fail to meet their mandates.[149] More than a decade after the federal government enacted funding legislation designed to protect against the over-reliance and abuses of foster care, the states pervasively fail to provide meaningful supports and responses to maltreatment. In fact, nearly half the states are under court supervision for failing to provide basic services to children in need of protection, which has led several to question the utility of the current approach which focuses on individual, case-specific response as opposed to broader institutional and societal reform that addresses the needs of poor families and those devalued by the dominant culture.[150]

Preliminary Conclusion

Despite the absence of analysis of the possible impact of human rights law on family violence experienced in the United States, a look at the different ways in which human rights are implemented and the divergence between international and U.S. approaches to family violence reveal a potential for impact. Although a narrow view of human rights may lead to the conclusion that human rights law would have a negligible impact on domestic policy, a more expansive view of how human rights operate leads to an opposite conclusion. A need to recognize international obligations, monitor and publicize the nature of family violence, ensure efforts for reforms at local levels, and attempt to move beyond viewing rights as solely judicial concerns leads to the conclusion that the substantive principles enshrined in human rights law differ enough to affect how the U.S. approaches family violence. Struggles to secure fundamental human rights ultimately remain local, and human rights progress only through domestic activism. Such advocacy suggests that human rights documents could make a difference in current U.S. legal approaches and obligations to children and families.

Conclusion

A review of current and evolving international mandates suggests that international law no longer can be dismissed as utopian and epiphenomenal to the realities of power politics abroad and at home. Despite limitations, the apparent narrowness of human rights law's margins and boundaries is not necessarily cause for apocalyptic prognostications. Rather, it is cause for suggesting, proposing, and promoting the directions its progressive development should take. Law-abiding States and peoples incorporate international law into their domestic legal and political structure. Nations do so in several ways that contribute to the construction of a culture of rights and a rights-conscious society.

Human rights principles were meant to be, and undoubtedly are, a milestone in a global strategy that aims to change our attitudes toward individuals and families. The human rights movement urges individuals to rethink current policies marked by contradicting visions about the proper role of children's voices, parents' authority and obligations, adults' rights and privileges, and states' responsibilities in matters concerning families. That fundamental mandate is the most critical contribution offered by the human rights movement to those interested in changing the place vulnerable individuals occupy in society.

Individuals must rethink the current discourse about human rights. Human rights instruments are "living documents." It would be unwise to preclude arguments about the aspirations of human rights treaties and guiding documents. In human rights law, this proposition is well-established. Human rights consist largely of norms *de lege ferenda*, the law that ought to be made, as opposed to *lex lata,* the law that is already made.

Because human rights law is about law that is about to be made, it makes sense to think about the transformative power of human rights law. Human rights law deals with cultural change, with the way in which cultures address competing interests, groups, and needs. Discourse should involve starting a discussion of the future of rights, not only of the ratification of specific instruments and their potentially narrow impact. The current approach that narrows the aspirations of human rights consistently fails to alter U.S. law: The history of ratified documents in the United States shows little impact; obligations were watered down to the point that they comported with U.S. law, and discussion about the treaties focused on how they would not change U.S. obligations. The failed impact is not surprising. A fundamental rule of legal interpretation mandates reliance on legislative history when there is ambiguity in legal texts. The failure to provide history with a broader vision of what may be found in human rights documents ensures that those who view no fundamental difference between U.S. and international mandates will prevail.

Legal documents play a critical role in cultural change. That is why human rights law focuses (see chapter 4) first and foremost on deliberation and the protection of deliberation. Advocates must aim not only to affect the law as it is but also to change the context of law and ensure that human rights principles infiltrate cultural and individual consciousness. The point is of utmost significance. Human rights gain their legitimacy from being rooted in the people. The faith in discourse actually reflects what both historical and modern developments in international law are all about. The basic faith in human interactions characterized by visions of a humanity that champion equality, inclusion, and respect for human dignity forms the very foundation of human rights law. The principles apply to what should be the goal not only for governments but also for individuals in their everyday interactions. That is why the human rights movement should be used to rethink U.S. law and why it is a mistake to propose that human rights instruments simply replicate existing conceptions of rights and that those that do not do not deserve consideration.

Although we already have seen the dramatic difference between human rights mandates and U.S. law as well as how human rights may change U.S. family policy, one question still remains. How can the movement help reform the substantive U.S. approaches to family violence? The remaining chapters address how current approaches to family violence would differ if the United States took its human rights obligations more seriously.

Endnotes

1. R. J. R. Levesque, "Educating American Youth: Lessons From Children's Human Rights Law," *Journal of Law and Education* 27 (1998):173–209.
2. Children's Convention, U.N. General Assembly, 44th Sess., Official Records, Supplement 49 at 166, Resolution 44/25, A/44/49; 28 ILM 1448, 1989.
3. *Cf.* C. P. Cohen and H. A. Davidson, Eds., *Children's Rights in America: U.N. Conven-*

tion on the Rights of the Child Compared With United States Law (Chicago: American Bar Association, Center on Children and the Law, 1990).

4. American Bar Association, *Report of the American Bar Association Working Group on the United Nations Convention on the Rights of the Child* (Washington, DC: Author, 1993).

5. S. P. Limber and B. L. Wilcox, "Application of the U.N. Convention on the Rights of the Child to the United States," *American Psychologist* 51 (1996):1246–1250.

6. H. H. Clark, "Children and the Constitution," *University of Illinois Law Review* 1992 (1992):1–41.

7. *See, e.g.*, G. B. Melton, "The Right to a Family Environment for 'Children Living in Exceptionally Difficult Conditions,'" *Law & Policy* 17 (1995):345–351.

8. *See, e.g.*, Cohen and Davidson, *Children's Rights in America*; J. Davidson, "A Model Child Protection Legal Reform Instrument: The Convention on the Rights of the Child and Its Consistency With United States Law," *Georgetown Journal on Fighting Poverty* 5 (1998):185–197.

9. *See, e.g.*, K. M. Smith, "The United Nations Convention on the Rights of the Child: The Sacrifice of American Children at the Altar of Third-World Activism," *Washburn Law Journal* 38 (1998):111–150.

10. *See, e.g.*, R. J. R. Levesque, "International Children's Rights: Can They Make a Difference in American Family Policy?" *American Psychologist* 51 (1996):1251–1256; Levesque, "Educating American Youth."

11. U.S. CONSTITUTION, Article II, § 2 clause 2.

12. Foster v. Nelson, 27 U.S. (2 Pet.) 253, 314 (1829).

13. *See* C. A. Bradley, "Breard, Our Dualist Constitution, and the International Conception," *Stanford Law Review* 51 (1999):529–566.

14. Whitney v. Robertson, 124 U.S. 190, 194 (1888); Reid v. Covert, 354 U.S. 1, 18 (1957).

15. Missouri v. Holland, 252 U.S. 416, 433–435 (1920); Zschernig v. Miller, 389 U.S. 429, 440–441 (1968).

16. *Reid*, 354 U.S. at 16.

17. Murray v. Schooner Charming Betsy, 6 U.S. (2 Cranch) 64, 118 (1804).

18. *See* A. Bayefsky and J. Fitzpatrick, "International Human Rights Law in United States Courts: A Comparative Perspective," *Michigan Journal of International Law* 14 (1992): 1–89.

19. L. Henkin, *The Rights of Man Today* (London: Stevens & Sons, 1979) at 50.

20. R. J. R. Levesque, "The Sexual Use, Abuse and Exploitation of Children: Challenges in Implementing Children's Human Rights," *Brooklyn Law Review* 60 (1994):959–998.

21. R. J. R. Levesque, "Maintaining Children's Familial Relationships With Mentally Disabled Parents: Recognizing Difference and the Difference That It Makes," *Children's Legal Rights Journal* 16 (1996):14–22.

22. *See, e.g.*, *Missouri*, 252 U. S. at 416.

23. U.S. CONSTITUTION, Article VI, § 2.

24. K. Wolfke, *Custom in Present International Law* 2d ed. (Boston: Martinus Nijhoff, 1993).

25. The Paquete Habana, 175 U.S. 677, 700 (1900).

26. *See, e.g.*, J. J. Paust, "Rediscovering the Relationship Between Congressional Power and International Law: Exceptions to the Last in Time Rule and the Primacy of Custom," *Virginia Journal of International Law* 28 (1988): 393–449.

27. *See* L. Henkin, "The Constitution and United States Sovereignty: A Century of Chinese Exclusion and Its Progeny," *Harvard Law Review* 100 (1987):853–886.

28. The Paquete Habana, 175 U.S. at 710–711.

29. *Murray*, 6 U.S. (2 Cranch) 64, 118 (1804).

30. *See* J. Turley, "Dualistic Values in the Age of International Legisprudence," *Hastings Law Journal* 44 (1993):185–272.

31. Thompson v. Oklahoma, 487 U.S. 815, 831 (1988).
32. Stanford v. Kentucky, 492 U.S. 361, 369, 369 (1989).
33. *See, e.g.*, A. Bayefsky and J. Fitzpatrick, "International Human Rights Law in United States Courts: A Comparative Perspective," *Michigan Journal of International Law* 14 (1992):1–89.
34. *Cf.* L. Henkin, "International Human Rights Standards in National Law: The Jurisprudence of the United States," in *Enforcing International Human Rights in Domestic Courts*, B. Conforti and F. Francioni, Eds. (The Hague, Netherlands: Kluwer Law International, 1997).
35. J. J. Paust, "Avoidant Fraudulent Executive Policy: Analysis of Non-Self-Execution on the Covenant on Civil and Political Rights," *DePaul Law Review* 42 (1993):1257–1285.
36. United States v. Belmont, 301 U.S. 324, 331-332 (1937).
37. United States v. Alvarez-Machain, 112 S.Ct. 2188 (1992).
38. *See* S. Wilske and T. Schiller, "Jurisdictions Over Persons Abducted in Violation of International Law in the Aftermath of United States v. Alvarez-Machain," *University of Chicago Law School Roundtable* 5 (1998):205–241.
39. *See, e.g.*, T. C. Barsumian, "Bail Bondsman and Bounty Hunters: Re-Examining the Right to Recapture," *Drake Law Review* 47 (1999):877–910.
40. *See* H. H. Koh, "The Haiti Paradigm in United States Human Rights Policy," *Yale Law Journal* 103 (1994):2391–2435.
41. The Paquete Habana, 175 U.S. at 677, 700.
42. Goldwater v. Carter, 44 U.S. 996 (1979).
43. *See* Fernandez-Roque v. Smith, 622 F. Supp. 887 (N.D. Ga., 1985); Garcia Mir v. Meese, 788 F.2d 1446 (11th Cir. 1986).
44. R. H. Gaskins, "Default Presumptions in Legislation: Implementing Children's Services," *Harvard Journal of Law & Public Policy* 17 (1994):779–800.
45. Children's Convention, 1989, Article 4 (emphasis added).
46. Economic and Social Covenant, U.N. General Assembly, 21st Sess., Official Records, Suppl.16 at 49, GA Resolution 2200 Annex, A/6316; 993 UNTS 3; 6 ILM 360, 1966.
47. Political Covenant, U.N. General Assembly, 21st Sess., Official Records, Suppl. 16 at 49, GA Resolution 2200, A/6316; 999 UNTS 171; 6 ILM 368, 1966.
48. Convention on the Elimination of All Forms of Racial Discrimination (1966, *opened for signature* Mar. 7, 1966), 600 U.N.T.S. 195.
49. Women's Convention, U.N. General Assembly, 34th Sess., Official Records, Suppl. 46 at 193, GA Resolution 34/180, A/34/46, 1979.
50. Torture Convention, U.N. General Assembly, 30th Sess., Official Records, Suppl. 34 at 91, GA Resolution 3452 (Dec. 10, 1984), 23 I.L.M. 1027, as modified, 24 I.L.M. 535.
51. *See* G. Kent, *Children in the International Political Economy* (New York: St. Martin's Press, 1995); *see also* chapter 5.
52. M. Longford, "NGOs and the Rights of the Child," in *The Conscience of the World: The Influence of Non-Governmental Organizations in the UN System*, P. Willetts, Ed. (Washington, DC: Brookings Institute, 1996).
53. *See* J. Best, Ed., *Troubling Children: Studies of Children and Social Problems* (New York: Aldine de Gruyter, 1994).
54. *See* C. F. Alger, "Citizens and the UN System in a Changing World," in *Global Transformation: Challenges to the State System*, Y. Sakamoto, Ed. (New York: United Nations University Press, 1994).
55. J. J. Paust, *International Law as Law of the United States* (Durham, NC: Carolina Academic Press, 1996) at 286–287, 318.
56. J. Brownlie, *Principles of Public International Law* 4th ed. (New York: Oxford University Press, 1990).
57. M. Ragazzi, *The Concept of International Obligations Erga Omnes* (New York: Oxford University Press, 1997).

58. Levesque, "International Children's Rights."

59. *See* R. J. R. Levesque, *Child Sexual Abuse: A Human Rights Perspective* (Bloomington: Indiana University Press, 1999).

60. *See* T. Meron, *Human Rights and Humanitarian Norms as Customary Law* (Oxford, England: Clarendon Press, 1989).

61. U.N. Charter, 1 UNTS xvi, 1945

62. *See* H. H. Koh, "Bringing International Law Back Home," *Houston Law Review* 35 (1998):623–681.

63. *See* M. Straus, *Beating the Devil Out of Them: Corporal Punishment in American Families* (New York: Lexington Books, 1994).

64. D. L. Coleman, "Individualizing Justice Through Multiculturalism: The Liberals' Dilemma," *Columbia Law Review* 96 (1996):1093–1107.

65. *See* Henkin, "International Human Rights Standards in National Law."

66. *See*, most notably, L. Brilmayer, "Federalism, State Authority, and the Preemptive Power of International Law," *Supreme Court Review* 1994 (1995):295–343.

67. Moore v. Ganim, 660 A.2d 742 (Conn. 1995).

68. Senate Committee on Foreign Relations, *Report on the International Covenant on Civil and Political Rights*, S. Exec. Doc. No. 23, 102nd Cong., 2nd Sess. (June 20, 1992) at 18.

69. 120 S.Ct. 1740 (2000).

70. P. L. 103–222, Title IV, 108 Stat. 1902, 1941–1942, 42 U.S.C. § 1398(b) (1994).

71. The general rule does have important exceptions. The federal government could be involved if the crimes implicated more than one state. Likewise, the federal government can encourage states to enact certain laws by making it a condition to partake of federal monies available to the states to fight crime.

72. P. J. Spiro, "The States and International Human Rights," *Fordham Law Review* 66 (1997):567–596.

73. Breard v. Greene, 118 S.Ct. 1352 (1998).

74. Bradley, "Breard, Our Dualist Constitution, and the International Conception."

75. *See, e.g.*, P. J. Spiro, "New Global Potentates: Nongovernmental Organizations and the 'Unregulated' Marketplace," *Cardozo Law Review* 18 (1996):957–969.

76. Children's Convention, Article 8.

77. *Id.*, Article 9.

78. Meyer v. Nebraska, 262 U.S. 390 (1923).

79. Pierce v. Society of Sisters, 268 U.S. 510 (1925).

80. *Id.* at 535.

81. Wisconsin v. Yoder, 406 U.S. 205 (1972).

82. B. B. Woodhouse, "Who Owns the Child? *Meyer* and *Pierce* and the Child as Property," *William & Mary Law Review* 33 (1992):995–1122.

83. L. L. Lane, "The Parental Rights Movement," *University of Colorado Law Review* 69 (1998):825–849.

84. Michael H. v. Gerald D., 109 S.Ct. 2333 (1989).

85. *Id.* at 2337.

86. For a review of cases, *see* R. J. R. Levesque, "International Children's Rights Grow Up: Implications for American Jurisprudence and Domestic Policy," *California Western International Law Journal* 24 (1994):193–240.

87. Troxel v. Grandville, U.S. S.Ct., No. 99-138 (June 5, 2000).

88. Washington Rev. Code, § 26.10.160(3) (1999).

89. *Troxel* at 57–59.

90. Children's Convention, Article 2.

91. *See, e.g.*, Universal Declaration of Human Rights, U.N. General Assembly, 3rd Sess., Official Records, *Part I. Resolutions*, Resolution 217A, UN Doc A/810, 1948, Preamble, Articles 1 and 2.

92. *E.g.*, Political Covenant, Article 17.
93. Hodgson v. Minnesota, 110 S.Ct. 2926 (1990).
94. For the most recent case in this area, *see* Lambert v. Wicklund, 520 U.S. 292 (1997).
95. For a review of these cases, *see* R. J. R. Levesque, "International Children's Rights Grow Up."
96. Prince v. Massachusetts, 321 U.S. 158 (1944).
97. Lassiter v. Department of Social Services, 452 U.S. 18, 27 (1981).
98. Santosky v. Kramer, 455 U.S. 745, 753 (1982).
99. Eisenstadt v. Baird, 405 U.S. 438 (1972).
100. Griswold v. Connecticut, 381 U.S. 479 (1965).
101. Eisenstadt, 405 U.S. at 453 (emphasis in original).
102. Bowers v. Hardwick, 478 U.S. 186 (1986).
103. This includes the right to protection against discrimination based on sexual orientation; *see*, *e.g.*, L. R. Helfer and A. M. Miller, "Sexual Orientation and Human Rights: Toward a United States and Transnational Jurisprudence," *Harvard Human Rights Journal* 9 (1996):61–103.
104. Children's Convention, Article 4.
105. *Id.*, Article 3.
106. DeShaney v. Winnebago County Dept. of Soc. Services, 489 U.S. 189 (1989).
107. *Id.* at 196.
108. *Id.* at 203.
109. *Id.*
110. Suter v. Artist, 112 S.Ct. 1360 (1992).
111. Adoption Assistance and Child Welfare Act of 1980, P. L. 96-272, 94 Stat. 500; 42 U.S.C.A. § 670–677 (1980).
112. 42 U.S. CODE, § 1983, 1994.
113. Roe v. Wade, 410 U.S. 113 (1973); Moore v. City of East Cleveland, 431 U.S. 494 (1977).
114. *Santosky*, 455 U.S. at 753.
115. Dandridge v. Williams, 397 U.S. 471 (1970).
116. *Id.* at 487.
117. 119 S.Ct. 1518 (1999).
118. *Id.* at 1526.
119. M. L. B. v. S. L. J., 117 S.Ct. 555 (1996).
120. Personal Responsibility and Work Opportunity Reconciliation Act of 1996, P. L. 104-193, 110 Stat. 2105 (codified as amended in scattered sections of 42 U.S.C.).
121. Convention on the Prevention and Punishment of the Crime of Genocide (1948, *opened for signature* Dec. 9, 1948), 78 U.N.T.S. 277.
122. R. J. R. Levesque, "Child Advocacy and the Power of Human Rights Law," in *Children as Equals? Exploring the Rights of the Child*, B. Klug and K. Alaimo, Eds. (Lanham, MD: University Press of America, in press).
123. Children's Convention, Articles 26 and 27.
124. *Id.*, Article 24.
125. *Id.*, Article 32.
126. *Id.*, Articles 19, 34, 35, and 36.
127. U.S. Advisory Board on Child Abuse and Neglect, *Neighbors Helping Neighbors: A New National Strategy for the Protection of Children* (Washington, DC: U.S. Government Printing Office, 1993).
128. Levesque, "Educating American Youth."
129. *Id.*
130. C. H. Kempe, F. N. Silverman, B. F. Steele, W. Droegemuerler, and H. K. Silver, The Battered Child Syndrome," *Journal of the American Medical Society* 181 (1962):17–24.

131. L. E. Walker, *The Battered Woman* (New York: Harper, 1979).
132. *See* R. A. Leo, "Recovered Memory and the Law: The Social and Legal Construction of Repressed Memory," *Law & Social Inquiry* 22 (1997):653–693.
133. R. J. R. Levesque, "The Failures of Foster Care Reform: Revolutionizing the Most Radical Blueprint," *Maryland Journal of Contemporary Legal Issues* 6 (1995):1–35.
134. *See* United States v. Lopez, 514 U.S. 549 (1995).
135. *See* J. E. Hasday, "Federalism and the Family Reconstructed," *UCLA Law Review* 45 (1998):1297–1400.
136. M. Griffith, "Battered Women Syndrome: A Tool for Batterers?" *Fordham Law Review* 64 (1995):141–198.
137. *Id.*
138. Violence Against Women Act of 1994, P. L. 103-322, 108 Stat. 1902–1955.
139. *See* R. M. Landers, "Federalization of State Law: Enhancing Opportunities for Three-Branch and Federal–State Cooperation," *DePaul Law Review* 44 (1995):811–824.
140. Child Abuse and Prevention Treatment and Adoption Reform Act of 1994, 41 U.S.C § 5106(a).
141. L. Mills, *The Heart of Intimate Abuse* (New York: Springer, 1998).
142. R. J. R. Levesque, "Prosecuting Sex Crimes Against Children: Time for 'Outrageous' Proposals?" *Law & Psychology Review* 19 (1995):59–91.
143. H. N. Ahn, "Cultural Diversity and the Definition of Child Abuse," *Child Welfare Research Review* 1 (1994):28–55.
144. K. Wang, "Battered Asian American Women: Community Responses From the Battered Women's Movement and the Asian American Community," *Asian Law Journal* 3 (1996): 151–184.
145. A. C. Mui, N. C. Choi, and A. Monk, *Long-Term Care and Ethnicity* (Westport, CT: Auburn House, 1998).
146. *See, e.g.,* M. H. Ruttenberg, "A Feminist Critique of Mandatory Arrest: An Analysis of Race and Gender in Domestic Violence Policy," *American University Journal of Gender & the Law* 2 (1994):171–199.
147. E. S. Cahn, "The Informal Economy: Reinventing Poverty Law," *Yale Law Journal* 103 (1994):2133–2155; M. Feldman, "Political Lessons: Legal Services for the Poor," *Georgetown Law Journal* 83 (1995):1529–1632.
148. R. J. R. Levesque, "Emotional Maltreatment in Adolescents' Everyday Lives: Furthering Sociolegal and Social Service Provisions," *Behavioral Sciences and the Law* 16 (1998): 237–263.
149. Levesque, "The Failures of Foster Care."
150. *See* A. R. Appell, "Protecting Children or Punishing Mothers: Gender, Race, and Class in the Child Protection System," *South Carolina Law Review* 48 (1997):577–613.

Chapter 7
CULTURAL LIFE, FAMILY VIOLENCE, AND U.S. LAW

Previous chapters highlighted the significant role cultural forces play in family violence, how human rights principles respond to cultural issues and family violence, and how the United States can respond to human rights concerns. This chapter explores the effect of human rights' challenges and principles on the U.S. legal system's approach to cultural forces that affect family violence. Despite commitment to cultural pluralism and the immigrant foundations of U.S. society, the legal system's approach to different cultural demands that relate to family violence remains generally unexplored and difficult to ascertain. An appropriate starting point for extrapolation undoubtedly involves the more blatant instances of cultural clashes and challenges to laws regulating family violence that emerge when immigrants treat their family members in allegedly culturally condoned ways that are nevertheless inconsistent with dominant legal values. Such an analysis exposes cultural forces at work in the legal system that foster and condone family violence.

Although understanding immigrants' challenges reveals much about the dominant legal system's approach to family violence and how it deals with dominant cultural values and forces, other reasons also suggest a need to investigate immigrants' issues. Understanding how individual family members from immigrant communities treat each other actually gains increasing significance in itself and creates renewed challenges to responses to family violence. Immigrants and others from insular cultural groups recently have contested the slew of new legal responses to the recognition of family violence. Their general argument is that their cultural beliefs justify or excuse their actions (which would otherwise violate U.S. laws). Although historically reticent to consider such evidence, the legal system increasingly receives and evaluates such arguments.

Numerous examples culled from recent cases illustrate the difficulties posed by cultural disagreement and the introduction of cultural evidence in legal responses to family violence. How should the law treat a mother who attempts suicide with her children but is rescued and explains she killed her children in a culturally appropriate response to her husband's infidelity? How should parents be treated if they follow their cultural principles, which compel them to force their 13- and 14-year-old daughters to marry and have sexual relations with adult men? What about parents who refuse medical treatment because cultural beliefs require them to shun medical assistance? What response should be taken to address practices that involve the partial excision of boys' and girls' genitals, practices conducted in accordance with apparently legitimate cultural beliefs? Should the legal system consider claims that men who kill their adulterous wives be excused because their culture sanctions such responses?

The legal system's response to these questions reflects its willingness to impose standards on other peoples' conceptions of family life and the extent to which it tolerates what it considers violence. Without doubt, the results of the actions contradict U.S. law's prohibitions against murder, child abuse, and other forms of assault.

Yet in the cases that have been brought forth (and reviewed below), the cultural evidence generally served either to exonerate assaulters or to mitigate their punishment. At its core, such tolerance for foreign practices and cultures raises two fundamental concerns regarding U.S. law's response to family violence. Consideration of the evidence involves deciding the manner and extent to which the legal system can permit abusive individuals to introduce evidence of cultural background without condoning violence against family members. The second concern becomes the extent to which the legal system must grant deference to cultural evidence in the negation or mitigation of state responses to instances of family violence.

How the legal system addresses these concerns becomes increasingly pressing and controversial. Numerous contemporary social forces make urgent the search for resolutions to the two challenges. The issues reflect an apparent collision course between the need to increase legal systems' responsiveness to claims of pluralism and efforts to take family violence more seriously. Family violence laws and the social recognition of child, elder, and partner maltreatment have gone through rapid transformations. Those transformations have been paralleled by renewed efforts to recognize different groups' civil rights and to respect different cultures.[1] In addition to apparent cultural clashes, the clashes take on renewed significance in that there continues to be an influx of individuals from different cultures who legitimately espouse traditional customs that conflict with U.S. law. Although different peoples always have come to the United States, two factors suggest contemporary differences. Recent decades have witnessed transformations in U.S. laws that allow more immigration of non-Western peoples who hold customs that may vary more from the mass of prior immigrants (or who at least offer the types of cultural evidence leading to current legal challenges).[2] Furthermore, numerous cultural groups in the United States are made up of foreign-born immigrants. For example, Asian Americans have a rate of foreign birth that is 10 times that for the general U.S. population; more than 60% are foreign born.[3] The result is that, in some communities, those who victimize and the vast majority of adult victims predominantly are foreign born and face different challenges.

In addition to population shifts and traditional tensions between mainstream and minority rights and obligations, the tensions take on new meaning with the rise of multiculturalism and the backlash against immigrants. For example, issues of multiculturalism increase awareness of the need to respect cultural life. As demonstrated throughout the previous chapters, settled human rights law demands respect for different cultural practices. That respect is buttressed by the U.S. ethos grounded in basic democratic principles that require respect for different conceptions of community life. Despite that increased awareness, there exists an uneasiness about immigration and about crimes committed by "aliens" and individuals from particular communities. Current responses to crime increasingly marginalize and assume that different groups of individuals pose a greater threat to the legal order. As scholars versed in critical and feminist legal theory convincingly purport, policy responses increasingly conflate immigrant status, lawbreaking, and race.[4] The most recent welfare and immigration regulations, for example, reduce social benefits on the basis of immigration status, undermine earlier legislation offering protection to immigrant family members at risk for family violence, and reflect the belief that those who are not fully part of U.S. society need not receive all of its benefits.[5]

Although offering pressing and somewhat novel issues, cultural evidence also presents familiar concerns. To enter legal responses to family violence, cultural issues need not deal only with immigrants' foreign ways of life. To a large degree, numerous examples of "cultural" defenses already exist in various guises. For example, the defenses are either explicit (e.g., states allowing religious defenses for actions that otherwise may constitute neglect) or implicit in that society pervasively does not even recognize the violence of some practices (e.g., various forms of corporal punishment and genital circumcisions).[6] In addition, the cultural forces may not even be recognizable as causes; a prime example involves the extent to which the legal system reinforces traditional values yet refuses to exonerate offenders who commit violence in response to those values. Likewise, issues surrounding the use of cultural evidence are not new to the extent that the legal system always makes use of cultural evidence. Both defendants and prosecutors routinely introduce cultural evidence in the form of social background and other evidence that permits triers of fact to understand the cases before them. Most notably, in cases involving capital sentencing, the U.S. Supreme Court requires states to admit "any relevant mitigating factor" that could affect jurors' decisions;[7] for example, child maltreatment is the paradigmatic mitigating evidence that allows juries to understand the crime within the broader context of the defendant's life.[8] Indeed, the existing legal defenses that take into account certain lack of mental states are themselves cultural; for example, states allow evidence of voluntary intoxication to negate the defendant's *mens rea*, to serve as a basis for an insanity defense, or to mitigate sentencing.[9] Moreover, the law already regulates expert testimony and the admission of novel evidence. Established rules of evidence make the use of cultural evidence somewhat settled and already offer ways to address cultural evidence. Yet rules of evidence remain pervasively ignored by commentators and, equally problematically, judicial decisions that examine issues of cultural evidence generally do not discuss how they applied the laws of evidence to allow or reject cultural evidence. These examples reveal how issues of cultural evidence seep into and already affect the adjudication of disputes.

Complications that arise from the effect of novel and familiar issues on the legal system's use of cultural evidence become considerably more complicated by laws that regulate family life and family violence. Unlike other legal contexts that use other novel defenses, such as those involving "abuse excuses" and psychological syndromes that require specialized testimony,[10] the laws regulating families actually involve two formal sets of laws. The first set involves traditional criminal law. That system places a focus on identification, punishment, and deterrence of offenders. The second system involves civil laws, such as child welfare laws that take the form of child abuse and neglect legislation. That system tends to focus more on identification of victimization, prevention, and rehabilitation of both victims and offenders. The systems pose different challenges to the use of cultural evidence.

Although the two sets of laws pursue goals that frequently intersect, these systems' differences necessitate considering them separately for at least four reasons. First, the two systems adopt different approaches to family violence and allow for different uses of cultural evidence. Second, those interested in cultural evidence in legal systems focus on criminal law and ignore how cultural information actually may be crucial to civil law. Third, both sets of laws operate in virtually all forms of family violence. For example, civil reporting laws relate to the victimization of children, women, and elderly people, and civil law provides remedies that include suits against offenders for harms and against the state for failure to provide social services;

criminal law affects all forms of violence, especially because it aims to control severe violence and to prevent such violence through threats that punishment comes to those who fail to restrain their actions. Failure to consider different legal approaches to family violence creates polarized debates, which do not recognize the realities of how family violence law operates and how victims gain protection. Unlike responses to other forms of victimization, civil and criminal legal responses to family violence allocate different weight to the needs and rights of victims, offenders, and society.

Although much may be settled in terms of legal doctrine and the rampant use of cultural information by litigants, the law faces the need to address the increasing use of cultural information and offer a more consistent, doctrinal, and reasoned approach to the use of cultural evidence when proffered by individuals from different cultures. This chapter details the contours of the current use of cultural evidence and proposes that both civil and criminal law must reform current approaches to cultural evidence. Instead of the current system, which actively seeks to ignore cultural evidence in criminal law yet embraces or condones cultural practices in civil law, the chapter proposes that family violence reform requires a similar interrogation of cultural evidence regardless of legal arena. The analysis delineates responses to likely objections to the proposed approach. The presentation highlights how systems now fail to find any accommodation at all between cultural information or receive cultural evidence in an unquestioning fashion and how both approaches send the unfortunate and inappropriate message that society tolerates culturally ingrained forms of family violence. To counter these limitations, the chapter offers concrete steps that can be taken to respond to cultural issues in a manner consistent with human rights principles.

Civil Law's Active Embrace and Approval of Cultural Practices

Although the civil regulation of family life generally involves disputes regarding divorce, child custody, and parental obligations, civil laws actually pervasively regulate and intervene in family life. That pervasiveness clearly affects cultural practices related to family violence. Understanding civil law's extensive control of family and cultural life and its relationship to family violence requires distinguishing issues relating to parent–child relationships and adult–adult relationships. Although both areas of law relate to each other and take similar approaches to family life, they offer different approaches to cultural practices: Civil laws regulating parents' and children's cultural practices actively support cultural life, whereas laws regulating cultural practices in adults' familial relationships generally seek to ignore cultural practices.

Embracing Cultural Protections for Children

Although an argument could be made that civil law generally seeks to ignore cultural beliefs that affect parenting (as would be supported by the myth that the government stays out of "private" family life), civil law does much more than that. The civil system seeks to protect cultural practices and especially does so in its responses to child maltreatment. Civil responses make extensive use of cultural information and generally aim to respect cultural dictates. Because the system seeks not to punish but, instead, to remedy the harms children face, the system generally views cultural evidence as useful in offering assistance to children, or the cultural information is used to deny services when the practices are perceived as permissible, alternative means to rear children. Although this area of law remains vast, both statutory protections and constitutional jurisprudence seek to ensure that child welfare systems respect, and sometimes even capitalize on, cultural information when the state intervenes to protect children.[11] This section delineates how laws typically allow for the protection of cultural practices.

The most explicit formulation of the need to protect cultural beliefs and practices comes in the form of statutory mandates that require consideration of parents' cultural practices in determinations of child maltreatment and appropriate interventions in response to those practices. Colorado law, for example, requires those investigating reports of child abuse to take into account accepted childrearing practices of the parents' culture.[12] Colorado also mandates that family preservation efforts must consider the cultural background of the family when assessing familial needs.[13] Likewise, California law provides that "cultural and religious childrearing practices and beliefs which differ from general community standards shall not in themselves create a need for child welfare services unless the practices present a specific danger to the physical or emotional safety of the child."[14] Other parts of the California statutes include a blanket requirement that child abuse prevention, intervention, and treatment organizations provide culturally appropriate services.[15] Other states simply provide that their entire child welfare system "must be designed to be child-centered, family-focused, community-based and *culturally competent* in its prevention and protection efforts."[16]

In addition to using culture as a factor to assist in determining and responding to child maltreatment, cultural practices help dictate what to do with children deemed in need of assistance or under state control. States consider cultural issues in many ways, three of which are illustrative. The first example involves how states explicitly protect certain groups. For example, states are required to do so under the federal Indian Child Welfare Act (ICWA).[17] The ICWA protects Native American populations against unnecessary removal of Indian children from their families and tribes. The law does so, for example, by involving tribes in child welfare proceedings and increasing the state's burden of proof before removing children from their homes. When children are removed from their homes, the law requires a focus on children's placement with Indian families and consideration of cultural and social implications of removal for the child and the tribe. New Mexico's statute illustrates the actual implementation at state levels; the statute requires dispositions of state child welfare interventions "to provide for a culturally appropriate treatment plan, [and for] access to cultural practices and traditional treatment for an Indian Child."[18]

The second example of statutory mandates that protect cultural life involves the provision by some states of culturally appropriate services and treatment for delinquent youth of minority backgrounds. Although several states and child welfare organizations may seek to do so in practice, some states statutorily require culturally fitting responses. These states, for example, encourage the development of alternatives to incarceration that involve culturally appropriate programming.[19] Thus, much effort, supported by law, seeks to provide culturally appropriate services in a culturally competent manner that integrates the needs and strengths of ethnic communities into the organization's mission, staffing, and programs. These efforts are part of a growing movement that seeks to respect and treat the youths' environment to which they will ultimately return and become reintegrated. Although some consider these laws extraneous to child abuse and neglect laws, they actually are related when focus moves to adolescents (rather than young children) and when one takes into account how delinquency, acting out, and criminal behavior clearly are related to difficult family environments.[20]

The third example involves the unwitting protection of cultural life offered by child welfare laws, even though the law may prohibit them from considering factors related to cultural life—the controversial prohibition in considering race in adoptions. Although federal statutes prohibit agencies from using race to determine the fitness of parents for adoptions, parents remain free to use racial preferences in their adoption decisions. Agencies facilitate the exercise of racial preferences by prospective adoptive parents because the agencies remain oriented toward fulfilling the preferences of adoptive parents.[21] The difficulties encountered by the legal removal of race consciousness in adoptions provides a measure of the formidability of barriers to removing cultural beliefs from child welfare law. Regardless of the relative appropriateness of considering cultural or racial backgrounds in responses to child welfare issues, the regulation of adoption does reveal how the law in theory and in practice considers cultural evidence, even when the law seeks not to do so.

Although some states explicitly provide for the use (or even nonuse) of an individual's cultural background to determine the presence of abuse and the state's response to children in need of assistance, other states do not. Those that do not explicitly protect cultural practices, however, frequently do so implicitly. Two examples illustrate the broad protection cultural practices enjoy.

The use of purposely vague child abuse and neglect laws serves to protect cultural practices. Although statutory definitions of child abuse vary from state to state, states typically provide relatively broad definitions of child maltreatment. Alaska's laws are illustrative; they define *child abuse and neglect* as "the physical injury or neglect, mental injury, sexual abuse, sexual exploitation, or maltreatment of a child under the age of 18 by a person under circumstances that indicate that the child's health or welfare is harmed or threatened thereby."[22] As with Alaskan law, other state statutes typically provide for physical abuse, sexual abuse, and neglect. Statutes also tend to focus on harm, or threat of harm, to the child. Some statutes, however, expand their ambit to include emotional abuse, although controversy arises when attempts are made to determine the harms and nature of such abuses.[23] States generally use a similar standard—the prudent parent standard—to determine whether the parent would be to blame, such as when statutes allow prudent parents to discipline their children through reasonable corporal punishment.[24] All of these definitions operate to provide latitude and discretion to those who intervene. Although the broad statutes have been understood to provide child welfare officials unchecked powers to intervene in family life, the mandates also protect parental and cultural practices so long as they can be construed as reasonable.

States also condone cultural practices through parental immunity doctrines. That immunity rests on the "reasonably prudent parent" standard, which is commonly found in judicial language and state statutes.[25] The doctrine exempts from tort liability actions that fall within parental discretion, such as decisions by parents to choose a family custom, tradition, or religious ritual. Generally, these exceptions involve cases where the alleged negligence constitutes an exercise of parental authority or ordinary parental discretion with respect to the provision of food, clothing, housing, medical and dental services, and other care.[26] Under this rule, reasonably prudent parents could insist that their actions are defensible given that they are customarily practiced within their culture. Even though some jurisdictions now allow some children to sue their abusive parents for sexual or physical abuse, many jurisdictions do not even allow such actions.[27] Despite reforms, then, parental immunities range broadly and allow for the persistence of cultural practices.

Both explicit and implicit statutory protections find parallels in constitutional jurisprudence regulating family life. The U.S. Constitution continues to provide families with control over the everyday lives of children. The U.S. Supreme Court, under the 1st and 14th Amendments, grants parents wide latitude in raising their children as they see fit. The 1st Amendment protects the exercise of religious traditions by parents in their children's upbringing. State invasions of these rights must be justified by interests "of the highest order."[28] In addition, the 14th Amendment also protects the fundamental right of "parental autonomy," which constitutes the parental interest in retaining substantial control over how parents raise their children. Indeed, the Supreme Court recognized that "the custody, care and nurture of the child reside first in the parents, whose primary function and freedom include preparation for obligations the state can neither supply nor hinder."[29] Parents, then, generally "have a right, coupled by a high duty, to recognize and prepare" their children for their current and future personal and social obligations.[30]

As with the statutory mandates, the constitutional right and duty to direct the upbringing of one's children has its limits. For example, the fundamental nature of parents' liberty to raise and control their children as they see fit ensures that parental rights do not "evaporate simply because they have not been model parents" and even abusive "parents retain a vital interest in preventing the irretrievable destruction of their family life."[31] However, state limitation of this interest may be justified by an equally compelling state interest.[32] In the words of the Supreme Court, "parents may be free to become martyrs themselves. But it does not follow that they are free . . . to make martyrs of their children."[33] Neither rights of parents nor rights of religion are beyond limitation. Thus, parents may be required to act contrary to their religious or cultural principles when the health, safety, and well-being of their children are at stake. The jurisprudence, then, reveals a limit to cultural practices, even though a considerable amount of protection for cultural backgrounds looms prominently in child welfare law.

Despite limitations, however, the constitutional standard provides parents with immense latitude. For example, if parents want to raise children to be sexist and racist, they can. If parents want to discriminate openly between their children according to sex, they can. Thus, parents could raise children so they do not like certain groups of people, and parents may refuse to pay for their daughters' college education at the same time they give every advantage to sons and finance their every effort to enter professional schools. Parents may do as they wish as long as they do not "abuse" their children. States justify intervention into cultural practices only in the name of protecting children from legally recognized harms. Indeed, parents have a right to avoid forming unwanted family ties and actually avoid giving birth to their children (as exemplified by the long line of birth control cases that recognize that right),[34] albeit a right that may be limited by the state, which may encourage birth over abortion by funding the former and not the latter[35] and which may grant potential fathers reduced rights when compared with potential mothers.[36]

Condoning Adults' Cultural Practices

The extent to which the child welfare system actively seeks to protect cultural values when it considers intervention in family life finds a similar parallel in protections offered adults. The extent to which the civil system respects the parental right to raise children as parents see fit equals the extent to which the laws protect adults' cultural values. When considering adult relationships, however, the protections deviate from active support. Three general rules emerge. First (and with some limits), adults' cultural practices relating to relationships with other adults remain protected through the broad principle of nonintervention. Second, as long as adults are in family relationships, they generally may practice cultural beliefs even when they limit the rights of others. Once outside of family life, however, the legal system increasingly operates to play down cultural practices. Third (and related to the first two), the more "traditional" the family or relationship, the greater protections it receives. Although the extent to which the system may affect ingrained cultural practices remains an area of dispute, it does seem that individuals within (traditional) families may practice cultural beliefs much more readily than adults who decide to exit their families or adopt alternative family lifestyles. These rules may not be obvious, for few cases offer cultural defenses to prohibit civil law's intrusion into adults' relationships that may be deemed violent or simply inappropriate. Yet the rules are important to understand because civil law still does regulate adults' cultural practices.

Three examples illustrate the extent to which the legal system seeks to support cultural practices within families. The first and most obvious way cultural practices gain protection involves privacy rights. U.S. law generally protects relationships, particularly heterosexual relationships, through the principle of nonintervention. Numerous U.S. Supreme Court cases, reviewed in the previous chapter, reveal the extent to which courts seek to protect adult' relationships by not intervening in them.[37] The court places familial relationships in a different order than those of unrelated companions. Relationships of the latter type do not receive protection; the court has not offered protection to unrelated individuals' rights to live together,[38] although it struck down ordinances barring extended family members from living together.[39]

The second way the Supreme Court protects cultural practices derives from the right to form marital relationships as fundamental. In *Loving v. Virginia*,[40] the court announced the status of the right as it invalidated state laws prohibiting interracial marriage. In regulating such fundamental rights, states could not inappropriately discriminate. Note, however, that the extent to which the right to found a nontraditional (nonheterosexual) family gains protection remains unsettled because states still may discriminate so long as they do so for "appropriate," compelling reasons.

The third way the legal system protects cultural practices involves the highly recognized right to protection from religious discrimination. By granting religious protections, the legal system inevitably affects the protections families receive. Just as the legal system protects the rights of parents through religious protections, it does so for adults. This doctrine reaches constitutional status and serves to support the view that families constitute a "private realm of family life which the state cannot enter."[41] Although the Supreme Court historically has protected religious beliefs absolutely but not actions,[42] it has held that the Free Exercise Clause protects some religiously motivated conduct: *Wisconsin v. Yoder*[43] reaffirmed the court's position that some religiously motivated conduct, related to family life, gains protection from the U.S. Constitution. Under this rule, then, religion properly belongs in a "private" sphere into which the government should not intrude.

Although the family constitutes a private realm that the state cannot enter, "the family itself is not beyond the public interest."[44] As with the protection of parental cultural practices, there are limits in the protections the legal system bestows on adults' abilities to pursue cultural interests and follow cultural dictates. The law, again, moves toward reinforcing traditional family life. Four examples illustrate the move toward encouraging traditional relationships.

1. In *Reynolds v. United States*,[45] the Supreme Court held that the practice of polygamy could be criminalized despite being derived from Mormon religious beliefs. The court rested its decision on two points: (a) the belief that monogamous marriage was the foundation of free government and that polygamy's link to political despotism threatened to undermine the liberal foundations of government and (b) the proposal that history and tradition had revealed that enlightened societies now condemned polygamy.

2. The Defense of Marriage Act[46] permits states to refuse to recognize same-sex marriages performed in other states. The new law also affirmatively preempts much of the effect that state recognition of such marriages would have. For example, the statute defines *marriage* as the union of one man and one woman for the purpose of all federal laws, rulings, regulations, and interpretations, and it denies federal benefits to same-sex couples. For all federal purposes, it makes any contrary state determination of family status irrelevant.

3. Federal laws, with some exceptions, encourage marriage through the social security system. Spousal benefits, for example, remain the main means by which most women receive social security. The system grants women the legal right to a higher payment by virtue of their marital status than they would have obtained if lacking the required familial relationship and depended only on their paid work histories.[47]

4. Civil (and criminal) laws historically have marginalized groups of immigrants. Underlying the management of different treatment is the country's deep normative vision of what America is and who is American. Thus, immigrants have been excluded from social and political participation and, as we have seen above, race-based immigration laws controlled prospectively the racial composition of incoming immigrants and thereby society at large.[48] Along with attempts to exclude, there have been aggressive and coercive attempts to assimilate. Laws provided effective financial deterrents and punishments for practicing family customs different from those of the mainstream society—restrictive efforts ranged from cemetery, laundry, and transportation laws to grooming and language laws.[49] Thus, history and tradition (particularly American tradition) are significant touchstones for defining the protections of family life.

The above examples illustrate the need to consider legislative attempts and their impact on cultural practices relating to family life. When individuals are within families, statutes tend not to regulate actions so long as individuals do not become overly abusive. For example, one spouse may control economic decisions or require their partner to perform certain traditional tasks; the other spouse has no recourse so long as the partner is not overly abusive. Indeed, even though a spouse may be emotionally abusive, the abused spouse may have no recourse in civil law, which may require separation or divorce to allow intrusion into the family domain in the form of civil remedies.[50]

Once outside of families, as when families break up through divorce or separation, numerous civil laws regulate the remaining relationship in a different manner. In general, there emerges a focus on treating individuals as autonomous adults and guarding against traditional practices that may harm. Numerous decisions relate to gender classifications, which the courts submit to intermediate scrutiny under the Equal Protection Clause. For example, in *Orr v. Orr*,[51] the Supreme Court found gender-based alimony laws unconstitutional. Likewise, the tender years doctrine, the policy that automatically gave custody of children under a certain age to the mother, either has been struck as gender discrimination or abolished by state legislatures.[52] Moreover, federal mandates create federal–state control over family life and take the form, for example, of far-reaching control of economic dispersements when couples separate: The Federal Child Support Enforcement Act[53] structures the creation of legally recognized parental relationships and helps define the rights and responsibilities of parents on the dissolution of their marriage or other relationship. Once outside of the marital relationship, former partners may use civil laws to hold abusive partners liable.[54]

However, even these developments that aim to treat individuals as autonomous adults have not moved far beyond the need to protect traditional values and have not necessarily enacted reform resulting in substantive changes in traditional roles and places of individuals. For example, civil damages for abuse leave considerable room for unrecognized forms of abuse to continue, and even extreme forms of abuse may not be redressible.[55] In addition, custody and visitation rights have had difficulty moving beyond traditional views: In *Michael H. v. Gerald D.*,[56] the U.S. Supreme Court granted greater protection to a "presumed" family as opposed to an actual family. In that case, the court found that a father who had formed a relationship with and provided economic support for his child born out of wedlock was not allowed to continue the relationship with his child when the mother returned to her estranged husband. The court found legitimate the legal rule that children may be presumed the product of a traditional marriage even when a biological relationship exists outside that family. Likewise, many vigorously dispute that divorce laws have benefited women and propose that family law has resulted in an "illusion of equality."[57] Thus, although seemingly moving beyond traditional values, the idyllic view of modern family law actually may continue to support them.

The above examples illustrate four important points regarding the civil regulation of family life. First, family relationships and their cultural practices receive constitutional protections. Second, family life is viewed as essential to the social order. That view allows for the protection granted to traditional values: Civil protection of families and their practices protect traditional families and traditional approaches to childrearing. Thus, the right to marry has been recognized, but that right thus far has been limited to the right to be free of obstacles to entering a traditional marriage; family and marriage rights have not been extended to require state recognition of nontraditional couples or groups of peoples as marriages or families. Third, adult family life (especially adult, heterosexual marital life) is a matter of privacy—it generally is beyond the jurisdictional competency and constitutional reach of the regulatory power of the state. Fourth, the legal rules regulating family life relate to civil law's other regulations. For example, religious beliefs may not be used to excuse criminal conduct. Again, so long as individuals remain within these broad boundaries, their interactions gain protection from intervention. That is, while within families, cultural practices generally gain protection. When individuals exit families, legal protections for cultural practices decrease as the legal system, at least in theory, aims to create greater equality.

Preliminary Conclusion

Child welfare law actually seeks to protect cultural practices and even seeks to harness them to protect children; it protects cultural practices by focusing on parents and their right to control their children, a right that subsumes children's rights and gains even greater force with the rise and rebirth of a parental rights movement.[58] So long as parents act reasonably and do not place their children in jeopardy, parents have free reign. Abuse only substantiates cause for intervention; and rehabilitation attempts take precedence over more punitive efforts that would sever parent–child ties or lead to the imprisonment of parents. Protections granted to parents reflect the rights adults enjoy—cultural practices deemed traditional and related to raising children form the general rationale to protect adult relationships and cultural practices; when adult relationships deviate from that rationale, they gain only reduced protections. Cultural evidence in civil law, then, remains far from controversial to the extent that simple rules regulate its use. Indeed, even when civil law reform efforts attempt to protect some individuals from traditional cultural practices and beliefs, the law faces considerable resistance and arguably results in limited reform. That generally uncontested response, however, differs markedly from the use of cultural evidence when family members' actions have been more extreme and have become subject to criminal jurisdiction.

Criminal Law's Hesitant Use of Cultural Evidence

Civil law regulations differ considerably from criminal justice approaches. Meeting the needs of victims or vulnerable parties is not the core responsibility of the criminal law and criminal courts. Criminal law focuses more on the offender and the need to determine appropriate sanctions. Given this focus, cultural evidence poses rather difficult issues for criminal law and challenges the criminal justice system's response to violent individuals. However, the cultural defense formally does not exist in criminal law.[59] Although this would seem to close any discussion, cultural evidence does seep into the criminal justice system's response to family violence. The extent and actual use of cultural information remains hotly debated. Those debates, rather than specific statutes and cases, necessarily form the basis of an inquiry into criminal law's use of cultural evidence.

The debates make sense from the perspective of the two core questions criminal law asks of any crime. First, should this individual be held guilty of a crime? Second, is this individual morally blameworthy? That is, the system focuses on the *mens rea* and the *actus rea* (guilty mind and guilty act) of a defendant to determine the legal response. Cultural evidence makes these determinations rather tricky. One ideological extreme urges use of cultural information to excuse an otherwise criminal act.[60] The other extreme, one more consistent with traditional law, urges exclusion of cultural evidence that demonstrates how a defendant's background diverges from the norm. Both extremes present important arguments that must be meaningfully considered to contend with cultural evidence in a legitimate, respectful manner.

Supporting Cultural Evidence

Cultural evidence sheds important insight into responses to the two questions criminal law seeks to address: holding individuals culpable and determining their relative blameworthiness. Cultural defenses allow for the contention that defendants are not completely morally culpable as individuals and that they may not have the necessary *mens rea* to commit the alleged act. Arguably, the defendants were merely following their culture's dictates. If defendants did so, their problematic actions could be interpreted as less morally blameworthy as would someone with heightened intent. In a sense, the act is not really the same as one committed by an individual who follows a different set of cultural strictures. Legal systems allow for considering different levels of blameworthiness. As the Supreme Court itself noted, states properly seek to protect those who are not blameworthy in mind from conviction of common-law crimes, and states continue to devise working formulae of guilty knowledge or permutations of intent to commit proscribed acts.[61]

In addition to addressing the legal nature of the act, use of cultural evidence supports fundamental legal values used to determine culpability and blameworthiness. Most notably, cultural defenses support the commitment to individualized justice. Cultural evidence may provide mitigating circumstances, which play a large part in criminal law. Evidence that individuals follow their own community's norms undoubtedly ranks high as a mitigating factor. For example, not only may offenders lack notice that such acts are proscribed (a major component of fairness in any social response to problem behavior), they also may lack a belief system that would allow them to resist actions inconsistent with their cultural beliefs. The argument has considerable merit. Cultural evidence allows for a sharper focus on blameworthiness, and cultural evidence assists each defendant to be judged according to his or her own level of guilt, all of which promotes individualized justice. From this perspective, cultural evidence would be used in a manner similar to the way insanity or provocation ("heat of passion") defenses are used: to excuse or partially excuse less blameworthy criminal behavior. Cultural evidence, then, potentially furthers the liberal legal notion of individualized justice required by criminal and constitutional law doctrines, which afford defendants a subjective evaluation of their moral culpability.

The defense also supports the notion of cultural pluralism, a fundamental component of any modern, liberal democratic society. Cultural pluralism requires respect for diversity of cultural identities as it seeks to preserve ethnic values. Under this argument, requiring newcomers or indigenous people to conform to the dominant population's values conflicts with the conventional American values of cultural and religious freedom. Recognizing cultural evidence preserves traditional cultures and enriches society. Admitting cultural evidence, then, potentially serves justice not only by the way it deals with individuals but also by the manner it addresses the rights and needs of groups that hold particular values.

Cultural evidence also potentially contributes to a different, and more accurate, understanding of crime. The effects of cultural life require an examination of the diffuse developmental processes rather than immediate and discrete cause-and-effect relationships characteristic of criminal law. Understanding the cultural roots of events brings society closer to the reality of criminal events and assists in shaping proper responses. The notion that social conditions contribute to criminal behavior comports with a broad literature that documents the effects of social conditions on the incidence of criminal behavior. For example, familial abuse, victimization, and war affect criminal behavior, and the law already allows for the use of those sources of violence to determine offenders' blameworthiness.[62] That approach to crime supports the understanding that would evolve from a closer examination of cultural beliefs that lead to harm against children.

Likewise, cultural evidence potentially contributes to a more sophisticated and accurate understanding of victimization and challenges dominant ideologies of victims' rights. The law narrowly defines victim status and assumes that responses to victimization are satisfied when a violation has been remedied (e.g., through punishment of offenders). A cultural understanding of harm suggests that narrow responses are problematic for several reasons. First, victimhood is not entirely circumscribed by the law. For example, the act of child maltreatment involves much more than an instance of child maltreatment; it also involves the place of the family in society, gender and class issues, and a host of other social forces that affect victimization. Maltreatment also involves more than legally defined instances of abuse. A focus on legally defined victims ignores other forms and sources of abuse, namely economic and other sources of power that place healthy child development at risk. Equally important, the focus on the legal victim ignores how those who abuse may have been victimized themselves and may not have had their victimizations addressed. Second, more than law is needed to protect victims. The law cannot protect all victims, and cultures may help as they buffer some children from certain forms of maltreatment. Most notably, for example, preventive efforts increasingly move toward community-based ways to support families so as to reduce maltreatment risks; such efforts are beyond the scope of criminal law, and the law has yet to be harnessed more effectively to assist communities in their protective efforts.[63] Third, the narrow focus on victims reinforces a growing focus on victims' rights and their role in the prosecutorial process, a process that does not necessarily lead to helping them recover from trauma.[64] Such focus, for example, has had the effect of increasing penalties and creating supercriminals who embody evil; it also has led to excusing other forms of victimizations and ignoring how victims may become perpetrators.[65] The result is a meaner, more stream-lined, and harsher criminal justice system, one that presumes that the excision of culture will lead to a culture-blind decision-making system that protects society.

The use of cultural evidence also finds support from several legal rules. Criminal law is premised on the notion of assessing individual culpability on a case-by-case basis. Individualized consideration of culpability arguably tips the balance in favor of not dismissing defendants' claims a priori. Under the current legal system, the law requires that defendants with legitimate claims be allowed to make their cases to jurors and others who will decide their fate. Indeed, when litigants are criminal defendants, the stance may be constitutionally mandated; defendants who stay within the bounds of the substantive law cannot be deprived from taking the stand and describing their own version of the facts.[66] As others have argued in different contexts, the criminal justice system also should be reluctant to prevent a retained expert from helping litigants tell their versions of disputed facts.[67] The biases found in criminal proceedings arguably make more pressing the admittance of cultural evidence. As several argue in the context of violence against women, the racism and sexism endemic to criminal processes already shape the perception of defendants (and victims), which make crucial the need to reason through cultural evidence.[68] Without doubt, the legitimacy of the criminal justice system rests on its willingness to ascertain the truth; preventing plausible claims from being heard likely undermines the trust individual litigants and society place in the system. When competing versions of truth exist, the legal system should allow those with the most at stake to tell their own version.

Opposing Cultural Evidence

Despite strong arguments in favor of allowing cultural evidence in the criminal justice system, several responses support the claim that criminal law must reject cultural information. Most fundamentally, regardless of excuses for violence, the result of the actions remains the same—violence against family members. This view proposes that the use of cultural information condones violence against children and other vulnerable family members because it simply arms those who inflict violence. Excusing criminal behavior on the basis of the accused's cultural background frustrates criminal law's effort to prevent injury to society at large and moves the system away from the ideal that the law entitles each societal member to protection from every other member's unlawful acts. Indeed, pluralistic societies make it even more imperative that one rule of law guides individuals' behaviors to prevent the disorder that would result from excessive pluralism in law beyond the already broad and acceptable variation between federal and state laws and among states themselves.

In addition to the need to ensure similar responses to family violence, the need to ignore cultural explanations and justifications arises from the new contexts in which the cultural beliefs are practiced. Rationales for the practices as they take place in countries of origin lose their rhetorical force when applied to new cultural situations and cultural life in the United States. For example, arguments from multiculturalists and relativists who find improper the imposition of U.S. values on immigrants lose their power because the situation facing immigrant children and parents in the United States differs from that facing them in other countries. Removing the cultural rationales that support particular socialization practices again results in harm to children being socialized for a world that espouses a different worldview than the one that leads to the harm. From this perspective, the use of cultural evidence undermines criminal law's goal of deterrence and education for American society and values. Punishment deters others from committing similar crimes and forces the alteration of traditions that conflict with U.S. law. Serving as an example, punishment results in the added benefit found in the acceleration of assimilation and child protection consistent with dominant values. Notably, the position does not necessarily assume that immigrants to the United States are moving to a more liberated, enlightened, and emancipated society and that immigrants require liberation into a more progressive society. Even though the United States may not be a better place for children and practices in this country may also contribute to violence against children, the argument simply reveals that U.S. laws and customs must be followed to gain a more consistent approach to child maltreatment and children's experiences in the United States.

Numerous practical considerations plague the use of cultural evidence, and those considerations often support the need to exclude such evidence. For example, even simple determinations of eligibility to use culture as a defensive measure raise vexing difficulties. Two issues exemplify potential problems. The first issue involves whether a defendant's culture actually can be determined. The amorphous concept of culture is not static over time, and members of the same cultural group may define and understand their practices differently. Because cultures are in flux, determining what is acceptable at various times proves exceedingly difficult. Thus, defining exactly what a culture is remains a controversial task, and the existence, prevalence, and legitimacy of any given cultural practice are prone to varying interpretations. The second concern involves determining who could use the evidence and providing rationales to distinguish them from a plethora of subgroups already in the United States who must go without the luxury of using cultural defenses. Even though one may not necessarily agree on what actually constitutes the majority culture, several groups' belief systems seemingly differ from popular perceptions of the more dominant culture. Providing every group with different rules would undermine the uniform application of law and fail to ensure all individuals equal treatment and equal protection of the law.

Even though it would seem necessary to respect different forms of relationships, basic standards for determining levels of care already have emerged that support the need to dismiss cultural evidence, which would constitute a defense to criminal law's intervention. Although the treatment of individuals does remain culturally determined and some customs could be excused for failure to understand the host culture, the international community (which controls all cultures and even seeks to protect them) increasingly sets basic standards relative to the manner in which people, including children, must be treated. The human rights movement recognizes, for example, the need to protect children from death, torture, sexual exploitation, excessive punishment, and even cultural practices detrimental to children's health. Likewise, the human rights movement also aims to abolish cultural practices that discriminate inappropriately between individuals, sexes, and cultural groups; the growing movement to combat gender discrimination within families illustrates the extent to which human rights law seeks to change cultural life. Thus, although it may be a noble aim to communicate to cultures that their practices are worthy of respect, not all customs can be afforded the same amount of respect, and legal machinery in the form of human rights law already aims to abolish those customs.

Despite the human rights movement's attempt to protect individuals from family violence, including protections against actions that may be culturally condoned by some societies, fundamental differences exist between that movement and the cultural defense. The human rights movement seeks to hold states and others responsible for actions occurring within particular jurisdictions, and it does so through encouraging reform and adopting an approach that views culture change as a process and cultures as worthy of respect. The cultural defense, however, runs the danger of viewing the culture as no larger than or as encompassing the practice for which the culture serves to explain or excuse. Cultural defenses, then, could operate to mark some cultures as irreconcilably different from the American mainstream, isolating immigrants for that difference, and subjectively judging them on that ground.[69] The danger creates the potential that when the dominant group essentializes a subordinate group by focusing on selected traits (i.e., it views the group as embodying a limited number of characteristics that encapsulate the totality of the culture and reduces diversity of ethnicity, religious, sexual orientations, and other traditions into one dominant culture), the cultural defense can be appropriated by the dominant group and used to further mark the group as subordinate. For example, a recent review of cases involving voluntary marriages of very young girls in the United States proposes that when an immigrant girl marries an older man, it is seen as reflecting cultural dictates; yet when a White girl marries an older man, it is seen as an idiosyncratic aberration and as cultural to the extent that White culture is individualistic.[70] When dealing with forced marriages of young girls, the prohibited behavior is conceptualized as a threat to "American" values when the perpetrator is an immigrant but not when the perpetrator is White.[71] As a result, the dominant (White) culture in the United States is deemed as one of individuals acting on their own accord outside of cultural dictates, whereas individuals from other (minority) cultures are deemed nonindividuals acting without their own sense of agency and a group threatening the American ways of life.

The process parallels that of orientalism, in which groups of people are divided into "them" and "us" (abuser–nonabuser, wife batterer–non-wife batterer), a process that the human rights movement seeks to avoid. Not only do such statements defining culture make dangerous generalization and essentialize other cultures, it does the same for the dominant culture as well. The argument becomes, then, that the criminal justice system could be more sensitive to different cultural values not through adoptions of different rules for those with different values, but by including people with those different values in the reformulation of legal rules.

The current legal system admits traditional defenses, which allow for the use of cultural evidence. Although cultural defenses tend to be portrayed as outrageous aberrations, they simply extend existing criminal doctrine commensurate with advances in law and more sophisticated understandings of crime. Thus, the proposed uses of cultural evidence and the way cultural evidence is used frequently can be subsumed within the existing structure of criminal law without major substantive innovation or expansion. As noted above, for example, cultural evidence simply enlightens the understanding of the defendant's mental state. The legal system does seek to understand that aspect of crime and allows evidence to determine the requisite level of intent or blameworthiness, particularly at sentencing phases of trials. This traditional use of evidence ensures that cultural information does not result in an expansive opening of floodgates to untold masses of defendants who will go excused, a result that would ignore the impact of defendants' actions on victims and society. In light of the discussion in previous chapters about the numerous roles cultural forces play in family violence, such absence of cultural discussions in response to family violence leads to important concerns, not the least of which is that violence would go ignored if certain cultural practices gained increased protection.

Preliminary Conclusion

Debates about criminal law's responses to cultural information suggest the following. Both sides of the debate present reasonable arguments, which suggests that neither position is likely to topple the other. It remains difficult to argue that certain cultural beliefs should result in complete and automatic defenses against family violence; it instead makes more sense to consider cultural evidence as other information relevant to determining guilt or imposing sentences. Cultural evidence may afford a more individualized and particularized justice and may lead to a more informed understanding of victimization. The actual use of cultural evidence may be fraught with difficulties, but addressing such difficulties may be a necessary part of contemporary life, of the need to acknowledge the concerns of diverse cultures and of diverse families and children in them.

Current Policy Resolutions: The Need to Reverse Orientations

Although meritorious ideological arguments may be made to both support and reject the legal use of cultural evidence, adoption of either approach ultimately turns on the consequences that could emerge from the evidence and how the legal system actually uses the evidence. Numerous commentators claim that the legal system unjustly uses excuses, which leads to recurring apocalyptic predictions of the demise of the U.S. legal system.[72] Yet cases that use cultural evidence to avoid criminal sanctions actually are rare; they are even more rare in instances of family violence that lead to criminal jurisdiction; and they are especially rare in cases that involve disputed cultural practices in child welfare law limited to abuse and neglect allegations. These cases provide information that is important but possibly misleading. The focus on reported cases runs the risk of masking the reality of what occurs when the laws described above actually are applied. Many cases may be neither reported nor challenged, and many challenges to the law's use of cultural evidence may go denied and simply not noticed. To address these concerns, I examine both reported cases and available social sciences evidence regarding the potential use of cultural evidence. Although it is difficult to locate cases in which cultural factors were dispositive or influential in determining outcomes, commentators and reviews of published and unpublished cases do report general trends in court findings. Available social sciences support the existence of those trends.

The Current Use of Cultural Evidence

Children's Cases

Published legal opinions do not recognize cultural evidence as admissible as a "cultural defense." Only two published cases involve disputes over cultural evidence pertaining to child victims. In *Quang Ngo Bui v. State*,[73] cultural evidence was admitted by the court but dismissed as irrelevant by a jury, which held the defendant guilty of murder for killing his three young children. In that case, Bui killed his children and attempted to kill himself when he suspected that his wife was to leave him. The expert testified that Bui was trying to "save face" in light of his wife's suspected infidelity and to protect his children from the harms they would suffer with another man. In *People v. Wu*,[74] a Chinese woman successfully challenged the failure to focus attention to cultural evidence through jury instructions. Instead of retrying the case to prove that cultural forces should not figure in holding her liable for killing her illegitimate 8-year-old son, the prosecution allowed a plea to a lesser offense.

Given the paucity of reported cases dealing directly with child maltreatment, interest in and information about cultural evidence derive mainly from media and other accounts. Although these sources make it difficult to evaluate precisely how the evidence was presented and its legal foundation, the reports do indicate that the evidence has served to reduce penalties, allow for acquittals, and dismiss charges. In a leading case, *People v. Kimura*,[75] a Japanese mother killed her two children and tried to drown herself; the prosecution allowed a plea to voluntary manslaughter because of cultural evidence that the acts were done in response to the shame of her husband's infidelity. Cultural evidence also served to acquit a father who had been charged with sexually abusing his daughter by rubbing her genitals during a basketball game.[76] Likewise, a reduced plea was offered to a father who was accused of imprisoning his daughter and endangering her life when the actions were presented as appropriate cultural norms.[77] In other instances, cultural evidence was used to drop charges altogether. For example a father was allowed to plead no contest to child abuse accusations and criminal charges were dropped after cultural explanations were used to justify the arranged marriages of his 13- and 14-year-old girls to Iraqi men and to justify 3 years of abuses that led to the marriages.[78] Likewise, charges were dropped against a father who held his daughter before relatives and kissed her vagina; the practice was viewed as a way Taiwanese mark the passage from infancy to childhood.[79] Similar charges were dropped when a court accepted the cultural explanation that a proper expression of love by an Afghanistan father, now living in Maine, involved kissing his baby boy's penis.[80] In accordance to customs of her native tribe, a mother made small slashes on her two young sons' cheeks to initiate them into the tribe of her ancestors from a different country; at trial, the judge dismissed the case when informed about the cultural meaning of the marks.[81]

In addition to media accounts, the social sciences literature reveals two important trends. The first trend involves the numerous commentaries that report on the increasing respect granted to certain practices viewed as abusive only outside of cultural contexts. Most illustrative are the different folk remedies that may be construed as abusive. For example, Vietnamese *cao gio* and Chinese *cheut sah* child-rearing practices involve "coining" or "spooning" the backs of children to ameliorate a variety of symptoms; both practices have been viewed as abuse by those who intervened but proposed by commentators as not abusive from a cultural perspective.[82] Likewise, cupping and scarification, practices found in Russian immigrant families as well as Asian and Mexican American cultures, may lead to scars and burns that result from efforts to remove burning cotton balls from cups as they are quickly placed on the child's back to create a vacuum that moves the blood to the surface.[83]

Like scarification, the vacuum created by cupping is deemed necessary to relieve a variety of symptoms such as pain, fever, poor appetite, and congestion.[84] Others have described *moxibustion* as appropriate, even though it involves burning little balls of yarn on the appropriate body part or using cigarettes that leave burns and scarring.[85] The practice is used as a folk remedy to cure abdominal pain, fever, and behavioral problems such as enuresis or temper tantrums and is found, in various forms, in Asian, Arab, and African cultures.[86] Hispanic communities also make use of remedies that leave burns as they use garlic and rue to treat the folk illnesses *mal ojo* (evil eye) and *empacho* (presumed intestinal blockage).[87] Hispanic communities use folk remedies to cure children from symptoms of traumatic events through, for example, holding them upside down by their ankles and shaking them, a gentle procedure that some inappropriately present as cultural excuses for behaviors that result in physical findings of shaken baby syndrome.[88] These examples illustrate how signs of abuse do not necessarily indicate intentionally abusive behavior and that the need to not view the practices as abusive receives support from professionals.

The second trend emerging from social sciences literature involves the extent to which less overtly cultural practices (e.g., folk medicines for the children's own good) actually do receive protection. The reality is that much remains unknown regarding the effect of cultural information on responses to child maltreatment, despite the remarkable extent to which the law seeks to protect cultural practices. Research reports, however, do reveal that those who respond to child maltreatment often do so in a manner that ignores cultural considerations. For example, researchers who examine intersections between religion and child abuse have focused more on extremes, such as satanic ritual child abuse, and have not examined the extent to which mainstream religion often excuses abusive behaviors.[89] Again, although religion may not cause child abuse, research generally stays clear of connections between child abuse and religion even though it is known that religion affects child rearing.[90]

Furthermore, the child welfare system is marked by practices that may be construed as racist and that privilege the White middle class. For example, Congress recognized the problems American Indian children face when placed outside of their tribe and family environments, such as a suicide rate twice that of the reservation suicide rate and four times that of the general population.[91] The federal government aggressively responded, through the Indian Child Welfare Act of 1978,[92] by implementing measures to limit Native American children's placement outside of their tribal and family environments. Yet placement of children outside of their families and tribes actually has increased—an increase attributed to the assimilationist views of those who intervene in American Indian families and to efforts to weaken the law's reach.[93] Research also documents how the child welfare system disadvantages minority groups and fails to protect them from harm. For example, research in the United States continues to identify Black and Hispanic children as suffering from higher rates of maltreatment.[94]

It remains controversial, however, whether higher rates of identified child maltreatment cases in minority and poor populations reflect actual abuse or biased responses. However, research does suggest that children from poor and minority families are more vulnerable to receiving the label "abuse" than children from more affluent households.[95] Although it is not clear why certain groups may be subjected to increased intervention, it is indisputable that those same groups also receive less therapeutic support. For example, compared with White children, African American and Hispanic American children who have experienced abuse are significantly less likely to sustain involvement in treatment after the first therapeutic contact.[96] Research persistently reveals that minority children receive less access to mental health treatment when they enter, leave, or remain in state custody.[97] In addition, as schools become the primary source of mental health and medical services for youth, minority's high dropout rates exacerbate difficulties.[98] Unlike the image that emerges from legal analyses, available social sciences findings suggest that cultural beliefs and differences may not receive much protection in practice.

Adults' Cases

As with children's cases, a most striking aspect of criminal law's responses to adult violence is the paucity of published cases that report an explicit use of cultural defenses in the context of family violence. Cases that have been reported relate to extremes: the murder of spouses. In *People v. Chen*,[99] a Chinese American confronted his wife about her adulterous relationship. After his wife told him she was having an affair, he hit her eight times in the head with a claw hammer, killing her. At trial, a judge admitted expert testimony to support the claim that "traditional Chinese values" about adultery (how a wife's adultery proves a man's loss of manhood and how divorce creates great shame on one's ancestors) drove Mr. Chen to kill his wife. The judge accepted the defense and sentenced Chen to 5 years' probation.[100]

Similar cases have arisen in reported opinions. For example, in the murder trial of May Aphaylath,[101] a trial judge excluded cultural evidence concerning Laotian culture and culture shock experienced by refugees. The defendant sought to introduce the evidence to explain how the defendant's jealous rage led him to stab his wife to death when he heard that she received a telephone call from a former boyfriend. The judge found that the jury did not require knowledge of Laotian culture to understand jealousy and that the witnesses could not assess whether the defendant acted on the basis of the alleged cultural imperatives. On appeal, the conviction was reversed for failure to admit cultural evidence; rather than being retried, the defendant accepted a plea bargain to a reduced charge.

Reported cases relating to adult family violence find parallels in cases that deal with gender violence. These cases are rather significant in that they illustrate the difficulty of raising and defending against cultural evidence. In *People v. Rhines*,[102] a Black (nonimmigrant) defendant, in response to a rape charge, offered cultural evidence of "cultural differences" in the social practices of Blacks and Whites as (a) a substantive cultural defense and (b) as cultural evidence to prove the element of voluntary consent of the Black victim. The court, however, rejected the defendant's proffered expert testimony. The court noted that the proffer was sexist, racist, and irrelevant. Other cases brought by men who offer culturally different explanations for their actions have been equally unsuccessful, such as evidence of Mexican masculinity to uphold a defense against murder charges that arose from sexual threats to the defendant's mother,[103] Italian masculinity for killing his wife and daughter after hearing of infidelity,[104] and "average servient homosexual" male's response of murder based on the partner's provocation by desire to end the relationship and by infidelity.[105]

Despite the tendency to reject cultural defenses from nonimmigrant defendants, theoretically similar defenses have been brought by immigrants who have different conceptions of sexual relationships. Illustrative of those defenses are cases that involve "marriage by capture." As explained in the leading case, *People v. Moua*,[106] the traditional practice involves a man's abduction of a woman who refuses his sexual advances and his "consummation" of the marriage. As with several other cases that have offered the defense, the evidence in *Moua* led to reduced charges and the unusual result of imposing a monetary fine for what otherwise constitutes rape.[107] The argument has been that, as long as conducted along the cultural ritual's tradition, sexual intercourse is consensual even without consent in fact. The practice directly relates to different perceptions of sexual relationships. In the capture case, the evidence centers on and celebrates the male sex right: kidnapping for marriage and consummation by force is marital sex, not rape. Thus, the legal system commutes a crime to a cultural ritual.

Although clear differences exist between immigrant and nonimmigrant cases, it is difficult to argue that the victims were treated equally and difficult to argue that the evidence of group differences should be allowed (and subjected to scrutiny) in one case but not the other. None of the cases presented evidence that could, on its face, gain definite support or rejection by a conscientious jury.

In addition to media accounts and published cases, it is again important to turn to what the social sciences literature suggests regarding the reality of how cultural practices gain protection. Although the literature again remains wanting, evidence does suggest that, even though the law may grant protection for cultural practices, responses to partner battering do not to the extent that they fail to protect victims. (Viewed from the perpetrator's point of view, evidence would suggest that responses do protect cultural practices to the extent that battering remains so difficult to combat and so pervasive.) From the victim's perspective, that intersection of racism and sexism exacerbates many problems commonly faced by women in battering relationships.[108] Racism operates, for example, to create more obstacles to leaving battering relationships and also to prevent individuals from recognizing that different responses to domestic violence may be required by women from different ethnic and racial backgrounds.[109] Racism and other cultural and community variables also help explain consistent differences in rates of abuse among Asian, Hispanic, Black, and White Americans.[110] Likewise, the failure to address cultural contexts results in law enforcement intervention that may lead to more negative outcomes for already vulnerable groups.[111] Although much remains unknown, what is known is that current approaches are problematic for the failure to recognize the extent to which cultural forces should factor in responses to adult relationship violence.

Preliminary Conclusion

Legal cases highlight several critical points about the use of cultural evidence in legal responses to family violence. The examples impart how cultural evidence may serve to mitigate sanctions in criminal law. Cases pervasively do not even report the use of cultural evidence. Some courts find cultural evidence admissible, some juries may find it useful, and some prosecutors find it useful enough that they drop charges. Cultural evidence is not generally offered as a novel form of excuse but rather to support existing categories of defenses, to avoid or alleviate guilt, or to mitigate punishment. Given the absence of official cases dealing with cultural information, it remains difficult to determine the extent to which cultural information gains proper respect.

Although limits in information about existing cases caution against extrapolation, existing reports reflect the mainstream U.S. legal system's views of family life and gender roles. The extent to which the circumstances strike a sympathetic chord with more mainstream culture seemingly matters. For example, Bui was given the death penalty for killing his children and trying to kill himself, whereas Kimura and Wu were seen as victims who actually did the same acts (for similar reasons), but received lighter punishments because they were interpreted differently in the immigrant culture and the United States. Chen's killing of his wife struck a chord with the judge's view of what a man should do; Moua's cultural traditions resonated with the judge who sympathized and allowed the defendant to plead to a misdemeanor and offer a monetary compensation rather than rape. The numerous instances in which parents were excused for otherwise maltreating their children reflects the powerful perception that parents have the right to control and raise their children as they (and their society) see fit. Despite cultural differences, then, all differences seemingly collapse into sameness, as influenced by the dominant culture's perception of, for example, appropriate gender and parental roles. The judicial process becomes an opportunity for mainstream society to restructure, reify, and reinforce expectations and explanations for family violence. The sameness is perhaps even more apparent in what the social sciences literature reveals. Although the legal system may allow for cultural protection, the current reality increasingly seems to be that those who intervene in families and enforce the law are allowed to actually ignore cultural practices, as exemplified by the differential treatment of minority children in social services systems and the failure to treat adults differently in the response to domestic violence.

The above conclusions suggest nothing radical about the current use of cultural evidence. Criminal law formally bars the use of cultural evidence, yet still allows, albeit hesitantly, the evidence to determine culpability and punishment. Cultural evidence remains rather uncontested in civil law, and cultural practices are condoned when involving intact family relationships (at least condoned by law but not necessarily in practice). Although the legal system allows those who implement laws to respect cultural differences, the extent to which they do protect practices by groups deemed different, as exemplified by the differential treatment of minorities, remains unclear. The following suggests that the current use of cultural evidence constitutes two policy directions that have things backward. In considering cultural evidence, the civil systems should hesitate more before protecting cultural practices, and the criminal justice system should hesitate less before ignoring cultural practices. Both areas of law require rethinking the use of cultural evidence.

Steps Forward: Interrogating Cultural Evidence

When approached from the view of family violence law as a whole (in terms of both civil law and criminal law), existing legal scholarship dealing with cultural evidence remains limited. Commentators pervasively ignore civil law. Those who examine criminal law advocate numerous and often conflicting positions. Some commentators advocate admitting cultural evidence in the name of cultural relativism,[112] excluding it in the name of assimilation,[113] including the evidence depending on the victims and offenders' situations in minority and mainstream society,[114] or simply excluding it as irrelevant.[115] These debates are significant: They reveal how family violence laws simply cannot adopt blanket approval or dismissal of such evidence. As the analyses presented above indicate, the various systems and goals of the different systems invite a deliberate approach. Both systems should adopt a more rigorous examination of cultural evidence.

Rather than providing a neutral process that uniformly resolves all cases, responses to cultural evidence must examine the cultural dynamics involved in the practice, and they must determine how the practice should operate in the legal system in a manner that also recognizes the cultural dynamics implicated in mainstream law and culture. Both analyses require an approach that interrogates—questions, examines, and determines the significance of—cultural authority found in the United States and in the community that surrounds the disputed cultural practice.

Reaching a legitimate conclusion on how cultural evidence should be used entails addressing at least four basic and interrelated concerns. These areas of inquiry all aim to increase information, uncover biases, and resist general invocations of culture that ignore the multiplicity of factors involved in specific maltreating environments.

Determine Relevance and Reliability

Regardless of the eventual use of the cultural evidence, the rules of evidence serve as a preliminary discussion point. Although intricate and often contentious, the rules of evidence simply seek to ensure that the legal system uses reliable information relevant to particular cases.[116] Other issues, such as the procedures of admission and the policy implications of such admissions, gain significance only after determining preliminary matters of reliability and relevancy.

As with other evidence, determinations of reliability hinge on the soundness of the social sciences reports, publications, and other documentation.[117] Thus, decision makers must scrutinize the presented evidence to ensure that it actually reflects the cultural dynamics from which it is purported to originate. In other words, are the presented truths likely to be accurate? These determinations may require a different view of expertise and an effort to involve individuals who are sensitive to their community's dynamics. A broader view of expertise may seem problematic, but it may be critical to dispensing justice.

Determinations of relevancy hinge on the extent to which the individual is influenced by cultural traditions at issue and the extent to which the issue relates to the particular legal issue at hand, such as the person's state of mind. That determination requires that information about a culture move beyond simple stereotypes. The investigation requires understanding the nuances of the challenged customs that are relevant to a full understanding of the evidence's value for purposes of legal analysis. For example, researchers challenge the conception that *caida de mollera* should be accepted to explain injuries from shaken baby syndrome.[118] *Caida de mollera* involves a folk remedy used to cure children from symptoms of traumatic events by holding them upside down by their ankles and shaking them. The gentle procedures have been inappropriately presented as cultural excuses for more violent behaviors that result in physical findings of shaken baby syndrome.[119] Likewise, an investigation of the cultural evidence requires that the practice be introduced and addressed in a manner that locates the individual within his or her community, diaspora, and history as well as the extent to which the belief system pervades the relevant community. This approach would take seriously the proposal that a mother who kills her children might be allowed to admit cultural evidence to mitigate her punishment if she can show that she too has been a "victim" of her culture's values.[120] The approach also would lead to the rejection of similar evidence by a father who did the same acts but had no evidence to support a claim that his cultural location similarly contributed to his actions.[121]

Although the rules of evidence serve as a springboard, the settings in which evidence is offered make a difference. In a criminal court arena, the potentially prejudicial nature of cultural evidence figures prominently in determinations of whether triers of fact should consider the evidence. This determination concerns the extent to which the evidence may unfairly prejudice, confuse, or mislead the trier of fact, especially given that expert evidence can be powerful and misleading because of the aura of credibility accompanying it. In civil court settings, consideration of biases and prejudices also figure prominently. However, civil settings may not mandate the heightened protections of criminal law and thus may allow for a more generous use of cultural evidence. The lowered threshold, however, does not vitiate the need for close scrutiny. The need for that scrutiny leads to the following areas of inquiry.

Consider Dissenting Voices

The presence of a practice does not constitute an acceptable means of proving its legitimacy. Considering cultural evidence may require more sensitivity to dissenting voices from the generally accepted, dominant voices found in legal settings. This consideration recognizes that numerous problems may arise from presenting cultures as bound by anthropological constructions such as rituals, customs, practices, and traditions. The main danger derives from conceptions of cultural life, which tend to be presented as monolithic and held by all cultural actors. As discussed in chapter 4, cultures do not possess monolithic, fixed, and static essences.[122] Presentations of cultures as immutable and singular do not take into account the role of external factors in determining a community's culture and how culture can be contested within communities.

Given the difficulty of defining what cultures are, dangers emerge in ignoring the beliefs and practices of disempowered subgroups within particular cultures. Particularly when dealing with entrenched cultural practices, the evidence may improperly focus on history and tradition and ignore how marginalized groups seek to redefine cultures and how lack of political voice may thwart those efforts. Subordinated groups, particularly children, lack the ability to define and shape the dominant culture, and their own views and needs may be preempted by existing powers, not the least of which relate to lack of social, economic, and political resources. The place of children and families in their indigenous communities also must be considered in light of the dominant forces that operate on the immigrant community, not the least of which may involve gender, economic, and racial discrimination.

Although commentaries focus on children, research also reveals how similar forces are at work with immigrant adults: Vietnamese immigrant women, for example, are at greater risk for violence because class, culture, and gender interact with immigration status and conflicts about changing norms and values relating to their familial roles,[123] a rather significant finding given the frequently observed proposition that immigration actually increases adherence to traditional values as immigrants cope with acculturation and assimilation.[124] For example, although female circumcision in the United States now violates federal law and several states ban the practice,[125] the most effective efforts to deal with eliminating the practice are those that aim to educate communities and consider the place of girls in their traditional society.[126] This example of the tendency to exclude certain groups from protections is particularly apt; within the broad group of children, boys do seem discriminated against to the extent that millions more boys than girls undergo circumcision that may be less severe but still pervasively goes ignored in law and social discussions.[127] In summary, the danger emerges that cultures are "essentialized" in a manner that privileges the dominant culture without regard for the various subcultures or subgroups that comprise any society and offer challenges to ingrained cultural beliefs.

In addition to considering the differences that may exist within cultures, responses must address the pressures individuals face both within and outside of their communities. Cultural differences may actually arise because of the relationship between the immigrant groups and the host community rather than the cultural differences imported from abroad. Immigrant workers, for example, do not gain protection from social services agencies, legal services, and unions.[128] That status may hamper their ability and willingness to seek assistance, a hesitancy likely due to the general unwillingness among people of different groups to subject their private lives to the scrutiny and control of the state.[129]

Language also may erect barriers to services. For example, researchers have noted that language skills present obstacles to obtaining health and social services such as medical attention and counseling and contribute to underreporting, hesitancy to seek law enforcement assistance, and inability to obtain prevention services (which are in any event targeted primarily to English-speaking victims).[130] In essence, responses must recognize how individuals may be less likely to have needs met because of their cultural backgrounds. Access to dominant groups' cultural resources, such as economic and educational means, social services, and shelters, affects victims as well as offenders. Although this information may seem to be the ordinary exculpatory or mitigating evidence presented in any circumstance, it is not systematically presented, which contributes to discrimination.

Weigh the Practice's Harms and Benefits

The previous point highlights how determining whether to count or discount cultural information must involve recognizing the manner in which individuals from different groups address basic needs. That consideration leads to the need to consider, for example, the extent to which certain groups and their members receive information regarding child rearing and how that information, if obtained, comports with their beliefs about particular practices. The result is that, in addition to looking at whether the interventions are fair and whether they adequately consider the different voices found in the culture, efforts must examine the impact of previous and current intervention efforts.

Experiences with minority populations reveal that culture blindedness can disadvantage individuals targeted for protection.[131] Efforts must take into account the relative value of prohibiting certain practices in terms of their impact on the practices and the ability of laws to protect individuals from harm. This approach challenges, for example, the presumption that U.S. law and culture protect children, when those mainstream forces may not reach certain segments of society and when there may exist other culturally envisioned ways of protecting children.[132] The same has been noted for the failure of laws to protect minority women from domestic violence, such as the law's failure to provide services and address structural forces contributing to women's inabilities to address abusive relationships.[133] In the end, practices need not lead to balance the rights of defendants over those of victims, or vice versa. Rights of some individuals need not trump the rights of others—an approach far from foreign to laws regulating family life and any other law that balances the rights of individuals with those of others and society.

It becomes admittedly difficult to determine the harms practices cause. However, weighing harms need not be done without guidance; three areas of inquiry immediately arise. First, harms and threat of harms must be viewed in terms of the impact on victims. For example, some practices are intended to protect children (e.g., coin-rubbing practices), whereas others do not necessarily do so (e.g., practices resulting in the shaken baby syndrome).[134] Because these practices are properly situated within their cultures and performed within their cultural strictures, it becomes difficult to determine that some lead to long-term harm. Second, in addition to the specific harms, it is important to consider the rationales for the behavior and the extent to which those rationales gain protection. For example, religious reasons have been viewed as legitimate sources to protect different cultural practices, as has failure to offer adequate economic resources needed for healthier child development.[135] Third, standards for deciding which harms are impermissible and in need of greater intervention already exist. Human rights law affords considerable guidance. For example, the death of children would mean more intervention, which would mean, in turn, efforts to prohibit it beyond particular cases that emerge. The rule is not new: The greater the harm, the more intrusive and aggressive the intervention. What is new is the need to move beyond one view of culture and one view of what may constitute harm.

Seek Alternative Responses

As evidenced by the previous discussion, where systems of culture, race, gender, class, and age converge, as they do in family violence, interventions require nuanced responses. Both victims and offenders may suffer simply because of numerous complexities. These complexities may include limited health care and educational opportunities, denial of economic and political agency, and other forces. Research does indicate, for example, that minority children have the least access to therapeutic services.[136] Rather than simply punishing offenders, responses arguably would focus on providing services to children in need, an effort that would seek to bring both criminal law and child welfare law into a concerted effort to protect child victims.[137]

The rehabilitative focus of child maltreatment law makes conceiving and implementing alternative dispositions even more pressing. It may seem unrealistic to transform the criminal justice system into a service provider, although in many instances it has become one (e.g., it may coerce therapeutic intervention). At the very least, the criminal justice system could better coordinate its responses with child protection systems aimed at service provision.

The search for alternative responses already results in parsimonious responses to acts conceived as maltreating by some but as culturally appropriate by others. Most notably, acts often depicted as barbaric practices imported to the United States have led to important controversy and thoughtful responses. The current responses to genital circumcision illustrates how cultures may be engaged and respected while efforts are made to protect children. Such responses aim to foster tactics for achieving a dialogue between cultures.[138] These responses aim to transform cultures by providing ways of approaching disputes that ensure greater participation of those involved and by offering alternative means of achieving similar ends. They also involve more concerted efforts to transform everyday relationships in accordance with long-standing principles of human rights.[139] Although not without controversy, the approach does reflect the need to balance the rights and responsibilities of any society and of those in any society's charge. The approach recognizes how law reform efforts must reach people's everyday lives to attain and sustain reform; it further recognizes how attaining specific reforms requires addressing numerous cultural forces.

Countering Objections to a Nuanced Approach

The use of cultural evidence engenders considerable debate in criminal law but considerably less in civil law. The polarized views ensure that objections arise from the proposed approach aimed to consider cultural evidence in existing legal responses to family violence. The approach, however, does address the most notable and foreseeable objections from existing sides of the policy debate.

The legitimacy of evaluating foreign practices has been questioned. Without doubt, ethnocentrism figures prominently in efforts to judge the morality of the cultural practices. Indeed, there is always a danger that discussing practices and behaviors may place immigrants on display and foster inappropriate comparisons to dominant approaches deemed more enlightened or progressive. However, it is important to consider nonmainstream and immigrants' struggles and cultural values, and it is appropriate to do so simply because the cultural practice is being judged in the United States and cultural diversity has its limits. Although a daunting task, evaluating the legitimacy of evidence is the role of juries, judges, and those who act to uphold the legal system. Despite numerous practical problems that may emerge from cultural evidence, it does seem fair to conclude that experts may be used to clarify issues and the legal system always must sort through exceedingly complicated evidence (and does so in a competent manner). As the dominant means U.S. society has chosen to resolve disputes, the legal system functions to weigh the merit of different evidence and fashion appropriate responses.

Some may wonder whether tools exist to make decisions about degrees of correctness, goodness, health, or optimal functioning. The above areas of inquiry confront these culturally sensitive issues and benefit from important developments in understanding cultural issues. A culturally sensitive approach can respect the uniqueness of cultures and allow for comparative standards. Psychologists concerned with cultural issues and establishing universals in human development, for example, make use of derived etics rather than etics or emics.[140] *Etics* generally are viewed as universal ideas, behaviors, and concepts, whereas *emics* are culture-specific ideas, behaviors, and concepts. Derived etics balance extremes between etics and emics as they seek to use culturally valid and relevant standards that can be applied in a comparative manner;[141] to put it differently, they seek to develop emic measurements of etic constructs.[142] Although these authors and even cross-cultural texts adopting this approach in their examinations of human development[143] do not examine issues related to family violence, this stand underlies intervention research as it moves researchers beyond analyzing, understanding, and explaining situations to a more active role in inducing change when faced with less-than-optimal fits between cultural values and practices and healthy developmental trajectories.[144] Like all evaluations and intervention efforts, cultural assessments, especially those for intervention, remain risky.[145] Yet even critics concur that risks can be alleviated only when efforts are made to better understand the "realities" of situations. Indeed, effective intervention requires a contextual analysis so that agents of change build on the existing strengths in changing conditions to promote sustained reform, a need that parallels efforts to increase respect for human rights.[146]

Some may object to a nuanced approach because it confers discretion on judicial and administrative personnel. Recall, for example, that criminal law seeks to exclude cultural evidence that would amount to an excuse and that civil law pervasively seeks to protect cultural practices. Without an explicit rule for or against cultural information, those who consider evidence run the danger of being swayed by their own prejudices. Rules that simply allow consideration of cultural evidence or leave broad discretion (as in the civil legal system) run the danger that those who implement laws actually advance discriminatory and prejudicial practices. Several responses may be made to the charge that there is no need for reform. First, the current legal system allows for reform. Those who implement laws already possess enormous discretion and always infuse morality into their decisions. That discretion derives from vague and broad rules of law prone to subjective interpretation. Second, instead of providing for more discretion, the framework checks subjectivity and its effects on individual cases. It provides for an explicit decision-making process and suggests that explanations be made for accepting or rejecting practices. The process exposes the decision makers' beliefs, prejudices, and ideological predispositions that ultimately serve to determine outcomes. Third, the process of addressing both cultures identifies power structures that lead to decision making and involves a rethinking of the system in which individuals operate.

The approach proposed here moves away from elegant simplicity and toward complicated rules of law. The approach resists dualism (us–them, proper–improper, civilized–uncivilized) in the construction of cultural life and recognizes the complexity of a multicultural society and the forces found in it. The proposed, more complicated approach may do so by offering a more involved approach to cultural rights. Protecting the rights of victims does not entail erasing cultural differences. Indeed, cultures provide important sources of protection and fulfillment of rights. The proposed approach recognizes social complexity by adopting an approach to crime that does not pit offenders against victims. In the parent–child suicide cases, for example, it makes sense to look beyond the legally defined victim and realize the position of parents who could also be considered victims. Regardless of the position taken, the effort recognizes the complicated interrelationships among parent, child, and society and that such relationships are central concerns in child maltreatment. The proposed approach also recognizes the complications cultural life brings to family violence responses. It recognizes intersectionality of how people's different identities (e.g., race, sex, cultural group, and age) affect their place in society and society's responses to them. The approach resists polarization of cultures at the same time that it seeks to identify basic forms of protection that could be afforded to those vulnerable to family violence. In other words, it recognizes the need not to erase intersections inhabited by people subjected to multiple oppressions of race, sex, age, class, and political power differences. Culture, rights, and crime constitute complex social phenomenon that are not best understood as unitary and as experienced similarly by different people. Multiple social forces affect lives experienced in similar and different cultures.

Reservations may be raised by the adoption of an approach that finds nothing peculiar about a move away from the criminal justice system. Indeed, to use the words of postmodernists, the approach "decenters" the state.[147] Rather than having the state appropriate the power to define and control cultural practices, it relies on numerous actors, including those outside of state control, such as community members. This effort simply comports with recent efforts that challenge the use of criminal enforcement as the dominant means to ensure protection from family violence[148] and, arguably more importantly, it recognizes the powerful role civil law plays in the creation and protection of victims. It also realizes that not only the law can protect victims; indeed, the failures of even the most radical and progressive laws run rampant.[149] The approach takes advantage of the rapid developments in understanding and ensuring human rights through addressing people's consciousness and, for example, moves to secure deeper cultural change in both the challenging and challenged culture. The approach recognizes how acculturation processes inevitably affect both host and immigrant cultural groups.[150]

Some objectors to the proposed approach may be concerned that recognizing cultural difference may jeopardize the uniformity of our law and nation. Four responses reveal how the fear may be unjustified. First, the approach simply recognizes that U.S. laws are not devoid of culture. Culture already infuses law and does not operate outside of it. Culture and law are not autonomous but mutually reinforcing. Second, it recognizes that U.S. culture is not necessarily unified and progressive. The history of ethnocentrism and gendered violence has been well documented; so too is its violence against children and the reworking of how to deal with different cultures. Third, it recognizes how cultural practices already are being respected by, for example, child welfare law and how foreign practices do manage to enter the criminal justice system and impact outcomes. Fourth, the approach recognizes how various systems of law remain far from unified, such as the civil laws that protect traditional, cultural values that contribute to violence, which the criminal justice system rejects.

The potential negative impact of using a more diffuse approach to cultural evidence also raises concerns. A more diffuse approach may well be problematic, but the approach to cultural information actually considers where cultural evidence is used most frequently. Although all legal commentaries dealing with cultural evidence focus on the judicial system, the court system actually makes the least use of cultural information, a point made obvious by the paucity of published legal decisions dealing with cultural evidence. The approach urges a focus on prosecutors, social workers, police, and other personnel who enforce law. It would behoove researchers and commentators to explore how these legal actors approach and view cultural evidence and determine what may be done to counter negative effects of improperly using cultural information. Existing evidence indicates that professionals lack considerable understanding of cultural issues.[151] The approach, however, also moves beyond state actors and urges a focus on cultural practices as experienced by the dominant culture and as experienced in everyday life.

Conclusion

Several sources provide impetus for interest in cultural issues for those who offer assistance. These range from a shift from melting-pot ideology to cultural pluralism, social and ethical responsibilities of service providers, political and social presence of diverse cultural groups, limitations of a purely biological model of human behavior, scientific advances in cultural psychology, global economic considerations, and national and international intercultural contact. These forces caution and heighten the need to consider culture conflict and cultural forces in cases involving individuals vulnerable to abuse and unable to act as their own advocates. Although states must be culturally sensitive, they must, at the same time, strive to respect fundamental human rights standards. Cultural considerations should not be viewed as extraneous to the law, and law cannot ignore culture's pervasive effects. Excluding cultural evidence may lead to an incomplete understanding of the circumstances and the continuation of violence.

The use of cultural evidence in legal responses to family violence reveals that different treatment may be helpful to differently situated communities. Instead of cavalierly rejecting or accepting cultural evidence, it should be examined with care. The need for a more deliberate response arises particularly because this area of law necessarily implicates individuals from minority, disadvantaged, and politically powerless segments of society. Injustice arises most obviously when cultural practices do challenge the reality of the current justice system and how the system regrettably seeks to ignore that challenges actually exist. Only a rigorous interrogation of cultural evidence—one that considers dissenting voices, deliberately weighs harms and benefits, and seeks alternative responses—can serve justice to those involved in family violence enmeshed by cultural practices.

Endnotes

1. R. J. R. Levesque, *Child Sexual Abuse: A Human Rights Perspective* (Bloomington: Indiana University Press, 1999).
2. D. L. Coleman, "Individualizing Justice Through Multiculturalism: The Liberals' Dilemma," *Columbia Law Review* 96 (1996):1093–1107.
3. K. Wang, "Battered Asian American Women: Community Responses From the Battered

Women's Movement and the Asian American Community," *Asian Law Journal* 3 (1996): 151–184.

4. *See* L. Volpp, "Talking Culture: Gender, Race, Nation, and the Politics of Multiculturalism," *Columbia Law Review* 96 (1996):1573–1617.

5. See, e.g., M. Goldman, "The Violence Against Women Act: Meeting Its Goals in Protecting Battered Immigrant Women?" *Family and Conciliation Courts Review* 37 (1999): 375–393.

6. R. J. R. Levesque, "Piercing the Family's Private Veil: Family Violence, International Human Rights, and the Cross-Cultural Record," *Law & Policy* 21 (1999):161–187.

7. Eddings v. Oklahoma, 455 U.S. 104 (1982).

8. P. L. Crocker, "Childhood Abuse and Adult Murder: Implications for the Death Penalty," *North Carolina Law Review* 77 (1999):1143–1222.

9. J. D. Marlow, J. B. Lambert, and R. G. Thompson, "Voluntary Intoxication and Criminal Responsibility," *Behavioral Sciences and the Law* 17 (1999):195–217.

10. *See* C. Slobogin, "Psychiatric Evidence in Criminal Trials: To Junk or Not To Junk," *William & Mary Law Review* 40 (1998):1–56.

11. State interventions typically occur in several stages. The first stage involves investigations following reports of suspected child abuse or neglect. In the second stage, the state assumes custody or care of the child if investigations indicate that children are at sufficient risk of harm; the state also may recommend efforts to rehabilitate parents or family members. In the final stage, if rehabilitative efforts do not create safe environments for children's return to the family, or if the children have been unsuccessfully returned, the state may seek termination of parental rights. To involuntarily terminate parental rights, the state must, at a minimum, show by clear and convincing evidence that parents were abusive or neglectful and that rehabilitative efforts have been unsuccessful. *See* Santosky v. Kramer, 455 U.S. 745 (1982).

12. COLO. REV. STAT. § 19-1-103(1)(b) (1997).

13. *Id.*

14. CAL. WEL. & INST. CODE, § 16509 (1996).

15. *Id.*, § 18961(a)(3).

16. S.C. CODE ANN. § 20-7-480(A)(7) (1996) (emphasis added).

17. Indian Child Welfare Act of 1978, 25 U.S.C. § 1901-63 (1994).

18. N.M. STAT. ANN. § 32A-3B-19(G)(8) (1996).

19. *See, e.g.*, WASH. REV. CODE, § 13.40.310 (1997); N.J. ADMIN. CODE, Title 13, § 13.90-3.6(b)(4) (1997).

20. R. J. R. Levesque, "Future Visions of Juvenile Justice: Lessons From International and Comparative Law," *Creighton Law Review* 29 (1996):1563–1585.

21. *See* R. R. Banks, "The Color of Desire: Fulfilling Adoptive Parents' Racial Preferences Through Discriminatory State Action," *Yale Law Journal* 107 (1998):875–964.

22. ALASKA STAT. § 47.17.290(2) (1998).

23. R. J. R. Levesque, "Emotional Maltreatment in Adolescents' Everyday Lives: Furthering Sociolegal and Social Service Provisions," *Behavioral Sciences and the Law* 16 (1998): 237–263.

24. R. J. R. Levesque, *Adolescents, Sex, and the Law: Preparing Adolescents for Responsible Citizenship* (Washington, DC: American Psychological Association, 2000).

25. For a review, *see* S. L. Haley, "The Parental Tort Immunity Doctrine: Is It a Defensible Defense?" *University of Richmond Law Review* 30 (1996):575–604.

26. For the leading case, *see* Goller v. White, 122 N.W.2d (Wis. 1963).

27. J. R. Tarpley, "Bad Witches: A Cut on the Clitoris With the Instruments of Institutional Power and Politics," *West Virginia Law Review* 100 (1997):297–352.

28. Wisconsin v. Yoder, 406 U.S. 205, 215 (1972).

29. Prince v. Massachusetts, 321 U.S. 158, 166 (1944).

30. Pierce v. Society of Sisters, 268 U.S. 510, 535 (1925).
31. Santosky, 455 U.S. 753.
32. *See, e.g.*, Parham v. J.R., 442 U.S. 584, 600 (1979).
33. Prince v. Massachusetts (1944) at 170.
34. *See* Belotti v. Baird, 443 U.S. 622 (1979).
35. *See* Harris v. McRae, 448 U.S. 297 (1980)
36. Carey v. Population Services International et al., 431 U.S. 678 (1977).
37. *See, e.g.*, Eisenstadt v. Baird, 405 U.S. 438 (1972).
38. Village of Belle Terre v. Borass, 416 U.S. 1 (1974).
39. Moore v. City of East Cleveland, 431 U.S. 494 (1977).
40. Loving v. Virginia, 388 U.S. 1 (1967).
41. Prince v. Massachusetts, 321 U.S. 158, 166 (1944).
42. Reynolds v. United States, 98 U.S. 135 (1878).
43. *Wisconsin* at 205.
44. *Prince* at 166.
45. *Reynolds* at 135.
46. Defense of Marriage Act, P. L. 104-109, 110 Stat. 2419 (1996), 1 U.S.C. 8 (Supp. II 1996) and 28 U.S.C.A. 1738C (West Supp. 1998).
47. K. Silbaugh, "Turning Labor Into Love: Housework and the Law," *Northwestern University Law Review* 91 (1996):1–86.
48. D. C. Chiu, "The Cultural Defense: Beyond Exclusion, Assimilation, and Guilty Liberalism," *California Law Review* 82 (1994):1053–1125; A. N. Ancheta, *Race, Rights, and the Asian American Experience* (New Brunswick, NJ: Rutgers University Press, 1998).
49. Chiu, "The Cultural Defense," *id.*; Ancheta, *Race, Rights, and the Asian American Experience, id.*
50. C. Dalton, "Domestic Violence, Domestic Torts and Divorce: Constraints and Possibilities," *New England Law Review* 31 (1997):319–395.
51. Orr v. Orr, 440 U.S. 268 (1979).
52. *See* L. Lacey, "Mimicking the Words, But Missing the Message: The Misuse of Cultural Feminist Themes in Religion and Family Law Jurisprudence," *Boston College Law Review* 35 (1993):1–48.
53. Federal Child Support Enforcement Act, P. L. 93-677, 88 Stat.2337 (1975), amended, 42 U.S.C. 651-669.
54. Dalton, "Domestic Violence, Domestic Torts and Divorce."
55. M. H. Weiner, "Domestic Violence and the Per Se Standard of Outrage," *Maryland Law Review* 54 (1995):183–241.
56. Michael H. v. Gerald D., 109 S.Ct. 2333 (1989).
57. M. A. Fineman, *The Illusion of Equality: The Rhetoric and Reality of Divorce Reform* (Chicago: University of Chicago Press, 1991).
58. *See* L. L. Lane, "The Parental Rights Movement," *University of Colorado Law Review* 69 (1998):825–849.
59. V. L. Sacks, "An Indefensible Defense: On the Misuse of Culture in Criminal Law," *Arizona Journal of International and Comparative Law* 13 (1996):523–550.
60. Generally, actors claiming either justification or excuse concede that they committed a criminal act but offer plausible arguments why they should not be punished. Defenses using excuses propose that defendants were unable to make responsible choices, that the circumstances were so limiting that their acts were not voluntary even though they knew the acts were wrong. Defenses involving justifications argue that defendants were advancing a social interest or redressing a wrong and that the acts were not wrongful. *See* R. P. Mosteller, "Syndromes and Politics in Criminal Trials and Evidence Law," *Duke Law Journal* 46 (1996):461–516.

61. *See* Morrisette v. United States, 342 U.S. 246 (1952).
62. P. J. Falk, "Novel Theories of Criminal Defense Based on the Toxicity of the Social Environment: Urban Psychosis, Television Intoxication, and Black Rage," *North Carolina Law Review* 74 (1996):731–811.
63. Levesque, "Piercing the Family's Private Veil."
64. L. Henderson, "Co-Opting Compassion: The Federal Victim's Rights Movement," *St. Thomas Law Review* 10 (1998):579–606.
65. Levesque, "Emotional Maltreatment in Adolescents' Everyday Lives."
66. *See* Rock v. Arkansas, 483 U.S. 44 (1987).
67. Slobogin, "Psychiatric Evidence in Criminal Trials."
68. *See* H. Maguigan, "Cultural Evidence and Male Violence: Are Feminist and Multiculturalist Reformers on a Collision Course in Criminal Courts?" *New York University Law Review* 70 (1995):36–99.
69. *See* Chiu, "The Cultural Defense"; F. S. Brelvi, "News of the Weird: Specious Normativity and the Problem of the Cultural Defense," *Columbia Human Rights Law Review* 28 (1997):657–683.
70. L. Volpp, "Blaming Culture for Bad Behavior," *Yale Journal of Law & the Humanities* 12 (2000):89–116.
71. *Id.*
72. *See*, most notably, A. Dershowitz, *The Abuse Excuse* (Boston: Little, Brown, 1994); and G. P. Fletcher, *With Justice for Some: Victims' Rights in Criminal Trials* (Reading, MA: Addison-Wesley, 1995).
73. Quang Ngo Bui v. State, 550 So. 2d 1094 (Ala. Crim. App. 1988).
74. People v. Wu, 286 Cal. Rptr. 868 (1991).
75. Unpublished decision, reported in T. F. Goldstein, "Cultural Conflict in Court: Should the American Criminal Justice System Formally Recognize a Cultural Defense?" *Dickinson Law Review* 99 (1994):141–168.
76. S. Jacobson, "Questions Persist," DALLAS MORNING NEWS (Nov. 29, 1995):A1.
77. R. Kim, "Clash of Cultures: Koreans Urge Leniency in Case of Locked-Up Teen," *Newsday* (May 5, 1998):A7.
78. P. Hammel, "Arranged Marriage Case Heard Iraqi Parents Plead No Contest to Neglect," OMAHA WORLD HERALD (Apr. 5, 1997):1.
79. L. Berger, "Learning to Tell Custom From Abuse," LOS ANGELES TIMES (Aug. 24, 1994):A1.
80. B. Crossette, "Testing the Limits of Tolerance as Cultural Mix," NEW YORK TIMES (Mar. 6, 1999):A15, A17.
81. Cited in M. Fischer, "The Human Rights Implications of a Cultural Defense," *Southern California Interdisciplinary Law Journal* 6 (1998):663–702.
82. *See, e.g.*, A. K. C. Leung, "Ecchymoses From Spoon Scratching Simulating Child Abuse," *Clinical Pediatrics* 25 (1986):98; and K. K. Hansen, "Folk Remedies and Child Abuse: A Review With Emphasis on *Caida de Mollera* and Its Relationship to Shaken Baby Syndrome," *Child Abuse & Neglect* 22 (1997):117–127.
83. A. Sagi, P. Ben-Mier, and C. Bibi, "Burn Hazard From Cupping—An Ancient Universal Medication Still in Practice," *Burns* 14 (1988):323–325.
84. Hansen, "Folk Remedies and Child Abuse."
85. K. W. Feldman, "Pseudoabusive Burns in Asian Refugees," *American Journal of Diseases of Children* 138 (1984):768–769.
86. K. W. Feldman, "Letter to the Editor," *Child Abuse & Neglect* 19 (1995):657–658.
87. A. L. Risser and L. J. Mazur, "Use of Folk Remedies in a Hispanic Population," *Archives of Pediatric and Adolescent Medicine* 149 (1995):978–981.
88. *See* Hansen, "Folk Remedies and Child Abuse."
89. B. L. Bottoms, P. R. Shaver, G. S. Goodman, and J. Quin, "In the Name of God: A Profile of Religion-Related Child Abuse," *Journal of Social Issues* 51 (1995):85–111.

90. E. T. Gershoff, P. C. Miller, and G. W. Holden, "Parenting Influences From the Pulpit: Religious Affiliation as a Determinant of Parental Corporal Punishment," *Journal of Family Psychology* 13 (1999):307–320.

91. L. M. Graham, " 'The Past Never Vanishes': A Contextual Critique of the Existing Indian Family Doctrine," *American Indian Law Review* 23 (1998):30, note 132.

92. *See* note 16.

93. Graham, "'The Past Never Vanishes.'"

94. National Research Council, *Understanding Child Abuse & Neglect* (Washington, DC: National Academy Press, 1993).

95. G. L. Zellman, "The Impact of Case Characteristics on Child Abuse Reporting Decisions," *Child Abuse & Neglect* 16 (1992):57–74; J. Waldfogel, *The Future of Child Protection: How to Break the Cycle of Abuse & Neglect* (Cambridge, MA: Harvard University Press, 1998).

96. K. D. Tingus, A. H. Heger, D. Foy, and G. A. Leskin, "Factors Associated With Entry Into Therapy in Children Evaluated for Sexual Abuse," *Child Abuse & Neglect* 20 (1995):63–68.

97. *See, e.g.*, C. Glisson, "Judicial and Service Decisions for Children Entering State Custody: The Limited Role of Mental Health," *Social Services Review* 70 (1996):257–281; and B. C. Feld, *Bad Kids: Race and the Transformation of the Juvenile Court* (New York: Oxford University Press, 1999).

98. J. D. Koss-Chioino and L. A. Vargas, *Working With Latino Youth: Culture, Development, and Context* (San Francisco: Jossey-Bass, 1999).

99. People v. Chen, unpublished decision, reported in N. S. Kim, "The Cultural Defense and the Problem of Cultural Preemption: A Framework for Analysis," *New Mexico Law Review* 27 (1997):101–139.

100. Wang, "Battered Asian American Women."

101. People v. Aphaylath, 502 N.E.2d 988 (N.Y. 1986).

102. People v. Rhines, 182 Cal. Rptr. 478 (Ct. App. 1982).

103. Trujillo-Garcia v. Rowland, No. 93-1506 (9th Cir., Oct. 10, 1993).

104. People v. Natale, 18 Cal. Rptr. 492 (Cal. Ct. App. 1962).

105. People v. Washington, 130 Cal. Rptr. 96 (Ct. App. 1976).

106. People v. Moua (1985), unpublished decision, cited in Chiu, "The Cultural Defense."

107. Kim, "The Cultural Defense and the Problem of Cultural Preemption."

108. K. Crenshaw, "Race, Gender and Violence Against Women"; E. M. Schneider, "Particularity and Generality: Challenges of Feminist Theory and Practice in Work on Woman Abuse," *New York University Law Review* 67 (1992):520–568.

109. V. Kanuha, "Domestic Violence, Racism, and the Battered Women's Movement in the United States," in *Future Interventions With Battered Women and Their Families*, J. L Edleson and Z. C. Eiskovits, Eds. (Thousand Oaks, CA: Sage, 1996).

110. For a review, *see* R. Hampton, R. Carrillo, and J. Kim, "Violence in Communities of Color," in *Family Violence and Men of Color*, R. Carrillo and J. Tello, Ed. (New York: Springer, 1998).

111. Schneider, "Particularity and Generality."

112. *See, e.g.*, A. D. Renteln, "A Justification of the Cultural Defense as Partial Excuse," *Southern California Review of Law & Women's Studies* 2 (1993):437–526.

113. *See, e.g.*, Coleman, "Individualizing Justice Through Multiculturalism."

114. Volpp, "Talking Culture."

115. Tarpley, "Bad Witches."

116. *See* Daubert v. Merrell Dow Pharmaceuticals, Inc., 509 U.S. 579 (1993).

117. A trilogy of U.S. Supreme Court decisions provides the frameworks for rulings on the admissibility of expert testimony and scientific evidence. In the first decision, Daubert v. Merrell Dow Pharmaceuticals, Inc., *id.*, the court construed the federal rules of evi-

dence to mean that expert scientific testimony is admissible only if it is relevant, reliable, and helpful, *id.* at 589; they listed factors that lower courts might consider in determining the reliability of expert testimony, *id.* at 593–595. Four years later, the court revisited the issue of admissibility in General Electric Co. v. Joiner, 118 S.Ct. 512 (1997), in which the court made clear that the trial judge's decision to admit or exclude scientific testimony can be reversed only for abuse of discretion, *id.* at 519. Finally, in the third decision, Kumho Tire Co. v. Carmichael, 119 S.Ct. 1167 (1999), the court established that *Daubert*'s requirement of relevance and reliability applies whether expert testimony is "scientific" or "non-scientific," *id.* at 1171. Although the decision does not necessarily apply to state courts, the emerging framework contributes to important controversies and commentaries offering guideposts to direct and improve judges' evidentiary decision making; *see, e.g.,* D. A. Krauss and B. D. Sales, "The Problem of 'Helpfulness' in Applying *Daubert* to Expert Testimony: Child Custody Determinations in Family Law as an Exemplar," *Psychology, Public Policy, and Law* 5 (1999):78–99.

118. *See* Hansen, "Folk Remedies and Child Abuse."

119. *Id.*

120. H. Maguigan, "Cultural Evidence and Male Violence: Are Feminist and Multiculturalist Reformers on a Collision Course in Criminal Courts?" *New York University Law Review* 70 (1995):36–99.

121. Volpp, "Talking Culture."

122. *See* R. Rosaldo, *Culture and Truth: The Remaking of Social Analysis* (Boston: Beacon Press, 1993).

123. H. N. Bui, "Domestic Violence in the Vietnamese Immigrant Community: An Exploratory Study," *Violence Against Women* 5 (1999):769–796.

124. C. Kagitçibasi, "Whither Multiculturalism?" *Applied Psychology: An International Review* 46 (1997):44–49.

125. E. Sussman, "Contending With Culture: An Analysis of the Female Genital Mutilation Act of 1996," *Cornell International Law Journal* 31 (1998):193–250.

126. Levesque, *Child Sexual Abuse.*

127. *Id.*

128. *See, e.g.,* J. Gordon, "We Make the Road by Walking: Immigrant Workers, the Workplace Project, and the Struggle for Social Change," *Harvard Civil Rights–Civil Law Review* 30 (1995):407–450; and V. P. Coto, "Beyond/Between Colors: Lucha, The Struggle for Life: Legal Services for Battered Immigrant Women," *University of Miami Law Review* 53 (1999):749–759.

129. K. Crenshaw, "Mapping the Margins: Intersectionality, Identity Politics and Violence Against Women of Color," *Stanford Law Review* 43 (1991):1241–1299.

130. Wang, "Battered Asian American Women"; B. E. Hernandez-Tryol, "Las Olvidadas—Gendered in Justice/Gendered Injustice: Latinas, Fronteras and the Law," *Journal of Gender, Race & Justice* 1 (1998):353–404.

131. Volpp, "Talking Culture."

132. *Id.*

133. *See* Hernandez-Tryol, "Las Olvidadas—Gendered in Justice/Gendered Injustice."

134. *See* J. Korbin, "Culture and Child Maltreatment," in *The Battered Child* 5th ed. rev., M. E. Helfer, R. S. Kempe, and R. D. Krugman, Eds. (Chicago: University of Chicago Press, 1997).

135. R. J. R. Levesque, "The Failures of Foster Care Reform: Revolutionizing the Most Radical Blueprint," *Maryland Journal of Contemporary Legal Issues* 6 (1995):1–35.

136. R. J. R. Levesque, "Prosecuting Sex Crimes Against Children: Time for 'Outrageous' Proposals?" *Law & Psychology Review* 19 (1995):59–91.

137. *Id.*

138. *See, e.g.,* I. R. Gunning, "Arrogant Perception, World-Travelling and Multicultural Fem-

inism: The Case of Female Genital Surgeries," *Columbia Human Rights Law Review* 23 (1992):189–248.

139. Levesque, "Piercing the Family's Private Veil."

140. J. W. Berry, Y. H. Poortinga, M. H. Segall, and P. R. Dasen, *Cross-Cultural Psychology: Research and Applications* (New York: Columbia University Press, 1992).

141. C. Kagitçibasi, *Family and Human Development Across Cultures: A View From the Other Side* (Mahwah, NJ: Erlbaum, 1996).

142. H. C. Triandis, *Culture and Social Behavior* (New York: McGraw Hill, 1994).

143. H. W. Gardiner, J. D. Mutter, and C. Kosmitzki, *Lives Across Cultures: Cross-Cultural Human Development* (Needham Heights, MA: Allyn & Bacon, 1998).

144. *See* Kagitçibasi, *Family and Human Development Across Cultures.*

145. For an analysis of how apparently equal treatment in defining neglect systematically discriminates against minorities, *see* K. J. Swift, "Canada: Trends and Issues in Child Welfare." In *Combatting Child Abuse: International Perspectives and Trends*, N. Gilbert, Ed. (New York: Oxford University Press, 1995).

146. *See* chapter 4.

147. *See, e.g.,* D. Otto, "Rethinking the 'Universality' of Human Rights," *Columbia Human Rights Law Review* 29 (1997):1–46.

148. R. J. R. Levesque, "Combatting Child Sexual Maltreatment: Advances and Obstacles in International Progress," *Law & Policy* 17 (1995):441–469.

149. Levesque, "The Failures of Foster Care Reform."

150. J. W. Berry, "Immigration, Acculturation, and Adaptation," *Applied Psychology: An International Review* 46 (1997):5–68.

151. *See, e.g.,* A. Gopaul-McNicol and J. Brice-Baker, *Cross-Cultural Practice: Assessment, Treatment, and Training* (New York: Wiley, 1998).

Chapter 8
RECONCEPTUALIZING FAMILY VIOLENCE, CULTURE, AND U.S. LAW

From a historical perspective, the developments charted in the previous chapters are nothing short of radical. Fifty years ago, the United Nations barely existed, and its path-breaking human rights documents and human rights machinery were far in the making. Thirty years ago, family violence received virtually no theoretical, empirical, or legal attention. Now, protections from family violence exist both in international human rights law and in virtually all countries. Both international and national protections from violence receive strong endorsement and concern.

Despite these formal dedications to international and national human rights commitments, gross and consistent violations of basic rights are recorded daily. Activist groups and nongovernmental organizations charge all governments with involvement or complicity in violating basic human rights and with the failure to live up to obligations they have set for themselves. The glaring disparity between apparent commitment in theory and law and poor compliance in actual practice constitutes the paradox of human rights law. The power of human rights law ensures that no government can openly reject its tenets. Yet governments continue to violate the most basic and fundamental rights. The previous chapters have sought to help resolve the paradox and bridge the gap between law and practice. This chapter brings together several strands of the book's overarching argument—that human rights law protects individuals from family violence—to focus more specifically on the power of a human rights approach and how it may alleviate family violence.

International Law and the Regulation of Families

Previous chapters posited that international law provides a useful basis on which to transform conceptions of individuals and of individuals within their families. Possible reconceptions, in turn, reveal how international law offers opportunities to rethink family violence. Before detailing the nature of these opportunities, it is necessary to revisit international law's approach to family life. Although international law approaches and affects family life in numerous ways, four basic developments in human rights law may serve as a springboard to rethink responses to family violence.

The primary transformation in legal approaches to family life concerns the simple fact that the modern human rights movement actually addresses families. Human rights law views families as the fundamental unit of societies and, as such, entitles them to protection and support. Rather than viewing families as out of the reach of governmental regulations, the human rights movement recognizes the need to support and protect families because they are the foundation for healthy individual and societal development. The allocation of rights to families derives from their functions. By implication, once families no longer perform those functions, families lose their rights and individuals within those families gain their own rights. Thus, human rights law bases itself on family life, recognizes its centrality to human existence, and seeks to protect families so they can shelter and foster human rights.

The second critical metamorphosis involves changing perceptions of the interactions individuals have with family members and members of other societal institutions. The movement appreciates how family members are individuals who are inseparable from their social fabric and assumes diversity among societies, families, and individuals. This assumption allows for attempts to ensure and recognize rights without inappropriately discriminating against family members on the basis of social position, particularly as reflected in their social class, gender, abilities, nationalities, and ultimate place of residence, and it allows for emphasis on legally protecting and fostering the development of all individuals as well as their social conditions. At its core, then, human rights principles establish the inseparability of all individuals from their collective, even global, condition.

The third revolutionary development follows from the recognition of the important place individuals occupy in society, the diverse situations in which individuals find themselves, and the need to foster their individual personhoods. This recognition dictates a new approach to the legal standards used to address family members' needs. International standards mandate that nations, societies, families, and individuals act in family members' best interests. This approach differs considerably from traditional notions of best interests. The need to recognize, respect, foster, and ensure family members' right to self-determination must now factor into determinations of what constitutes best interests. This development constitutes the foundation of the human rights movement's most radical development. The foundational nature of this reconceptualization requires special elaboration of its implications for both individual family members and their cultures.

In terms of individual development, self-determination needs coupled by the mandate that societies act in family members' best interests actually switch the current starting points in thinking of families in societies and the law. In terms of families themselves, this conception of rights radically departs from the adult, family-centered conceptions of family rights—it departs from what some would characterize as the patriarchal foundations of family life. For example (and sweepingly stated), the family-centered approach equates children's familial interests with those of adults, ignores the need to ensure children's independent access to courts and legal services, places societal priorities on economic interests rather than on children's needs, and plays down concern for the manner in which individual societies treat their children in favor of nations' treatment of each other. The international conceptual revolution seeks to rebalance concerns toward children's best interests and rethink the nature and influence these cultural institutions have on children. In that process, the development gives children greater voice and control in determining how all institutions affect their lives. The human rights movement demands changes in the adult-centered focus approach even as it applies to adults. Adults who may be vulnerable to family life, typically women and elderly people, gain their own independent rights so that one family member's interests cannot dominate the interests of others. As with children's own interests in self-determination, the human rights movement seeks to put in place sociolegal mechanisms that allow individuals in families access to services and institutions outside of their families, such as access to education, work, public service, and protections from violence.

Reconceptualization of self-determination also supports another emerging development in international human rights law—cultural self-determination. At cultural levels, the developments allow for rethinking the diverse institutions that constitute cultures. Prior to these developments, conceptions and proposals for cultural self-determination remained vulnerable to charges that they allowed traditional practices to control vulnerable individuals and allowed repressive regimes to oppress vulnerable constituencies. Although these charges still remain, modern conceptions of cultural self-determination and of "culture" itself address these problems. Modern conceptions counter these criticisms through a focus that aims to respect difference and engage in exchanges. The belief is that cultures recursively affect one another and that the nature of imperialism has changed even to the extent that some global forces operate largely independently of individual cultures. Modern international law moves away from focusing solely on how nations and cultures within them must behave toward one another. Modern international law now includes a move toward taking greater advantage of the natural involvement cultures have with one another and capitalizing on "indigenous" beliefs to develop and foster more global human rights.

The fourth development encapsulates and energizes the previous three developments. International law characterizes human rights as both fundamental and inherent to every human because of their humanness. This approach to international human rights law demands much more than technical adherence to justice and equality. The international instruments expressly reject the dehumanization of both human people and the human condition. Because individual rights are inalienable to both their human personhood and the human condition, responsibility for protecting rights rests both on individuals and States. All must be enlisted to recognize, respect, and ensure fundamental rights. As we have seen most explicitly in chapter 4 but implicitly throughout the other chapters, this conception of rights and obligations adopts a very expansive view of law. Under this approach, law is much more than what courts and lawyers do. Law fundamentally involves the manner people treat one another. Human rights law deals most fundamentally, then, with human relationships and the need to recognize others' humanness.

Although drastically distilled to its fundamentals, the four central developments reveal radical transformations in international law's conceptions of individuals and their families. The global community now agrees that individual family members must be provided with rights; that those rights adhere to them as individuals, which allows them to control the exercise of these rights; that families are inseparable from their cultural location; that human rights seek to transform both individual relationships and cultural forces; and that an urgent need exists for greater commitment to developing and ensuring those rights. The development and investigation of cultural practices that serve to foster or hamper development of those rights grows from these recognitions and demands that international law places on everyone. International law, then, calls for investigations like the one offered in previous chapters.

The Cross-Cultural Record's Lessons for Reform Efforts

Despite an international obligation to investigate, challenge, and, where necessary, reform individuals' experiences of family life, human rights law and reform efforts still readily face serious obstacles. These obstacles account for the massive failure of societies, families, and individuals to fulfill their obligations. The obstacles also reveal the challenges that confront human rights efforts to affect family violence.

Although the obstacles are numerous, previous chapters revealed the essentially cultural nature of the most ingrained and problematic obstacles. Commentators and researchers may disagree about the interactive nature of law and cultural forces and even prefer to examine social or economic considerations, but the relationship between various cultural forces and their impact on law are integral to any analysis. The previous chapters described several effects of cultural life on conceptions of violence and efforts to alleviate such violence. Chapter 2 noted how cultural practices influence societies' definitions of experiences as maltreating, create climates conducive to violence, buffer some individuals from violence, and affect intervention efforts. Chapter 3 explored how reform efforts meet cultural resistance and how such resistance ensures the failure of local human rights efforts. Most notably, the resistance takes the form of existing discriminatory laws, customs, religious traditions, and differential allocations of basic social resources that place individuals at risk for maltreatment. Taken together and addressed from a human rights perspective, these obstacles reveal three fundamental concerns and challenges to human rights: visibility, legitimacy, and rigidity.

Overcome Invisibility

The first obstacle faced by a human rights approach involves the diverse manner in which institutions foster family violence and the extent to which harmful beliefs and practices remain largely invisible. Indeed, numerous institutions render some forms of maltreatment invisible, and some forms of maltreatment thrive because of their relative invisibility.

The invisibility permeates societies' treatment of some family members. Some family members' rights remain essentially invisible because families seek to protect other individuals and societies seek to develop individuals into productive members of society. For example, some societies do not view children as individuals in their own right; instead, they view children as exchangeable, familial property, which makes it difficult to accept that children should not be married, sold, or rented to profit others. These societies provide a cultural framework that condones the negative effects of these practices. Likewise, problematic practices often coincide with efforts to buffer some family members from certain harms. For example, commentators report the pervasive double standard girls face regarding their sexual activity, which seem to protect girls as they reduce their availability to certain sexual partners. In addition, the pervasive notion of family privacy guards against intrusion to protect individuals from maltreatment, and the approach to family life allows families to operate without state control and develop individuals into societal members without much governmental support. These examples underscore how cultural practices unwittingly condone or foster maltreatment. The complexity, cultural embeddedness, and utility of practices and beliefs render cultural institutions unable to recognize how certain forms of relationships and potentially problematic practices may contribute to or actually constitute maltreatment.

Human rights law expressly seeks to address issues of invisibility. Indeed, the major goal of human rights law involves the need to increase visibility of rights abuses. Visibility provides human rights law's fundamental method of enforcement against state failure to protect human rights: The international human rights machinery focuses on record keeping, consciousness raising, and challenging states. Human rights law focuses on offering individuals mechanisms to participate in their social institutions and have their concerns addressed, as most obvious and significant in our above discussion of self-determination. Human rights protect deliberation about human rights issues involving social processes, evolution, and aspiration and attempt to reform, recognize, and ensure the rights of all.

Much of the discussion found in previous chapters highlighted how international law does not necessarily resolve disputes; it (more importantly) provides methods of deliberation and accommodation. For example and as with other human rights advocacy, published reports, use of the media, and international law's usual methods can be used to cajole, push, threaten, and punish actors who fail to make progress in attempts to address the needs of families trapped in violence. Such advocacy remains important not only for action at the Nation–State level, but also for action directed toward individual actors who implement laws at their discretion as well as those subject to that discretion. Existing evidence suggests that such efforts are far from futile. For example, the development of a documentary record of maltreating experiences already contributes to a deeper understanding of the difficulties individuals face; recall that documentary records effectively have placed several forms of family violence on the public agenda. Put into the perspective of this analysis, these efforts work simply because they appropriately aim to make maltreating experiences, and their sustaining forces, visible. Human rights law holds promise because it offers principles and mechanisms that ensure consideration of individuals' own interests and that capitalize on the natural transformation of cultural life.

Increase Legitimacy

The inability to view some forms of beliefs and practices as problematic makes suspect efforts to include practices into conceptions of what violates basic human rights. Cultures maintain problematic practices by simply not recognizing how their belief systems place individuals at risk and involve human rights violations. They may marshal locally legitimate arguments that allow them to view practices as unproblematic and to argue that human rights law inappropriately usurps local values and traditions better left unchallenged and unchanged. As a result, concepts of rights and justice remain distant from the lives of those involved in family violence, who do not recognize that they have legitimate claims to safety.

This investigation revealed numerous examples of arguments and rationalizations, many of which appear reasonable, that challenge efforts to conceptualize practices as constituting family violence. These arguments were especially strong in defense of female genital operations, child marriages, dowry deaths, and ways some societies let older people die with dignity. Some of the major arguments against including these practices as potential violations of fundamental human rights included the proposal that cultures simply do not necessarily view the practices as harmful. For example, some propose that the practices outsiders would view as child maltreatment are in fact permissible child labor or proper socialization for adulthood. Other major arguments against conceiving numerous practices as maltreatment rested on the proposition that the practices remained critical to healthy development and "proper" gender roles. For example, much of the violence perpetrated within families has been linked to traditional gender roles, which leave individuals vulnerable to the control of others. Some practices are argued to be legitimate responses to social pressures, which required the allocation of scarce resources. For example, if boys could earn more and return those earnings to their families, it would make sense for families to focus on ensuring that boys reach their highest earning potentials. Likewise, if societies have to spend too many resources on those "decrepit" and near death (and those who do not contribute to societal resources), they could justify allocating those resources to benefit more individuals and families. Justifications for abusive practices directly challenge the legitimacy of conceptions that would view the practices as maltreating.

The second point of legitimacy involves challenges to human rights as originating from outside of local cultural life. As demonstrated in chapter 4, frequent charges include, for example, the claim that human rights are imperialist, that they derive from sources of human rights foreign to many of the world's cultures, and that they do not account for local variation in the manner societies approach and respect people and their surroundings. These are important arguments that constitute powerful obstacles against including many of the reviewed practices into the concept of maltreatment.

Local arguments remain difficult to counter. The arguments pose much more fundamental challenges than their appearance as reasonable and their view of outsiders' intrusive efforts as impermissibly imperialistic. The fundamental challenge is that naked imperialism simply does not work and contravenes basic democratic, international principles. As revealed in chapters 4, 5, and 6, when applied in different cultures that resist the imposition of alien standards, international law and national laws that take human rights seriously simply aim to provide principles of deliberation and respect for diversity. For example, instead of saving individuals from cultures, human rights advocates seek to use indigenous concepts and basic values to foster rights. As we have seen, child protective strategies reach effectiveness when they connect basic children's rights themes with localized and widely shared values. For example, the universal recognition that children should not be exploited offers an important opportunity. The goal would be to delineate more precisely what constitutes exploitation and the conditions under which it is tolerated. Efforts to characterize practices as torturous also reflect this approach's effectiveness, as most obviously seen in efforts to catalyze responses against genital alterations and partner battering. Reform attempts that frame practices, such as physical punishment, as violations of basic human dignity and equality also increase the likelihood of reform simply because human rights policy making places strong emphasis on the concept of human dignity and equality of treatment. Also powerful are efforts that link the universal right to life with practices that lead to the early death of elderly people or the violent death of battered women. By linking international values with local values, human rights law provides a common language that serves as a stepping stone for changing approaches to protections from family violence.

The third point of legitimacy involves the extent to which rights remain removed from the ways family members envision wrongs, injustice, and deprivations in their daily lives. People's interactions with those charged with law enforcement dictate views of law and justice. Individuals frequently experience law as oppressive, corrupt, ineffective, and even dangerous to their personal safety. As a result, they view rights as inapplicable to their conditions. For example, immigrants and individuals from impoverished communities may experience a very sharp distrust of police, government officials, hospitals, clinic personnel, and any notion that formal systems may protect their rights and interests. Receiving protection undoubtedly remains obstructed by presumptions that systems cannot deliver justice.

Rather than imposing standards, then, human rights law seeks legitimacy. Human rights law seeks to infiltrate individual consciousness and to internalize values that offer and develop legitimate ways to deal with violence. Again, those means of achieving justice include not only public or institutional means but also less formal changes and more subtle forms of individual development. Human rights law seeks legitimacy instead of simply ensuring that nations mandate an end to violence without actually intending to alleviate such violence. More important, it does so without usurping traditions that seem problematic from an outsider's point of view yet actually protect individuals from violence.

Resist Rigidity

Human rights law is challenged by the difficulty of pressing for changes in culturally embedded practices, even though the practices may be recognized as problematic and worthy of response; the perception of cultures as static, never changing, and monolithic; and the ingrained belief that international law deals with nations' treatment of one another and not their treatment of their own citizens or citizens' treatment of one another.

Numerous practices continue despite condemnation from outside and inside the observed societies. Child sexual abuse, as conceptualized in Western countries, provides a powerful example of a form of maltreatment subjected to numerous legal and policy responses fueled by intense public concern. Yet the sexual abuse of children continues essentially unabated in every Western country studied by researchers. Child neglect continues to be the most documented form of maltreatment. The history of support services for the poor reveals how they began as reasonable, if not adequate, efforts that quickly lost perspective or were overwhelmed. Efforts to assist have been marked by a chronic sense that arrangements for providing help are inadequate, in need of reform, or worse, that they actually contribute to the problems and are fundamentally destructive. Much of the failed responses, then, remains attributable to responses to social problems that necessarily must accommodate to rigid approaches and values.

Rigid cultural practices and beliefs pose difficulties for efforts to combat the above social problems. One difficulty derives from the failure to reconsider how to make the internal workings of families more public and offer greater protection to individual members. Family privacy hinders intervention efforts to help individual children and offer services. A second difficulty emerges with the conceptualization of maltreatment, which leaves entire groups of children at risk. Policy makers have failed to recognize the extent to which boys may be abused, particularly by other boys, and how their socialization makes it difficult for them to disclose, seek assistance, or simply acquire skills to avoid maltreatment. Conceptions of masculinity, views of homosexuality, and impressions of how the sexes interact hinder attempts to assist boys. Properly addressing the abuses boys suffer necessitates confronting traditional views and values. These examples reveal how pervasive forms of maltreatment remain difficult to combat even though the relevant societies exhibit a sincere public commitment to address all forms of maltreatment. Thus, maltreating "practices" continue largely because certain sex role socializations and familial patterns leave individuals vulnerable. The failure to combat this and other forms of maltreatment is related to the inability to accept how certain cultural beliefs place individuals at risk and to the fear that addressing the problems will intrude impermissibly on deeply rooted cultural values.

Perceptions of what constitutes cultural life contribute to rigidity. The pervasive view of culture is one in which societies are authentic and which consist of individual autonomous and internally coherent universes. Cultures are thought to be the vehicle through which one generation passes on to the next its ways of seeing, experiencing, interpreting, and being. From this view, culture serves to teach new generations ways of coping and surviving in the world as the previous generation understood it. As such, cultures are thought to be readily identifiable groups that differ from other groups in the way they believe, act, and adapt to their surroundings. Legal systems tend to adopt a similar view and embrace cultures as groups with strict, discernible boundaries. This approach to cultures differs considerably from other conceptions of cultural life that focus less on intergenerational transmission and more on the process in which people engage in the continual process of accounting for what they do, say, and think. From this perspective, cultures simply provide general guidelines for interpreting dispositions.

Cultures do not signify a static group; cultures only serve as useful analytical abstractions. This perspective interprets culture as the system of values and symbols reproduced by a specific group or groups within those groups, a system that provides individuals with the required signposts and meanings for behavior and social relationships in everyday life. The perspective encourages a focus on sets of subsystems or domains of shared knowledge and the realization that intracultural differences may exceed intercultural differences. The perspective realizes that a focus on intergenerational transmission of cultural practices misses how those who ostensibly receive cultures (e.g., children and immigrants) are far from passive recipients and actually actively participate in defining cultural practices. One's cultural identity, then, constantly evolves in a dynamic manner as one moves from one context to another and as one incorporates such broad influences as education, religion, ethnicity, language, nationality, gender, age, geographical location, and socioeconomic status.

Human rights law must counter the rigid and continued belief that it does not necessarily affect how nations treat their citizens and how citizens treat one another. Most notably, for example, and as discussed in chapters 1, 4, 5, and 6, the perception that state sovereignty guards from outside influence unnecessarily adopts a rigid view of international law, which neglects international law's mandate to intervene in other nations and the need for other nations to ensure not only that they respect internationally recognized rights but also that they seek to ensure that other nations do so. Likewise, although human rights laws move beyond states, the image still tends to be that only governments commit human rights violations and that only they can provide recourse to human rights violations. Thus, not only do perceptions unnecessarily take a narrow view of state sovereignty, but they also fail to consider how institutions other than the state can violate human rights and can also alleviate human rights violations. Individuals are not always conscious of how law exerts authority in their lives because they understand important aspects of their lives through the language of law, which suggests that law plays a more pervasive and less perceptible role in ordering familial relationships.

Preliminary Conclusion

The analyses of obstacles to human rights reform suggest that the fact that problematic practices are situated in cultures restricts attempts to envision and propose different approaches. Many of the cultural forces that support the practices are not well suited for (or never make it to) the sociopolitical agenda. Indeed, some of the practices receive considerable protection, such as the right to practice one's religion and participate in cultural life. Another conclusion to be drawn from the analyses is that responses to the central obstacles identified by existing commentaries may be necessary, but they remain insufficient to protect individuals from family violence. Rampant failures to protect family members do not necessarily rest on failed efforts to provide resources, the inability to enact specific responses to maltreatment, the failure to aggressively enforce criminal sanctions, or a general lack of political will to address maltreating practices. Instead, the analyses suggest that the basic obstacles to protection from violence deal more with the cultural saliency of the practices and the contributing forces that remain culturally condoned.

These two conclusions acquire significance when considered in light of the often-repeated proposal that failures in protection generally arise from the inability to take seriously individual family members' rights and to recognize the importance of the human rights framework. The next section revisits how the human rights movement provides people with an opportunity to rethink cultural frameworks that leave individuals vulnerable to violence in family life, particularly in terms of family life in the United States. The ultimate goal of human rights reforms requires a renewed focus on increasing visibility, gaining legitimacy, and fostering less rigid views of cultural and state life.

Implications for U.S. Policy

Skepticism about the extent to which human rights law may assist individuals subjected to family violence may be measured by the number of commentaries urging reform. As discussed in the Introduction and chapter 6, few advocate a turn to human rights law and those who do most often find that the effect of incorporating human rights mandates into U.S. law would be negligible. Prognostications of doom reflect how the United States officially remains opposed to the imposition of international human rights law onto its laws. The United States continues to resist ratifying numerous treaties and those that it does accept are ratified in a manner that ensures no direct additional obligation.

Despite these tendencies, it would be a mistake to conclude that U.S. laws and policies remain hostile to international human rights' basic principles. Many of the principles enshrined in human rights law already are part of U.S. laws. Indeed, the extent to which U.S. law already protects many human rights principles often serves as a reason to ignore international mandates. More important (and as argued in chapter 6), the impact of human rights law is much broader than generally imagined. Human rights law affects how people approach family life and seeks to enlist the international community, nations, states, communities, families, and individuals in that reform effort. Although basic obstacles complicate analyses and question the eventual impact of the major transformations in human rights related to family life, a close reading of the nature of these obstacles reveals that they do not vitiate the potential contributions of human rights responses and human rights analyses. Indeed, obstacles make analyses of family violence and of human rights law's potential impact even more critical. This concluding section highlights the potential benefits of the international human rights approach and provides concrete examples of feasible contributions.

Although international law offers an expansive, if not idealistic, vision that may remain far from reach and subject to constant refinement, the international movement does spur forward some minimal reconceptions that may play central roles in efforts to combat family violence. A reasonable way to present the human rights movement's potential contributions is to return to the four major developments delineated at the beginning of this chapter and pinpoint how they may contribute to uncovering and dealing with family violence and how the envisioned approach diverges from prevailing responses to such violence.

Recognize Individuals Within Families

In the regulation of families, laws have transformed themselves only to return to similar outcomes. Common law historically has provided men with the right to chastise (beat) their spouses. Common law also provided parents with ultimate control over their children. During the past several decades, those common-law rights generally have been abolished, and the legal system has replaced them with other rights. Most notably, the rights have been replaced with the right to privacy. States now resist intervention in families on grounds that interference would violate the privacy necessary to foster marital relationships and to promote domestic harmony. Likewise and in terms of children's lives, attenuation of the parental right to control their children has been replaced by the family's right to family privacy; and the parental right to control their children still draws on parental property interests in children of the sort long recognized in the Anglo-American common law tradition. Resistance to intervention preserves authority relations between husband and wife, parent and child, and even among families of different social classes.

One of the most fundamental metamorphoses in human rights law involves changing perceptions of the interactions individuals have with family members and members of other societal institutions. As reviewed in chapters 1, 4, 5, and 7, human rights law seeks to recognize that individuals within families have rights. Although it would be inappropriate to conclude that U.S. law does not already recognize individuals' rights within families, particularly in terms of adults' rights, it does seem appropriate to conclude that individuals' rights remain rather limited. For example, individuals may have gained a right to protection from some forms of violence, but their other rights remain limited in terms of access to education, health, work, and other services; and those limitations relate to familial situations. The human rights movement urges us to rethink how certain individuals within families (e.g., women and children) may differently enjoy familial rights, privileges, and protections. Understanding the impact of the recognition of rights, however, requires understanding who actually controls the rights individuals ostensibly possess. That is, it requires an analysis of whether parents, spouses, families, or some other entity controls the rights of individuals within families.

Provide Individuals Control of Their Rights

One of the most revolutionary fronts of human rights law involves its attempt to make individuals within families subjects of their own rights. This development significantly departs from traditional law that holds that parents and society control the limited rights children have as well as the nature of those rights. The development also departs from traditional family law that allows even adults, through protection of family privacy, to control many of the rights of other adults in their families.

Nowhere is the movement more significant and illustrative than in attempts to make children subjects of their own rights. Under the human rights approach, children own their rights. For example, current law generally defers to parental rights when issues arise concerning whether children should have access to certain educational resources, social services, and supports. In terms of family violence, the recent developments mean that children's own primary interests, not those of their parents, would dictate whether they have access to services. For example, parents would not possess nearly unilateral control over the information children receive. Thus, children's own interests would dictate their access to education and the content of their education. At a minimum, the switch would result in concern about the inadequate and scarce amount of available information, both in terms of professional knowledge and the information communities seem willing to convey to children and youth. The orientation would affect the extent to which children and youth receive adequate information about gender, sexuality, violence, and their own rights. The development conceivably could go further.

Recognizing that children are legally independent entities with a need for and right to individual consideration in all matters concerning their treatment by others would lead to a reconfiguration of family life, particularly of family privacy, and could allow for greater "intrusion" into family life to protect children. This could mean, for example, important reform to the extent that current law assumes that parents act in the children's best interests and generally allows state intervention only in instances of harm or potential harm. Taking human rights seriously would mean allowing intervention when it could be in the best interests of the child, which would allow more freedom to displace the role of parents. Again, this may seem radical, but even the current legal system allows some third parties (e.g., teachers, physicians, children's relatives) to assume parental roles even without evidence of harm or potential harm to the child. In addition, the realities of everyday living mean that third parties (e.g., peers and the media) affect child development in ways beyond parental control. Indeed, a fundamental premise of this volume is that cultural forces beyond familial control affect family life. This view of human development suggests that legal systems must acknowledge and address children's own claims and not render them invisible by allowing parents or other caretakers to control rights that the global community recognizes as belonging to children.

The international movement also addresses the rights of other individuals within families as well as outside of families. The discussion has demonstrated how efforts are made to balance adult family members' rights and obligations within families, ranging from access to educational and economic opportunities to cultural events. Rights need equal recognition when individuals exit families. If taken seriously, these developments offer enormous implications. For example, some researchers report that up to 70% of reported injuries from domestic violence occur after separation. Such evidence suggests a need to consider child custody, access to children, child support, and other issues differently when family violence issues arise. Likewise, although arrest and incarceration for domestic violence has been viewed as the most successful effort to stop violent men, others find that arrest may increase violence, especially when men do not have close community ties or need for social conformity. Ironically, then, strategies that seek to terminate abuse and the relationship through legal interventions may prove more, rather than less, dangerous. The result is that some interventions, even the most innovative ones, which potentially subject batterers to incarceration are effectively unthinkable and unusable for many victims. Understanding these limitations requires understanding victims' cultural location and the significant role such location plays in victims' efforts to seek, obtain, and maintain assistance. Law, then, must seek to appreciate the complex cultural contingencies of everyday violence.

Recognize the Significance of Cultural Location

The legal system has difficulty taking into account the ethnocentricity of its responses to family violence. That failure has resulted in calls for greater appreciation of both abuser and victim's cultural location. The appropriate means to do so remains elusive and uncertain. Chapter 7 discussed the vexing questions posed by cultural differences when considering legal responses to family violence. Two fundamental issues illustrate the challenge.

The first issue raised by cultural sensitivity deals with the continued indeterminacy of such sensitivity. Those who address human rights and professionals who deal with family violence acknowledge the need for "cultural sensitivity" in dealing with family life issues, but it is unclear what exactly this sensitivity entails and how it may be translated into policy and practice. Most important (and as seen in chapter 7), the legal system affirmatively protects cultural practices when intervening in families. Investigators, adjudicators, and treatment professionals generally must take cultural concerns into account in performing their role, and policies should not be made strictly from the perspective of the dominant cultural values and practices. Indeed, even the criminal justice system, which formally opposes cultural excuses and justifications, actually allows for considerable cultural sensitivity, but it remains generally haphazard and unregulated. How these sentiments are to be put into practice remains to be determined and addressed, and the human rights movement may prove helpful in this regard. The movement does aim to set basic standards for human interaction. It also attempts to do much more: It provides ways to determine which practices deserve protection, as is discussed below.

The second challenge posed by cultural sensitivity deals with the need to address root causes of violence based in cultural beliefs. Observing that cultural differences exist in how families treat their members is not necessarily a justification for accepting all sorts of behavior. Yet it is essential to recognize that the different views reflect a deeper, more basic, disagreement about the nature of individuals and family life. Cultural and familial norms, for example, variously contribute to silencing those who endure abusive relationships. The deeply rooted nature of cultural life is of considerable significance. For example, even massive resources in the form of antipoverty programs do not suffice to alter or respond to practices that place children at risk. The obstacles are also more fundamental than the belief that maltreatment continues because of the failure to criminalize certain family patterns and relationships. In fact, criminalization often fails or exacerbates matters, and many practices legitimately may be viewed as part of a continuum of violence against family members that requires a variety of responses that make variable use of fiscal, educational, therapeutic, and criminal justice resources. Likewise, the obstacles are even more fundamental than the lack of political will to foster reform. Several recent legislative efforts consider aspects of the reviewed practices; local and customary laws also often recognize aspects of the problematic practices and aim for ideals that often diverge from everyday reality. Although addressing obstacles identified by commentaries certainly could alleviate some maltreatment rates, they would not necessarily address root causes of family violence, which have more to do with the problematic cultural beliefs and practices that remain invisible, the culturally salient beliefs that rationalize problematic practices, and the culturally ingrained socialization patterns that leave individuals vulnerable to forms of abuses societies mark for eradication. Although commentaries often play down these root causes in favor of a push for resources, tougher law enforcement, and an increase in political will, this volume highlights what researchers and those who work with family violence know: The desire to help family members, strict legal sanctions, and the infusion of resources remain far from enough.

Statistical realities of the rampant abuses and failures of the legal system make clear that the responses must do more than attempt to eradicate and control specific forms of violence. That is something the legal system, as one component of cultural forces imbuing societies, cannot do alone. Instead, the legal system must recognize and foster the need to transform both individual relationships and cultural practices.

Transform Both Individual Relationships and Cultural Practices

The need to recognize cultural location and the need to foster greater protections from family violence lead to the fourth contribution of the human rights movement: its important focus on self-determination both at individual and cultural levels. Both levels are important to consider.

Increasing legal independence in the form, for example, of ensuring victims right of access to information and social services is significant. Although the example applies to all vulnerable groups, such as battered woman and older people, the most radical reorientation human rights law asks of societies relates to children's rights to services. The international development in this area requires that children's sense of agency be made more visible and even harnessed in efforts to assist. Currently, perceptions of children's incapacities and dependencies primarily guide legal approaches to children's lives. Current responses to child sexual abuse are illustrative of the limitations of the current approach. The past decade's legal reforms largely focused on protecting children who became involved in legal processes that attempted to punish offenders or, in the alternative, focused on not prosecuting offenders for fear that children were suspect witnesses. These concerns with children's abilities ignored children's realities. Child victims make numerous decisions, including the decision whether they should tell about abuse. Indeed, the majority of children, like adults in comparable situations, decide not to disclose. Yet the law uses children's reticence to exclude their testimony.

Given the psychological and social complexities involved in disclosure, legal reconceptions could, for example, rethink the role of disclosure in prosecutorial and therapeutic efforts. At a minimum, concern for children's self-determination may be used to question whether there should be greater respect for those who would prefer not to disclose, or at least greater respect for having children determine the outcome of their cases. If the proposal for reform were taken seriously, it could mean that, as for adults, the law would not mandate children's therapists to disclose their clients' sexual victimization and violate patient–therapist confidentiality. Instead, the law simply could mandate therapists to take appropriate steps to determine whether abuse has stopped or to protect the child from further abuse, much as the law requires therapists to take action with other forms of abuse. These reforms would ensure that the law acts therapeutically and place greater emphasis on children's interests.[1] Reforms that increase children's self-determination clearly would be controversial. However, it is only in considering such possibilities that more effective means will emerge to deal with disclosure, treatment, and prevention.

In fact, the proposal is not as radical as it may appear. Children in some jurisdictions already essentially possess the power to veto prosecutors' decisions or affect sentencing outcomes. For example, Washington state, which has taken the lead in getting tough on sex offenders, has a sexual offender treatment alternative to sentencing that exhibits a preference for sentencing family members to treatment while sentencing the stranger to prison, and the treatment alternative requires the child's consent.[2] Likewise, prosecutors systematically forgo some prosecutions, especially incest cases, and rely heavily on the child's ability to be an effective witness when they decide whether to accept cases for prosecution and carry the cases forward.[3] Although these instances may be seen as moving toward taking family abuse less seriously, it could lead to the opposite outcome: Children could be appointed guardians *ad litem* or separate attorneys to safeguard their unique interests when legal parties and therapists propose to reunify the family and have a voice in determining the extent they have a relationship with perpetrators.[4] Again, although perhaps initially outrageous, thinking of how else to treat children and other vulnerable family members helps further their rights and may lead to the realization that present legal systems already allow for more enlightened reforms consistent with respecting the rights of victims.

The need to consider cultural self-determination relates to rethinking individual self-determination. This development suggests a need to resist the conclusion that individuals must be saved from their cultures. The approach that aims to protect cultural self-determination by linking global to local standards offers important opportunities to ensure protection from family violence.

Links can be made between children's basic rights and the highly touted concept of family values. The approach is useful to the extent that the latter may help address the former. That is, when the rationale that families exist to protect children serves to decrease intrusion into family life, the failure to protect children erodes the power of the rationale to resist intervention. The difference in stance toward child protection is significant. The approach suggests that concern for child protection would increase willingness to intervene prior to discovery of abuse, even though the legal system currently waits to intervene after the discovery of problems. Again, such approaches may be controversial. However, some societies readily intervene in families to support children even without proof or allegations of abuse; these societies simply use nonintrusive techniques, such as offering social services and community support programs, instead of waiting until coercive and punitive measures become the only available response. Likewise, the legal system already affects and controls family life, yet those controls remain largely ignored and their potential impact replaced by a myth that the legal system must remove itself from families presumed to be functioning.

Links also may be made between ideals of self-sufficiency and democratic life and action to reduce rates of family violence. The United States grants educational institutions the task of furthering democratic ideals, particularly with regard to individuals' economic self-sufficiency. The basic democratic commitment to providing children with educational opportunities coincides with protecting them from maltreatment. Ensuring children's own educational rights means, for example, providing resources to poor families so they can see to it that their children are ready for schooling; securing access to quality education that prepares children for rapidly changing societal mores; and increasing the availability of social services, including therapeutic and family planning services, to children who come from disruptive homes and those who have become sexually active. In brief, education that takes children's interests seriously fosters all of children's rights and prepares children for living in the type of world envisioned by modern human rights law. These examples reveal the potential effectiveness of strategically connecting children's needs to widely shared values and means of achieving culturally settled ideals consistent with global conceptions of human rights.

The human rights movement and the current understanding of family violence confirm the need to foster diverse ways to protect individuals. Protection must remain flexible, comprehensive, and placed within a larger social context. In terms of children's rights, the development translates into approaches to child protection that accept the duties of parents and community members and offer them requisite support to help prevent child maltreatment. In terms of women's rights, the development means more effort to create opportunities that respond to women's particular needs. These responses challenge a unidimensional criminal response and attempt to devise a legal resolution that meets the varying emotional, cultural, and financial needs of victims; a need illustrated by recognition of the difficulty raised by terminating a relationship that is needed culturally, emotionally, and financially but which may be severed with appropriate community-based support.[5] In terms of the rights of the elderly population, the dominant demographic developments in their care and social networks reveal the failure of social networks to replace levels of care that families may provide as well as a reduced ability and availability of families to care, especially for certain sectors of the older cohort—women, people who are very old, those

who are frail, and those who migrate. Yet the continued and growing preference for
the traditional and familial-oriented base of elderly care continues and places older
people at risk for violence. The findings suggest the need to reconcile the demonstrated reduction in resilience of family networks, the limited role of informal and
formal support structures, and the enthusiasm of "back-to-the-family" and
"community-care" policies for elderly life. Although controversial moves, the development recognizes the reality of victims' lives. For children, the legal system
must recognize and respond to what has been called the "silent ecology of abuse."[6]
For women, the legal system must address how different communities respond differently to legal intervention, which runs the danger of sending victims further un-
derground rather than offering assistance. For older people, overstretched and un-
derresourced systems of family or informal care can only increase the risk of
maltreatment, particularly when the majority of those sources of care generally involve a very limited number of individuals who also tend to be at risk: women and
elderly people with few limited resources. The cultural focus realizes that societal
imperatives structure lives and highlights how demands for rights can achieve their
goals only if they consider and aim to restructure these imperatives. At its core, then,
the transformation in approaches to family members' rights recognizes that prevailing
conceptions of family life are ideological artifacts that may hinder ways to assist
maltreated family members and that may foster maltreatment.

Conclusion

Recent global developments mark a sweeping approval of human rights instruments
and unprecedented advances in human rights law. Whether reluctantly or eagerly, all
nations aim to accept, understand, and respect the moral aspirations of modern notions of human rights. The result is that the notion of human rights expresses the
norms of the international community and no longer is reducible to any single State's
interpretation. Ultimately, national laws and practices increasingly will become accountable and subordinate to norms embodied in international law. In the process,
States will increasingly accept criteria by which to judge the treatment of everyone
within their jurisdictions. This is international law's radical vision. At no other time
has international law aimed to be so extensive. Individuals as well as States and
nongovernmental organizations are asked to identify, respect, and actively ensure
human rights the international community has made part of its laws regulating human
relations, not the least of which includes fostering discussion of how to recognize
and respond to harms individuals may suffer in families.

The broadening acceptance of the power of international law, its expanding
moral vision, and its novel approaches to ensuring that societies respect the rule of
human rights law make momentous the accompanying formulations of human rights
principles relating to family violence. In light of invigorating developments in international law, emerging conceptualizations of rights attain unprecedented significance. International human rights mandate fundamental transformations in laws and
policies that regulate families and cultural life. Precisely how the movement will
affect U.S. laws and responses to family violence remains unsettled. Although much
does remain for debate, one firm conclusion remains. As with all other nations, the
United States cannot ignore basic human rights commitments, which create duties

that increasingly infiltrate family and cultural life. Those obligations require response, not the least of which includes fostering discussion of how to recognize and respond to harms individuals may suffer in families.

Endnotes

1. For a review, *see* R. J. R. Levesque, *Child Sexual Abuse: A Human Rights Perspective* (Bloomington: Indiana University Press, 1999).
2. WASH. REV. CODE, § 9.94A.120, (1998).
3. For a review, *see* A. R. De Jong, "Impact of Child Sexual Abuse Medical Examinations on the Dependency and Criminal Systems," *Child Abuse & Neglect* 22 (1998):645–652.
4. *See* L. M. J. Simon, "Sex Offender Legislation and the Antitherapeutic Effects on Victims," *Arizona Law Review* 41 (1999):485–533.
5. C. M. Sullivan and D. I. Bybee, "Reducing Violence Using Community-Based Advocacy for Women With Abusive Partners," *Journal of Consulting and Clinical Psychology* 67 (1999):43–54.
6. Levesque, *Child Sexual Abuse.*

TABLE OF AUTHORITIES

Numbers in italics refer to listings in endnote sections.

Federal Law, Regulations, and Rules

U.S. State Laws, Regulations, and Rules

International Materials

Cases

AUTHOR INDEX

Numbers in italics refer to listings in endnote sections.

SUBJECT INDEX

Numbers in italics refer to listings in endnote sections.

ABOUT THE AUTHOR

Roger J. R. Levesque received his JD from Columbia University School of Law and his PhD in cultural psychology from the University of Chicago. He recently was appointed associate professor of psychology and law at the University of Arizona. Before joining the University of Arizona's Psychology, Public Policy and Law Program, he was an assistant professor of criminal justice at Indiana University—Bloomington and was a Fellow in the Law & Psychology Program at the University of Nebraska—Lincoln. He has published more than 40 scholarly articles and book chapters that deal with family life, maltreatment, and the law. His most recent books include *Child Sexual Abuse: A Human Rights Perspective* (Indiana University Press, 1999) and *Adolescents, Sex, and the Law: Preparing Adolescents for Responsible Citizenship* (American Psychological Association, 2000).